Palestinian Islamic Jihad

Palestinian Islamic Jihad

Islamist Writings on Resistance and Religion

Erik Skare

I.B. TAURIS
LONDON • NEW YORK • OXFORD • NEW DELHI • SYDNEY

I.B. TAURIS
Bloomsbury Publishing Plc
50 Bedford Square, London, WC1B 3DP, UK
1385 Broadway, New York, NY 10018, USA
29 Earlsfort Terrace, Dublin 2, Ireland

BLOOMSBURY, I.B. TAURIS and the I.B. Tauris logo are trademarks of
Bloomsbury Publishing Plc

First published in Great Britain 2021
This paperback edition published 2023

Copyright © Erik Skare, 2021

Erik Skare has asserted his right under the Copyright, Designs and
Patents Act, 1988, to be identified as Author of this work.

For legal purposes the Acknowledgments on p. ix constitute an extension
of this copyright page.

Cover image: Young Palestinian during a military-style graduation organised by Islamic
Jihad, in Gaza City July 4, 2019. (© Majdi Fathi/NurPhoto/Getty Images)

All rights reserved. No part of this publication may be reproduced or transmitted
in any form or by any means, electronic or mechanical, including photocopying,
recording, or any information storage or retrieval system, without prior
permission in writing from the publishers.

Bloomsbury Publishing Plc does not have any control over, or responsibility for, any
third-party websites referred to or in this book. All internet addresses given in this
book were correct at the time of going to press. The author and publisher regret any
inconvenience caused if addresses have changed or sites have ceased to exist,
but can accept no responsibility for any such changes.

A catalogue record for this book is available from the British Library.

A catalog record for this book is available from the Library of Congress.

ISBN: HB: 978-0-7556-3592-4
PB: 978-0-7556-3596-2
ePDF: 978-0-7556-3593-1
eBook: 978-0-7556-3594-8

Typeset by Deanta Global Publishing Services, Chennai, India

To find out more about our authors and books visit www.bloomsbury.com and
sign up for our newsletters.

This is the history of the superpowers' relationship with the oppressed peoples.
                                          Fathi al-Shiqaqi, March 1980

*For my parents, Roswitha and Olav Skare, and my brother, August.
They are my first and finest teachers.*

Contents

Acknowledgments ix
Notes on Transliteration x

Introduction 1

Part I Facts and Stances

1 What Is Palestinian Islamic Jihad? 9
2 Excerpts from *Facts and Stances* 17
3 Political Document of Palestinian Islamic Jihad 25
4 Islamic Principles and Concepts 44

Part II PIJ, Colonialism, and the Palestinian Cause

5 Why History? 55
6 The Palestinian Cause Is the Central Cause of the Islamic Movement ... Why? 66
7 Excerpts from "Afghanistan The Roots of the Conflict ... The Revolution ... The Future ... Is It a New Resurgence of the Crusaders?" 82
8 The Centrality of Palestine and the Contemporary Islamic Project 95
9 Palestine Is on a Collision Course with the Western Colonial Project 120

Part III Iran and the Shiites

10 Excerpts from *Khomeini: The Islamic Solution and Alternative* 129
11 The Sunni and the Shiite: A Fabricated and Regrettable Pandemonium 154
12 Excerpts from *Facts and Stances* 175

Part IV State, Violence, and Civil Society

13 Restructuring the PLO: The View of Palestinian Islamic Jihad 185
14 Principal Notes on the Issue of a Palestinian State 192
15 Fundamentalism and Secularism 200
16 Excerpts from "The Islamic Movements and the developments of the Palestinian Cause" 208
17 Creedal and Intellectual Foundations for the "Culture of Resistance" 212

18	The Philosophy of Martyrdom	221
19	Excerpt from *The Jihadist March of Palestinian Islamic Jihad*	244
20	Anwar Abu Taha on the Arab Spring and PIJ's Position	249

| Bibliography | 253 |
| Index | 257 |

Acknowledgments

A number of colleagues and friends assisted me with this book when I was stuck; when there were Islamic, historical, or political references I did not get; and when I was uncertain on how to best convey the meaning of the original text. I have thus incurred a great debt to Eva Marie Håland, Ghazi al-Omari, Carla El Khoury, Zehad Sabry Mohamed, Mansour al-Omari, Asaad Almohammad, Stephan Guth, Albrecht Hofheinz, Jacob Høigilt, Erling Lorentzen Sogge, K. S. Batmanghelichi, and Samad Alavi. Their advice and suggestions were inestimable.

I would also like to thank the team at I.B. Tauris: my editors Sophie Rudland and Yasmin Garcha, who accepted the project and who saw it through until the end. I also extend my gratitude to the anonymous peer reviewers for their valuable critique and feedback.

Needless to say, any error or weakness in this book remains my responsibility alone.

Notes on Transliteration

The following study employs the transliteration guide of the *International Journal of Middle East Studies* (IJMES).

ء—ʾ	ذ—dh	ظ—ẓ	ه—h
ب—b	ر—r	غ—gh	و—w
ت—t	ز—z	ف—f	ي—y
ث—th	س—s	ق—q	ة—a, in
ج—j	ش—sh	ك—k	construction -at.
ح—ḥ	ص—ṣ	ل—l	ال—al-
خ—kh	ض—ḍ	م—m	
د—d	ط—ṭ	ن—n	

The long vowels are transliterated as follows:
ى—ā   ي—ī   و—ū

Doubled: Diphthongs: Short vowels:
يّ—iyy, with final form ī   ي—ay   a, u, i
وّ—uww, with final form ū   و—aw

- Full transliteration is primarily employed for technical terms, names, and noncognate words whose meaning English readers cannot easily discern. These are without exception fully italicized.
- Transliteration has not been employed for personal names, place names, and organizations following accepted English spelling. ʿAyn and *hamza*, however, are preserved, except for initial *hamza*.
- I have to the fullest extent possible avoided Anglicized plurals on fully transliterated words (such as *fuqahāʾ*, and not *faqīh*s).

Introduction

Today, they obsessively scream: Save us from this hell... Today, they realize they are losing and that they will never be able to survive among us ... Today, they are fully aware that we have nothing to lose and that we love martyrdom more than they love life.
—PIJ communiqué, December 11, 1987

Although Palestinian Islamic Jihad (PIJ) issued its first public statement on December 11, 1987, its existence had been one of the worst-kept secrets of the Palestinian resistance. Founded in the Gaza Strip in 1981 by a group of Palestinian students who had never touched a rifle, PIJ commenced employing violence against Israeli targets in 1984, five years before Hamas. The movement grew notorious while doing so, for the spectacularity of its attacks and its uncompromising stances against the Israeli occupation. The slogan they proposed was "Islam, jihad, and Palestine": Islam as the starting point, jihad as the means, and the liberation of Palestine as the goal.[1] No negotiations, no two-state solution, and no recognition of Israel.

The Oslo Agreement and the establishment of the Palestinian National Authority (PA) almost eradicated the movement in the 1990s, with most of its militants either imprisoned or assassinated. Yet, the world witnessed PIJ's resurgence with the eruption of the Second Intifada in 2000. Continuing its use of suicide bombings, shootings, and stabbings, PIJ firmly established itself as one of the Palestinian resistance's main players. It became the third-largest Palestinian armed faction in the Occupied Palestinian Territories by the end of the second uprising, and then the second-largest armed movement in the Gaza Strip following the legislative electoral victory of Hamas in 2006. Indeed, popular support for PIJ was polled at over thirty percent in Gaza at its peak in September 2014.[2]

Palestinian Islamic Jihad thus matters. Little is nonetheless known about the actual political thought and ideology of the movement despite its relevance. While the literary works and speeches of al-Qaida, Taliban, Hezbollah, and the Islamic State (IS) have been translated and published for an English-speaking audience, the same cannot

---

[1] For a history of Palestinian Islamic Jihad, see Erik Skare, *A History of Palestinian Islamic Jihad: Faith, Awareness, and Revolution in the Middle East* (Cambridge: Cambridge University Press, 2021).
[2] Rasha Abou Jalal, "Islamic Jihad Gains Support in Gaza as Hamas Declines," *al-Monitor*, April 10, 2014, https://www.al-monitor.com/pulse/originals/2014/04/islamic-jihad-support-gaza-expense-hamas.html [accessed: September 3, 2019].

be said about PIJ.³ In fact, when analyzing political Islam, we often refer to Hassan al-Banna and Abul A'la Maududi as its trailblazers, and Hassan al-Turabi, Rachid Ghannouchi, Yusuf al-Qaradawi, Muhammad Khatami, Sayyid Qutb, Ali Shariati, and Ayatollah Khomeini as its ideologues and intellectuals.⁴ PIJ's founding father, Fathi al-Shiqaqi, on the other hand, is rarely, if ever, mentioned. Yet, he was a remarkably prolific intellectual and ideologue with an oeuvre spanning from 1979 until his assassination on October 26, 1995. The same can be said about other PIJ thinkers such as Ramadan Abdallah Shallah, Anwar Abu Taha, Yusuf Arif al-Hajj Muhammad, and Abdallah al-Shami.

We often refer to PIJ as an ideologically strict movement, but seldom as an intellectual one. Still, its founding fathers were avid readers and bookworms, and violence and intellectual immersion were not mutually exclusive. The omission of PIJ from research on Islamic political thought is thus undeserved—imbued as the movement is with ideological influences and theoretical and religious references. While Fathi al-Shiqaqi argued that God predestined the victory of the Palestinians, this victory would also introduce independence for all states in the Global South under the shade of Western colonialism. While PIJ's principal tool for Palestinian popular mobilization in the First Intifada was religious symbolism, its analysis of the conflict in the same period was, and still is, largely secular. While being one of the least compromising Palestinian factions regarding cease-fires with, and armed struggle against, Israel, it is also one of the most ardent proponents of dialogue and peaceful discussions in intra-Palestinian conflict.

Indeed, al-Shiqaqi always seemed more infatuated with history and historical analysis than religious exegesis, and the Arab Nahda movement of the nineteenth century seems to have been more relevant for him than the first five centuries of Islam (known as the Islamic golden age). Al-Shiqaqi's analysis of the Afghan-Soviet War (1979–89), for example, had an exclusive focus on the economic driving forces behind Western colonialism. His attempt at conciliation between Sunnis and Shiites was visibly motivated by the need for a united Islamic front as the only realistic defense against colonial adventures.

Palestinian Islamic Jihad: Islamist Writings on Resistance and Religion is an annotated collection of PIJ texts translated into English dating from 1979 until 2018—including booklets, articles, studies, and interviews. The book is intended to be a resource and an intellectual introduction to PIJ for historians on the Israeli-Palestinian conflict, and scholars on political Islam in general and Palestinian Islamism in particular, in

---

[3] See Gilles Kepel and Jean-Pierre Milelli (eds.), *Al Qaeda in Its Own Words* (Harvard: Harvard University Press, 2010); Laura Mansfield, *His Own Words: A Translation of the Writings of Dr. Ayman al Zawahiri* (Old Tappan: TLG Publications, 2006); Alex Strick van Linschoten and Felix Kuehn (eds.), *The Taliban Reader: War, Islam and Politics in Their Own Words* (London: Hurst & Company, 2018); Nicholas Noe (ed.), *Voice of Hezbollah: The Statements of Sayyed Hassan Nasrallah* (London and New York: Verso Books, 2007); Donald Holbrook (ed.), *Al-Qaeda 2.0: A Critical Reader* (London: Hurst & Company, 2017); Haroro J. Ingram, Craig Whiteside, and Charlie Winter (eds.), *The Isis Reader: Milestone Texts of the Islamic State Movement* (London: Hurst & Company, 2019).

[4] See, for example, John L. Esposito and Emad al-Din Shahin (eds.), *The Oxford Handbook of Islam and Politics* (Oxford: Oxford University Press, 2016); Shahram Akbarzadeh (ed.), *Routledge Handbook of Political Islam*, 1st ed. (New York: Routledge, 2011).

addition to students of the Middle East. Compiled through years of research, most of these sources were found online, while others required fieldwork in the Middle East—most notably at the Institute for Palestine Studies in Beirut, Lebanon. What the selected texts have in common is that they represent a cross section of PIJ's political thought and ideology.

This cross section deserves some attention because ideologies are typically mixtures of analytical and descriptive elements, on the one hand, and moral and technical prescriptions, on the other.[5] Ideologies thus combine factual content and moral commitment in a coherent system, which lends them their action-guiding power. Ideologies are hence capable of preparing its members with goals, motivations, prescriptions, and imperatives. Essentially, ideologies "lend coherence to the groups or classes which hold them, welding them into a unitary, if internally differentiated, identity."[6] As Gunning notes in his research on Hamas, an actor's political practice cannot be understood without a thorough understanding of its political theory because ideas are translated into action,[7] and due to the pervasiveness and durability of certain texts and doctrines, we may generally assume that they encode, in however mystified a way, genuine needs and desires.[8]

That is not to suggest that the following texts should be read uncritically. First, because the ideology of many Islamist movements is characteristically orthodox, relying too heavily on texts has traditionally meant depicting these movements as driven by rigid ideological ideals with little room for pragmatic maneuverability in their daily practices.[9] Indeed, even if the ideological literature production of PIJ is a truthful representation of the thoughts and beliefs of the movement, it is nonetheless a human organization—and its internal practices both imperfectly reflect its ideals and simultaneously suffer from the contradictions within those respective ideals.[10] Second, as Hegghammer notes, Islamist movements tend to have end goals that essentially are "very vague, similar and utopian"—all of which can be used to rationalize a vast range of political and military strategies. Just like the declared aim of a "better world" tells us very little about the political preferences of Western political parties, Islamist slogans such as "establishing the Caliphate" are too vague to tell us anything about the expected political behavior of a group in the short- or mid-term.[11] In other words, "what [Islamists] write or say must be placed within context of what they actually do."[12]

---

[5] Martin Seliger, *Ideology and Politics* (London: Allen & Unwin, 1976), 119–20. Seliger's analysis was initially found in Terry Eagleton, *Ideology: An Introduction*, new ed. (London and New York: Verso Books, 2007), 48.
[6] Eagleton, *Ideology: An Introduction*, 45.
[7] Jeroen Gunning, *Hamas in Politics: Democracy, Religion, Violence* (London: Hurst & Company, 2009), 16.
[8] Eagleton, *Ideology: An Introduction*, 12.
[9] Khaled Hroub, "Introduction," in *Political Islam: Context versus Ideology*, ed. Khaled Hroub (London: Saqi, 2010), 13.
[10] See Gunning, *Hamas in Politics: Democracy, Religion, Violence*, 95.
[11] Thomas Hegghammer, "Jihadi-Salafis or Revolutionaries?: On Religion and Politics in the Study of Militant Islamism," in *Global Salafism: Islam's New Religious Movement*, ed. Roel Meijer (Oxford: Oxford University Press, 2013), 259.
[12] John L. Esposito, *The Islamic Threat: Myth or Reality?* 3rd ed. (New York and Oxford: Oxford University Press, 1999), 263.

This also applies to the translated texts in this book. Authored by several of the movement's theoreticians in various, yet specific, historical periods with their own set of pressing issues, grievances, and conflicts, they contain several anachronisms and contradictions. For example, PIJ states, on the one hand, that the Jews are the historical and inevitable enemies of the Muslims. On the other, PIJ also states that the movement is not against Jews because of their religion but because of the occupation—and it distinguishes between Israelis and people of Jewish faith who are not involved in Israeli settler-colonialism. The same contradiction applies to Christians, who are an inseparable part of the Palestinian people and the Arab and Islamic nation while also being allies of the Jews. It should thus be noted that publishing these texts in translation does not imply any support for their problematic aspects, and they should be read as critically as any other text.

What are then the significance and aims of this book? *Palestinian Islamic Jihad* matters because research on Palestinian Islamism has largely focused on Hamas.[13] While this research has been pioneering in its own right, it cannot provide the entire picture if one wishes to understand Palestinian Islamism. Because of the lack of research on PIJ,[14] a number of myths and misunderstandings consequently persist about the movement, and little is known about its actual thought—and why PIJ believes what it believes. *Palestinian Islamic Jihad* is the first work to provide the ideology of PIJ in its own words with comments and introductions to its key texts. Like van Linschoten and Kuehn in *The Taliban Reader*, I hope that this book will "help reset the research agenda."[15]

Notes on Translations

The main goal of these translations has been to convey the true referential and expressive meaning of the original text (adequacy), while also adhering to the linguistic

---

[13] See, for example, Hroub, Khaled, *Hamas: Political Thought and Practice* (Washington DC: Institute for Palestine Studies, 2000); Shaul Mishal and Avraham Sela, *The Palestinian Hamas: Vision, Violence, and Coexistence* (New York: Columbia University Press, 2006); Azzam Tamimi, *Hamas: Unwritten Chapters* (London: Hurst & Company, 2009); Gunning, *Hamas in Politics: Democracy, Religion, Violence*; Beverley Milton-Edwards and Stephen Farrell, *Hamas: The Islamic Resistance Movement* (Cambridge: Polity Press, 2010); Michael Irving Jensen, *The Political Ideology of Hamas: A Grassroots Perspective* (London: I.B. Tauris, 2010); Sara Roy, *Hamas and Civil Society in Gaza: Engaging the Islamist Social Sector* (Princeton, NJ: Princeton University Press, 2011); Paola Caridi, *Hamas: From Resistance to Government* (New York: Seven Stories Press, 2012); Tristan Dunning, *Hamas, Jihad and Popular Legitimacy: Reinterpreting Resistance in Palestine* (London and New York: Routledge, 2016); Björn Brenner, *Gaza under Hamas: From Islamic Democracy to Islamist Governance* (London and New York: I.B. Tauris, 2017); Tareq Baconi, *Hamas Contained: The Rise and Pacification of Palestinian Resistance* (Stanford: Stanford University Press, 2018).

[14] For works on PIJ, see Skare, *A History of Palestinian Islamic Jihad: Faith, Awareness, and Revolution in the Middle East*; Meir Hatina, *Islam and Salvation in Palestine* (Tel Aviv University: The Moshe Dayan Center for Middle Eastern and African Studies, 2001); Ziad Abu-Amr, *Islamic Fundamentalism in the West Bank and Gaza* (Bloomington, IN: Indiana University Press, 1994); Beverley Milton-Edwards, *Islamic Politics in Palestine* (London and New York: I.B. Tauris, 1999).

[15] van Linschoten and Kuehn (eds.), *The Taliban Reader: War, Islam and Politics in Their Own Words*, 5.

and stylistic norms of the language into which the text is translated (acceptability).[16] The inherent tension between "adequacy" and "acceptability" means that there are a number of challenges and strategies facing the translator—primarily the contradiction between domestication and foreignization. While the former aims to make the translation as clear as possible by aligning it with our own cultural references, the latter focuses on "authenticity" by preserving that which is "culturally foreign" in the text— although translations frequently combine the two as the case may require.[17]

One example from this book is the Arabic word "Allah", which I have translated as "God" without exception. The same applies to variants thereof such as "God willing," "praise be to God," and so on. Similarly, when I have employed already-existing translations of the Qur'an in the following translations, I have replaced the word with "God."[18] Admittedly, I find writing "Allah" in English as misleading as suggesting that the English believe in "God" as opposed to the Germans who believe in "Gott" or the Spanish who believe in "Dios."

Second, the selection of the following texts has necessarily been an issue of prioritization, and there are a number of key texts that were excluded simply because of the scope of this book. Moreover, certain parts of the following PIJ texts do not necessarily contribute equally to our understanding of the movement. Al-Shiqaqi's analysis of the Afghan-Soviet War is one example, as it elucidates how PIJ assesses international society, law, and relations, in addition to the uneven development between the Global South and Global North. Yet, the article also contains a largely encyclopedic listing of the various Afghan parties and factions, which adds little analytical value. Consequently, when I have excluded parts of a text, I provide the marker "℃" for the sake of clarity.

Third, the following translations are rich in literary, historical, religious, and political references, and I provide explanatory footnotes when specific persons, phenomena, or terms are mentioned in the text. Examples include when someone such as the Iraqi Islamic scholar Abu al-Thana' al-Alusi is mentioned, or there is a reference to Sufi concepts such as "unveiling" (*kashf*) or "conjunction" (*ittiṣāl*). These annotations are not meant to be exhaustive explanations, but brief guidance only. In addition, articles (*maqālāt*) and monographs (*dirāsāt*) authored by scholars (*'ulamā'*) on the Middle East (*al-sharq al-awsaṭ*) are often brimming (*ṭāfiḥ*) with Arabic terms (*muṣṭalaḥāt 'arabiyya*) provided in brackets (*aqwās*). I have avoided doing so in the translations for the sake of readability, except in notes when explaining specific terms.

Notes on Structure

Palestinian Islamic Jihad is divided into four parts, each with its particular thematic focus.

---

[16] Gunnvor Mejdell, "Kulturelle og språklige utfordringer i oversettelse av arabisk litteratur," *Babylon. Nordisk tidsskrift for Midtøstenstudier*, no. 2 (2012): 16.
[17] Mejdell, "Kulturelle og språklige utfordringer i oversettelse av arabisk litteratur," 16.
[18] The Qur'anic translations referenced in this book are without exception taken from The Noble Qur'an, https://quran.com/.

Part I serves as a general introduction to PIJ and the movement's own narration of how and why it was founded in the Gaza Strip in the early 1980s. Providing the standard narrative of PIJ, it tells how the movement emerged due to its founders' estrangement by the PLO's secularism and increasing willingness to compromise with Israel, and the Palestinian Muslim Brotherhood's refusal to participate in the armed struggle.

Part II introduces PIJ's analysis of the Palestinian cause and its historical, de facto, and Qur'anic dimensions. These three dimensions constitute what we may term the ideological foundation for PIJ's armed struggle against the Israeli occupation. They entail the causes not only of the Palestinians' predicament but also of the underdevelopment of the Global South in its entirety. Although the Qur'anic dimension is the religious analysis of the conflict and its divine predestination, this part shows how PIJ largely relied on a secular (and, at times, even materialist) analysis of colonial interests, economic driving forces, and Israel as the embodiment of western hegemony in the Global South. The selected text thus illustrates how a two-state solution and peace with Israel is an oxymoron for PIJ not simply because of creedal tenets, but because it considers the State of Israel as a precondition for continued Western colonial domination.

One of the most peculiar characteristics of PIJ is its relationship with its patron, Iran. Part III thus focuses on PIJ's view on the Iranian revolution in general and the Shiites in particular. As a continuation of the preceding part, this part shows how PIJ perceived religious sectarianism between Sunnis and Shiites as weakening the ecumenical front against Western colonialism. Moreover, it shows how the Iranian revolution was a great inspiration for PIJ, not merely for striking at Western colonialism while basing it on perceived Islamic values but also by virtue of Khomeini giving sufficient credence and importance to the Palestinian cause when doing so.

The last part of the book focuses on PIJ's conception of the future, ideal organization of Palestinian society after liberation, and its view on resistance and violence against the Israeli occupation. Most notably, the selected texts on future society illustrate how PIJ desires an Islamic society, yet the movement does not seek the establishment of a strong Islamic state. On the contrary, the movement's belief resembles that of classical liberalism in which a strong state may threaten the harmony of society. Yet, it also shows how there are clear structural limitations as politics and democratic practice can only be negotiated within, and cannot abandon, a religious framework.

Further, the texts on violence highlight how PIJ's discourse on violence is largely determined by contemporary conflicts; the position of the movement thus partly depends on what debate and period to which one refers. For example, this part shows how PIJ condemned the terrorist attacks on the United States on September 11, 2001, because al-Qaida targeted US civilians, while the movement simultaneously had to legitimize its own suicide bombings during the Second Intifada by negating the status of Israelis as civilians. Essentially, while stating that there are limitations to violence, PIJ outlines a thesis of resistance as a universal and inalienable right by virtue of man being God's creation.

Taken together, these parts show the historical longevity and the ideological depth of a group that is all too often dismissed as Hamas' more violent and uncompromising little brother.

Part I

Facts and Stances

What Is Palestinian Islamic Jihad?

Published as several pieces in al-Mujāhid, no. 146-149, June-July 1992.

PIJ was in many ways a response to the void appearing in the Palestinian resistance by the 1980s. The Palestine Liberation Army (PLA) had been defeated in the Gaza Strip in 1971/1972, the PLO had been exiled to Tunisia in 1982, and the Palestinian Muslim Brotherhood (later Hamas) refused to engage in armed struggle. There was simply no credible organization in the Occupied Palestinian Territories if one wished to resist violently at the time.

PIJ's formation process commenced in Egypt in the mid-1970s when a number of Palestinian students began discussing the Palestinian cause. It was there that the future leaders of the movement met—such as Fathi al-Shiqaqi, Ramadan Shallah, Nafidh Azzam, Abdallah al-Shami, and Muhammad al-Hindi. Reading Shakespeare and Dostoyevsky, Sayyid Qutb and Muhammad al-Ghazali, and Mahmud Darwish and Badr Shakir al-Sayyab, these students began stressing the necessity for the Islamic movement to lead the armed struggle for Palestinian liberation.

Returning to the Gaza Strip in 1981 following the assassination of Egyptian President Anwar al-Sadat, the Palestinian students soon engaged in fierce debates with the Palestinian Muslim Brotherhood on the necessity of violent resistance. While PIJ's founding fathers stressed the necessity of resistance now, and not later, the Brotherhood and its spiritual leader Sheikh Ahmad Yassin stressed the importance of proselytization and the strengthening of Islamic values first. As the sympathizers of Islamic armed struggle were assaulted both physically and verbally by Brotherhood sympathizers, the former soon seceded to form their own project.

Spending the first years building an organizational base in the Gaza Strip, PIJ commenced employing violence against Israeli targets in 1984—five years before Hamas. As the organization received attention for the spectacularity of its attacks, most of its leaders were arrested and imprisoned by the mid-1980s by the Israeli occupation authorities. Between 1987 and 1989 several were also deported to Lebanon in an Israeli attempt to quell the insurgency.

As al-Shiqaqi and the PIJ spiritual leader, Abd al-Aziz Awda, found themselves in foreign lands, the deportation had unsuspected consequences for their movement. Primarily, it meant that the PIJ leadership could travel freely, cooperate with others, and broker alliances with Iran, Syria, and Hezbollah. From initially being a group of students who had never touched a rifle, PIJ had become a force to be reckoned with by 1992.

The following text thus matters because it is PIJ's own recollection of its history up until 1992, which includes its view on the PLO and its role in the Palestinian resistance. Although the author is unknown, this text features in the collected works of Fathi al-Shiqaqi, who is most likely the author.

Palestinian Islamic Jihad is a Palestinian Islamist fighting organization that crystallized organizationally in the early 1980s in occupied Palestine. It did so after an intellectual and political dialogue, which commenced in the mid-1970s among some Palestinian students during their time in Egypt. This dialogue included methodological issues related to understanding Islam, the world, and reality, and how to see and understand history in general and Islamic history in particular.

The starting point was the systematic understanding of Islam as a creed, of the principles of religion, of jurisprudence, and of law, based on the Qur'an and the sunna. The early movement's consciousness of history, and its deep sense of this method, was a way of seeing the world as it was. It thus facilitated awareness and discerning the means for change, which led to the realization of Palestine's particularity in the contemporary Islamic problem. Palestine was therefore considered the central cause of the Islamic movement and of the Islamic umma. This assumption was based on the Qur'anic understanding, as explained in surat al-isra' and several other verses in the Holy Qur'an and the prophetic hadith.[1] The systematic discernment of history and reality contributed to the formulation of this theorem: the centrality and particularity of Palestine.

The trajectory of contemporary history is embodied in the colonial activity against the Islamic homeland that has lasted for two centuries. This activity has centered and focused on Palestine after it overthrew the Islamic political system, and it did so with the establishment of the territorial state and the promotion of Westernization as a model for culture and life in Muslim societies from Egypt via Turkey to Iran. Reality confirms that the peak of evil and the satanic colonial polarization embody themselves on the land of Palestine through the Zionist entity allied with the colonial West.

The aforementioned intellectual and political dialogue among some of the Palestinian Muslim intellectual youths during their studies in Egypt in the late 1970s turned into a political climate from which an organizational nucleus emanated. This nucleus later set out for occupied Palestine in order to build the revolutionary Islamic movement, surrounded by the aware masses, enthusiastic for the salvation of self and homeland under the banner of Islam. The goal was to realize the neglected duty in order to solve the existing problem at the time with nationalists without Islam and Islamists without Palestine. The Palestinian nationalist movement excluded Islam as an ideology, with its absence from its programs. The traditional Islamic movement, on the other hand, postponed answering the Palestinian question and jihad in Palestine for both objective and subjective reasons. Palestinian Islamic Jihad thus came to answer

---

[1] According to PIJ mythology, allegedly evidenced by sūrat al-isrā', the Israelites had grown in power and corruption in the Arabian Peninsula only to be defeated by Prophet Muhammad and his followers of true Muslims. Yet, God had predestined that they would rise, and fall, once more. Israel was for PIJ this second manifestation, and as the Prophet had defeated the Israelites before, the true Muslim Palestinians would defeat Israel once more. For an analysis, see Skare, *A History of Palestinian Islamic Jihad: Faith, Awareness, and Revolution in the Middle East*.

the Palestinian Islamic question, and it raised the slogan: Islam, jihad, and Palestine. Islam as the starting point, jihad as the means, and Palestine as the goal for liberation.

Palestinian Islamic Jihad passed from its inception through three main stages. The first included mass, political, media, and tactical work. The second witnessed armed jihad and fighting against the enemy. The movement entered its third stage on October 6, 1987, with the eruption of the popular intifada in Palestine.

The First Phase

The first phase commenced with the return and settlement of the first nucleus, which was formed during the studies in Egypt. This stage witnessed mass work, political work, media work, and strategic work, which the land of Palestine was thirsting for. This phase thus witnessed an Islamic and jihadist discourse paving the way to realize the neglected duty as long as the believing Palestinian masses yearned for it.

The movement's student role emerged in all of the universities and institutions in the West Bank and the Gaza Strip at that stage. At the end of 1981, the student block representing Palestinian Islamic Jihad, The Independent Islamists, was formed in the Islamic University in Gaza. It received positive results in the first elections that took place in January 1982, although the movement had existed only for a short period. The idea of Palestinian Islamic Jihad soon spread quickly in most of the Palestinian refugee camps, all of the cities, and a great number of villages, and the followers of the movement were concentrated in a number of mosques in addition to the universities.

The movement began to issue the magazine *The Light* (*al-Nūr*) in Jerusalem from early 1982. It was originally the magazine of the Society of Muslim Youth in Jerusalem, which had ceased for more than a year before some brothers in Palestinian Islamic Jihad began working secretly with the Society's management to reissue the magazine. Indeed, the magazine continued to be published intermittently until the end of 1982 and it expressed the ideological and political position of the movement. The movement began to publish the magazine *The Islamic Vanguard* (*al-Talī'a al-Islāmiyya*) in the United Kingdom by the end of 1982, and it expressed the same ideological and political line. *The Islamic Vanguard* was secretly reprinted in Jerusalem and spread throughout Palestine a couple of days after first being issued in London.

The *Islamic Vanguard* had an important impact in the Palestinian street, which pushed the Zionist authorities to find out how it was printed and distributed. The authorities consequently carried out an arrest campaign in August and September 1983, which included dozens of the movement's members—among them Dr. Fathi al-Shiqaqi. The interrogation of the detainees lasted for five months in the worst conditions of torture, and the case was called the Islamic Vanguard Case as it became one of the greatest political and security issues in that period. The investigation shifted after five months from the publications and the incitement for revolution and jihad to a search for political and security organizational structures, and thus shifting to a search for weapons and military cells. This Islamic group, which included dozens of Palestinian Islamic Jihad's sons, was considered the first Islamic organization arrested since the Zionist occupation of the West Bank and Gaza in 1967. The traditional

Islamic position had in other words avoided a direct political or security clash with the occupation authorities until 1983!!

In those years, Laylat al-Qadr[2] in the al-Aqsa Mosque witnessed gatherings and mass demonstrations under the care of Palestinian Islamic Jihad, as the movement brought the Palestinian masses out into the open for Eid prayer in several areas as an expression of challenging the occupation. Such was the movement's increasing role at that stage regarding tactical, political, and media work through its role in the universities and in the mosques in all of the cities, villages, and camps.

The Second Phase

Armed jihad against the Zionist enemy was the main justification for the advancement of Palestinian Islamic Jihad from the onset, despite the importance of its intellectual contributions and its distinguished Islamic political line. However, this matter—armed jihad—remained the most important for the Palestinian Islamic movement as it rose to form a new and real addition to solve the problem that existed between the nationalists without Islam!! and the Islamists without Palestine!! Armed military cells belonging to the movement were therefore organized within Palestine under the highest secrecy the first weeks of the movement and from the first beginnings of the first stage. There is thus no automatic separation between the two stages. The political, tactical, and mass work was growing with the launch of Palestinian Islamic Jihad, of course.

In the summer of 1981, the first military cell was organized. However, the armed work began gradually, slowly, and in complete secrecy between 1983 and 1985. Although the enemy raised the issue of armed military cells and the presence of weapons in the movement through its arrest campaign in 1983—the Islamic Vanguard Case—it failed completely in seeing a breakthrough.

The enemy caught Dr. Fathi al-Shiqaqi on March 2, 1986, for the second time, and it was two weeks after the latest military operation carried out by the movement in the Palestinian arena—in Gaza City on February 18, 1986. It was a hand grenade attack on a gathering of Zionist soldiers during a patrol change, and it was connected to the same place that Zionist soldiers martyred a Palestinian citizen one day before that operation. The masses thus considered this courageous operation as a response to the martyrdom of al-Akluk in Palestine Square in Gaza City.[3] Dr. al-Shiqaqi was arrested,

---

[2] The Night of Destiny (*laylat al-qadr*), the night when the first verses of the Qur'an were revealed to Prophet Muhammad. The night is commemorated on one of the last ten days of Ramadan.

[3] There is possibly an anachronism in this account as PIJ presumably refers to Rami al-Akluk, a fifteen-year-old Palestinian from Deir al-Balah refugee camp, Gaza Strip, who died from severe head injury after being clubbed by Israeli soldiers. Yet, this occurred on February 8, 1988, and could thus not possibly be the cause of the operation on February 18, 1986. I have found no accounts of one al-Akluk being killed in February 1986. Even if it is a typo, referring to the operation being carried out on February 18, 1988 instead of 1986, it would still not correspond with al-Shiqaqi's second arrest in 1986. See John Kifner, "Five More Dead in Arab Protests," *New York Times*, February 8, 1988, https://www.nytimes.com/1988/02/08/world/five-more-dead-in-arab-protests.html?searchResultPosition=1 [accessed: August 5, 2019].

and the incident was accompanied by the discovery of eight military operations carried out by the movement.

The year 1986/1987 was the year of militant Islam in Palestine. At a time (before the intifada) when the Palestinian nationalist action entered a bottleneck and suffered multiple defeats, Palestinian Islamic Jihad proceeded to lead the armed jihad and to carry out the most important military operations. The operations began with the Buraq operation on October 16, 1986,[4] by the Islamic Jihad Brigades,[5] and then proceeded to the al-Shuja'iyya operation on January 6, 1987.[6] These operations were carried out with several stabbing operations in between. There was also the great escape from Gaza Central Prison led by Misbah al-Suri and Muhammad Sa'id al-Jamal, which included six mujahidin from the movement, and there was the killing of Colonel Ron Tal, the commander of the military police in Gaza on August 3, 1986. Yitzhak Rabin,[7] the war minister at the time, described the killing of Tal "as an exceptional operation that would receive an exceptional response." There were other heroic operations as well, and the brave heroes of al-Shuja'iyya—Muhammad al-Jamal, Sami al-Shaykh Khalil, Zuhdi (Fayiz) al-Gharabli, and Ahmad Halis—headed for their heroic operation and illustrious martyrdom. Indeed, Misbah al-Suri had been martyred days earlier.

The heroes of al-Shuja'iyya were those who led the great escape from Gaza Central Prison on July 5, 1986, which was considered one of the most important prisons of the occupying state and a castle for the Zionist army, police, and intelligence. So the escape of six mujahidin from this prison—this castle—was a miraculous strike. They struck their roots into the depths of the people who embraced them for five full months as they carried out the most dangerous military operations at the gates of al-Shuja'iyya, despite the desperate attempts by the enemy to find them.

Indeed, it was an epic: the pure, faithful youth and memorizers of the Qur'an, who the people hurried to pray behind, met face to face with the Zionist enemy. They raised their weapons and rifles, stared into the eyes of the enemy, and opened fire. Their blood thus marked the entry of the people and of Palestinian Islamic Jihad into a new phase: the intifada.

---

[4] The Gate of Moors Operation was carried out by the Islamic Jihad Brigades, a Palestinian jihadist subcurrent of former Fatah Maoists who relied on logistical and financial support from the PLO, on October 16,1986, killing one and injuring seventy others after throwing hand grenades at a group of Israeli soldiers near the Wailing Wall in Jerusalem. Al-Shiqaqi either mixes the date or there is a typographical error in the text, as he dates the operation to October 6, 1986.
[5] Consisting of several former Fatah Maoists turned Islamists, the Islamic Jihad Brigades was responsible for several operations inside Israel in 1986 while being logistically and financially dependent on the PLO. For an elaborate analysis of the Islamic Jihad Brigades, see Manfred Sing, "Brothers in Arms: How Palestinian Maoists Turned Jihadists," *Die Welt Des Islams* 51 (2011): 1–44.
[6] The al-Shuja'iyya operation refers to the violent clash in Gaza City, in October 1987, between Israeli soldiers and the PIJ cell of Misbah al-Suri, Muhammad Sa'id al-Jamal, and Sami al-Shaykh Khalil who escaped from Gaza Central Prison in 1986. The cell carried out several military operations from 1986 until 1987.
[7] Yitzhak Rabin (1922–95) served as prime minister of Israel in the period between 1974 and 1977, and from 1992 until he was assassinated in 1995. He served as Israeli minister of defense in 1988. Rabin became known as "the bone breaker" in the First Intifada due to his Iron Fist policy, with which Israeli forces were ordered to use "force, might, and beatings" to suppress the uprising.

The Third Phase: The Intifada (October 6, 1986)

The spilled blood of Palestinian Islamic Jihad's heroes at the gates of Gaza City that day was a lightning message igniting the great Palestinian hidden meaning. It was the spark ignited by years of occupation, with all of its coercion and the darkness of its nights. It discharged the experiences of the Palestinian struggle, which had accumulated seventy years. It was the Palestinian hope's disappointment in the official Arab reality those days that reached its limit, and Islam was ascending as a model of this phase, as it was deeply rooted in the conscience of the people, returning to lead the march of jihad again.

Palestinian Islamic Jihad did not cause the intifada, because the intifada is greater than all groups, parties, organizations, and factions. Nor did it set the time for its launch, as it is impossible for anyone to set the hour for the launch of a miracle. We affirm, however, that the mass rally into the streets was our dream from the first day. When the movement called to enforce the religious slogans, called to Eid prayer outside, and called to Laylat al-Qadr ceremonies in the al-Aqsa mosque, it dreamt of seeing the masses going out in the streets to begin the march of jihad. Islamic Jihad thus accompanied the intifada hour by hour, and day by day, from October 6. It issued statements and publications calling on the masses to disembark, calling on resistance and on jihad in the path of the martyrs of al-Shuja'iyya. December 8/9, 1987, came to be two days of complete escalation and resoluteness as the intifada arrived in every city, village, and camp in the West Bank and the Gaza Strip.

Those who return to the Palestinian and Arab literature between October 6, 1987, and December 9, 1987, will see that the discussion centered on the intifada of the Palestinian people in the occupied homeland. The trailer incident that occurred in Jabalya on December 8, 1987, became an opportunity to transfer the tension and clashes in the Gaza Strip, and some parts of the West Bank, to everywhere. The trailer incident was a response to the killing of a Zionist settler by the mujahidin of Palestinian Islamic Jihad in the Gaza Strip. A statement was given by Yitzhak Mordechai[8] in December 1987, which attributed the operations of the intifada and its escalation to the trailer incident, and thus to the decision to deport Sheikh Abd al-Aziz Awda, issued on November 17, 1987.

Palestinian Islamic Jihad bore the burden of the occupation's response together with the masses throughout the first weeks of the intifada until the rest of the Islamic and nationalist forces awakened for the intifada to include all forces, groups, and classes. Indeed, the movement paid a dear price when the most important cadres were arrested from the onset, when some of its leaders were deported, and when the harshest types of oppression was perpetrated against it, as it was subjected to campaigns of elimination and weakening. This only increased the power of Palestinian Islamic Jihad, however, which avoided eradication according to the Zionist thinker Mikhail Zilg: "It is the movement that pops up [in] one place if you remove it in another."

---

[8] Yitzhak Mordechai (1944–), a former Israeli politician and minister of defense, who served as commander of the Israeli Southern Command (Padam) in 1987, a regional command of the Israeli army responsible for the Negev, the Araba, and Eilat/Umm al-Rashash.

The activism of Palestinian Islamic Jihad continued through approximately five years and the movement is still determined—God willing—to escalate the intifada and continue on the road of jihad as long as the occupation is there. The participation of Palestinian Islamic Jihad in the intifada does not come at the expense of the work on the political level, or its mass mobilization and armed jihad, which continues despite the calls to stop armed jihad against the enemy.

What Is the Position of Palestinian Islamic Jihad on the PLO?

The Palestine Liberation Organization (PLO) was born at the hands of the official Arab order, as represented by the resolution of the Arab summit no. 1/1964,[9] and by a Nasserite effort. It also emerged from Palestinian pressure, however, in search for representation and a national identity.

The first Palestinian National Council (PNC)[10] was held in Jerusalem on May 28, 1964, where the organization was announced, and it decided on its Palestinian national charter. Ahmad al-Shuqayri[11] was removed from the leadership of the organization in 1966. The Palestinian fighting factions took over (under the leadership of Fatah,[12] the authority of the PLO), and its role subsequently emerged after the nakba of 1967.[13] The current stage of the Palestinian people's struggle was defined as the stage of nationalist struggle. It was also categorically emphasized that all compromise projects for the Palestinian cause were rejected.

Those days gave the Palestinians a strong sense of self and national identity. However, the Palestinian national project (the PLO) began to slowly leave its fundamental tenets. It came to recognize the legitimacy of the enemy on eighty percent of the land of Palestine in less than a quarter of a century, and it prepared to accept self-rule on the remaining five percent of the land. In addition to this great political retreat, the chaos of ideology prevailed in the ranks of the PLO before it in the last years lost its ideology completely. Not one single faction denies the administrative corruption and organizational failure of the PLO.

In light of this suffocating crisis, there must be a search for a way out, or for an alternative!

* * *

---

[9] The 1964 Arab Summit in Cairo was the first summit of the Arab League. The Palestine Liberation Organization (PLO) was founded to represent the Palestinian people with its stated goal to liberate Palestine in its entirety through armed struggle.
[10] The Palestinian National Council (PNC) is the legislative body of the PLO and is responsible for formulating the policies and programs of the organization.
[11] Ahmad al-Shuqayri (1908–88), the first chairman of the PLO from 1964 until 1967 when he resigned after the Six-Day War.
[12] Fatah, Palestinian-secular nationalist political party founded in 1965, and the largest faction in the PLO.
[13] The Palestinians often refer to the two catastrophes (*nakba*), the establishment of Israel and the ethnic cleansing of the Palestinians in 1948, and the Arab defeat in the Six-Day War in 1967.

There is nothing in the publications of Palestinian Islamic Jihad that indicates that it has presented itself as an alternative to the PLO. Neither is there in its publications any clear opposition against the PLO as an inclusive framework for the political forces of our people. However, the movement considers that it is its right and duty to present a fighting ideology against the ideological chaos, its alienation, and retreat. Palestinian Islamic Jihad considered that this living ideology is Islam, the creed of the umma, and the axis of its history and heritage—Islam, which the PLO factions generally excluded, and which some fought relentlessly at some point, if not continuously.

Palestinian Islamic Jihad considers Palestine—all of Palestine—the common denominator bringing together all political forces that fight for its liberation. The movement affirms the possibility of cooperating with these factions regardless of ideology, and despite the importance of this issue... Affirming the importance, gravity, and sanctity of the Palestinian cause, and the unity of all Palestinian political forces regardless of ideological particularities or legal reasoning... All this does not only allow, but does also invoke and underline, the need for all Palestinian forces to meet in the confrontation with the Zionist enemy for the liberation of all of Palestine through armed jihad.

Hence, Palestinian Islamic Jihad has never disputed the PLO as an inclusive framework for the political forces of the Palestinian people. However, the movement does dispute the content and its meaning. The strength, credibility, and legitimacy of the PLO as a political or organizational framework, therefore, do not come from the number of embassies or from its presence in diplomatic forums. They can only come from escalating the armed struggle, mobilizing the umma, embodying its unity, and by mobilizing its potentials and its mujahid forces as a necessary condition to break and overcome the balance of unjust forces relying on fragmentation and colonial domination, in order to rebuild a balance of power in the interests of our just cause. This is also a prerequisite for any achievement at the international level.

Palestinian Islamic Jihad sees that the greatest danger for our people and its cause lies in tearing apart the program and orientations of our struggle and jihad. The unity of the struggling line and its solidity comes before the unity of the framework. What is the point of asking all Palestinian political forces to abide by the PLO if its program declares and abandons the right of our people to their homeland, and their right to jihad and armed struggle for its liberation? From here, Palestinian Islamic Jihad refuses to compromise for a number of seats in the PNC, or for organizational and administrative guarantees, because the most important issue is the solidity of the jihadist line and the program of struggle. It refuses to recognize the legitimacy of the Zionist enemy on any inch of Palestine. It considers armed struggle and jihad as the road to the liberation of Palestine—without any abdication on the national charter, which affirms the right of the Palestinian people to their homeland in its entirety.

Islam must also be rehabilitated as the framework of our civilizational conflict against the Zionist attack, which Palestinian Islamic Jihad sees as a necessary condition to cooperate with all of the Palestinian forces within an inclusive framework such as that of the PLO. We would like to affirm that our ideological and political differences with any party or with any part of our Palestinian people can only be solved through intellectual and political dialogue, however, and far from violence, as violence is only directed against the Zionist enemy.

2

Excerpts from *Facts and Stances*

2007, published by muʾassasat al-aqṣā al-thaqāfiyya, Damascus, p. 17–26.

While PIJ had reached a preliminary military peak in 1993, it was almost eradicated with the introduction of the Palestinian National Authority (PA) as a product of the Oslo Agreement. One cause of the movement's decline was the security cooperation between the Israeli occupation and the PA, which led to the imprisonment and assassination of PIJ cadres and members. Another was the hope of the Palestinian population that the peace process would bring a Palestinian state to fruition, and both PIJ and Hamas plummeted in the polls as they persisted with their armed attacks against Israeli targets. Indeed, many believed the movement had disappeared by the late 1990s.

The eruption of the Second Intifada in 2000 signified the comeback of the movement. While the lawlessness in the Occupied Palestinian Territories eased militant action once Israeli-Palestinian security cooperation halted, so did the Palestinian belief in armed struggle facilitate the resurgence of PIJ. Employing ambushes, mortars, shootings, and suicide bombings against both Israeli soldiers and civilians, the movement grew into the third largest Palestinian armed faction. Yet, as the impetus of the uprising began to dwindle and the Israeli counterinsurgency gained ground, PIJ was defeated militarily in the West Bank in 2005, with its concentration in the Gaza Strip from then on out.

This document is an excerpt from the book Facts and Stances (2007) by PIJ's second secretary-general Ramadan Abdallah Shallah. Although this document too is a historical account of the movement's development, it matters because much had changed between 1992 and 2007—both for PIJ and for the Palestinian political arena. Here we can read Shallah's account about his movement's development and the commencement of Palestinian suicide bombings, about the emergence of Hamas and its violence against Israeli targets, about the return of the PLO leadership to the Occupied Palestinian Territories and the introduction of the Oslo Agreement, and about the Second Intifada.

☾

Can you introduce Palestinian Islamic Jihad, its emergence, what its intellectual premises are, and its effort on the Palestinian arena?

Palestinian Islamic Jihad originated from the intellectual and political discussions and efforts inside the Palestinian Islamic movement since the mid-1970s. The discussions centered on the place of Palestine and of jihad in the program of the Islamic movement. The founders settled for Palestinian Islamic Jihad, led by the martyr doctor Fathi al-Shiqaqi—may God have mercy upon him—and they were instructed by the necessity of forming a new organization that prepared for jihad and resistance on an Islamic basis.

The first nucleus of this project was formed by organizing students, including dozens of Palestinian students during their university studies in Egypt in the late 1970s. The student organization did not have the name Palestinian Islamic Jihad from the first day, but it began to crystallize in that direction in the mid-1980s when it formed its first military cell and began working in the resistance against the occupation, first in the Gaza Strip... The motives for establishing the movement welled up: first in regards to the reality of the Islamic movement we were a part of, for its neglect of the Palestinian issue in the dimension of struggle, and for presenting alternative priorities than jihad and resistance. Thus, jihad was in our view the neglected duty for Palestine, and we looked for those who called for it.

Second was the reality of the nationalist movement led by the Palestine Liberation Organization (PLO) with its secular factions, which carried out armed struggle and overlooked Islam's role in the conflict against the Zionist project. We stood in front of Islamists who waved the banner of Islam without Palestine as a military cause, and without jihad or resistance—regardless of the reason why. We similarly stood in front of the nationalists who waved the banner of Palestine and the armed struggle without any creed or Islamic identity to protect the cause and the struggle for Palestine from negligence and resignation, into which the PLO subsequently fell.

So Palestinian Islamic Jihad raised the motto, "Palestine is the central cause for the Islamic movement" according to an integrated vision based on three dimensions in the diagnosis of the conflict over Palestine: The first is the religious and legal dimension, which presents Palestine in the religion as a blessed land in the text of the Qur'an, as the first *qibla*[1] of the Muslims, and as the place of our Prophet Muhammad's departure to the seventh heavens with Archangel Gabriel—peace be upon him. This dimension also shows the inevitability of confrontation between us and the Jews, and this is what is confirmed by the Qur'an and the sunna, in particular by surat al-isra' and its glad tidings to the Muslims about the entry into the al-Aqsa mosque.[2] Then it is the Islamic ruling that jihad in Palestine is an individual duty.

The second is the historical dimension that places the Zionist offensive within the context of war, the Jews as historical enemies, and their cunning against the religion since the emergence of the sun letters[3] until the present day. It also includes the

---

[1] Qibla is the direction Muslims face when in prayer. While Muslims originally faced Jerusalem in prayer, this changed to the Kaaba in Mecca approximately one and a half years after the *hijra* of Prophet Muhammad. See, for example, Heribert Busse, "The Sanctity of Jerusalem in Islam," *Judaism* 17, no. 4 (Fall 1968): 441–68.

[2] See "The centrality of Palestine and the Contemporary Islamic Project" in Part Two of this book for a more elaborate analysis of Palestine's Qur'anic dimension.

[3] Letters are divided into two groups in the Arabic language: sun and moon letters, based on whether they assimilate the letter "lām" in the Arabic definite article "al-".

Western enemies since the Battle of Muta[4] and Tabuk[5] via the crusader wars down to the inculcation of the Zionist entity into the heart of the umma, Palestine. That is, the Zionist entity as the spearhead of the Western project, and as the culmination of its recent attack on the Islamic East, which began as the campaign of Napoleon in the late eighteenth century, perceived by some Arab intellectuals, unfortunately, as the beginning of the modern Arab renaissance.

The third is the de facto dimension, appearing through what "Israel" represents in current reality as a colonialist base and military barracks to protect Western and American interests in the region, and through what is caused by its presence and role in the region. "Israel" is thus a threat not only to Palestine but also to the whole umma.

Through its practice, Palestinian Islamic Jihad was thankfully the forerunner to the spark of jihad under Islam's banner in the contemporary Palestinian revolution. It had a more prominent role in the creation of a jihadi climate, and in the mobilization of a whole generation to ignite the spark of the First Intifada. This was witnessed by the Zionist enemy, which told its sources: "It is the right of Islamic Jihad's members to be proud of their movement, which rolled the rock of the intifada." This is known and acknowledged. We do not mark these words as a matter of pride or self-promotion, but to recall the facts that are sometimes obscured and absent in the historiography of the Islamic movement and its role in jihad and resistance in Palestine, in which some consider the history of jihad, resistance, and martyrdom to be the history of their particular faction or party. The people and the cause are consequently summed up in this faction or this party. We, therefore, do not claim that Palestinian Islamic Jihad is the one that ignited the intifada or planned it, as some do, because the intifada was, as a miraculous and iconic event, the product of the Palestinian people with all its groups, classes, and strength, and it cannot be attributed to one faction's strength or primacy of its role.

The establishment of Hamas, and its engagement in the intifada and armed jihad, was a huge addition to the march of the Palestinian struggle, and it was evidence of the success of Palestinian Islamic Jihad's idea and of its goal to awaken the Islamic option and attract it to the field of confrontation. When the First Intifada was coiled and miscarried by the settlement process and the signing of the Oslo Accords, it was the steadfastness of Palestinian Islamic Jihad and its sister organization Hamas, and their insistence to stick to the fundamentals, that were the most important factors for maintaining the cause—that is, their rejection of the Oslo approach and its concessions, and their adherence to jihad and resistance, the perseverance and steadfastness of the Palestinian people, and their insistence to continue on the road of jihad and liberation.

The attacks of Oslo and the entry of the PLO leadership into the settlement tunnel as the only option for the Palestinian people were a serious turning point, and a tragic decline in the history of the Palestinian struggle. The martyrdom operations organized by Palestinian Islamic Jihad and Hamas, however, were a bright spot and a historic

---

[4] The Battle of Mu'ta (629), fought between Prophet Muhammad and his followers, and the Byzantine Empire in present-day Karak Governorate in Jordan.
[5] Battle of Tabuk (630) refers to the expedition of Prophet Muhammad to Tabuk in present-day northwestern Saudi Arabia in order to confront the Byzantine invasion. Spending almost three weeks at Tabuk, Prophet Muhammad returned without any encounter.

station for the jihad of the Palestinian people. Hope returned to the hearts of millions of Arabs and Muslims, and confidence in the Palestinian people and their ability to deliver the battle into the enemy's heart was revived in the darkest circumstances.

One of the highlights of the martyrdom operations at that stage was the "Beit Lid Operation"[6] conducted by two mujahidin from Palestinian Islamic Jihad, which resulted in the killing of twenty-two Zionist soldiers and injuring eighty-seven others. The Beit Lid Operation stunned the world and shocked the Zionist mind, and it was even said that it was the direct cause of pushing the Zionist enemy to liquidate the leader and founder of Islamic Jihad, the martyr and doctor Fathi al-Shiqaqi, who was assassinated at the hands of Zionist Mossad in Malta on October 26, 1995.

The al-Quds Brigades[7] arose in the blessed al-Aqsa Intifada, the new name of the movement's military wing, as a new birth for the movement during which it contributed to jihad and martyrdom next to the rest of the factions and the military wings—especially the Izz al-Din al-Qassam Brigades and the al-Aqsa Martyrs' Brigades in the creation of a new stage in the history of the conflict over Palestine.

The funds of Palestinian Islamic Jihad in the march of the Palestinian struggle, which we sacrifice in anticipation of God's reward in the Hereafter, are not a subject of pride and partisan propaganda. Rather, they are wounds weakening the body of the movement, and they are burdens that weigh heavily. Yet, they have never prevented the movement from continuing the march. Indeed, the movement has since its inception carried out thousands of military operations in different forms against the occupation, and presented thousands of martyrs, wounded, prisoners, and detainees. There are today approximately 2,500 imprisoned sons, mujahidin, and leaders of Palestinian Islamic Jihad languishing in the occupation prisons. This is only in addition to the movement's role in the field of proselytization, education, culture, and society via the mosques, the centers for the memorization of the Qur'an, and the welfare associations that suffer from the lack of material possibilities and from the pursuit of the Zionist enemy.

However, the most important and significant contribution of Palestinian Islamic Jihad in the history of the cause is essentially its rise and advancement—and filling the gap between Islam and Palestine with its jihad. It has managed to attract a new Islamic generation to the contemporary Islamic movement, a generation that thinks of Islam from the position of jihad and resistance, and which thinks of the struggle and resistance from the position of Islam. It has today become the Islamic movement in Palestine, a stream that imposes itself on reality with force—a force that cannot be exceeded in drawing and determining the future of Palestine.

There are those who think that the Islamic movement in Palestine has not neglected the issue of jihad and resistance, and that Islamic Jihad is the one that rushed into it,

---

[6] Beit Lid Operation, the double suicide bombing carried out on January 22, 1995, by the PIJ members Anwar Sukkar and Salah Shakir at the Beit Lid junction in the Israeli Sharon region.

[7] The al-Quds Brigades is the military wing of PIJ, and was founded with the eruption of the Second Intifada in 2000. The foundation of the al-Quds Brigades was largely cosmetic and a direct continuation of its former military wing The Islamic Mujahid Forces (abbreviated to *Qassam*), formed in 1992. See Skare, *A History of Palestinian Islamic Jihad: Faith, Awareness, and Revolution in the Middle East*.

as the issue requires intellectual and spiritual preparations, which cannot be ignored. What is your opinion?

First, we must necessarily identify here what the Islamic movement is. Before the emergence of Palestinian Islamic Jihad, the Islamic movement in Palestine basically consisted of two groups: the Muslim Brotherhood and Hizb al-Tahrir,[8] which was founded in Jerusalem in 1953 by Sheikh Taqi al-Din al-Nabhani.[9]

So let us begin with Hizb al-Tahrir, because its position is known and clear. I must discuss the beginning as we respect and appreciate the views of our brothers in Hizb al-Tahrir, and we value them for their eagerness and zeal for Islam. This does not prevent us from differing from them, however, especially on the issue of jihad and resistance. For Hizb al-Tahrir does not in practice adopt the option of jihad, and it does not follow the road of resistance, despite the party and its founder's awareness of the Palestinian cause's depth in its creedal dimension, the civilizational dimension, and the gravity of the colonial Zionist project—even despite their conviction that Palestine can be liberated only through jihad. It argues, instead, that its priority is the establishment of the state or the Islamic caliphate, and that jihad should not be carried out by the general Muslims in the absence of the Caliph or the Muslim Imam who shall call them to war.

This deduction is unfortunately based on a misguided understanding and diagnosis of the nature of the aggression, which the umma is exposed to in Palestine, and the nature of the jihad required to protect it. Thus, for the majority of the umma today, jihad is defensive and not offensive. The defensive jihad against the invading enemy into the lands of the Muslims is thus an individual duty[10] for the people of the country subjected to aggression—groups and individuals, men and women. It is even said that a woman can go out without the consent of her guardian. If the people of the country are not sufficient, then the duty is extended to those of the Muslims who come after them, and then those coming after that, and so on until it includes the rest of the Muslims everywhere on Earth. Hizb al-Tahrir has postponed almost everything until the establishment of the state or the Islamic caliphate, leading to a very negative situation for that party. We are today seeing a resurgence of the party in the Islamic world and in the Palestinian street. We welcome it, and we hope that it cuts the rest of the road and engages in jihad and resistance in order to strengthen the march.

Considering the Muslim Brotherhood, the martyr Fathi al-Shiqaqi and some of his brothers and co-founders of Palestinian Islamic Jihad were members of the group. Some of his brothers and co-founders were not members of the Brotherhood, however, as was the case with me and others. We thus educated ourselves in the thought of the martyr Hassan al-Banna, the writings of Sayyid Qutb, and the rest of the thinkers and sheikhs of the Islamic awakening. When the martyr al-Shiqaqi—may he rest in

---

[8] Hizb al-Tahrir is an internationalist pan-Islamic political party working to re-establish the Islamic caliphate. While supporting jihad, it believes it can be carried out only under the leadership of the Caliph, and thus postpones any armed struggle in occupied Palestine.
[9] Taqi al-Din al-Nabhani, (1909–77), Islamic Jerusalemite scholar and founder of Hizb al-Tahrir.
[10] Individual duty (*farḍ ʿayn*) is a religious duty that must be performed by each individual, contrary to the sufficient duty (*farḍ al-kifāya*), which is a communal obligation.

peace—presented the issue of jihad and the necessity for the Brotherhood to take the initiative, and initiate jihad and armed resistance, it was not a departure from the group, nor was it an attempt to divide or weaken it. It was a historical response, however, and an attempt to correct and direct the course in Palestine. It was a compass in the mind and consciousness of Imam al-Banna, and to accept the correct priorities: Is it reasonable that Palestine is a priority in the program of the Islamic movement in Egypt, or that their children come to fight the Zionist enemy in Palestine, while we have other priorities? Is it permissible for us to carry out jihad, whatever the obstacles and excuses, or to leave it to the others in the secular and leftist organizations, whom we criticize while they fight? This is the essence of the debate that Palestinian Islamic Jihad raised.

Considering the theoretical, educational, and moral preparations, no one denies their importance, but the question is until when?! How many years do we have to wait and prepare, while the enemy stretches, expands, and grows its power, perils, and ambitions every day? The spiritual postponement, delay, and excuses cannot therefore produce a jihadist situation. The companions of the Prophet[11]—God's blessings upon them—and the pious predecessors[12] raced toward jihad, despite all the legal excuses and obstacles that were raised to exempt them.

Ibn Umm Maktum[13]—may God be pleased with him—was blind. He was made "disabled,"[14] but he nonetheless went for jihad. He used to say: "Raise the banner for me, for I, who am blind, is incapable of fleeing, so put me between two rows." It is said that he attended the Battle of Qadisiyya[15] with a black flag and armor, and some accounts say that he was martyred on the day of the battle!!

Sa'id ibn al-Musayyib[16] left for jihad and even missed an eye. It was said to him that his injury was an excuse. So he answered: "God has called upon the light and the heavy, and if I cannot fight I will increase our numbers, and guard the possessions."[17]

---

[11] The companions of the Prophet (al-ṣaḥāba), followers of Prophet Muhammad who saw and met him, and thus were physically present.

[12] The pious predecessors (al-salaf al-ṣāliḥ), reference to the first three generations of Muslims, which includes the generation of Prophet Muhammad and his followers (al-ṣaḥāba), their successors (al-tābi'ūn), and the successors' successors (tābi' al-tābi'īn). These three generations are often considered as the perfect example of good and rightly guided Muslims.

[13] Abdallah ibn Umm Maktum (d. 635), companion of Prophet Muhammad. He was born blind, and his mother was called Umm Maktum (the mother of the veiled one).

[14] The term Shallah employs is directly translated as "Other than the disabled" and refers to sūrat al-nisā': 95. "Not equal are those believers remaining [at home]—other than the disabled—and the mujahideen, [who strive and fight] in the cause of God with their wealth and their lives. God has preferred the mujahideen through their wealth and their lives over those who remain [behind], by degrees. And to both God has promised the best [reward]. But God has preferred the mujahideen over those who remain [behind] with a great reward."

[15] The Battle of Qadisiyya (636), a decisive battle between the Muslim army and the Sasanian Empire (last kingdom of the Persian Empire before the rise of Islam) leading to the conquest of present-day Iraq and subsequent battles at Jalula (present-day Iraqi Diyala province) and Navahand (near Iranian Hamadan).

[16] Sa'id ibn al-Mussayib (642–715), one of the pious predecessors and fiqh (jurisprudence) authority.

[17] The term "light and heavy" may refer to rich and poor depending on interpretation. I have chosen to translate it according to sūrat al-tawba: 41. "Go forth, whether light or heavy, and strive with your wealth and your lives in the cause of God. That is better for you, if you only knew."

The profound and famous story is that of George, one of the Roman leaders who embraced Islam and fought his people together with the Muslims, and who was martyred on the day of Yarmouk.[18] How long had he been in Islam? Two years? Days? Hours? Or minutes!? What did he know about Islam's legal rulings and its law? Khalid ibn al-Walid[19]—may God be pleased with him—did not send him to attend some educational seminars to be authorized for jihad in the ranks of Muslims. He moved from the row of infidelity to that of faith on the battlefield, he fought, and he was martyred. All his registry of Islam was the saying: "There is no God but God, and Muhammad is the Messenger of God."

Accordingly, assuming that the group holds the conviction, will, and understanding under the right circumstance, the outcome of our position on jihad is acceleration, not postponement. Spiritual and educational preparation and promotion is through the practice of jihad, following what is said: "And those who strive in Our (cause), We will certainly guide them to our Paths: For verily God is with those who do right."[20] Palestinian Islamic Jihad has taken this verse as a slogan which expressively indicates that jihad is the path of guidance, purity, and serenity to the extent that it releases the word "those who do right," and that the guidance, in turn, must lead to jihad. Thus, the milestones become clear through this miraculous Qur'anic argument, which leads to standing up and not sitting down, and in our pious predecessors we have a good example.

The story of Abu Mihjan al-Thaqafi[21] and his bravery in al-Qadisiyya informs us with the lesson that jihad is the path of guidance, repentance, and cleansing the heart of the filth of sins. Abu Mihjan, as these accounts narrate, was addicted to wine, and he was punished several times. When fighting erupted at al-Qadisiyya, however, Sa'd ibn Abu al-Waqqas[22]—may God be pleased with him—detained Abu Mihjan to keep the ranks clean. Yet, when there was fierce fighting, he went out and participated in combat after Sa'd's wife untied him. The story is famous, and what transpired between Abu Mihjan and Sa'd after the fighting is well known. What matters to us is that Abu Mihjan became a new person after this event, who repented, and who refrained from the sin of drinking wine. Abu Mihjan was a sinner, but he loved God and his Prophet, and he epitomizes the situation of Gaza quite a bit. There are a good number of our people and community who still remain Muslims no matter how they have departed from the right path. All they lack is the presence of a faithful and determined vanguard, calling

---

[18] George, unit commander in the Byzantine army who according to tradition rode up to the Muslim army and converted to Islam. He died in battle that same day.
[19] Khalid ibn al-Walid (585–642), companion of Prophet Muhammad and army commander under the first caliph of the Rashidun Caliphate, Abu Bakr, and its second caliph, Umar.
[20] See sūrat al-'ankabūt: 69.
[21] Abu Mihjan al-Thaqafi (d. 637), Arab poet before and after the advent of Islam. Converted to Islam and participated in the Muslim conquest of Persia. Imprisoned for intoxication, his wife obtained a temporary release for al-Thaqafi so he could participate in the Battle of Qadisiyya, which subsequently made Sa'd ibn Abu Waqqas, a companion of the Prophert, grant him full pardon.
[22] Sa'd ibn Abu Waqqas (595–674), a companion of Prophet Muhammad primarily known for commanding in the Battle of Qadisiyya and in the conquest of Persia.

them to jihad, and marching with them to al-Qadisiyya, Yarmouk,[23] Badr,[24] Hittin,[25] and Ain Jalut[26] anew.

This was the significance of Palestinian Islamic Jihad and its project, and it hastens—thank God for that—as it is a confirmation of God's saying: "I hastened to You, my Lord, that You be pleased."[27]

₡

---

[23] Battle of Yarmouk (636), major battle between the Muslim forces and the Byzantine Empire near the Yarmouk river at the present-day borders of Syria and Jordan. The Caliphate's victory at the battle marked the first wave of Muslim conquests.

[24] The Battle of Badr (March 13, 624) is considered a decisive battle and a turning point for Prophet Muhammad and his struggle against the Quraysh in Mecca.

[25] Battle of Hittin (July 4, 1187), battle between the crusaders and the forces of Saladin. The triumph of the latter made the Muslim forces the main military power in present-day Palestine with its re-conquest of Jerusalem.

[26] Battle of Ain Jalut (September 1260), battle between Muslim Mameluks and the Mongol forces in present-day Galilee, the Jezreel Valley, and outside of present-day Nazareth.

[27] See sūrat al-Ṭaha: 84. "He said, "They are close upon my tracks, and I hastened to You, my Lord, that You be pleased."

3

Political Document of Palestinian Islamic Jihad

Published by Palestinian Islamic Jihad in February 2018.[1]

Although PIJ calls this text a political document, and not a document of principles, it outlines the movement's main positions on itself, on Palestine, on Israel, on the international community and its complicity in the oppression of the Palestinians, and the means and role of Palestinian resistance.

Undoubtedly, this political document is a product of its time and the changes taking place in the Palestinian resistance after the 1990s. After Hamas won the Palestinian Legislative Elections in 2006, for example, it took control over the Gaza Strip after a short-lived "civil war" with Fatah in 2007. PIJ decided that a split was against the interests of the Palestinian cause, and that the Palestinian gun had only one legitimate direction: against the Israeli occupation. It thus refused to take sides and cooperated with the Popular Front for the Liberation of Palestine (PFLP) and the Democratic Front for the Liberation of Palestine (DFLP) to repair the relationship between Fatah and Hamas and to stop infighting in the streets of Gaza. In this period, the Israeli infrastructure of control expanded with the separation wall in the West Bank, the blockade on the Gaza Strip, and the growing number of Palestinian 'enclaves' surrounded by Israeli settlements. The PA's main strategy was to pursue negotiations and international recognition through the United Nations (UN) and its agencies—with little success.

With this background in mind, we may appreciate the perceived necessity to publish this document. As PIJ states in the preface, negotiations have led nowhere, the Palestinian people and their resistance are divided, and Israeli settlements and colonial control are expanding. In other words, the two-state solution is dead, and the Palestinian national project is at an impasse. While later texts in this book will illustrate the more pragmatic traits of PIJ, this document outlines some of the constant features of the movement's thoughts and position—any negotiations with the Israeli occupation are illegitimate, any partition of Palestinian land is impermissible, only armed struggle can liberate Palestine from the Jordan River to the Mediterranean Sea (from "the river to the sea"). Thus, PIJ rejects any notions of the feasibility and legitimacy of a two-state solution.

---

[1] I am grateful to Musa Abu Samir, leader of PIJ in South Lebanon, who sent me this text shortly after publication.

This document matters because much remains unknown about the political thought of PIJ, and the movement has received little attention when studying Islamist movements. The political document of the movement is thus a short, candid, and concise introduction to its main positions—on the nature of Palestinian land and its blessedness, the Palestinian people, on Israel and the Jews, on the two-state solution and negotiations, the international situation, the Palestinian situation, and on armed struggle.

Preface

Palestine has since the dawn of history been the homeland of the Palestinian people, and it is an integral part of the Arab and Islamic homeland. Encouraged and assisted by Western colonial forces, it was usurped by Zionist Jews who established the Israeli entity there after killing, displacing, and replacing most of its people.

The Palestinian people did not hesitate to defend their land and sanctities since the commencement of the conflict, whether in the past or in the present, providing thousands of martyrs, injured, and prisoners taken from the finest of its children. The Arab umma fought battles and wars, and provided generations of martyrs for the liberation of Palestine, which the umma considered the central cause of the Arabs and Muslims.

The disastrous Oslo Agreement was the major turning point in Arab history, and it marked the transformation of the Arab-Zionist conflict with its bet on "the impossible peace" with "Israel." As the PLO, which was established to liberate Palestine, recognized the Zionist entity, the Palestinian trauma suddenly unfolded a paradox in which the victim turned into the guardian of its executor!

After a quarter of a century of official Palestinian dependency on the compromise approach, giving the Israeli entity more than it could ever dream of and robbing the Palestinians of the rest of their land and rights, the Palestinian arena fumes with a new stage of intellectual malady and political despair, circling in a vicious cycle. It does so only to replicate its bet on the illusion and mirage of compromise while dissipating the fruits of steadfastness, blood, and sacrifice, which revealed the fragility of the Jewish entity. At a time when the madness of blood sweeps the region, some Arabs are preoccupied in examining the principles that will expand the Israeli domination in the Arab world, for "Israel" to write a new and different history of the region as it becomes the sole fixed value while the rest is alien and unstable!

Before this collapse in this painful Arab-Palestinian moment—when everything is confused, the vision is blurred, the collusion on reality intensifies, and injustice is condoned—our confidence in adhering to the absolute right and the "complete liberation" of our nation until martyrdom is strengthened.

Confirming this, and in order to preserve the clarity of vision, and the unity of spirit and goal, far from the intellectual chaos predominating the Palestinian scene, Palestinian Islamic Jihad has decided to formulate this internal document. It does so to proclaim and confirm the central ideological features and principles of its jihad and its positions to move on solid ground on this long and bitter road to Palestine, all of Palestine.

I. Presenting the Movement and Its Identity

Presenting the Movement

Palestinian Islamic Jihad is a Palestinian resistance movement, its reference is Islam, its goal is the liberation of Palestine from the Zionist entity, and its means is jihad.

Identity and Belonging

1. The Islamic reference of Palestinian Islamic Jihad is based on Islamic sharia, adhering to it as the most appropriate way of life, and on the work to embody its meanings, values, and ethics in thought, behavior, and jihad; to exalt the symbols of God; and to sublimate the importance of belonging to the homeland and to the umma.
2. Palestinian Islamic Jihad is an independent movement originating from a conscious Palestinian will to fulfill the legitimate duty—sensing a national, Arab, Islamic, and moral responsibility. It is a response to the demands of the complete confrontation with the Zionist project on the land of Palestine.
3. In keeping with its founding principles and objectives, the movement's main priority and mission is to fulfill the duty of jihad and resistance for the liberation of Palestine without neglecting its other national, Arab, and Islamic responsibilities toward its people and umma.
4. Palestinian Islamic Jihad is a national-Islamic liberation movement, and it is one of the links in the Palestinian people and umma's jihad against the invaders and colonialists throughout our history right up to the Zionist invasion that usurped Palestine. It is an integral part of the contemporary Palestinian national movement.
5. The movement sees itself as a part of the general Islamic current in the world, without organic links to, or dependence on, any other group. It sees Islam as the source of our strength and pride, and as the secret of our distinguished identity among nations, integrated with all living forces in the umma. The movement expresses its will and aspirations to fulfill the duty of jihad and resistance in Palestine.
6. The movement affirms the interdependence between its Islamic commitments, its pride in its Arab and Islamic identity, and its firm belonging to the homeland and pride in its national identity. The movement is thus emotionally linked to the umma and organically linked to the homeland, and the defense of any of them is reflected positively on the other. The enemy of the umma, and the enemy of the homeland, is one.

II. Palestine

The Land of Palestine

1. Historical Palestine, as known during the British occupation, extends from the Jordan River in the east to the Mediterranean in the west, and from Ra's

al-Naqura in the north to the Gulf of Aqaba in the south. It is a single, indivisible territory, and it is the land and homeland of the Palestinian people. It is unlawful to give up any part of it in any way.
2. Palestine is an Arab-Islamic land and it is a part of the greater Arab-Islamic homeland, and the Islamic umma in which it resides has a natural, religious, and historical right to it. It shall not be abandoned or given up under any pretext.
3. There is no right for Jews in Palestine to usurp the land, expel its people by force, and to establish an entity on it. The fact that some of our people and umma have recognized this entity does not give it any right, and it does not dissolve the constant and legal right of the Palestinian people in all of Palestine. Nor does it dissolve the legal sovereignty of the Palestinian people, which is not removed by the military occupation or the coercive political domination of the Israeli entity.
4. The land of Palestine is a direct axis of the conflict with the Zionist project. It is so because of its sanctity and its place in history, and it is distinguished by its geographical location as it represents the key to the East and to the Islamic world. It thus embodies the conflict in all of its dimensions, which will not end before the liberation of every inch of Palestine.

The People of Palestine

1. The Palestinian people—with all of their generations, faiths, ideological currents, political and struggling forces, social groups, everywhere in Palestine and outside—are one, and their cause is one. The Palestinian people are a genuine and vital part of the Arab and Islamic umma.
2. The Palestinian Christians are an inseparable part of the Palestinian people and of the Arab and Islamic umma. They are partners in the homeland who have made great sacrifices for their Muslim brothers. Prominent political and militant leaders, in addition to cultural and economic elites, originated from them. They have thus had a profound impact on the march of the Palestinian struggle.
3. The Palestinian people did not leave their land, Palestine, of their own volition and will, or on the request of the Arab states or Palestinian leadership. Instead, they were uprooted and expelled from their land by the force of arms, terrorism, and Zionist massacres. The Jews then seized the land and property.
4. The right of the Arab Palestinians in all of their land and homeland, Palestine, is a universal and inalienable right, including the right to own land and to liberate it through resistance. It includes the right of self-determination with full sovereignty on the land, the right to return and live in the homeland, to embody its political choices with which it preserves its belonging and identity, and to affirm its natural position as a part of the Arab and Islamic umma.
5. The national character of the Palestinian people is deep-rooted and distinct. It is derived from the values, principles, and ideals emanating from the people's creed, history, heritage, and continuity on this blessed land, and from its struggle to liberate it. It is a character affiliated with the Arab and Islamic umma, and

interacting with the world in which we live. It is thus a character and identity integrated with its national, Arab, Islamic, and human components.
6. Any political projects or programs based on dividing the Palestinian people or removing any part, or violating the components of its national character, is devoid of legitimacy. They do not represent the Palestinian people and do not express their will.

Palestine in the History of Islam and the Arabs

1. Palestine is the place where the Arab Canaanites, who came from the Arab Peninsula thousands of years ago, lived. Our ancestors, the Jebusites, were one of the first to inhabit Jerusalem more than 4,000 years ago. The present people of Palestine are descendants of the Arab Canaanites intermingled with Arab peoples and tribes. Since ancient times, and despite the numerous invasions, the people of Palestine have maintained their ownership of the land and their presence up until the Zionist invasion.
2. Palestine was the land of salvation and emigration for Prophet Abraham—peace be upon him. "No, Abraham was neither a Jew nor a Christian. He was of pure faith, a Muslim." From his descendants, God sent the Arab prophet, Muhammad—peace be upon him—as affirmed in the Qur'an: "Indeed, the most worthy of Abraham among the people are those who followed him [in submission to God] and this prophet, and those who believe [in his message]." This does not include the Jews who claim affiliation with him, and who fabricate a lie against God claiming he promised the Holy Land of Palestine to the oppressors.
3. All the apostles and prophets, including those dispatched to the Tribe of Israel and those who believed in them, were Muslims united by God. The prophets of the Tribe of Israel were not Jews, and there is no description in the Torah of their being so, so their religion was Islam. Their history is thus regarded as part of Islam's history, and not the Jewish history that commenced with the formation of the Jewish religion in Babylon, and which was based on injustice, corruption, fighting the Truth, and disavowing the prophets and killing them. The Jews thus brought upon themselves the fury of God who destined them to exile on the land.
4. Archaeological research has not verified the Jewish allegations on kingdoms established by invaders from the Tribe of Israel in Palestine. If they existed, then they were small and limited kingdoms in time and space, and their ephemeral and sporadic existence does not prove the right of Jews in Palestine. If it were the right of every tribe and nation to return to, and control, land that it at some point invaded in any part of the world, then it would change the existing shape of the world and its maps.
5. The Arab Muslims liberated Palestine from the Roman occupation through the Islamic conquest of Jerusalem in the seventh century. Most of Palestine's inhabitants embraced Islam, fulfilled their Arabism, and, from that time, gave rise to one people united in origin, language, culture, religion, the creed

of Muslims, and the culture of Christians. They all established a permanent presence in Palestine, where they lived for more than 1,350 years, until the nakba of 1948.

6. The bond of Palestine to Islam is a bond of creed as it is a holy and blessed land. It was the first *Qibla* of the Muslims, the point of departure for Prophet Muhammad's midnight journey to the seventh heaven—peace be upon him—and from where he ascended to heaven. It is where the al-Aqsa Mosque is placed, which God blessed and connected in the Qur'an to the Great Mosque of Mecca. It is the land of the frontier post of the upholders of Truth to the Day of Resurrection.
7. Under the rule of Islam, Palestine was challenged by the invasions of European crusaders, the Tatars, and Mongols, which swept the Islamic world. Muslims thus rose up, took up jihad, resistance, and battles of liberation against them. They were able to defeat them and to liberate Palestine until the new colonialists returned when British colonialism occupied Palestine in 1917 and subsequently gave it to the Jews.
8. The Muslims of the Palestinian people are proud that their land, Palestine, is the birthplace of God's prophet Jesus—peace be upon him. The Muslims have since the Islamic conquest preserved the monuments, symbols, and places of Christian worship, especially the Church of the Holy Sepulcher in Jerusalem as well as others. Muslims have similarly worked to preserve and protect them since the age of the Umayyad.

Jerusalem

1. Jerusalem is the heart of Palestine, its capital, and the symbol of its sanctities. Jerusalem is a religious, historical, and cultural place in the heart and mind of all Arabs and Muslims. It is with all of its Islamic and Christian sanctities a constant right of the Palestinian people and property of the umma in its entirety—in the past, present, and future—as is all the land of Palestine. It is unlawful in any situation to relinquish any part of it, or to compromise even an atom of its dust.
2. All the aggressive plans, procedures, and work in Jerusalem—aiming to change the religious, historical, and cultural features of the city, its social fabric and composition of the population, by displacing the Palestinians there and blurring and falsifying the Arab and Islamic identity through destruction and Judaizationt—have no legitimacy.
3. The blessed al-Aqsa Mosque, the Dome of the Rock, and the Wailing Wall, which is an integral part of the Temple Mount, are all exclusively Islamic property, and a constant right of our people and umma. The Jews do not have any right to it, and all of the aggressive plans and procedures of the occupation authority with the attempts by the Jews to seize the al-Aqsa Mosque and to divide it temporally and spatially, or to deny Muslims the right to pray inside, are unlawful and illegitimate.
4. All solutions canceling the rights of the Palestinian people, the Arabs, and Muslims in Jerusalem—whether in the eastern part, the Old City, or anywhere else known as Jerusalem—or limiting their relationship with it, in any form

of religious sovereignty, without emancipation from occupation and the full sovereignty of our people and umma, are illegal and rejected.
5. Dealings with the Zionist occupation authorities by any party—whether Arab, Islamic, or international—in any form that can be invoked as an implicit recognition or acceptance of the fait accompli imposed by the Jews, declaring Jerusalem as an eternal and unified "capital" of the Israeli entity, are illegal and rejected.

The Refugees and the Right of Return

1. The Palestinian refugees are those of the Palestinian people who were thrown out from their homes and rooted out from their land by oppressive and aggressive force during and after the two nakbas in 1948 and 1967. They were prevented from returning to their homeland, their homes, their land, and properties, which were seized by the Zionists and provided as accommodation to the Jews imported to Palestine from different states in the world.
2. The right of the Palestinian people to return to their land, homes, and properties is a natural, individual, communal, legitimate, hereditary right from generation to generation, and does not wither away with time. It is unlawful to give it up, partition it, or to compromise it. No side has the right to violate it or to dispose of it.
3. Any decisions issued by any state, or a national, regional, or international authority, that impinge on the right of return or offer compensation as an alternative to it are all unlawful and rejected. This applies to all projects or attempts to liquidate the cause of the refugees, and in particular the alternative homeland projects with the resettlement of the Palestinians where they are, outside of their homeland, Palestine.
4. The Palestinian cause is not a refugee cause, but a national Arab-Islamic human cause to liberate the homeland of the Palestinian people for them to live in it with freedom and dignity like the rest of the peoples in the world. The refugees' right to return to their land and homes from which they fled is a right derived from this ownership, and it is the right of the Palestinian people throughout their homeland, Palestine.

The Zionist Project

1. The Zionist project is the project of a settler-colonial invasion. It is a racist, aggressive, and expansionist project based on Jewish religious allegations, myths, and political lies. Slogans such as "the promised land," "God's chosen people," and "a land without a people" display the identity and essence of "the Israeli entity" in particular as a phenomenon of religious revisionism and settler-colonialism.
2. The Zionist project was based on the organic link with the forces of Western colonialism, which worked to get rid of the Jews and to solve the "Jewish problem" in Europe by planting an entity for the Jews in Palestine. The

deportation of the Jews began before the declaration of the Zionist project in 1897 as the Arabs and Muslims had to pay the price for the West's persecution of the Jews, who conversely had lived their happiest times in security and peace under the protection, and in the homes of, Islam and Muslims.

3. The usurpation of Palestine by the Zionist project is a part of the historical clash of the West with Islam. It began with the Covenant of the Prophet via the so-called "Reconquista" of the land conquered by Muslims, which began with the fall of Toledo in Andalusia in 1085. Then came the crusader wars, and all that followed, until the overthrow of the Ottoman Caliphate, the division of its domain, the British occupation of Palestine, the declaration of it as the homeland of the Jews, and the establishment of the Israeli entity on its territory.

4. The Israeli entity is a settler-client entity, and its persistence is essentially related to the role assigned to it. It is a tool for the project of colonial domination and control in Palestine, and the Israeli entity is its aggressive base in the region and its advanced regional center. It principally derives all of its material and moral strength from the strength and capabilities of the West, in particular the United States of America, in the international power balance. Any weakening of this force will automatically lead to the weakening of the Israeli entity.

5. The establishment of the Israeli entity embodies the will of the Western colonial forces, its desire to establish a human and geographical barrier entity, to separate the east of the Arab homeland from the west. It embodies the will of the Western colonial forces to isolate Egypt from the Levant, robbing it of its strategic position and central role in the region; to prevent any Arab or Islamic unity; to consecrate division and dependency; and to serve the interests of Western colonialism.

6. The support for the establishment of Israel was not limited to Western, capitalist countries. The socialist communist states, led by the former Soviet Union, were among the first countries to recognize the entity in 1948, providing it with political and military support, and opening the gates of Jewish emigration to Palestine.

7. The danger of the Israeli entity does not stop by the borders of Palestine, as it has its eyes on the umma in its entirety—its units, states, and people. It works with absolute American and international Zionist support to bolster its force and to consolidate its presence as a "Jewish superpower" that dominates the people of the umma, depletes it of its capacities and abilities, and aborts any attempt to obtain renaissance or independence.

8. The conflict with the Israeli entity, with all that it represents, is not solely a conflict over land, riches, or strategic sites. It is equally not solely a conflict of class where Arab and Jewish laborers and proletarians are lined up against the bourgeoisie or capitalist class. It is, instead, a complete civilizational conflict, complex and multicircuit, encompassing all religious, historical, geographical, political, military, security, economic, and cultural spaces and dimensions of life.

9. The conflict with the Israeli entity on the land of Palestine is a conflict of existence, not a conflict about borders. Nor is it a conflict against a system of racial discrimination, "apartheid." "Israel" exists to keep Palestine out of

existence, and the foreign Jews are where they are because the Palestinians, the legitimate owners of the land, were expelled from the land of their fathers and forefathers by the force of arms and Zionist terrorism.
10. The Israeli entity is unique in terms of the importance of military power in its structure and role. The Israeli entity is the instrument of Jewish Zionism, and it is its military fortress, armed with the latest and most lethal weapons, including nuclear ones, playing the guardian of the colonial powers' interests, which sponsor it in the region. Military life in the entity is the basis, all other segments of life are in the service of the military structure and role, and every individual of the entity is a soldier on temporary leave. Therefore, in order to overcome and defeat this entity, one must target their military forces and subvert their prestige, as they are the source of its power, tyranny, and superiority.
11. The Jews are not a nation, nor are they a homogenous people of one origin assembled by one history and one language. Yet, the Zionist movement gathers them in the Israeli entity with all of their various nationalities, languages, and customs, which despite its contradictions mixed the Jewish religion with Zionist policies. This entity thus became the heart in the identity, belonging, and loyalty of the majority of Jews in the world.
12. Our conflict for Palestine is with the Israeli entity, the usurper of our homeland, the enemy of our people and umma. Any Jew outside this entity—wherever (s)he is—who does not follow "Israel" and does not support it, who does not usurp our land and our rights, and who is not hostile to us, we do not consider an enemy of ours. Thus, the criterion for our position toward the others is their position on Palestine, regardless of belief or origin.
13. The Israeli entity, despite its character, is the last bastion of settler-colonialism in the world, and it will fall just as all the other bastions fell. With all that symbolizes and embodies it of usurpation, occupation, injustice, and aggression, the entity is an illegal and illegitimate entity forbidden to be recognized. It has no right to exist on any part of Palestine, or on any part of Arab and Muslim lands.

The Palestinian Cause

1. The Palestinian cause—with its religious sanctity, historical depth, and strategic and civilizational importance—is not the cause of the Palestinian people alone or the cause of the Arabs alone. It is the central cause of the Arab and Islamic umma in its entirety, and it is of concern to all people and nations preoccupied with establishing peace and stability in the world based on Truth and justice, and not on aggressive force and coercion.
2. The Palestinian cause is not the cause of Palestinian land occupied in 1967 or a part of it, but it is the cause of all the occupied Palestinian land, from the river to the sea. It is not the cause of a particular generation of Palestinians, Arabs, or Muslims, but the cause of all generations, handed over by grandparents and parents to their children until God permits victory and liberation.

3. The Palestinian cause is critically linked to all the causes of the Arabs and Muslims. The Arabs and Muslims will never be liberated from the reality of division, underdevelopment, and dependency—all of their problems—unless Palestine is liberated. The transformation of the umma's situation and the liberation of Palestine are thus complementary and integral issues, as one predisposes the actualization of the other. The renaissance of the umma, its independence, and its unity is the road to liberate Palestine, while the work to liberate Palestine is the path to the renaissance and unity.

Jihad and Resistance

1. The right of the Palestinian people and the umma to wage jihad and resistance against the Zionist enemy usurper of Palestine—with all means and methods, primarily armed struggle—to liberate the land, and to recover their rights and dignity, is a legitimate right established by all heavenly laws and by international conventions and charters.
2. The armed struggle against the Zionist enemy is the main method and strategy in our struggle, and it is a religious, national, Arab, and moral duty. It is not allowed to abandon it before the aggression is gotten rid of, the land is liberated, and the rights are recovered. To disengage from the armed struggle is thus a defiance of religion, to give up the homeland, and to betray the charters, covenants, and the values upon which societies, states, homelands, and nations are built.
3. The experiences of all liberation movements in the world, and the experiences of the umma in its long conflict with the Zionist enemy and all colonists, affirm that the approach of jihad and resistance is the most realistic and useful approach for liberation. This was confirmed by the Lebanese resistance's liberation of southern Lebanon from the Zionist occupation and by the Palestinian resistance's liberation of the Gaza Strip from the Zionist occupation and its settlements.
4. Armed jihad is considered the main method of the resistance. Yet, it does not prevent the use of other means and forms, especially the "popular intifada," in which different arts and tools for confrontation are brought together innovatively and creatively.
5. Martyrdom in Palestine in all of its forms is the highest degree of self-defense against the terrorism of a Zionist enemy carrying out a racial extermination of our people—from men and elders to women and children—in view of the world's failure to prevent the oppressive occupier, or to protect our oppressed people.
6. Palestinian Islamic Jihad stresses the absolute right of the Palestinian people and the resistance forces to acquire weapons and as much of them as possible, to manufacture and develop arms, and the absolute right to refuse abandoning the arms of resistance and to reject any attempt by any party to violate it.
7. Palestinian Islamic Jihad affirms that the strategic goal of the jihad and resistance of the Palestinian people is the recovery of all land and rights. It similarly sees, unconditionally, the defeat of the Zionist occupation forces on any part of

Palestine through resistance as a national achievement and a step on the road toward full liberation.

8. The constant approach of jihad and resistance is the continued confrontation with the Zionist enemy—exhausting its energy and capabilities and destabilizing its security and stability—to force it to leave our land, and lead to the full liberation of Palestine. It is a great historical and human task to be achieved by the generations of the Arab and Islamic umma and its vanguard, the Palestinian people, which requires the support and assistance of all the free people of the world.

The Approach of Compromise

1. It is impossible to have peace with the Zionist project because peace is incompatible with its settler nature and its racist and aggressive essence. The peace that the Israeli entity desires is the peace of a fait accompli imposed by force, a functional peace. Its goal is to loot the rest of Palestine, Judaize it, and declare the entity a "Jewish state" exclusive to Jews on the entire land of Palestine.
2. All projects and resolutions made by states or by international bodies to establish a political state or entity for the Jews in Palestine—such as the Balfour Declaration, the bill of the British Mandate, the resolution to partition Palestine in 1948, and other similar resolutions—are invalid from their issuance until today.
3. All settlement agreements and peace treaties concluded by the Israeli entity and some of the Arabs and Palestinians (such as the "Camp David" agreement, the "Israel-Jordan peace treaty," the "Oslo" agreement, and what followed) recognizing the right of "Israel" to exist at the expense of Palestine and its people are considered invalid, do not express the will of the umma, and do not commit it to anything.
4. Palestinian Islamic Jihad refuses to recognize the Israeli entity, to reconcile with it, or to negotiate with it because our right in Palestine is not a relative right, but an absolute right that cannot be divided or compromised, and because to recognize the "entity" means to erase Palestine's existence, and to recognize the right of foreign Jews to live and rule on the land of Palestine means the non-recognition of the Palestinian people and their inherent right to live and rule over its entire national territory in Palestine.
5. Palestinian Islamic Jihad refuses to relegate the right of our people and our umma in Palestine to a Palestinian state within the 1967 borders as a solution to the Palestinian cause. Palestinian Islamic Jihad rejects a 1967 state because it means to compromise most of the land of Palestine, to recognize the right of the Israeli entity to exist, and to waiver the right of return, the right of self-determination, and the right to liberate Palestine.
6. The Israeli entity is an intrusive and alien entity in an environment hostile to it, and it will disappear no matter how long it takes. The imbalance of power, and the inability of the Arab states to confront it, do not justify surrendering to it or to recognize the legitimacy of its existence on Arab and Islamic land. It does not exempt states and regimes from the responsibility of preparing for all possible

force. Neither the peoples nor the governments are exempt from the duty of supporting the forces of jihad and resistance, which are engaged in a conflict with the enemy on behalf of the whole umma.
7. Palestinian Islamic Jihad rejects all attempts to fuse the Israeli entity into the region as a natural entity with the consequence of redefining the region as "the new Middle East." It has the purpose of dismantling the Arab and Islamic identity of the region, fragmenting its states and entities, and dividing it on religious, sectarian, and ethnic grounds to justify the existence of "Israel" as a "Jewish state"—enabling it to control and dominate the nascent entities and draw them into the Zionist embrace.
8. The process of compromise, making the relationship with the Israeli entity reach an unprecedented level, led to the end of the official Arab commitment to the Arab-Zionist conflict and its values, guidelines, and obligations. It turned it into a conflict for the Palestinians in particular, then to a power struggle within the Palestinian ranks while it turned into a sectarian, creedal, and ethnic conflict between Arabs and Muslims themselves as an alternative enemy to "Israel."
9. Palestinian Islamic Jihad rejects the normalization of the Israeli enemy in any form by any Arab or Muslim country on any level. It affirms the necessity of reviving and implementing the Arab boycott resolutions of the entity, and of resisting all Zionist attempts to penetrate the Arab and Islamic world in all political, economic, social, cultural, and media areas, to mention a few.
10. The true peace sought by the Palestinian people and the people of the umma is the peace based on the realization of rights; the abolition of oppression, aggression, and occupation; returning Palestine, from its river to its sea, to its people and indigenous holders; and returning them to the land and homes from which they fled.

The Internal Palestinian Situation

A. The Nature of The Stage

1. Palestine in its entirety is still occupied. The enemy is the one who acts on the land, has sovereignty, and controls the population. The Palestinian National Authority (PA) is set up on a part of the land in the West Bank and in the Gaza Strip without any real sovereignty.
2. The stage in which the Palestinian people live, as evidenced by the facts, is still the stage of national struggle to liberate the land and recover the rights under conditions and circumstances unique and different from the experiences of other national liberation movements against colonialism.
3. The nature of the stage is the stage of struggle for liberation, which determines the nature of the national Palestinian project. The nature of the stage defines the form of the struggle and its appropriate tools against the enemy that continues to loot and Judaize the land, and to displace and expel its people, and it regulates the relationship between the components of the Palestinian national movement.

Accordingly, the original Palestinian project is the project of liberating all of Palestine through the strategy of jihad and resistance.

4. In the stage of national struggle for liberation, it is not permissible to shift from the approach of jihad and resistance to the approach of compromising land and rights. Alternative priorities may not be created, such as electoral conflict or competition for power and representation under occupation, which will divert our struggle from its rightful path and our people from the duty of resistance and liberation.
5. In the stage of national liberation, the main historical contradiction of our people and its fighting force is that with the Zionist enemy. Any contradiction or dispute in the Palestinian rank is treated according to its connection with the main contradiction with the enemy.

B. *The Palestine Liberation Organization (PLO)*

1. The legitimacy of any Palestinian institution or body, and its eligibility to represent the Palestinian people, is derived from its full commitment to its homeland, Palestine. It is derived from its jihad to recover it, its rejection of any compromise that detracts it from the homeland, and its representation of the national identity with all of its components and its embodiment of the unity of the people everywhere.
2. The Palestine Liberation Organization (PLO) was founded to liberate Palestine through armed struggle. Yet, it has abandoned this goal, recognized the legitimacy of the Zionist entity, signed the Oslo Agreement, and it has renounced the resistance and criminalized it, which amounts to a coup d'état against the PLO and the constants stipulated in its charter. It thus amounts to a departure from the history of the Palestinian struggle.
3. A large part of the Palestinian people is represented by Hamas and Palestinian Islamic Jihad together with broad Palestinian factions not involved in the framework of the PLO, which means that it does not currently constitute a framework for the whole spectrum of the people and its components. This weakens its representational legitimacy and does not reflect the full will of the Palestinian people.
4. The restoration of the PLO's status as the representative of the Palestinian people requires it to be reconstructed in a democratic and patient manner so that it becomes a comprehensive framework for all Palestinians. It is as such based on new intellectual and political foundations, and is essentially on the basis of two charters, the national and Arab-national. It is based on not abandoning an inch of Palestine within a framework of a comprehensive national struggle to achieve the goals of the Palestinian people in the liberation of all of Palestine.

C. *The Palestinian National Authority*

1. The Palestinian National Authority (PA) is a self-governing authority created by the illegal and illegitimate Oslo Agreement, which was signed in isolation

from the will of the Palestinian people and which bestowed legitimacy upon the occupation. The PA does not have any sovereignty on the ground and is limited to executive, civilian, and service functions within a framework allowed by the enemy, provided in return for the security coordination to protect the occupation and the settlements.
2. The project of the PA does not include all of the Palestinian people but is only for the Palestinians in the West Bank and in the Gaza Strip. It thus ignores the Palestinians in the diaspora, in the occupied 1948 areas, and subsequently the people of Jerusalem. It is in other words a project that has abandoned the unity of the land and the unity of the people. It threatens the unity of the Palestinian identity and makes our national cause a cause of a minority population within the framework of Israeli sovereignty.
3. Palestinian Islamic Jihad deals with the PA as a reality while still adhering to the right to challenge its project, its approach based on compromise and forfeiture, and its abandonment of the National Charter and of the unity of the land and people, as the PA submits to the pressures and dictates of the United States and the Zionists and, instead, favoring the enemy's security demands at the expense of the demands and security of our people and their national cause.

D. National Relations

1. Palestinian national unity, based on resistance against the occupation, is the most urgent necessity to confront the Zionist scheme of transforming the conflict from that between the Palestinian people and the Israeli occupier to an internal one between Palestinians themselves.
2. The work to achieve unity does not eliminate differences in vision, or in objectives and means, among the Palestinian forces and factions. Rather, it aims to make the national action meet on commonalities—based on "strengthening what we agree upon, and discussing what we disagree on"—in order to protect the essentials, and to confront the projects attempting to liquidate the cause.
3. Palestinian Islamic Jihad affirms the necessity of cooperation and coordination between the forces of jihad and resistance. It sees the necessity to unite their efforts, strengthen their alliance, and to exchange experiences and capabilities in order to improve the capacities of the resistance, the ways of confronting the occupation, and everything that will achieve the goals and aspirations of the Palestinian people.
4. Palestinian Islamic Jihad rejects clashes or using violence to solve internal Palestinian problems. It adopts, instead, an alternative, the method of purposeful and constructive dialogue with all Palestinians, and it stresses the necessity of directing all Palestinian rifles against the occupation.
5. Palestinian Islamic Jihad refuses to reduce the principle of national partnership, in competition or consensus, to a sharing of self-authority, which depends entirely on the Israeli entity holding all aspects of life, and on external support conditioned by the PA's implementation of the Oslo Agreement, repressive

measures against our people, threatening their unity, and dispelling their objectives and aspirations.
6. A real national partnership means the participation of all Palestinian frameworks, organizations, and activities in national decision-making, which stems from the right of our people in the whole of its homeland, Palestine. This requires the reconstruction and reframing of the Palestinian national institutions fitting a national liberation movement that embodies the unity of the land and the people struggling for the recovery of their land and their rights.
7. Palestinian Islamic Jihad affirms the importance of liberating the Palestinian will and the independence of the Palestinian national decision, and it must be far from any dependence on third parties or an obedience to the American and Zionist dictates. The Palestinian national decision must be far from that distorted practice of "independent resolution," which was merely a means to bring the Palestinian cause out of its Arab and Islamic depth and an excuse for some Arabs to disengage from their obligations toward Palestine.

E. National Issues and Tasks
1. Civil society is the historical cradle of the Palestinian national struggle's march, and stresses the role of different cultural, religious, professional, or unionist groups and segments in the struggle. Heeding the youth generation, enabling them to rise in all fields, it is a national demand to secure the widest popular participation in order to achieve our national goals.
2. Providing the requirements of our people's steadfastness and their attachment to the occupied land throughout Palestine, to confront the policies of Zionist oppression aiming to displace Palestinians from their land, who either search for a living or dispose of the hell of living under occupation.
3. Liberating the prisoners and the detained from the occupation prisons is one of the central and important causes of Palestinian Islamic Jihad. This entails providing the necessities and needs of our prisoners, care for their families, cooperating with all forces of our people in the work to liberate them, and supporting and assisting their struggle to secure a decent life until God grants them freedom.
4. Strengthening the fighting role of women, promoting their level of participation in the resistance, in the national and Islamic practice, asserting their rights and duties, accomplishing their dignity and status in society, as they are an essential pillar providing the resistance and liberation project with the most important reasons for strength persistence.
5. The Palestinians inside the occupied 1948 areas are an inseparable part of the Palestinian Arab people. With their persistence and steadfastness on the Palestinian land; with their struggle to consolidate and maintain their Palestinian, national identity; with their protection of our Arabic-Islamic culture from Judaization; with their resistance against all Zionist projects and plans aiming for their expulsion from their land and its Judaization; and with the confrontation of all forms of Zionist oppression and racism against them, the 1948 Palestinians contribute to achieving the full national goals of the Palestinian people.

6. The Palestinians outside Palestine are an authentic part of the Palestinian people and their struggling march. They embody the unity of the land and the people through the support of their people at home, through the struggle to preserve their national identity, and by adhering to the right of return and refusing the resettlement of the refugees. The whole Palestinian movement shares the responsibility to defend their interests and to demand their legitimate civil and social rights wherever they are.

III. The Arab and Islamic Umma

1. Palestinian Islamic Jihad believes that the Palestinian cause is the central cause of the Arab and Islamic umma.
2. Palestinian Islamic Jihad believes in the unity of the umma with all of its various components. Yet, the principle of unity has been absent for decades, replaced by a reality of fragmentation, division, and narrow interests, which are often characterized by either hostility, tensions, or tepidness at best.
3. The reign of fragmentation and division in the umma, and the absence of support for Palestine and its people from the Arab League and Organization for Islamic Cooperation, does not cancel the concept of the umma's unity in the Arab and Islamic consciousness. It also does not exempt the rulers and the people from the responsibility and duty to defend the fateful causes of the umma, foremost of which is the Palestinian cause.
4. The failure to realize "the centrality of the Palestinian cause" in the contemporary Arab and Islamic reality, with the Arabs' and Muslims' preoccupation with their internal affairs and regional conflicts, does not negate the Arabism of Palestine and its Islamic nature, nor does it diminish its priority or centrality, because the Palestinian cause is the central cause on which the fate of the Arab and Islamic world depends.
5. Palestinian Islamic Jihad is determined to open up to various countries in our Arab and Islamic umma to establish positive relations with all for the support and service of our cause and people. The position of Palestinian Islamic Jihad on this or that side is determined by its position on the Palestinian cause and the level of material and moral support. At least its support and assistance for the steadfastness of our people and its permanence on its land, and its right, in resistance, to defend itself, its land, and its sanctities in the face of persistent Zionist aggression.
6. Palestinian Islamic Jihad affirms the importance of building and strengthening cooperative relations with all existing and active Arab and Islamic forces that support the Palestinian cause, the steadfastness of the Palestinian people, their jihad and resistance, and their right to liberate the homeland, and which refuse to recognize the Israeli entity and any forms of American-Zionist domination over the region.

7. Raising the level of interaction with the Palestinian people and their resistance among the Arab and Islamic people, and providing all forms of material and moral support required, is the responsibility of all forces and parties, associations, organizations, youth frameworks, women's bodies, scholars, preachers, and intellectuals. It is the duty of governments to shoulder their responsibilities and to cease all restrictions on popular initiatives in support of Palestine.
8. Palestinian Islamic Jihad stresses the necessity of distancing the Palestinian cause from the engagement in any alignment or axis in the context of wars, and internal and regional conflict, among the people of the umma, which distracts our people and their resistance from the central cause, and corrupts the compass of their jihad and struggle in the conflict with the Zionist enemy.
9. Palestinian Islamic Jihad sees the necessity of deepening the culture of dialogue, consultation,[2] and democracy, and respecting political pluralism; human, material, and moral rights; public freedoms; and the preservation of identity as a prerequisite to overcoming internal crises, strengthening the capabilities of the umma, achieving development and progress, confronting foreign challenges, and escorting the zeitgeist.
10. Palestinian Islamic Jihad denounces ethnic, sectarian, and creedal strife and conflicts, particularly between Sunnis and Shiites, which only serve the enemies of the umma, ensure their cunning plans against it, and consolidate the abhorrent occupation of its land and sanctities. The movement calls for adherence to national unity among all Arabs and Muslims in confrontation with the attempts at fragmentation and dismantlement, and for the adoption of national dialogue as the means to resolve conflicts, far from violence and foreign interference in the internal affairs of the umma.
11. Palestinian Islamic Jihad calls for a comprehensive Arab-Islamic reconciliation, starting with the reconciliation of the governments and their people. It calls for the reconciliation between the Arab countries themselves, and between the states and people of the Islamic umma, in particular neighboring countries such as Iran and Turkey. Palestinian Islamic Jihad calls for adopting a positive dialogue to build confidence, to work to resolve the problems and disputes by peaceful means, to achieve cooperation for the promotion of common interests, and to confront the challenge of the Zionist threat.
12. Palestinian Islamic Jihad calls for the rejection of foreign military presence on any Arab or Islamic land and all forms of foreign domination. The movement condemns the response of the American administration, and its Zionist tool in the region and the world, under the pretext of combating terrorism. The ugliest form of terrorism is the American "state terrorism," which it practices in several places in the world, and the terrorism of the Israeli entity, which it practices daily in Palestine against its defenseless people.

---

[2] Consultation (*shūrā*), a principle referring to the Prophet's injunction to consult with his followers. Considered by numerous modern Islamists as the basis for the implementation of democracy. See Oxford Islamic Studies, "Shura," http://www.oxfordislamicstudies.com/article/opr/t125/e2199 [accessed: October 24, 2019].

13. Palestinian Islamic Jihad calls for the abolition of peace treaties and agreements with the Zionist enemy signed by some of the Arabs and Muslims, and the termination of all forms of normalization and security cooperation with it. It calls for closing all embassies, consulates, and commercial and cultural attaché- and liaison offices, both public and private, between the entity and some of the Arab and Islamic countries, and withdrawing from the "Arab peace initiative."
14. Palestinian Islamic Jihad affirms the important role of Arab and Muslim intellectuals in promoting their mission to defend the cultural components of the umma and its identity; to protect its historical memory; and to strengthen future generations, their values, and the curricula to raise, educate, and develop them and their spiritual and national formation away from the culture of resignation and defeatism that distorts the concepts of the Arab-Islamic-Zionist conflict and wipes Palestine and jihad from the culture, mind, heart, and conscience of the umma.
15. Breaking the wall of the negative Arab and Islamic position toward Palestine and its sanctities, and curbing the eagerness of some to normalize and ally with the Zionist enemy, primarily requires the Palestinians to restore the initiative by liberating themselves from the program of compromise and the Oslo Agreement. They must rehabilitate the resistance and its escalation, and to commence the intifada, which has always proved its ability to regain the world's attention to the Palestinian cause.

IV. The International Situation

1. The Western forces controlling the contemporary international system are still haunted by the West's historical animosity to Islam, which it classifies as the main enemy of Western civilization. It sees any attempt to reach the Arab and Islamic renaissance as a threat against the West and considers any form of resistance against American and Zionist domination in the region and in the world as "terrorism."
2. The Western position on the Palestinian cause stems from the centrality of the Israeli entity in the culture of the West and its policies. The United States is the greatest patron of the entity and the guarantor of its existence, security, continuance, and its military, security, economic, and technological superiority. Europe, on the other hand, does not overstep the American policies in this era, whether in the Arab and Islamic east, or anywhere else in the world.
3. The absolute bias of the United States—its comprehensive and continued support for the Israeli entity and its persistent aggression against the Palestinian people, their land and sanctities—represents a position hostile to the Arabs and Muslims in general and a blatant aggression against our people in particular, which denies them all established and legitimate rights in their homeland, Palestine.
4. The American administration and the European states have included movements of jihad and resistance against the Zionist occupation, and some of its leaders and

symbols, on what is called a "terror list," while the occupation is directly involved in the attack on our people, our umma, and our right to resist to liberate our land. It is an explicit authorization for the Israeli entity to continue its aggression and terrorism to shed the blood of our people, plunder our land, and Judaize our sanctities.

5. The recognition of the Israeli entity by the PLO, and some of the Arab states, led to the expansion and development of the former's international relationships in all fields. It strengthened its infiltration into Africa and the countries of the Nile Basin; in Asia, and in particular in China and in India; it consolidated its relationship with Russia so as to not remain dependent on the United States' international power alliances, contemporary or in the future.

6. We cannot rely on the so-called "international legitimacy" to determine the fate of our people and their cause. This alleged legitimacy, which paved the way for the establishment of "Israel" and recognized it as a "peace-loving state," and which continues to protect and sponsor it, ignores its continued refusal to implement any resolutions condemning its crimes and wars against our people, denying our most basic national and human rights.

Palestinian Islamic Jihad believes in the importance of communicating and cooperating with all forces and currents in the world sympathetic to the Palestinian cause. The movement criticizes the racism of the Zionist entity and its policies in order to mobilize international opinion in support of the Palestinian people, and the legitimacy of resistance against the occupation, condemning the crimes of the Zionist entity and its terrorism, and addressing the schemes against Palestinian national rights.

4

Islamic Principles and Concepts

Written by PIJ's second secretary-general Ramadan Abdallah Shallah and published on February 1, 2018.

This text is an appendage to the preceding political document, and these two pieces should therefore be read together. This document is also a product of its time. While the introduction to the preceding text focused on the national Palestinian context, Shallah reveals another one: the regional chaos raging through the Middle East following the Arab Spring.

The Arab Spring mattered to PIJ. One reason was that Egypt acquired an increasingly important role in Palestinian politics following the Israeli blockade in 2007. PIJ's relationship with the rulers of Egypt thus became increasingly important—whether it was with the Egyptian Muslim Brotherhood or, subsequently, the regime of al-Sisi. Another was the fact that its main patrons and allies—Iran and Hezbollah—became involved in the Syrian civil war. As PIJ stressed its neutrality in the conflicts to keep the Palestinian cause away from regional turmoil, Iran pressed the movement to side with the Syrian regime—and later with the Houthis as Saudi Arabia intervened in the Yemeni civil war.

It is not clear what the movement means when it refers to "this chaos of concepts in the Islamic and national arena." While it may refer to the wars, infighting, and chaos in the Middle East in general, it may very well allude to the growth of elements such as the Islamic State (IS), with the excommunication and bloodshed of other Muslims. Indeed, although PIJ may come forth as an uncompromising jihadist movement, it distanced itself early from other currents such as Egyptian Islamic Jihad (EIJ) and the Islamic Group (al-jamā'a al-islāmiyya) due to their domestic violence. In this document, we thus see PIJ stressing that there is no compulsion in religion (i.e., non-Muslims cannot be forced to convert); that non-Muslims are a part of Islamic society; that one must be exceedingly careful in regard to excommunication; and that one must work against Muslim infighting, fragmentation, and bloodshed.

This document matters because it is one of the few texts by PIJ which point by point discuss and clarify the movement's view on Islamic concepts and ideas. As the movement writes below, this document "represents the general framework defining the features of PIJ's Islamic identity and the creedal and intellectual premises governing its positions." While some of the terms are general—such as "independent reasoning" and "renewal"—it also clarifies the movement's position on excommunication (takfir) and reconciliation with Jews. The document also matters because it is one of the last *known texts written by Shallah before he died in 2020 after a long period of illness—with the subsequent election of Ziyad al-Nakhala as the third secretary-general of the movement.*

In the name of God, the Merciful and Beneficent

Preface

Praise be to God, Lord of the Worlds,
and peace and blessings upon our prophet, Muhammad, his family, and companions.

Palestinian Islamic Jihad is an Islamic mujahid movement, and its goal is the liberation of Palestine through jihad and resistance. Since its inception, the movement was launched on the Islamic idea and the specificity of Palestine's link with Islam. It was a pioneer in its presentation of its vision on the conflict over Palestine, and its religious, historical, and de facto dimensions—covering all political, economic, cultural fields, to mention a few, at the international, regional, and national levels.

This intellectual vision crystallized, and was established through the developing stages of the movement—through practice, efficiency, and vitality, far from stagnation—which distinguished the movement and gave it the ability to adhere to the principles and strategic objectives no matter how circumstances changed. It provides it the flexibility to respond consciously and responsibly according to every change and development at all stages.

In the context of this chaos of concepts in the Islamic and national arena, accompanied by the disorder and imbalance of values in the dominant culture, it is essential that Palestinian Islamic Jihad presents its elaborate vision in a well-defined intellectual structure, thus contributing to the consolidation of the sense of the members' belonging, and protecting the intellectual forts of the movement and society. It was from this point that Palestinian Islamic Jihad decided to present this intellectual document, complementing the "political document," with the essential concepts of the movement. It is from these that the movement commences its process of intellectual and struggling formation, within its general approach derived from the Islamic approach of building the individual and educating the community.

Certainly, the movement does not claim that this document formulates the final truth or concludes its understanding of Islam. Rather, it is a modest independent reasoning[1] of Islam in "a time of conflict over Islam" in order to answer the question: What Islam? For what world? The document thus represents the general framework defining the features of Palestinian Islamic Jihad's Islamic identity and the creedal and intellectual premises governing its positions on issues at stake in various fields. It is based on the way of the people of the sunna and the community—open to all

---

[1] Independent reasoning (*ijtihād*), one of four sources of Sunni law and principally the practice of developing legislation and legal provisions through rational reflection, contrary to blind imitation (*taqlid*) of preceding jurists, where the Qur'an and sunna are silent. See Oxford Islamic Studies, "Ijtihad," http://www.oxfordislamicstudies.com/article/opr/t125/e990?_hi=1&_pos=1 [accessed: August 29, 2019].

constituents of the umma. It is based on the Book of God and the true prophetic sunna according to the independent reasoning of the pious predecessors and from the noble Islamic idea acceding to time, which takes advantage of the extensive experience of human thought so as to not contradict the teachings of our true religion, its values, and its supreme purposes.

In doing so, while I write these specific and summary concepts, I would like to thank and extend my respect to all the brothers and friends who have read this document, and influenced it through their remarks when discussing it. It is with the hope that the Muslim youth, and particularly the sons of Palestinian Islamic Jihad, will find answers to their doubts and questions after a deliberate and conscious study of the document, to help them appear from the fog of conflicting ideas of Islam to the clarity of the vision closest to the light of inspiration and spirit of time.

I pray to God Almighty to assist me in explaining these features and pillars in order to form a valid ground and cornerstone for a new stage of development and bestowal in the march of blessed jihad.

May God grant us success in this endeavor, and He alone is the guide on the path.

Dr. Ramadan Shallah, Secretary-General of Palestinian Islamic Jihad

Islamic principles and concepts

1. **The definition of Islam:** Islam is a submission to God, the religion of God, and the religion of natural disposition.[2] It was transmitted by all the prophets and messengers, which God sealed through the prophecy of Muhammad—peace be upon him—who God sent to all people with the religion of Truth, and which he perfected for his followers.
2. **Islam is a way of life:** Islam is a complete and comprehensive religion, and a way of life. It is a divine creed that gives rise to a complete vision of the universe, man, and life, and a valid law for humanity anywhere and anytime. It governs religious observances, dealings, and ethics in order to achieve pride and happiness in this world and in the Hereafter.
3. **The Islamic reference:** The Holy Qur'an and the true prophetic sunna is the reference of the Muslim in his religion and worldly affairs. God preserved the Qur'an and it is comprehensible, including its legal and linguistic rules. In light of the overall purposes, they are used as tools for understanding the sunna, besides the science of hadith.
4. **The benevolence of the umma:** The Muslim umma is—on the condition of faith, doing good, and resisting evil—the best of nations brought to man, and a proof to them by delivering Islam to them after the seal of the prophecy, representing its noble values and ethics. This is not a racist selection, however, of a specific

---

[2] Natural disposition or primordial nature of the human being (*fitra*) is typically referred to as the pureness of infants in which they are naturally inclined toward the Oneness and religion of God.

race or a chosen people, but for all human beings if they follow the religion of Truth and the approach of God.

5. **The unity of the umma:** Islamic unity is one of the greatest goals in Islam, and Muslims are one nation in the religion of God. The brotherhood of Islam gathered them with different races, languages, colors, homelands, and doctrines. To reject fragmentation, and to denunciate division and conflict, and to achieve harmony and unity among them are a legal obligation and a necessity of life.
6. **The Islamic call:** The Islamic call, with wisdom and gentle exhortation, by enjoining virtue and prohibiting vice, is one of the highest Islamic duties to make the Muslims aware of their religion, and prompting them to adhere to its teachings and values. It is the purification of society and the preservation of its identity, and protecting it from intellectual, moral, and behavioral deviations, yet far from any compulsion.
7. **Ethics:** Ethics in Islam are the true mirror of devoutness and the measure of the integrity of faith. It is a set of fixed individual and societal principles and values prescribed by Islam. It is based on obligation and responsibility to guide the life of man, and to regulate his behavior and relationship with others in a manner worthy of his humanity, thus realizing its very existence.
8. **Moderation:** Islam is the religion of moderation and balance in regard to man, society, history, politics, and the world. Moderation means obligation to Truth and Justice by the guidance of Islam and its approach to life—far from excess and negligence or immoderation and waste.
9. **Excommunication:** Excommunication is a legal ruling not to be taken lightly, or to be embarked upon with uncertainty and suspicion due to the consequences of its provision and its hazardous acts. It is illegal to excommunicate a Muslim who has avowed the Islamic profession of faith and who adheres to the pillars of Islam and the faith, unless he publicly declares himself a blasphemer or knowingly disaffirms what is obligated by religion, or does something equaling unbelief.
10. **Jihad:** Jihad in the path of God is Islam's peak of the hump. It was imposed by God to defend the sanctity of religion, the shrines, and homelands, and to defend the rights and dignity of humans. Jihad is not limited to fighting, however, but is a struggle that encompasses all aspects in the life of the individual and of the community.
11. **Peace:** Peace is the foundation of Muslims' relationship with others. Religious differences are not to be a cause for enmity and fighting, and bloodshed is impermissible. Nothing can alter this peaceful relationship except the aggression of non-Muslims against Islam and Muslims. The law of Islam is thus peace with those peaceful, and jihad against the aggressors.
12. **Resisting aggression:** If the enemy invades or occupies a part of, or a country in, the land of Islam, as is the case in Palestine, jihad becomes an individual duty for its people, and then for all Muslims, to resist the aggression and liberate the land until it is returned to the Muslims.
13. **Reconciliation with the Jews:** It is impermissible for the Arabs and Muslims to make peace with the Jews usurping Palestine in any manner making them permanent in this blessed land as a state. Rather, the Arabs and Muslims must

cooperate in jihad to liberate Palestine, Jerusalem, and the blessed al-Aqsa Mosque.

14. **Violence and terrorism:** Islam does not endorse the violence and terrorism targeting our umma and world, whatever the motives, and whether individuals, groups, or states practice it. It is consequently rejected and condemned. One must differentiate between prohibited or forbidden violence and the use of legitimate and appropriate force, meaning jihad against all foreign enemies as is the case in Palestine.

15. **Islam and governance:** Good governance is a legal obligation and one of Islam's handholds. It is a fort to defend the religion, and to preserve society and Islamic life. Justice is the basis of governance, consultation is its pillar, and all people have the right to choose the method to achieve this, suitable to their circumstance and age.

16. **Democracy:** Democracy is a Western system with its own particular philosophy and vision of the universe and of life. The democratic mechanism, however, does not contradict the teachings of Islam and its purposes—with the people choosing their own rulers in free and direct elections with a peaceful transfer of power within the framework of the Islamic reference. Rather, it is in this age just one form of implementing consultation.

17. **Secularism:** Secularism is the separation of religion from the state, to exclude it from the matters of public life, or to restrict it to individual rituals and rites of worship. It is an imported idea alien to the creed of Islam and its code, derived from the concepts of others in their struggles and experiences in religion and life.

18. **Nationalism and the citizen:** The interconnection of Islam and nationalism is close and well established. The love for the homeland comes from the religion, and the defense of the former is one of the religion's highest duties and obligations. Citizens in the Muslim state include Muslims with their faith and their loyalty to the Muslim community, as well as the non-Muslims with their loyalty to the state. All of them constitute an Islamic society together, the people in it notwithstanding, except when religious distinction is required.

19. **Islam and Arabism:** The relationship between Arabism and Islam is one of harmony and amity. The Arabs were the constituent of earliest Islam and of the campaign of dispatching it to the world; God thus celebrated them for it. God immortalized their language, spread it, and preserved it through the Qur'an. Arabic is the language, and Arabism is a cultural identity and not a form of nationalism or an ethnicity. The bond of Islamic brotherhood is the connecting bond of the Muslims.

20. **Difference and diversity:** Difference and diversity is one of God's rules in the universe and in life. Accordingly, Islam respects religious, ethnic, linguistic, cultural, and political pluralism. It does not mean the elimination of differences between religions and doctrines, however, and Islam calls for toleration and coexistence between human beings so as to not threaten the identity of society, its unity, and its cohesion.

21. **No coercion in religion:** A constant in the Islamic creed is the noncoercion of non-Muslims to convert to Islam, by the people of the Book and by those in

power. It entails enabling them to practice their worship in the abode of Islam and to organize their personal and religious affairs according to the teachings of their religion.

22. **Women:** Women are the sisters of men, and Islam has established justice and equality between them in human nature, esteem, and legal entrustment. Islam has induced the preservation of women's rights and their individual and societal duties, ensuring their participation in building society and in jihad to defend the homeland, within the limits of Islamic regulations and rules.

23. **The family:** The family is the foundation of the Islamic society, based on religion, morals, and belonging to the people and homeland. Parents and children have shared rights and duties toward each other to form a virtuous family, which is considered the main pillar of good society.

24. **Islam and science:** Islam is the religion of faith and of science, and there is no contradiction between the mind and the true tradition. Muslims are called upon examining, thinking, reflecting, and acquainting themselves with the ordinances of God in the selves, outlooks, and societies. Islam is not the cause for the Muslims' backwardness. On the contrary, it opens the road to the renaissance and to progress, and it interacts with civilizations and cultures according to its perspective stemming from the creed of monotheism.

25. **Human rights:** Human rights are ensured in Islam, and they are comprehensive and irrevocable. They are based on the unity of humanity and the equality of people in human dignity and in commitment and responsibility without discrimination, in compliance with the principles and purposes of the sharia.

26. **The Islamic economy:** The economy in Islam is based on the principles of sharia and its purposes in order to ensure dignity, justice, sufficiency, and development. This requires acknowledging property of all types, the controlled freedom of moral values, fighting poverty, imposing zakat,[3] emancipation from usury, preventing the hoarding and monopolization of wealth, and considering the umma as one body and working on interdependence and integration for its constituents, and so on.

27. **Independent reasoning and renewal:** Independent reasoning and renewal in Islam is a religious obligation and a human necessity. Independent reasoning is to be conducted only within legal controls, and by its people in their place. Renewal is to be conducted within religion, and it shall not alter its constants to keep up with time or to justify reality. Rather, renewal is to be appropriate in order to deduce the Text, actualize it in reality, and meet its requirements in accordance with the method to facilitate it in jurisprudence and non-binding legal opinions, in order to achieve the purposes of the religion.

28. **Ends and means:** The end does not justify the means in Islam. Islam is a religion that struggles for the highest goals and the noblest of purposes. It is not sufficient for the end to be legitimate, but the means must also be in accordance with the teachings and rulings of Islam.

---

[3] Religiously obligated alms and one of the five pillars of Islam.

29. **The Islamic idea:** The Islamic idea is not Islam, as Islam is the divine revelation in the Book of God and in the true prophetic sunna. The Islamic idea is the Muslim scholars' perception of Islam, their independent reasoning and opinions, where no text is provided. That is, it is a human idea based upon the circle of Islam.
30. **The Islamic heritage:** The heritage is what the predecessors left behind, with the revelation being the exception. The Islamic heritage is thus not infallible or non-negotiable, and a balanced position is neither to sanctify it, nor to disassociate oneself from it, or to reject it. Rather, it is to filter it and to employ everything good in it—thus contributing to the elevation of the umma's presence and its historical and civilizational continuity.
31. **Innovation:** Innovation in religion is to add what does not belong to it. Yet, not everything new is heresy. Rather, it is forbidden to make a command in the religion without any basis in sharia, or which contradicts a principle of sharia and its purposes.
32. **Globalization:** Islam is a world religion aiming to become acquainted and cooperate with other nations in everything that benefits, and is good for, humanity. Western globalization, on the other hand, seeks the domination of one global pole to impose cultural, economic, and civilizational dependency on the world.
33. **The Islamic history:** The Islamic history is the register of the umma's life, including its strengths and weaknesses. It cannot be interpreted as a material explanation denying the Concealed[4] and prophecy, or any other method raising suspicion about the history of the Prophet, the Qur'an, the companions, the successors, or the civilizational achievements of the umma. Rather, it must be understood and comprehended according to the Islamic approach, which recognizes the revelation of the Prophet and the conventions of God, and acted upon in history and in life.
34. **The companions and the household:** The honorable companions of Prophet Muhammad are the best generation of the umma, and the faith and virtue testify for them, as do their love and reverence. To love the household of God's messenger and to exalt his wives, the mothers of the believers, and to recognize them for their contribution, is the grace of Islam and the faith. To hate the companions or the wives and to slander them, on the other hand, is an abuse of Islam and the Messenger of God.
35. **The Muslim societies:** The contemporary societies of Muslims are Muslim societies. The corruption of Muslims' conditions, their deviation from the virtue of true Islam, and the weakness of both their individual and collective devoutness are flaw and forfeiture that need to be addressed and reformed, but they do not negate the status of Islam from these communities.

---

[4] The Concealed (*al-ghayb*) is a concept referring to the unseen, unknown, and hidden, and it encompasses the realm of the divine and the future, which only God can perceive.

36. **People of the sunna and the community:** The Sunnis are the majority of the umma, and they include the Ash'arites,[5] the Maturidi,[6] and the Salafists who follow the four schools of jurisprudence and others, in contrast to the Mu'tazilites[7] and Kharijites.[8] The entire creed of the Sunnis is derived from the Qur'an and the sunna. As for some verbal details, these are a matter of independent reasoning where differences are admissible.

37. **Shiism:** The Shiites are not one sect, although the majority of them are Twelvers or Ja'faris.[9] They are Muslims, coming together with the Sunnis through the bond of Islam. There are historical differences between the two on issues such as the Caliphate or the Imamate, which extend to some issues of belief and jurisprudence, but they do not secede from the religious community.

38. **Sufism:** Sufism, or mysticism, is a particular approach to education and worship. It has multiple approaches with the intention of purifying the self and reviving the heart in accordance with the Book of God and the prophet's sunna—peace and blessings upon him. It is thus acceptable, and that which is in conflict with the two is unacceptable.

39. **Salafism:** Salafism is a school of thought to understand and practice the religion based on the affiliation with the pious predecessors of the umma. It is not one current, however, and its trends are divided between the traditional preaching current in its different colors and the current of violence in its various stages and groups. The salafi trend claims it is the only representative of true Islam and of the people of the sunna and the community.

---

[5] Ash'arism, one of the main theological schools in Sunni Islam, named after the Islamic theologian, Ali bin Isma'il al-Ash'ari. While initially adhering to Mu'tazilism, al-Ash'ari made a compromise between the overly rationalist approach of the Mu'tazalites and the literalism of Hanbalism, dismissing human reason and adhering to the literalist reading of the Qur'an and hadith alone.

[6] Maturidi, one of the main theological schools in Sunni Islam, named after Abu Mansur Muhammad al-Maturidi. Relying on the Qur'an without reasoning or free interpretation, the maturidis claim that any interpretation is innovation (bid'a), equaling heresy. With their reliance on literalist readings of scripture, the maturidis emphasize man's complete freedom to act. See Encyclopædia Britannica, "Māturīdīyah," https://www.britannica.com/topic/Maturidiyah [accessed: August 22, 2019].

[7] Mu'tazila, a formation of Islamic theological thought in the ninth century. It postulates that human reason is capable of understanding and appreciating God and his creation and thus equally bestowed with the ability to resonate what is good and what is not. Consequently, mu'tazilites hold that Truth and the rulings of God can be achieved through rational and intellectual deduction.

[8] Kharijites, a group of Muslims who seceded from Caliph Ali's army because he arbitrated with Mu'awiya I, whom they deemed an infidel. Infamous for their theological rigidity, they deemed all who sinned as infidels, avowed the legality of rebelling against unjust rulers who failed to rule according to religion, and rejected arbitration to choose the leader of Muslims. While rejecting the infallibility of the leader, they believed that all Muslims could become Caliph, and not merely the members of Quraysh. See Nelly Lahoud, *The Jihadis' Path to Self-Destruction* (London: Hurst & Company, 2010); and Patricia Crone, *God's Rule, Government and Islam: Six Centuries of Medieval Islamic Political Thought* (Columbia: Columbia University Press, 2004).

[9] Twelver Shiites are the majority of Shiite Muslims, often referred to as ja'faris due to their following the ja'fari school of law named after the sixth imam Ja'far al-Sadiq. While basing their legal reasoning on the Qur'an and the sunna, Twelver Shiites and Zaydis put greater emphasis on reason ('aql), both pure and practical, than the Sunni schools of law. See Najam Haider, *Shi'i Islam: An Introduction* (Cambridge: Cambridge University Press, 2014).

40. **The Islamic movements:** The work to revive the role of Islam in life is a legal obligation. Any Islamic group or movement seeking to achieve this goal is not entitled to claim it is *the* group of the Muslims. It is, instead, just one part, or one group, of Muslims, with rights and wrongs in its ranks. The unification of their ranks to serve Islam does not require them all to gather in one particular group or movement.

Part II

PIJ, Colonialism, and the Palestinian Cause

5

Why History?

Published in al-Ṭalīʿa al-Islāmiyya *(The Islamic Vanguard), no. 11, November 1983, by Fathi al-Shiqaqi.*

The main grievance for the PIJ founding fathers was the absence of an Islamic movement in the armed Palestinian struggle. While the Palestinian Muslim Brotherhood stressed the need for proselytization and Islamic values in society first, Hizb al-Tahrir believed that jihad could only be waged with the permission of the caliph. The thesis of Palestine as the central cause of the Islamic movement pushed the PIJ nucleus to bitter disputes with the Muslim Brotherhood in Egypt. Conflict then erupted with the Gazan Brotherhood in the 1980s on the need for the Islamic movement to lead the armed Palestinian struggle. This struggle was particularly hostile and bitter, as the Palestinian Brotherhood refused to start an insurgency for fear of Israeli repression.

This article was authored by Fathi al-Shiqaqi in these times of conflict with the Palestinian Brotherhood. It was also published one year before PIJ launched its first attacks against Israeli targets. At first glance, it seems to provide a brief history of the Muslim Brotherhood—from Hassan al-Banna until the 1980s. Yet, its intention was to pose a challenge to the Brotherhood leaders who were perceived to have deviated from the original course set by their founder. Indeed, the first generation of the Muslim Brotherhood constituted the generation of the renaissance, as they stood up against colonialist deculturization and Westernization. They thus embodied the peak of awareness as they restored the pride of the Muslim community. Yet, the leadership later devolved into a generation of hesitation and distress, as the leftist and secular-nationalist currents emerged in the Middle East. In the eyes of al-Shiqaqi, if anything marked this new generation it was their impotence and their lack of a clear strategy and analysis. It was thus up to the third generation—the generation of al-Shiqaqi and his comrades—to light the torch anew. They were the generation of awareness and revolution. The context of the following piece is thus the ideological, political, and strategic conflict in the early 1980s between the PIJ founding fathers and the Brotherhood.

This document matters for three reasons. First, although the existing literature already describes the conflict between the Palestinian Muslim Brotherhood and the PIJ nucleus in the early 1980s, this piece offers some insight into the arguments and rhetorical devices employed. The Muslim Brotherhood was not simply wrong, but the movement had also deviated from its supposed essence and purpose. Second, this text *also matters because it illustrates how little al-Shiqaqi relied on Qur'anic verses and religious references when entering polemics and debates with other Islamic actors. Instead, he employed historical lessons in order to convince his opponents. Although religion permeates his writing, al-Shiqaqi's analysis in nonetheless quite secular by nature.*

History was, and still is, the cause of man since time immemorial, which is affected and constructed by objective conditions that pass through the stages of human history, and by the cosmic laws laid down by God Almighty.

When a nation is subjected to a violent jolt at some point in its life, either it wakes up from its sleep to look at its history and to reexamine the conditions for its very existence, or it wakes up from its sleep to look askew at history, accusing it before the nation returns to its deep sleep again. Likewise, when a nation or a group is exploited, it begins to take notice of its history. It proceeds to study, to analyze, and to examine it closely. It realigns and reconfigures it to discern its current positions, and then, the way forward. The groups sleeping through its history (in a situation of impotence and estrangement), on the other hand, take a negative and accusing position toward it.

It is here that we—the true sons—realize the importance of an awareness of history, and that this awareness is the key in our hands to understand the consciousness of our past and to learn from its lessons and experiences. We influence our present accordingly, and we are not satisfied sitting in the spectator's seat. This understanding, and this history, will thus lead to the possession of the future. We have suffered greatly from the decline in our historical awareness, and we have thus lost our identity and pedigree. We have found ourselves incapable to determine where we stand—let alone to look ahead.

Countless Islamic movements did not escape this trap as the Islamic homeland lived through this absence. We believed until recently that these movements had realized the subjective requirement for their existence, although not yet realizing the objective condition. We have made great mistakes for two reasons:

1. How can it be said that someone who has lost his historical awareness has discovered himself or the subjective requirement of his existence?
2. This is a fantasy ignoring the dialectical relationship between subjective and objective awareness. Despite the relationship of trust covering the conduct of many organizations in the ranks of the Islamic movement today, we see—from an objective study—that these organizations are in a state of alienation. This state puts its members in a cycle of collapsing values and an anarchy of concepts, and then, ever so often, despair.

Our interest in history is thus not for entertainment, pleasure, or excitement when approaching the biography of the pious predecessors. Rather, our interest is in it as a continuity subjected to study, analysis, and close examination through a particular approach and vision. That is, through the religion of God Almighty: "[And say, "Ours is] the religion of God. And who is better than God in [ordaining] religion?"[1]

---

[1] See sūrat al-baqara: 138.

Although the Islamic movement as a modern concept first crystallized after the dangerous contact between the Crusader campaign, led by the young Corsican adventurer Napoleon Bonaparte, and the Islamic homeland, we cannot lose sight of the Wahhabi movement's role, as the first symptom of the struggle to return to the purity of the pious predecessors. It was therefore the first serious movement, centuries after the emergence of the great renewer of the faith,[2] Ibn Taymiyya. Because we look at the Crusade led by Napoleon as the starting point for the most serious confrontations the Islamic homeland has faced since its inception, it is here that we start our chronology of the Islamic movement, without ignoring Wahhabism as a pioneering movement.

Although the martyrs provided by the Islamic masses confirmed their excellence as an important part of the Islamic homeland in the confrontation with the crusader invasion's first vanguards, before the latter could settle in Egypt, the trauma was nonetheless severe. We discover isolation, stagnation, and failure of independent reasoning and renewal. This was the issue enabling those crusader vanguards and the following generations to succeed—and the Islamic political system to fall. Our abidance by the sharia fell after the expeditions to Paris and to Europe penetrated our eyes and the pores of our skin, which then returned to destroy our morals and our culture as some of them—perhaps initially in good faith—outlined the Western vision for life and modernization.

These expeditions continued en masse to enable this challenge… this invasion… this colonialism, to form a generation of thinkers carrying our names and our thoughts. Their bodies resided in our land, but their hearts were attached over there. This filthy rash of defeated intellectuals on the face of the Islamic homeland, and the books by dogs and pigs, is nothing but another continuation of this sequence. So, bit by bit, things in front of us became clearer, until we found ourselves in five situations, or in five categories, that were manifestations of the challenge, or a response to it, in one form or another:

1. **The traditional Muslims:** Who have been completely absent as they lived in a state of alienation from the self and from the cause. Those who were told about the coming challenge by them felt that it was a pure evil, and the preachers remained on the pulpits of the sultans who had left centuries ago.
2. **The conservative Salafis:** Such as the Wahhabis, Mahdists, and Senussists, and we will talk adequately about them a little later.
3. **The enlightened Salafis:** Led by Jamal al-Din al-Afghani, and we will also return to them later.
4. **The fourth group:** This is what some writers call the "secular Muslims." We apologize for employing this contradictory term, as it is necessary to use it temporarily in order to distinguish between the third and fifth group. In order to be clearer, we note:

    The second word of this term refers to the group of people who initially adhered to Islam, while the first word refers to the reality of their position. The

---

[2] Renewer (*mujaddid*), person who appears at the turn of every century of the Islamic calendar to revive Islam, cleansing it of extraneous elements and restoring it to its pristine purity.

essence of their thinking rejects Islam as a true revival and real authority, and it approaches the Western vision of separating religion and the state. Although they took a conditional position on secularization, stopping it by the confines of the creed, the pioneers of this group gradually and logically ended up carrying a fully secular vision. Foremost in this group are Qasim Amin,[3] Saad Zaghlul,[4] Ahmad Lutfi al-Sayyid,[5] and Taha Hussein.[6]

5. **The Westernized and estranged Christians:** The term here, like the preceding one, is one proposed by Dr. Hisham Sharabi. They are Westernized because they felt Western about the Islamic homeland, and they emigrated because they realized their adherence to the values and goals of the West. Its civilizational vision saved them from the suffering of estrangement in the Islamic homeland.

These attempts led to the secularization of our homeland because these Christians understood it was impossible to solve the problem of their alienation in it without secularizing the historical vision, the institutions, and the foundations upon which this society and state rest—that is, a strike against the process reviving Islam as an ideology capable of acting in the face of the coming challenge (Farah Antun,[7] Shibli Shumayyil,[8] and Louis Awad[9]).

We are here studying the modern Islamic movement in the confrontation with the modern Western challenge in its two great phases. The first commenced with the French campaign and lasted until 1928, while the second began in 1928 and has lasted until this day. We will observe that the second and third group were part of what is termed the first phase of the modern Islamic movement.

The Salafists were divided between those who were conservative, enlightened, or revolutionary. They were the first true response to the coming challenge and a sign of this religion's unique ability to overcome the challenge and to act. This movement was thus truly a key factor in the modern Islamic awakening. It resisted the intellectual invasion and valiantly fought the colonial crusader schemes. We do not forget to

---

[3] Qasim Amin (1863–1908), Egyptian Islamic modernist and a co-founder of the Egyptian nationalist movement.
[4] Saad Zaghlul (1859–1927), leader of the Egyptian nationalist liberal Wafd Party, and prime minister of Egypt from January 26, 1924, until November 24, 1924.
[5] Ahmad Lutfi al-Sayyid (1872–1963), Egyptian anti-colonial intellectual and leading personality in the Egyptian nationalist movement.
[6] Taha Hussein (1889–1973), Egyptian modernist author and symbol of the Egyptian Renaissance cultural movement.
[7] Farah Antun (1874–1922), Syrian Christian largely influenced by the Enlightenment and French Romanticism. While rejecting Arab nationalism, Antun publicaly supported secularism and equality regardless of creed.
[8] Shibli Shumayyil (1850–1917), Lebanese Christian intellectual and one of the first to popularize Darwinism and Socialism in the Arab world. Shumayyil published the magazine *The Future* (*al-Mustaqbal*) with Salama Musa.
[9] Louis Awad (1915–90), secularist Egyptian author and English professor at the Cairo University until he was forced to resign in 1954 following the Egyptian July 23 Revolution.

mention the role of al-Ghazali,[10] Ibn Taymiyya,[11] and Ibn Qayyim al-Jawziyya[12] in this period.

Thus, if we look to each of the groups separately, we see that the Wahhabis emerged approximately half a century before the advent of the French campaign (Muhammad bin Abdel Wahhab was born in 1703). They thus represented the first powerful rejection of the corruption spreading in the Islamic community and a serious attempt to restore Islam to its initial attributes prevailing in the era of the Prophet (peace and blessings be upon him), the Rightly Guided Caliphs, and the pious predecessors. Ibn Abd al-Wahhab saw that the problem of the Muslims was the weakness of their creed and that the solution was returning to the Qur'an and the sunna, to fight innovation, and to apostatize exegesis. He called on the Muslims to adhere to asceticism, abstinence, and jihad in order to build the Islamic society, as well as opening the door to independent reasoning, which had been closed for a long time.

Then came the Senussist movement (founded by Muhammad ibn Ali al-Senussi, 1787-1859),[13] which was greatly influenced by Wahhabism in terms of restoring Islam to its first attributes and returning to the Qur'an and the sunna, fighting innovation, and opening the door for independent reasoning. However, they also believed in the vision of conjunction and unveiling,[14] with which the Sufis deal. This movement was able to succeed in reforming the Bedouin community and transform it into a cooperating and producing society, to impose Islamic authority in its areas, and to spread the flag to the corners of the African desert, reaching the pagan tribes there and spreading Islam among them. Despite the mistakes committed by al-Mahdi al-Laban in the attempt to keep away from conflict, the movement had to declare jihad under his leadership when the French enemy's progress in the desert put things in perspective, and war and jihad became unavoidable as a way of persistence.

There was in addition al-Mahdi in Sudan (the first al-Mahdi was born in 1844 and died in 1885),[15] who also called on restoring Islam to its initial purity, uniting the Sunni schools of law, and fighting innovation and political corruption. Al-Mahdi gathered his followers after that, and he declared revolution against England. He managed to inflict great defeats on them, and he intended to invade Egypt after the occupation of

---

[10] Abu Hamid Muhammad ibn Muhammad al-Tusi Al-Ghazali (1058–1111), considered one of the most influential Sunni philosophers and theologians, and a *mujaddid* (a renewer of the faith).
[11] Taqi al-Din Ahmad ibn Taymiyya (1263–1328), medieval Hanbali theologian and reformer. He is considered to have particular influence on contemporary Wahhabism, Salafism, and Jihadi-Salafism.
[12] Ibn Qayyim al-Jawziyya (1292–1350), Hanbali medieval theologian who was a disciple and follower of ibn Taymiyya.
[13] Muhammad ibn Ali al-Senussi (1787–1859), Muslim theologian and leader of the Senussi mystical order, which assisted in liberating Libya from Italy during the Second World War.
[14] Conjunction (*ittiṣāl*) is the connection obtained between the worshipper and the Divine. Unveiling (*kashf*) is to obtain revelation of the "concealed", the divine, which is unattainable by reason alone.
[15] Muhammad Ahmad bin Abdallah (1844–85), Nubian religious leader in Sudan. Leading the war and victory against the Ottoman-Egyptian rulers and later against the British, his disciples proclaimed him Mahdi in 1881.

Khartoum and appoint governors to the Levant and Marrakesh, without his political powers reaching outside the borders of Sudan.

The Salafist movement was not limited to these major trends, but there were the Alusis in Iraq connected to Abu al-Thana' al-Alusi[16] who called for purifying religion from impurities and following the pious predecessors in the matters of creed. There was also the movement of al-Shawkani in Yemen (born 1760), the author of *Nayl al-Awtar*, which was in fact an echo of Wahhabism in the Arabian Peninsula.[17] There was also the movement of Mulay Slimane[18] in Morocco, who received the call of Muhammad bin Abd al-Wahhab from the pilgrims, by which he was impressed and worked to spread. In addition came Mulay Hassan, Sheikh Hassan Abu Shu'aib al-Dukali,[19] and Sheikh Ibn al-Arabi al-Alawi.[20]

Yet, despite the great role played by the conservative Salafists, they had difficulties overcoming the modern Western challenge. This was so because they failed to recognize the objective condition, which made them lose an important and dangerous weapon in the great battle. This is what the enlightened Salafists, led by the great revolutionary Jamal al-Din al-Afghani,[21] identified from the beginning: "The cure for every sick Muslim is in the Qur'an."

One of the most important causes that al-Afghani raised was the necessity of the Islamic renaissance, and that Muslims understood their religion correctly and applied its teaching. He was at the same time interested in making the Islamic homeland a successful political force. He kept shouting in all places, calling on Muslims to the renaissance, to reject the occupation, and to fight it. He also rejected educational reform, later an approach adopted by his student Muhammad Abduh,[22] as a decisive means for change and restoring the glory of Islam. Instead, Abduh believed in political revolution as the best means to restore Islam. His magazine *The Indissoluble Link*[23] analyzed the situation of the Muslims and the reason for their backwardness, explaining the meaning of the Caliphate and the reasons for its deterioration, calling for its preservation as the last bastion to bring the Islamic umma together. He had a benign hope in the Mahdist revolution, to change the situation in Iran and to reform the Caliphate.

---

[16] Abu al-Thana' al-Alusi (1802–54), Iraqi Islamic scholar known for his exegesis of the Qur'an. See Basheer M. Nafi, "Abu al-Thanaᵉ al-Alusi: An Alim, Ottoman Mufti, and Exegete of the Qurᵉan," *International Journal of Middle East Studies* 34, no. 3 (2002): 465–94.

[17] Muhammad al-Shawkani (1759–1839), Yemeni scholar, jurist, and reformer whom Yemeni Salafis claim to be an intellectual precursor. See Bernard Haykel, *Revival and Reform in Islam: The Legacy of Muhammad al-Shawkānī* (Cambridge: Cambridge University Press, 2003).

[18] Mulay Slimane (1766–1822), sultan of Morocco from 1792 until 1822.

[19] Abu Shu'aib al-Dukkali (1878–1937), Moroccan theologian known for spreading the reformist ideas of the nahḍa in Morocco.

[20] Muhammad ibn al-'Arabi al-Alawi (1880–1964), Moroccan reformist in the Salafi reform movement and anti-colonialist.

[21] Jamal al-Din al-Afghani (1838/1839–97), Islamic anti-colonial thinker and co-founder of Islamic Modernism. See Albert Hourani, *Arabic Thought in the Liberal Age, 1798-1939* (Cambridge: Cambridge University Press, 2003).

[22] Muhammad Abduh (1849–1905), Islamic jurist, scholar, and liberal reformer. Co-founder of Islamic Modernism and disciple of Jamal al-Din al-Afghani.

[23] *Al-'Urwa al-Wuthqa* (*The Indissoluble Link*), newspaper published in Paris from 1884 by Jamal al-Din al-Afghani and Muhammad Abduh.

Albert Hourani writes in his book *Arabic Thought in the Liberal Age* that "[o]n all who knew him he left a strong although not wholly pleasant impression: of a man devoted to his convictions, obstinate, ascetic, quick to anger when honour or religion was touched, wild and untameable." Muhammad Abduh describes him thus: "He was the fiercest I have seen in preserving the principles of his doctrine."

Although the opinions almost converge in that al-Afghani was a Shiite, his doctrine, which Imam Muhammad Abduh referred to, was nonetheless the true doctrine. He always called for the removal of differences between Muslims, even those between Shiites and Sunnis. He called upon the Afghans and Persians more than once to unite, although they were Sunnis and Shiites. However, it does seem that al-Afghani—and this is pretty ingenious—came forth as a distinct and sublime individual of his age, at a time when ignorance and backwardness prevailed, when independent reasoning had been deserted, and jihad was abandoned in the phase of the colonial crusader tide in the entire Islamic homeland. Despite all that, his theses remained a beacon for generations to come.

Muhammad Abduh stood with Jamal al-Din al-Afghani at this stage as an enlightened Salafist, particularly in the first stage of his life when he was deeply influence by Jamal al-Din al-Afghani. He was often the official spokesperson of al-Afghani at that time and expressed his ideas (al-Afghani did not like writing very much). When al-Afghani went abroad once Great Britain entered Egypt, Muhammad Abduh went to prison for—finally—standing beside the 'Urabi movement[24] and participating in it. He then left the country and joined al-Afghani, moving from Beirut to Paris, then to London and to Tunisia. Muhammad Abduh tried to enter Sudan through Egypt after that in disguise to contact al-Mahdi but failed and returned to Beirut once again.

Imam Muhammad Abduh returned to Egypt in 1888 to begin a new phase in his life, during which he revealed the absence of al-Afghani's influence, his adoption of the reformist educational trend, and his rejection of the political struggle as a means for revolution. Thus, this stage of his life is not beyond particular reproach as he returned to official work after his exile once pledging passivity to the Khedive of Lord Cromer[25] who interceded on his behalf. The Muslim activist Mustafa Kamil[26] took a critical and rejectionist position in this phase and rebuked him for his interest in public influence. Muhammad Abduh, in contrast, was suspicious of the expected results of Mustafa Kamil's political struggle. This is what makes us say that the second stage of the life of Imam Muhammad Abduh is not beyond reproach: not only because of what we have noted so far but also because of the row of secularists who had been taught by the imam. Rashid Rida[27]—a student of Imam Abduh, who is considered a Salafist pioneer—does not deny this, and these students came from the line of the imam.

---

[24] Egyptian nationalist movement named by its leader Ahmad 'Urabi (1841–1911), an Egyptian nationalist and officer in the Egyptian army who participated in the 1897 mutiny against the administration of Mohamed Tewfik Pasha.

[25] Reference to Mohamed Tewfik Pasha (1852–92), Khedive of Egypt and Sudan from 1879 until 1892, who largely ruled on behalf of French and British colonial interests.

[26] Mustafa Kamil Pasha (1874–1908), Egyptian lawyer, journalist, nationalist, and co-founder of the Nationalist Party.

[27] Rashid Rida (1865–1935), Islamic reformist deeply influenced by early Salafism and the Islamic Modernism of Muhammad Abduh.

Before we end our talk about this stage, it is necessary to refer to the circle of Sheikh Tahir al-Jaza'iri (1851–1920)[28] in Syria where the subject of the main circle was the cause of the Islamic renaissance, overcoming the crisis of the challenge, and uniting the Islamic world. Nor can we overlook the elements of Islamic and enlightened revolutionaries such as Mustafa Kamil and Abdallah al-Nadim[29] as well as Muhammad Iqbal[30] in Pakistan, who called for the combination of reason, conscience, and will to build an Islamic society through a new philosophy and a magnificent poetic structure.

This is how this stage ended for a new one to commence in the shadow of the escalating liberal-secular intellectual and political threat, in the shadow of danger resulting from the fall of the Caliphate under the influence of the ideas of al-Afghani, Rashid, Iqbal, and the current of the Islamic community in general. A new stage began in 1928, the stage of an effective social organization represented by the Muslim Brotherhood in Egypt and in the Arab world, and which was to subsequently include the Islamic homeland and Jamaat-e-Islami[31] in Pakistan and India.

If al-Afghani stands on top in the first stage, then the martyr Imam Hassan al-Banna stands on top in the second. This stage—characterized by three generations—commenced in 1928.

The First Generation (1928–49), or the Generation of the Renaissance

In this generation, the martyr imam al-Banna presented Islam in all its comprehensiveness as a code regulating all aspects of life from economy and politics to society, in addition to creed and worship. The imam was able to inspire this umma throughout twenty years from under the debris, and to develop the concepts of the movement with revolutionary and refined acceleration—inspired by the Qur'an, the sunna, and the way of the pious predecessors, in addition to the daily practices guiding these concepts. This generation of the [Islamic] movement was able to restore confidence in the Muslim individual, the Muslim intellectual, and the Muslim community, and to present Islam in a revolutionary way against the secular alternatives presented by colonialism since the challenge appeared and up until that point.

The Palestine War fought by the Islamic movement was the peak of that generation's awareness and understanding of the nature of the modern Western challenge, which began manifesting itself in Palestine as an inevitable military clash... Bullets of

---

[28] Sheikh Tahir al-Jaza'iri (1852–1920), Islamic reformer referred to as the "Syrian Muhammad Abduh."
[29] Abdallah al-Nadim (1842–96), Egyptian journalist, poet, politician, and nationalist revolutionary. Al-Nadim is often described as the orator of the 'Urabi revolt.
[30] Allama Muhammad Iqbal (1877–1938), largely considered to have inspired the Pakistan Movement (Tehrik-e-Pakistan) and is called the "spiritual father of Pakistan."
[31] Jamaat-e-Islami, Islamic and right-wing nationalist movement founded in British India in 1941 by Abul A'la Mawdudi. Considered one of the most influential Islamic organizations alongside the Muslim Brotherhood.

treachery were fired in February 1949, however, and the imam's pulse stopped in order for the features of a new generation to commence.

The Second Generation (1949–67), or the Generation of Hesitation and Distress

We cannot say that the renaissance process commencing with the first generation actually stopped. There is no doubt, however, that a severe blow—a very severe one, indeed—was directed against the Islamic movement, which was caught in a state of confusion and disintegration.

As much as the 1954 defeat[32] had external dimensions, it equally carried—perhaps even more so—strictly internal factors. One aspect of the analysis was that the defeat meant the Islamic movement was unable to absorb the blow of the martyred imam for five years. Indeed, with the obvious floundering, the coup d'état of July 1952 led to a split in the Muslim Brotherhood movement with some elements resigning—even some in the Constituent Assembly[33] and the Guidance Bureau.[34] Although the strike was directed in 1954, the organizational analysis of this generation became apparent in the late 1950s when so many of the detainees who denounced the organization were released, after bowing their heads to the authority. Some elements remained in the Special Apparatus,[35] however, while another minority suffered the authority's terror, which pulled the rug from under the feet of the Islamic movement.

We do not deny the severity of the terrible secular tide in that phase. Nor do we deny the emergence of the so-called revolutionary national movements, whether with the fall of the Dutch Empire in the far east of Indonesia or the fall of France in the countryside of Morocco and Algeria on the Arab side. Although it was Islam that ignited the spirit of jihad on this polar axis and its extension (the Tangier Jakarta axis, according to the expression of Muslim thinker Malik bin Nabi),[36] the Islamic features were concealed with the so-called nationalist leadership's takeover of power... until these features were on the verge of disappearing completely.

Moreover, this was because of the complete absence of the Islamic movement as a revolutionary movement with an integrated theory in the confrontation with Western

---

[32] The 1954 defeat refers to the suppression of the Egyptian Muslim Brotherhood after the assassination attempt against Egyptian President Gamal Abdel Nasser. Following the attempt, Nasser outlawed the Brotherhood, imprisoning thousands of members.

[33] The Constituent Assembly (*al-jam'iyya al-ta'sīsiyya*) was the legislative body of the Muslim Brotherhood.

[34] The Guidance Bureau (*maktab al-irshād*), the top level of the Muslim Brotherhood consists of fifteen Muslim Brothers, led by the Supreme Guide (*murshid*). The Guidance Bureau executes decisions made by the shura council.

[35] Special Apparatus (*al-niẓām al-khāṣṣ*), military apparatus of the Muslim Brotherhood founded in 1940, mainly as a response to the failure of the 1936 Uprising in Palestine. See Omar Ashour, "Myths and Realities: The Muslim Brothers and Armed Activism," *Aljazeera*, August 12, 2014, https://www.aljazeera.com/indepth/opinion/2014/08/myths-realities-muslim-brothers--20148129319751298.html [accessed: July 26, 2019].

[36] Malik bin Nabi (1905–73), Algerian author and philosopher focusing on alienation in Arab society and the fall of the Islamic civilization.

technology and its agents. Its vision was blurred because of the lack of scientific analysis and the chaos of concepts—incapable of envisioning the goal, the starting point, and the means—in addition to the absence of a historical awareness and the lack of education among the movement's cadres—in short, an ignorance of most elements of the proposed main equation: counterbalancing the modern Western challenge against the Islamic homeland.

In addition to the spread of these so-called national revolutionary phenomena, this generation was also confronted by the emergence of the left—otherwise known as the social ideologies with progressive content—as a new trend with particular appeal. It too stood passively, however, unable to present an alternative, and it remained absent in front of this great colonial flood. In the midst of all this, the second generation withdrew... to relive its pains and the glories of the pious predecessors far and near. It even stood accused of rejecting attempts to renew.

Even so, before we leave this generation, it is necessary to refer to Hizb al-Tahrir's attempt to break out of the cycle of hesitation and distress.[37] Yet, was the party really able to break out, and to what degree? What did it offer? All this must be the task of an expanded study, God willing. Another attempt was the earnest effort of the martyr Sayyid Qutb[38] to save the Islamic movement by introducing concepts in a radically confined and revolutionary manner. However, this attempt, visible in the organizational form that Sayyid Qutb presented in his pioneering book *Milestones in the Road*, in addition to his great interpretation *In the Shadow of the Qur'an*... This attempt left a real impact on the third generation and the youth of this generation, more than it was reflected in the second generation. The latter failed to absorb Qutb's attempt, and it even adopted a skeptical, hesitant, and uninterested position toward it.

While we note the seriousness and greatness of this attempt, we stand firm in our critical position toward those who called themselves Qutbists and those who followed in their footsteps in the arbitrary interpretation of Sayyid Qutb's ideas. This arbitrariness eventually led to the emergence of The Group of Muslims, the so-called Takfir wa-l-Hijra.[39]

The Third Generation (1967 Until Today), or the Generation of Awareness and Revolution

Suddenly, everything was revealed in the skies of the region, and it turned out that this revolutionary nationalist tide was nothing but a great ruse in our lives. Suddenly it turned out that colonialism, which had withdrawn militarily, had returned more viciously with

---

[37] Hizb al-Tahrir (The Islamic Liberation Party), founded by the Palestinian Islamic scholar Taqi al-Din al-Nabhani in 1953. It believes that jihad is permissible, but only under the leadership of the Caliph. Hizb al-Tahrir thus postpones armed struggle in order to focus on the reestablishment of the Caliphate, which will subsequently liberate Muslim lands under occupation.

[38] Sayyid Qutb (1906–66), Egyptian author and Islamic theoretician of the Muslim Brotherhood focusing on the spiritual decline in Muslim society, most known for his works *Milestones in the Road* and *In the Shadow of the Qur'an*, to mention just two.

[39] The Group of Muslims (*jamā'at al-Muslimīn*), better known as Excommunication and Exile (*al-takfir wa-l-hijra*), was an Islamist group founded in Egypt in 1960 by Shukri Mustafa. It was crushed in 1970 after the group's execution of Egyptian Minister of Religious Endowments Husayn al-Dhahabi.

economic or political means, in addition to other concealed ones. What was called the stage of nationalist revolution was nothing but a latency period during which colonialism stripped off its skin and returned even more ferociously. Suddenly, it became evident that the colonialist countries lived in abundance, while our backwardness increased. They thus advanced as productive societies, while we were defeated as animals of consumption.

The nakba of 1967 was a dramatic and bewildering transformation that froze everything in its place in order to awaken our umma, becoming aware of this stage in its entirety... A brutal end reached through a long phase of squandering and loss.

Yet, did one really have to succumb to the enemy? Were the values of submissiveness and consumption imposed by technology to be easily withdrawn from our lives? Did the Iranian revolution have to walk on a road paved with flowers to achieve its stunning victory over the values of submissiveness and consumption? The victory of faith, of virtue, and of spirit in the era of technology... Certainly not... Things seemed to become worse at first... The client systems, which arose colored in various ways... And the US intelligence, or the French National Security Agency, were found controlling the course of events officially and semi-officially in plenty of states in the Islamic homeland and other regions in Latin America and in Africa... This came in addition to the cancerous presence of the multinational monopoly companies in the same region.

> Islam alone, as a religion and as a civilization, is the only prerequisite for our survival and persistence as a nation and culture in the face of the modern Western challenge, whether politically or culturally. (Tawfiq al-Tayyib)

Thus, the generation of awareness and revolution will transcend the stage of distress and hesitation, and it will advance the process of revival to its logical end in the Arab region, inspired by the experience of the martyr imam Hassan al-Banna, presenting the thesis of awareness, revolution, and martyrdom. The emergence of this generation was inevitable, both on the internal and external level, and immobility, stagnation, and calcification could not persist.

The absence of such a generation could not continue, and the colonial secular alternatives had to collapse and fall. From the beginning, this generation had to fight its battle on two levels: The first was the decisive battle against ignorance, tyranny, and the worn-out remnants of the alternatives presented by colonialism. The second one was the battle in its midst within the various wings of the Islamic movement itself. It happened as these wings failed to understand themselves, others, this age, and existing relationships... or those wings focusing on one side of Islam and ignoring the others, or those accepting reconciliation with the infidel regimes and thus betting on the dark side of history, as happened to some extent in Jordan and Egypt.

There are daunting tasks in front of the generation of awareness and revolution to prepare itself... The young men of the Islamic revival and the continuation of the revolution after defining the concepts, premises, means, and goals in a scientific way through serious studies, analysis, and critique... Awareness means here a deep awareness of Islam and of the contemporary Islamic problems, which requires a belief based on reason and science... A political awareness of the reality of this age... and a moral commitment to the criteria of Islam.

6

The Palestinian Cause Is the Central Cause of the Islamic Movement . . . Why?

Published in al-Mukhtār al-Islāmī *(The Islamic Digest), no. 13, July 1980 (p. 28–41), by Fathi al-Shiqaqi (pseudonym Izz al-Din al-Faris) and Bashir M. Nafi' (pseudonym Ahmad Sadiq).*

Meeting as young students in Egypt in the 1970s, the PIJ founding fathers used the Islamic journal al-Mukhtār al-Islāmī as one of the most important channels for their ideological maturation. It was in this intellectual outlet that they composed the ideological basis for the centrality of the Palestinian cause. That is, the Palestinian cause had to be the central cause of the contemporary Islamic movement. The logic of their argument was quite straightforward. The Global South in general and the Arab-Islamic world in particular was exploited and oppressed by the Western colonial project. Israel was similarly established as a settler-colonial entity and partner of the West in order for this colonial project to succeed in the Middle East. Israel was thus not just a bridgehead to the neighboring states of Palestine, but the very precondition for the continued subjugation of the Palestinians and everyone in the Global South. As long as Israel existed, the oppressed would not succeed in their liberation struggle. The first step was to remove Israel in order for justice and independence to be restored.

Al-Shiqaqi and his companion Nafi' attempt to explain this historical trajectory in the following piece. Yet, perhaps surprisingly, they do not commence with the establishment of Israel in 1948 but, instead, with the colonial adventures of Napoleon in Egypt in the late eighteenth century. What marks the Middle East is thus its continued struggle against Western colonialism for the past centuries, which always attempted to weaken Islam as the creed capable of withstanding the assault.

This text matters for two reasons: First, although PIJ is often perceived and analyzed as a radical religious movement, this article demonstrates how al-Shiqaqi was far more infatuated with history and historical analysis than Qur'anic verses and exegesis. What appears is a largely secular analysis of colonial developments, strategic miscalculations, and Palestinian defeat. Second, the following text matters because it may inform us of the potential intellectual influences in the life of al-Shiqaqi. While the existing literature on PIJ, and al-Shiqaqi himself, suggest the notable influence of Sayyid Qutb, it is difficult to discern these intellectual traces in the writings of al-Shiqaqi. The question is thus whether the influence of Qutb on al-Shiqaqi was emotional rather than cognitive—given that the former was martyred by the

Egyptian regime of Gamal Abdel Nasser for speaking the truth. Al-Shiqaqi wrote, instead, more positively about, and with far more references to, other intellectuals and historical figures such as Jamal al-Din al-Afghani and Izz al-Din al-Qassam.

The positions of the Islamists on the Palestinian cause vary to a surprising degree. Some of them ignore it as if it—as a political cause—were nothing more than a disagreement between the emirate of Ras Al Khaimah and the emirate of Ajman. They think—as usual—that the establishment of an Islamic state in the region will finally end the problem and resolve the long conflict, returning Palestine back to its people in a matter of hours… If I ask them about the Islamic state they envision, one hears nothing but one thing: "It is not our business to think about it or to plan it, our duty is to work and only to work." They are unfortunately ignorant of their stage and of their tools because they are ignorant of the essence of the ongoing conflict in the land of the Islamic homeland, brought forth by their ignorance of the Palestinian cause and its position in this stage and the cycle of conflict.

Among the Islamists are those who fight the Palestinian cause, and who present their position as an expression of the Islamic position—as they believe—when dealing with it and the political conflict cycle around it. This way, they vacillate between political concession in analysis and vision on the molecules offered to us by the great powers as if they were the universals of the cause, and the non-analytical and emotional position seeing Palestine as the land of Islamic sanctities to be liberated by pure, Islamic hands. May God protect the believers from the evils of education, awareness, and analysis.

The truth is, all of these positions are based on a superficial understanding—or no understanding at all—of the tasks of the contemporary Islamic movement and of the origins of the Palestinian cause. These are alien positions in the legacy of the Islamic movement. When the martyr imam Hassan al-Banna—may God have mercy upon him—went to Palestine to establish new Brotherhood bases, and when the Islamists offered their finest martyrs on the land of Palestine between 1947 and 1948, they were actually dedicated to the flame of luminous awareness of the Palestinian cause as the central cause for the Islamic movement. This is the flame that the mujahid sheikh Izz al-Din al-Qassam advanced in the mid-1930s in the first attempt to light it.

We have to consult the trajectory of history beyond the Islamic homeland's territory precisely as a tool facilitated by the logic of God, the logic influencing this universe. We have to do so in order to grasp the roots of the Islamic homeland as a whole; if we really want to understand our stage, our goals, and our tools; and if we want to draw closer to the flame of awareness and revolution as al-Qassam and Hassan al-Banna once attempted.

Palestine and the Trajectory of Modern History

The Ottoman Empire ruled Palestine as an important part of the Islamic land. When the Jewish Zionist trends set out for Palestine during the end of the last century, the administrative establishment in the region was reorganized so that Palestine became an administrative unit directly subordinate to the Grand Commander in Istanbul…

This is how the Islamic principles dealt with the Islamic land. The concept of the homeland's historical borders had not yet appeared, which would later form the basis of the nationalist trends in the Arab region as for the Zionist expansionist idea.

However, the persisting, fierce conflict between Islam as a society and a system, and non-Islam as ideological and social trends—continuing throughout the nineteenth century on the territory of the Islamic homeland—managed to achieve very dangerous results on the threshold of the twentieth century... From the French campaign [of Napoleon] until the First World War, the West attempted by all means to shatter the Islamic wall, which prevented it from controlling the world's reserves of wealth—constituting an inherent threat to it, its values, and the structure of its system. The West employed its military bayonets, its missionaries, and its secular schools. In a broad and persistent attack, the most dangerous tool was those models of the Islamic community that had been defeated spiritually and intellectually. They served as a tool for the secularism of the West and its Arab-nationalist political treatises, and in particular against their homeland.

With the beginning of the twentieth century, it was the Party of Union and Progress in Turkey[1] that called for Turkish nationalism in Turkey. There were also Arab associations and parties such as the Young Arab Society,[2] the Covenant Society,[3] Beirut Reform Society,[4] and the Decentralization Party,[5] and many more, calling on Arab nationalism and Arab states independent from the Caliphate. On the other hand, the Zionist movement—as an expression of the historical Jewish idea—sharpened its political features in Europe as a genuine and "intellectual" ally of the imperialist colonialism against the wealth of the peoples and the Western attack on Islam and its homeland. Such was the Arab nationalist movement born as a legitimate son of the Western attack against the Islamic homeland, and the Zionist movement commenced as a genuine part of that attack with all of its features.

Against that stage, communication commenced[6] between al-Sharif Hussein,[7] the representative of the Arab nationalist movement, and Sir McMahon,[8] "Representative of

---

[1] Party of Union and Progress (İttihad ve Terakki Fırkası), formed in present-day Istanbul on February 6, 1889. Commencing as a liberal movement initially calling for reform and democratization of the Ottoman Empire, its goal was the return to the former strength of the Empire.
[2] Young Arab Society (jamʿiyyat al-ʿarabiyya al-fatā), underground Arab nationalist movement formed after the Young Turk Revolution in 1908. Its primary goal was the independence and unity of Arab territory under Ottoman rule.
[3] The Covenant Society (jamʿiyyat al-ʿahd), a group organized in 1913, mainly by Iraqi officers in the Ottoman army, which called for the independence of Iraq with subsequent union with Syria.
[4] Beirut Reform Society (jamʿiyyat Beirut al-iṣlāḥiyya), a secret society working for the decentralization and modernization of the Ottoman Empire, leaving internal affairs to the local population in the different governorates.
[5] The Decentralization Party (ḥizb al-lāmarkaziyya al-idāriyya), established in 1912 in Egypt by a group of Syrians aspiring for reform of the Ottoman Empire and for administrative decentralization.
[6] Refers to the McMahon-Hussein Correspondence (July 1915–March 1916), a series of letters between Hussein bin Ali, Sharif of Mecca, and Lieutenant Colonel Sir Henry McMahon. The correspondence led to an agreement on British recognition of Arab independence after the First World War in exchange for an Arab uprising against the Ottoman Empire.
[7] Hussein bin Ali (1853/1854–1931), Hashemite Arab leader and Sharif of Mecca.
[8] Sir Henry McMahon (1862–1949), British High Commissioner in Egypt from 1915 until 1917. He resigned after the Sykes-Picot Agreement was leaked by the Bolshevik government in November 1917.

His Majesty the King of Britain"... Al-Sharif presented his vision of the future, assuring an establishment of an Arab kingdom, which was to be independent from the Ottoman Empire. This was supposed to include the Arab region east of the Suez Canal and the Arabian Peninsula. McMahon refused to engage in the details of borders, however, and after some persuasion, he agreed to that with the exclusion of Palestine and some parts of the Levant from the requested state. The British offered no real guarantees to the Arab nationalist dreams, and the Arab nationalists nonetheless entered the war, with Britain against the Ottoman Empire... The Arab kingdom desired by the first generation of Arab nationalists was a retreat from the large and comprehensive Islamic state for a number of separate nationalities.

In the First World War, Britain occupied Palestine and announced the Balfour Declaration.[9] The Syrian National Congress was also convened,[10] which gathered representatives of Greater Syria, including Palestine, and Faisal bin al-Sharif Hussein[11] was declared "king" of Greater Syria. When the government of Faisal was defeated in front of the French forces, he and his family later accepted the British compromise of declaring him king of Iraq. This generation of Arab nationalists—most of them belonging to a class of large landowners—largely forgot the old idea of establishing a greater Arab state. Their interests were divided between a Syrian state including Palestine and several small independent states... The nationalist landowners stood in the eastern Arab region of the Islamic homeland with an idea of independence from the Ottoman Empire as an expression of their intellectual, spiritual, and economic defeat in front of the West's secular-nationalist idea. It was also an expression of their ambitions for economic independence from the central government in Istanbul. (There is no fear for the future as long as they are the ones governing that future state...)

This is the general framework governing the trajectory of the conflict in the region as a whole between the two wars and between the Balfour Declaration and the first nakba of 1948.[12]

So how did things transpire in Palestine in that period?

Palestine... Those Leaders and That Collapse

The end of the First World War led to an increasing Jewish immigration to Palestine after the British occupation, and directly so after the Balfour Declaration. The Palestinian masses moved with their historical sense against the attack. The dignitaries and the landowners who carried out the secession from the Ottoman Empire allied

---

[9] The Balfour Declaration (1917), named after British Foreign Secretary Arthur Balfour, which announced British support for establishing a national home for Jews in Palestine.
[10] The Syrian National Congress was convened in 1919 in Damascus to assess the future of Greater Syria after the Ottoman Empire had been expelled.
[11] Faisal I bin Hussein bin Ali al-Hashimi (1885–1933), king of the Arab Kingdom of Greater Syria in 1920, and king of Iraq from 1921 until 1933.
[12] The first nakba of 1948 refers to the establishment of the State of Israel and the ethnic cleansing of the Palestinians.

themselves with Britain, however. They returned once more under a complete political and civilizational decline in order to lead the masses and their trajectory.

Islamic and Christian associations were established in the Palestinian cities (in the wake of secularism, it should be noted) under the leadership of dignitaries and merchants, and the representatives of these associations held the first Palestine Arab Congress in January 1919.[13] There were twenty-seven participants: eleven associates of Britain, two of France, two were independent, and twelve were supporters of Arab national unity, according to a British intelligence officer in Palestine. It was evident that the congress and its leader, Musa Kazim al-Husayni,[14] would adopt appeasement with Britain, and that the congress' general tendency would be to conceive the conflict as a conflict with the Zionists only.

When Britain announced Mandatory Palestine and appointed the Zionist Herbert Samuel[15] as the High Commissioner in Jerusalem, to expedite the implementation of the Balfour Declaration by establishing a national homeland for the Jews, Samuel formed an advisory council of Jews, Muslims, and Christians. The most prominent members of the council among the Arabs were Isma'il al-Husayni,[16] Farih Abu Mudayn,[17] Sulayman Nasif,[18] and Abd al-Razaq Tuqan.[19] All belonged to the class of dignitaries and landowners, and were associates of Britain. This same group would form the National Defense Party,[20] led by Arif al-Dajani,[21] Raghib al-Nashashibi,[22] and Suleiman [al-Taji] al-Faruqi,[23] as a tool against the homeland along with Britain.

---

[13] The Palestine Arab Congress does not refer to one event but to seven congresses held by the Palestinians in Mandatory Palestine between 1919 and 1928. The first congress of 1919 was convened in response to Jewish immigration to Palestine before the First World War.
[14] Musa Kazim Pasha al-Husayni (1853–1934), mayor of Jerusalem from 1918 until 1920, and head of the Palestinian nationalist Executive Committee of the Palestine Arab Congress from 1922 until 1934.
[15] Herbert Louis Samuel (1870–1963), politician and leader of the Liberal Party. An avid supporter of Zionism, Samuel was appointed as High Commissioner for Mandatory Palestine in 1920.
[16] Isma'il al-Husayni (1860–1945), Mufti of Jerusalem in the beginning of the 1900s and one of the city's most prominent dignitaries. Al-Husayni adopted a cooperative attitude toward the British occupation following the First World War and participated in several consultative meetings.
[17] Farih Abu Mudayn (1871–1955), mayor of Beersheba from 1922 and member of Herbert Samuel's advisory council (representative of Beersheba).
[18] Sulayman Bey Nasif (unknown), Protestant entrepreneur, lawyer, and merchant affiliated with the Arab Office in Cairo and member of Samuel's advisory council (representative of Haifa).
[19] Sulayman Abd al-Razaq Bey Tuqan (1893–1958) became a member of Samuel's advisory council (representative of Nablus), and was mayor of Nablus from 1925 until 1950.
[20] The National Defense Party was set up by Raghib al-Nashashibi in 1934. Though it rejected the Balfour Declaration and called for an independent Palestine, the party was considered collaborationist for its assistance to the British occupation during the Arab Revolt from 1916 until 1918.
[21] Arif Basha al-Dajani (1856–1930), Palestinian politician and mayor of Jerusalem from 1917 until 1918. He was co-leader of the Palestine Arab Congress when it was convened in 1919.
[22] Raghib al-Nashashibi (1881–1951), wealthy Palestinian landowner and mayor of Jerusalem from 1920 until 1934.
[23] Suleiman al-Taji al-Faruqi (1882–1958), originally president of the Patriotic Ottoman Party (founded in Jaffa in 1910), al-Faruqi subsequently became founding member and first head of the Palestine Arab National Party in November 1923.

The Palestinians carried out three bloody uprisings before the early 1930s. The first one was in 1920,[24] and the second was in 1923. Both were based on their leaders' theses—that is, they were uprisings only against a Zionist presence. In 1929, however, when the Jews attempted to draw near the Islamic sanctities in Jerusalem, the masses left their leaders behind as they rose against the Jews, in addition to Britain and its men, police, and government institutions. It became clear that the conflict was with the attack from both Britain and the Zionist movement, despite the misinformation from the Palestinian leaders, dignitaries, and landowners. The Young Men's Muslim Association in Haifa[25]—closely related to Sheikh Izz al-Din al-Qassam[26]—was at the head of the organizations advocating an attack on Britain.

The so-called Pan-Islamic Congress was held in Jerusalem in early 1931,[27] and was to be dominated by the same leaders and dignitaries. The Congress was thus unable to bring the conflict forward—despite its inclusive representation of Muslims in the world with Sunnis and Shiites in the Arab region, in India, and in Iran. The political currents on the Palestinian scene became clear and distinct immediately after the Congress: the traditional nationalists preserved their idea and method of working in the Independence Party[28] of 'Ajaj Nuwayhid, As'ad Daghir, Izzat Darwaza, and Subhi al-Khadra. The dignitaries associated with Britain formed the National Defense Party of Raghib al-Nashashibi, and the al-Husayni family presented its moderate nationalist vision through the Palestine Arab Party[29] of Jamal al-Husayni with the blessings of mufti al-Hajj Amin al-Husayni. The Palestine Arab Party was a mixture of nationalist dreams, hopes for national independence, and something of an Islamic perception. Given their association with the Islamic intellectual positions, however, none of those currents were able to determine the essence of the conflict and move toward its resolution.

The masses, with their Islamic sense and historical awareness, had to offer their vision and approach. Thus came the movement of Izz al-Din al-Qassam. The conflict continued to escalate between the masses, on the one hand, and Britain and the Zionist movement, on the other, while the dignitaries still climbed on the shoulders of the

[24] The 1920 Jerusalem Riots (also known as 1920 Nebi Musa Riots), occurred between April 4 and 7, 1920, in and around the Old City of Jerusalem and was named after the Nebi Musa festival with which it coincided. It followed the rising tensions between Arab Palestinians and Jews. Five Jews and four Arabs were killed, with several hundreds being injured.

[25] The Young Men's Muslim Association (YMMA) was a youth organization originally founded in Egypt in 1926, and was established in Haifa, Mandatory Palestine, as a reaction to the Christian YMCA and reflecting the need for an organizational structure expressing the need of Muslim urban youth. See May Seikaly, *Haifa: Transformation of an Arab Society, 1918-1939* (London: I.B. Tauris, 1998).

[26] Izz al-Din al-Qassam (1882–1935), Syrian Islamic preacher who first fought militarily against French colonialism in northern Syria, before fighting the British in Mandatory Palestine in the 1930s. He was the leader of the Young Men's Muslim Association in Haifa. Killed by British forces in 1935, al-Qassam has inspired both PIJ and Hamas, with the latter naming its military wing after the Syrian militant.

[27] There is possibly an anachronism in al-Shiqaqi's account as he is likely referring to the Pan-Islamic Congress that was held in December 1931.

[28] The Independence Party (*hizb al-istiqlāl*) was a Palestinian nationalist party founded in 1932 in response to the rivalry of the al-Husayni and al-Nashashibi clans, which paralyzed the Palestinian resistance in the 1930s.

[29] The Palestine Arab Party, founded in 1935 by the al-Husayni family as a response to the National Defense Party of their rivals, the Nashashibi clan, and was the largest Palestinian political party throughout the 1930s.

masses as an official leadership. The leadership of the revolution was formed by Awni Abd al-Hadi,[30] Ahmad Hilmi Pasha,[31] Raghib al-Nashashibi, Jamal al-Husayni, Abd al-Latif Salah,[32] and Husayn al-Khalidi[33] when the conflict erupted violently in 1927. The same faces and practices thus persisted, and they were the representatives of this stage in its entirety. Consequently, while the masses offered their blood in the field of jihad, it was those outside who led the battle! So after six months of hunger, oppression, and blood, they and the Arab leaders in the Arab kingdoms (Egypt, Jordan, Saudi Arabia, and Iraq) came to command the masses to stop the battle because their friend Britain would understand our claim in the next negotiation sessions!!

The stage had not ended. The 1940s witnessed the first seed of the conflict for Palestine, and Western colonialism stood with all its might behind the Zionist movement to establish Israel by 1947—a critical moment in the attack on the Islamic homeland… On the other side stood the Arab monarchist leaders, the dignitaries, and the landowners of Palestine. They were brought up in the arms of the Western attack, and they led the process of shattering the Islamic state fifty years ago. Yet, today, they stand against the West and the Zionist movement. Is there room for any more surprise and astonishment!? It was also here that the Islamic masses could present a real and authentic way. Islamic brotherhood factions entered the center of the conflict from Egypt, Syria, and Jordan, and the Islamists were steadfast and seeking martyrdom when everyone was defeated and had retreated.

The stage was greater than their capacities, however, and the Zionist-Western coalition managed to establish the State of Israel in the end, as the societal and persisting incarnation of the fierce attack on the Islamic homeland. All old visions for the region's future fell after the defeat of the Islamic homeland… It fell because its leaders never really fought against the invasion but, instead, were on its side—intentionally or not—and they led a false battle against the conflict without grasping its essence. These leaders thus portrayed the Jews as the only party in this conflict until 1929, while the masses with their Islamic sense felt that also Britain was one.

When the mosque imams called on the masses to boycott the taxes of the British infidel government to escalate the conflict, the landowners and dignitaries stood against the call, as they feared for their property following a British response. When the revolutionary Islamic movement led by Izz al-Din al-Qassam proposed raising arms against the British, these so-called leaders did not encumber themselves walking in the martyrs' funerals. The masses were martyred in the heat of the first nakba's battles, and the leaders negotiated. The masses starved, and the leaders divided what was left of the land. The masses were determined to continue the conflict with their religion, and the leaders signed armistice agreements.

---

[30] Awni Abd al-Hadi (1889–1970), founding member of the Young Arab Society and subsequently representative and secretary of the Arab Executive Committee's congress.

[31] Ahmad Hilmi Abd al-Baqi (1883–1963), prime minister of All-Palestine Government established by the Arab League on September 22, 1948, which governed the Egyptian-controlled Gaza Strip.

[32] Abd al-Latif Salah (1882–1953), a local leader in the Tulkarem-Nablus area and founder of the National Bloc in 1935, a Nablus-based Palestinian political party calling for an independent Palestine.

[33] Husayn al-Khalidi (1895–1962), mayor of Jerusalem from 1934 until 1937 and founder of the Reform Party in 1935. He subsequently became the representative of the Reform Party in the Arab Higher Committee.

Their arrangements, ideas, and approaches had to fall one by one, as they led the stage from the beginning of the century until the first nakba. They gave the umma nothing but hunger, forfeiture, and loss of self—establishing the bases of the Western colonial attack on the land of Palestine along the Islamic homeland, exposing it to their parties, ideas, values, and defeat...

They were an integral part of the attack.

From the First to the Second Nakba

It was natural for the Islamic movement to take the lead in the second stage. However, the political, social, and economic conditions of the late 1940s and early 1950s, and the violence of Western intervention in the Islamic homeland, did not allow it to do so (there is not sufficient space here to study those reasons in detail). The first nakba ended with a great blow to the hopes of the masses, their religion, and their land, and the military elements came to power in continuous coup d'états to advance their new Arab-nationalist theses. They confirmed their tie to the West—whether capitalist or communist—and proclaimed to the umma that they had come to restore the unity of the land, build its future, and achieve social justice, prosperity, and progress for it.

However, their adherence to secular Arab nationalism in the 1950s and to secular socialism in the 1960s completely restricted their position on the struggle's cause on the land of the Islamic homeland. They were only a new thesis to the Western attack against Islam. With the West (whether capitalist or communist) always being against the independence of their umma, they were accompanied by oppression, arrests, and assassinations against the religion of the umma and the freedom of its intellectuals and men. They worked for their own prosperity and wealth against the umma's aspirations of growth, progress, and welfare.

This was the framework of the coming stage from the first nakba in 1948 until the second nakba in 1967. Even in the purely Palestinian domain, the same trends developed as those of the Arab military regimes. With the complete absence of awareness at that stage, the essential, historical, and proper awareness of the Palestinian cause was lost once again. Moreover, various trends now exist in the Palestinian arena in the framework of resistance organization, which are rooted in that stage and perhaps a little earlier. The second nakba in the summer of that difficult year of 1967 was a systemic collapse for the socialist revolutionaries, from their militaries and regimes to their programs and deception. First when their promises perished in practice did they fall, and they fell once more when they handed over the rest of the land and history as a price for the existence and survival of their authority over our umma's spirit.

The umma began returning to its firmness, its Islamic sense, and its historical awareness after the second nakba. It had become conscious and was beginning to feel its way after years of negligence and breakdown. It was bound to recognize any precipice coming along after losing its Islamic identity and after its leadership had surrendered to their enemies and their rightful students. With the beginning of the 1970s, the comprehensive Islamic tide in the Islamic homeland was the natural and practicable response to the preceding stages, which had led our umma to the two terrible catastrophes in less than twenty years. The theater of conflict revealed an escalating Islamic current advancing to resolve this conflict in favor of the umma's authenticity, independence, and real progress. The forces of the colonial West and their extension of Arab-nationalist, socialist, and nationalist systems and parties, on the other hand, stood next to Israel as the embodiment of the attack on Islam.

Palestine Remains Our Central Cause

The modern history of the Palestinian cause reveals two very clear and important principles or lines to us:

First: The Palestinian cause was part of the basic features of the non-Islamic leaders, who punished countermeasures to lead the trajectory of the masses or who took power at the turn of the century, in the period following the defeat of the Islamic state. Those leaders represent the persisting decline in front of the Western-Zionist challenge that came to abolish history, to eliminate the awareness of the umma, to tear down the solid Islamic wall, and to seize the land, wealth, and future. Just as those leaders failed in 1948, they did so again in 1967. Their inability to continue the conflict—due to their inability to understand—subsequently led to, as we now see, their accepting anything as a solution to the cause. This is evidenced by the practices of everyone and their announcement of projects to solve the cause—from Arab regimes of all types to those of any faction claiming to lead the Palestinians. It seems that only Islam—as a religion, as a history, as a civilization, as a system, and as a practice—is capable of confronting the crisis, understanding it, leading the trajectory of the conflict, and solving it as it is the true party. It is the awareness and sense of the umma.

Second: The non-Islamic attack, and its essential party, is the West. The West could only establish Israel as a whole entity—as an idea and system; as a civilization and objective—when it was able to insert its institutions, apparatuses, and currents into, and around, the region of the Islamic homeland. Israel was thus a central part of its attack on the Islamic homeland. Today, the Islamic movement must either obtain an awareness of the attack and challenge it with all its aspects, potentials, and tools, or to remain where it fluctuates between progressing once and retreating recurrently. It is either to fully understand the essence of the conflict and the role of the Palestinian cause in it, or it is to be faced with the foulest age in the territory of the Islamic homeland—one looming on the horizon—and that is the Israeli age.

Al-Qassam... The First Pioneer of the Islamic Movement's Vanguard in Palestine

A forenoon in witnessed history, the people of paradise's young master, al-Hussein ibn Ali,[34] stood on the square of Karbala to present us with a scene that will forever remain

---

[34] Husayn ibn Ali ibn Abi Talib (625–680), grandson of Prophet Muhammad and the third Shiite Imam.

in the memory of history, a unique human symbol of martyrdom for the sake of Truth, justice, and duty. Thirteen centuries later, in one of the honorable days and on the path of extended continuation—the continuation and persistence of this great religion—came the last Husseini pioneer called Izz al-Din al-Qassam. He raised his small hand[35] in the face of the next crusader invasion. Confronting the foul Britain and its Zionist affiliate, Al-Qassam fell as a Husseinian martyr on the mountains of Palestine. The earth drank his pure blood and the trees absorbed his blazing spirit. He entered the funnels of the poor and into the water mugs with a holy fire—a holy fire and an endless joy entered our blood.

What is impressive about this encounter between al-Qassam and al-Hussein… a few believers confronting large armies, yet with the triumph of the sacred duty in the essential and possible conflict. A responsible and conscious spirit amid a sea of indifference and inaction. Al-Qassam was a symbol of faith, awareness, and revolution in the 1920s and 1930s—a symbol of determination not to compromise, as he rejected the bribe of an insured future, just as al-Hussein was at the dawn of the first movement.

Al-Qassam and the Qassamists Are the Symbol of Faith

Al-Qassam was a Muslim believing scholar who did not stop chanting the verses of jihad, struggle, and sacrifice, while calling on the people, as noted by David Hirst in his book *The Gun and the Olive Branch*, for the "emulation of the heroes of early Islam." Hirst adds: "And everywhere, but especially in the mosques, he looked for disciples among the pious and God-fearing." Al-Qassam thus chose his companions from the people of religion and true creed, each of whom carried the Holy Qur'an in his pocket and adopted it as an ideal as he found happiness in martyrdom, in the transition to the Hereafter, and in enjoying what God has prepared for the mujahidin and martyrs in Paradise.

The inhabitants of the village of Ba'bda—where the Muslim fighter and his brothers were stationed—also say that the Qassamists went to the caves during the day to pray and read the Qur'an; at night the Arab band of thirteen went out to fight. Ibrahim al-Sheikh Khalil, one of the brothers of al-Qassam, narrates that the martyr commander called for jihad on religious grounds, for jihad in the path of God, to claim the homeland, and to push back the oppression of its citizens. Then he says: "There was one slogan covering all concepts of the revolution." This was jihad: victory or martyrdom. Abd al-Wahhab al-Kayyali[36] says that Sheikh al-Qassam addressed the masses raising the slogan: The book of God in one hand, and the rifle in the other.

According to the Zionist authorities, copies of the Qur'an were found on the bodies of al-Qassam and three of his brothers who were martyred in the battle with him.

---

[35] "His small hand" is possibly a literary device employed by al-Shiqaqi referring to the Islamic militant organization that al-Qassam led, the Black Hand. Founded in 1930, the organization attacked British forces and Jewish settlers.

[36] Abd al-Wahhab al-Kayyali (1939–81), secretary-general of the Arab Liberation Front (ALF) from 1972 until 1974, and member of PLO's executive council from 1973 until his death in 1981.

When one of the Qassamists, Subhi Yasin,[37] published the names of forty distinguished brothers of al-Qassam, we see that thirty-six of them had the title of Sheikh. All of this forced a Palestinian communist, Abd al-Qadir Yasin,[38] to note that "this confirms that religion was the conscience of al-Qassam's movement."

The faith of al-Qassam reached its peak in that tragic and everlasting moment when a British force of around 300 to 600 men surrounded him and ten of his brothers. The battle began in the morning and continued until noon. Throughout the violence, the invaders attempted to tempt him with money and positions until they eventually offered him the job of deputy mufti. However, the Muslim hero answered them: "We will never surrender as this is jihad in the path of God and the homeland." He then turned to his comrades saying: "We die as martyrs."

Al-Qassam Is the Symbol of Awareness

Throughout his struggle, al-Qassam was not only a hard and stubborn fighter but also an aware thinker who enjoyed a mature and clear vision at the social and political levels. He fought a continuous battle before going out to fight.

Al-Qassam realized that the ignorant umma would never be able to resist an octopus harnessing science to serve all of its purposes. He was thus a scholar who taught at the Islamic school in Haifa and in its mosques—in the Istiqlal Mosque, in particular—and he spread his ideas among the workers, peasants, and merchants. His experience of establishing a night school to teach illiterates was a pioneering experience on the social level. Al-Qassam is said to have had great interest in the role of women. He attempted to develop the awareness of the women who had a strong relationship with the political organization in order for them to become working members.

After al-Qassam settled in Haifa, he engaged in social activity. He became a member of the Young Men's Muslim Association where he was subsequently elected president. He also took advantage of his role as an official who was authorized to perform civil marriages, and he attended the celebrations to get to know the masses and understand their mentality, thus making it easier for him to connect with other classes. Al-Qassam strongly resisted spending waqf funds on hotels and decorating mosques in a period of conflict with the enemy and in a time of increasing displacement and expulsion of farmers because of their inability to resist the economic pressure they were suffering. This was on the social side.

On the political side, the movement of al-Qassam and the effectiveness of his political organization became stronger. It happened in light of the increasing Israeli immigration and in light of the land passed from Palestinian farmers to the Jews, who enjoyed rights and advantages completely absent for the Arabs. While the Arabs lost

---

[37] Subhi Yasin (1920–68), a Palestinian militant born in Haifa who participated in military raids against Jewish settlements in the 1930s. Yasin was also a soldier in the Salvation Army in the Arab-Israeli War in 1947–1948. He was assassinated in Jordan in 1968 by unknown assailants.

[38] Abd al-Qadir Yasin (1937–), a Palestinian Leftist political analyst and author of *Misconception about the Palestinian Revolution*, *The History of the Palestinian Working Class*, and *The Crisis of Fatah*.

the land; the Jews acquired it. While the wages of the Jews rose, the wages of the Arab workers remained low. While the Jews enjoyed a trade union organization, the Arab workers were denied this and they suffered from underdevelopment, unemployment, and the absence of security. The Jews, on the other hand, had guarantees providing them with protection. All of this happened under persisting British occupation, which limitlessly stood behind the ambitions of the Jews and which equally fought and ridiculed the hopes of the Arabs.

The leaders of the Palestinian nationalist movement, on the other hand, suffered severe divisions and conflicts. One of the most important ones was the traditional and persisting disagreement between the al-Husayni family and the al-Nashashibi family, who fought for the leadership of the Palestinian nationalist movement in that period. These leaders were mostly hesitant cowards seeking their own interests and thus avoided clashing with Britain as it was sufficient to submit complaints and statements to them while being oblivious to the victims presented by the masses in demonstrations and riots. They always attempted to divert the attention from the key role of Britain, instead regarding the Jews as the only enemy! They regarded it as necessary to reason with Britain to make it stand with us against the Jews, thus forgetting and ignoring that Zionism is no more than another imperialist face of Britain, and that both embody the modern Western challenge in the most precious part of the Islamic homeland. In short, it was thus difficult for many of the Palestinian bourgeoisie elements to resist Britain, which was raised in their arms.

With all this, al-Qassam came... fleeing from his death sentence for participating in a revolt against the clans of Zion in Syria... As a Muslim revolutionary scholar and as a militant intellectual he understood that Britain was the main enemy, and that the means of passive struggle had been torn apart, incapable of deceiving anyone, especially after the 1929 Palestine riots.[39] He realized, however, that this umma, which the enemies attempted to isolate from Islam (its only revolutionary ideology), would never be prepared for jihad without special preparation. Only a Muslim revolutionary vanguard could embark upon this task... and a "solid" and effective organization embodying a clear revolutionary ideology was one of the most important factors for victory over a developed enemy in both quantity and quality.

Al-Qassam Is the Symbol of the Revolution

It is difficult to deduce the concepts of revolution and awareness, except through a dialectical relationship between the two, and it is therefore difficult for us to talk about awareness and revolution as two separate things. We mean then that this section's

---

[39] The 1929 Arab Riots (also known as the Buraq Uprising) was a series of riots, demonstrations, and protests that erupted when the long-lasting conflict between Palestinian Muslims and Jews over access to Jerusalem's Wailing Wall developed into violence. See Avraham Sela, "The 'Wailing Wall' Riots (1929) as a Watershed in the Palestine Conflict," *The Muslim World* LXXXIV, no. 1–2 (April 1994): 60–94.

discussion is an extension of the previous one—an extension of one language and one meaning.

Al-Qassam began by assessing the situation and investigating from where in the region he could begin. This area was in northern Palestine where the objective conditions were riper; despite our belief that the restriction to northern Palestine was only a weakness by making it easier for the enemy to encircle the movement militarily. Al-Qassam thus moved from one village to another, observed the people, and met with them. It is said that he assessed the worshippers while he was in the pulpit, and he joined the elements he deemed to be well prepared for action.

He subsequently prepared an organization of people, or the first secret vanguards of the organization, and each person was subjected to a period of assessment and testing before being recruited. He then joined a secret group consisting of five members with a commander. Periodic secret meetings were held to prepare them educationally through studies of what Islam represented as an idea and as an active, political, and military behavior. The member was required to buy a gun at his own private expense and to hand over what he could to the movement. The monthly contribution of each was ten percent of his income, and the person would write his will the hour he was accepted into the organization as an active member.

That is how the Qassamists became a new organization with elite vanguard elements of the Palestinian people. Although al-Qassam's organization was not a class organization, the poor and the well-off were in it together. Al-Qassam saw the workers and the peasants as the sincerest groups, however, and the ones most willing to sacrifice. We must nonetheless keep in mind that although the main motivation behind the Qassamists' movement was economic oppression, these were not the most afflicted classes as he who armed himself was economically capable and al-Qassam himself enjoyed a stable economic position. The faith in the hearts of this vanguard, and the awareness of the confrontation and the battle's significance, was the most importance factor behind the creation of the "jihadist" organization.

As building the revolutionary organization continued—vanguardist and clandestine—five committees or units emanated:

1. The unit calling for revolution and the mobilization of the masses, led by Sheikh Kamal al-Qassab.[40]
2. The unit for education and military preparation, led by a Muslim officer who had served in the army of the Ottoman Empire.
3. The unit for training, storage, and securing weapons, led by Sheikh Hassan al-Bayir and Sheikh Nimr al-Sa'di.[41]
4. The reconnaissance and intelligence unit whose mission was to spy on the British and the Jews. Several in this unit worked in government departments and in the

---

[40] Kamal al-Qassab (1853–1954), a religious scholar and student of Muhammad Abduh. Travelling to Mandatory Palestine, al-Qassab met and joined Izz al-Din al-Qassam in Haifa.

[41] Hassan Ibrahim al-Bayir (1895–1984), a Palestinian militant and follower of Izz al-Din al-Qassam. He survived the clash between al-Qassam's group and British soldiers in Yab'ad in 1935, and was subsequently sentenced to fourteen years in prison. He settled in Damascus where he lived for the rest of his life.

police, and one division worked with the Jews to identify their secret activity and their troops. One member of this unit was Sheikh Naji Abu Zayd.[42]

5. The unit for political and foreign communication. One of the known persons in this unit was Sheikh Mahmud Salim al-Makhzumi.[43] This unit communicated with the Italian consul in Jerusalem and with the Turkish consul with the intent of buying new weapons.

Some worked in the administrations, and they were one side of the coin in al-Qassam's movement. The other side was the revolutionary theory by virtue of the intellectual maturity and clarity of vision.

1. Al-Qassam was able to understand and to analyze the community and the political conditions, and he employed this analysis to choose the appropriate moment for the eruption. He was not in a hurry when some of the brothers presented the declaration of the revolution to him after the 1929 Palestine riots because of the lack of an efficient organization and because of the unripe conditions. He also rejected some of them for their desire to bring in money through violence, believing and declaring that the masses would side with the revolution once it began.
2. Contrary to the leadership of the nationalist movement, which hoped for benefits from Britain, al-Qassam's view was that Britain was the main enemy and that the Zionists followed. In addition, peaceful political struggle was no longer useful, and one had to, instead, adopt armed struggle.
3. Just as al-Qassam was forthright and correct when identifying the enemy, he also had to identify the true ally. Despite his belief that the Muslim Arabs in the neighboring countries were a strategic dimension for the Palestinian people and their revolution, the problems these countries were suffering under the brunt of colonialism made him convinced that the Palestinians had to rely on themselves first. Domestically, he deemed the workers and peasants to be the sincerest ally of the revolution and its continuation. Therefore, we found the street kerosene vendors, Abd al-Qasim and Mahmud Za'rura, in the highest leadership of the organization.

   He also did not overlook the importance of al-Hajj Amin al-Husayni as the most senior leader of the Palestinian nationalist movement, and al-Qassam thus attempted to contact him. It was also al-Qassam's belief that al-Hajj Amin was still the center of the masses' movement in all of Palestine. However, as his brothers observe, al-Qassam was disappointed when he did not find anything more than a rebellious nationalist in the mufti, who did not live up to the level of the revolutionary Muslim. Perhaps the mufti was mistaken about his analysis of the issues or about his choice of the ideal method. Yet, it is also clear that he feared for

---

[42] Nimr Husayn Abd al-Rahman al-Sa'di (1910–48), a Palestinian militant and follower of Izz al-Din al-Qassam. He survived the military clash between al-Qassam's group and British soldiers in Yab'ad in 1935, when he surrendered while severely wounded.

[43] Mahmud Salim al-Makhzumi (d. 1966), originally from Ramleh, al-Makhzumi joined al-Qassam and participated in the Palestinian resistance until 1948 before he moved to Syria where he died in 1966.

his family's interest, which made him reluctant to adopt armed struggle as the way of fighting at that stage, "knowing that a change in his position had subsequently occurred." His answer then was that the time was not right for that kind of work, and that the political efforts being made were sufficient to grant the Arabs of Palestine their rights.

Although the sources of the Arab Higher Committee subsequently alluded that al-Qassam was very close to the mufti who supported him, his brothers affirm that al-Qassam did not belong to a non-"jihadist" organization founded by him. In fact, al-Qassam contacted the mufti who refused to even appoint him as a temporary preacher to prepare for the revolution: "We work to resolve the cause peacefully." Al-Qassam, as a pioneering and revolutionary Muslim, thus understood that a phase like this—a phase of looking into independence and freedom—had to be about blood and revolution, while the bourgeoisie raised the banner of wisdom and understanding!!

4. Al-Qassam identified the nature of the battle through intellectual distinctness, as he identified the camp of the enemy and the camp of the revolution. He identified the tasks and stages of the struggle, which could be divided into four:

   a. The stage of self-preparation and mobilization of the masses, which lasted for three years.
   b. The stage of preparing and implementing secret courses, which began in 1925 and through which the vanguard organization was prepared educationally, politically, and militarily.
   c. The stage of testing the firmness of tactics and their effectiveness, and the Qassamists managed to produce "Sheikh Ahmad al-Ghalayni"-grenades and use them in some limited battles, and in assassination attempts of British officers and those who cooperated with them.
   d. The stage of declaring the revolution, which began the night of November 12, 1925, the night when al-Qassam left Haifa for the villages of Jenin in order to form revolutionary centers. These were methods the Algerian Muslim revolution adopted two decades later, and which Ernesto Guevara adopted in Bolivia thirty years later. Al-Qassam thus went out to call on the people to join the revolution. It is said that he intended to advance and occupy Haifa from the Jenin Mountains after the revolution ignited, and to announce the birth of a great popular revolution!

But what happened after that!?

We have pointed to the grenades that the Qassamists produced and employed in their first test battles in which some of the homes of some Jewish guards were blown up in 1933, killing some of them. They subsequently surprised the Jews in the Atlit settlement, where they killed several of them, and attacked some cars with Jewish workers near the village of Yajour. Before the famous night of the departure, the Qassamists sold the jewelry of their wives, and armed themselves with bullets and rifles. They then rushed to the mountains of Jenin, and one of them killed a Jewish guard who exposed them on the way.

Before al-Qassam's movement grew among unpredicted and unintended conditions, the decisive battle descended unexpectedly upon everyone—including the British themselves. The battle was between an estimated force of 300 to 600 British, and al-Qassam and ten of his brothers, who were besieged by that force. The battle continued for approximately six hours… They asked him to surrender… The great al-Qassam, however, "the symbol of the free and of non-compromise," shouted to them that they would never surrender… That this was jihad in the path of God… So they tempted him with money and the job of deputy mufti… Yet, the Muslim fighter mocked the bribe of this insured future, so he exhorted his brothers: "Die as martyrs." Al-Qassam was thus martyred standing as one of the greatest heroes of the epics in human history.

Once the masses learned the news of his martyrdom, they went out to mourn his death in the mosques and minarets everywhere in the occupied homeland. They walked in his glorious funeral and carried his coffin for ten kilometers. Naturally, most of the nationalist movement's leaders took a cowardly position toward the body of the great man, so they refused to participate in his valediction with the exception of Akram Zuaiter[44] who called upon them but to no avail. Settling for the conventional telegram, they sent a note to the British authorities: "If they do not receive their note, irresponsible extremist views will prevail, and the situation will deteriorate rapidly." Thus, the great al-Qassam passed into the history of our umma as a wonderful flash after serving as an example and a model with his blood. He was thus the first beginning of the revolutionary and organized armed action… far from the delusion of the dignitaries and the dominance of the traditional leaders who revealed their ugly and hesitant face to the movement of al-Qassam.

To those trying to wipe out the signposts of this unique Islamic personality under the auspices of the abundance of secular-nationalist and left-wing ideas, we state with absolute clarity that he was nothing but a natural Islamic model… and the true Qassamists are coming with a new dawn. The communists who try to blur our identity, stood nowhere at that time except in the ranks of the Jews, asking the Arabs to stand in solidarity with them, as Walter Laqueur writes in his book, *Communism and Nationalism in the Middle East*.[45] Conversely, a Palestinian Marxist, Naji Alush,[46] writes in his book *The Palestinian Nationalist Movement* that the communist party participated in the 1929 Palestine riots with the defense of the Jewish neighborhoods, accusing the British authorities of being responsible for the massacres, as he called them.

These are our symbols, and this is our sequence, from Muhammad bin Abdallah[47] to the last martyrs. So where are their symbols!?

These are our symbols, O young men of Islam. We are burdened with restoring them and carrying the flag of their continuance on the path to God.

---

[44] Akram Zuaiter (1909–96), co-founder of the Independence Party in 1932. He spent the years between 1937 and 1951 in exile in Iraq, Syria, and Turkey following his role in the 1936 Revolt. Subsequently, he became secretary-general of the Islamic Conference convened in Jerusalem in 1959, and later worked as a Jordanian diplomat.
[45] Walter Laqueur (1921–2018), American journalist and historian.
[46] Naji Alush (1935–2012), nationalist Fatah intellectual who left the Fatah Revolutionary Council in 1977 in order to found and lead the Palestinian political faction, the Arab People's Movement.
[47] Muhammad bin Abdallah, full name of Prophet Muhammad.

7

Excerpts from "Afghanistan The Roots of the Conflict . . . The Revolution . . . The Future . . . Is It a New Resurgence of the Crusaders?"

Published in al-Mukhtār al-Islāmī *(The Islamic Digest), no. 9, March 1980 (p. 27–43), by Fathi al-Shiqaqi (Izz al-Din al-Faris) and Bashir M. Nafi' (Ahmad Sadiq).*

There never were any close connections between PIJ and the Afghan Mujahideen in the 1980s, and we do not know of any PIJ militants who travelled to Afghanistan. To this translator's knowledge, the most significant contact between the two was an interview with al-Shiqaqi featured in al-Mujahidun—*a magazine published from the mid-1980s until the mid-1990s by the party of Burhanuddin Rabbani, Jamiat-e-Islami. Moreover, Hamas quickly appropriated the Palestinian leader of the Services Bureau, Abdallah Azzam, after his death in 1989. As Abdallah Anas, the son-in-law of Azzam, noted: Neither al-Shiqaqi nor PIJ received any significant attention from the Afghan-Arabs or from the Afghan Mujahideen.*[1]

This does not mean that al-Shiqaqi was oblivious to the Afghan-Soviet War, however. Indeed, one of the many conflicts between the PIJ nucleus and the Egyptian Muslim Brotherhood was the perception that the latter's interest in the Afghan cause came at the expense of the Palestinian one. Moreover, as the following document illustrates, al-Shiqaqi did spend some time to analyze the war and its causes. For the sake of readability, I have removed al-Shiqaqi's section listing the Afghan parties and movements as it adds little to our understanding.

Many similar tropes are repeated in the following piece. Colonialism attempted to weaken the Arab-Islamic lands, which was accelerated by the introduction of secular-nationalist regimes. In the eyes of al-Shiqaqi, this was no different for Afghanistan—although Russia is the main colonial agent. This document nonetheless matters because it adds to our understanding of how al-Shiqaqi read contemporary conflicts in the context of colonial interests. History, as always, permeates his publications, while religious analysis is conspicuously absent. Yet, what distinguishes this text from the preceding ones is that al-Shiqaqi does not merely discuss historical trajectories, but, instead, puts greater focus on economic driving forces in order to understand the impetus of Western colonial adventures. Although al-Shiqaqi was far from Marxist, there are nonetheless traces of a materialist analysis in the piece below. Attempting to

---

[1] Abdallah Anas, interview with translator, September 4, 2017, Oslo.

explain Western aggression, al-Shiqaqi and Nafi' state that the West must maintain its growth rates and economic and social prosperity, and the North is thus kept rich while the South is kept poor. Last, the document matters because this is one of few commentaries by al-Shiqaqi on international law and his perception of (the lack of) international justice. International law is thus not a neutral means to obtain justice for the downtrodden, but a tool to keep them in place. As the authors ask: "What international law is this when only the Muslim peoples and the oppressed nations in the world lose? Why are our dreams confiscated and our wealth stolen, while they advance, and their people thrive? Is this law not a Western law?"

Has Peter the Hermit[2] been resurrected—and in a Marxist form this time—to be reawakened decaying and vicious in the earth? Does that which now happens in Afghanistan bring those barbaric campaigns to mind, which were prepared by the Catholic Church in Europe to overthrow the Muslim world in an attempt to destroy and eradicate it?? Or is it the position of Tsarist Russia toward the Ottoman Caliphate in the eighteenth and nineteenth centuries when it established itself in the name of the Orthodox Church—in an attempt to atone for its sins by not participating in the first Crusades, to protect the Christians who lived safely in the Caliphate? In the name of that task, Tsarist Russia launched fierce crusader wars and several Islamic states ended up in the belly of the Russian bear as a result. Many other states were separated in the name of liberating the Christian people...

In order to understand what is happening, we have to turn back.

Since Islam entered the land of Khorasan in the era of Caliph Uthman, the Possessor of Two Lights,[3] this land found itself in the religion and believed in it. It was broken in order to subsequently become a stronghold exercising its role in spreading its message and standing as a reliable bulwark in the face of the ferocious attacks to which it was exposed. Afghanistan and its environs were included under the rule of Suleiman the Magnificent,[4] to become a part of the broad body of the Caliphate. The situation remained as such until 1747 when Ahmad Shah[5] declared the secession from the Caliphate. This created the State of Afghanistan, leaving the Ottoman Caliph with only nominal power.

A dark page in Afghanistan's history was opened in February 1919 when Amanullah[6] ascended the throne to succeed his father, the slain despot. He thus completed a dangerous triangle in the history of the Islamic umma (Mustafa Kemal in Turkey, Amanullah in Afghanistan, and Rada Khan in Iran) as modern Western colonialism

---

[2] Peter the Hermit (1050–1115), priest of Amiens, emotional revivalist, and considered one of the most important preachers of the First Crusade (1095–99).
[3] Caliph Uthman was according to tradition so loved by the Prophet that the former was called "the Possessor of Two Lights."
[4] Suleiman the Magnificent (1494–1566), the tenth Sultan of the Ottoman Empire from 1520 until 1566.
[5] Ahmad Shah Durrani (1722–72), founder of the Durrani Empire (also known as the Sadozai Empire or Afghan Empire) and is often considered the founder of present-day Afghanistan.
[6] Amanullah Khan (1882–1960), the emir and subsequent king of the Kingdom of Afghanistan from 1919 until 1929. Known for his attempts to modernize Afghanistan by emulating the West, Khan abdicated and fled Afghanistan with the ensuing Afghan civil war (1928–29).

flowed into the mind and sense of our umma with its armies of Westernization to counterfeit and falsify them.

The West left Amanullah breathless, and he was greatly impressed by Mustafa Kemal and his approach of Westernization. However, his understanding of the West and its culture was more superficial, and he thus saw nothing more than a call for the secularization of education and the removal of the veil. He strongly called for it, and his wife appeared unveiled during their tour in Europe. As a result of this, and due to the exorbitant taxes that Amanullah imposed on his people for his personal spending, there were several successive revolutions in Afghanistan that have continued for several years, and which only ended with his overthrow and exile to Europe in 1929.

There were several other episodes in the list of rulers of defeat and Westernization in Afghanistan. To pass through the names: Naji Saqqa (the bandit), Muhammad Nadir Shah,[7] and Muhammad Zahir Shah[8]—each of them striking with a new pickax at the edifice of truth, and each adding a new brick in the attempt to counterfeit the umma's awareness and to falsify its historical perception. The episodes then follow in succession to present us with new names. They begin with Muhammad Daoud[9] and end with Babrak Karmal[10] for Afghanistan to assume the other face of Westernization on the Marxist road in continuation of the same attempt and following the same line.

In the second half of the nineteenth century, the Islamic world was a theater for the colonialist conflict between the three great colonialist crusader forces at that time: Tsarist Russia, Great Britain, and France. In the Islamic Gulf and in Iran in particular, the conflict was at its strongest between Russia and Great Britain in the attempt to control this important region, which controls the lifeblood of Europe as represented in the main maritime trade routes between India—the colonies' jewel in the British crown—and the European continent… That conflict which was clearly reflected in the region of Central Asia and Tibet.

The British policies in the region were at that time based on a belt of buffer states to the south of Russia. These states were politically independent, but only to the degree of preventing the advancement of the Russians to the south in its attempt to achieve their historical dream by finding a port by the warm ocean waters. Great Britain attempted in these times to implement its policies in Iran, maintaining absolute sovereignty for itself in its southern regions overlooking the Gulf in front of the Russian practices to the north. The reach of the Russian bear's claws aimed at Afghanistan, and its interest in it—especially after losing its naval bases in the Black Sea following the signing of the Treaty of Paris in 1856,[11] depriving it of its absolute privileges to harass—made

---

[7] Muhammad Nadir Shah (1883–1933), king of Afghanistan from 1929 until his assassination in 1933 at the hands of Abdul Khaliq, a Hazara student.

[8] Muhammad Zahir Shah (1914–2007), the last king of Afghanistan (1933–73) who introduced free elections, parliament, and universal suffrage to the country.

[9] Muhammad Daoud Khan (1909–78), prime minister of Afghanistan from 1953 until 1963 and president from 1973 until 1978 with support and assistance from the Soviet Union. He was assassinated in 1978 in the Saur Revolution (more reasonably described as a coup d'état) at the hands of the People's Democratic Party of Afghanistan.

[10] Babrak Karmal (1929–96), installed as president of Afghanistan by the Soviet Union following the latter's invasion in 1979.

[11] The Treaty of Paris (1856), agreement to settle the Crimean War between Russia and the alliance of the Ottoman Empire, the French and British Empires, and the Kingdom of Sardinia. Al-Shiqaqi

Britain look differently at the issue when it came to Afghanistan... fighting with its armies in two failed attempts to occupy it... each time forced to retreat after losing entire armies on its land... Russia, in return, refused to recognize the British in their absolute preference in the region. As expressed in the newspaper *Petersburg Zeitung*, "The Tsar's government is ready to work on the British question in the Arabian Gulf on the condition that the British leave their special claims that India's borders end in Iraq (and Kuwait)." It also wrote: "Asia will find room for Russian colonialism as well as for British colonialism."[12]

Russia translated its position through its numerous attempts to break this preference; perhaps most notable was the economic plan drawn by Count White to be implemented in Iran, as well as its alliance with the French at the turn of this century against Britain in an attempt to exploit the French fleet in the Indian sea. The collapse of the enormous Russian force facing Japan in 1905 terminated the hopes of Russia to advance to the south, however, and forced it to sign a treaty with Britain in 1907 recognizing the latter's undisputed right to Afghanistan, Iran, and the Gulf.

The Second World War's negative impact on the Afghan economy, and the emergence of the United States on the international scene as a superpower rich in technical and industrial goods without any apparent political ambitions—in addition to Britain's exit from India in 1947 and the resultant increase of Russian pressure on Afghanistan—was a direct influence pushing Afghanistan to link itself to several American companies, which in 1943 began to implement several important projects. Ambassadors were exchanged between the two countries in 1948 in order to give Afghanistan an American loan of $21 million for construction projects. American money in the Gulf region and in Iran—through the petrol companies—increased steadily in the following years to form a close link between it and its foreign policy, while British control ebbed, and ended completely by the early 1970s.

Russia, on the other hand, was living in a period of passivity, preoccupied with what was happening domestically after the socialist revolution [in 1917] until the 1940s. Russia appeared before the outside world with its ideological cause in the 1940s, ending the stage of passivity (the revolutionary phase) in order to commence a new role of colonialism... It approached the Gulf waters with extreme caution; yet it seems its view of Afghanistan was closer.

Thus, in 1955, in the era of Muhammad Zahir Shah's rule, the prime minister of Afghanistan, Muhammad Daoud, decided to worsen the Pakhtusa crisis[13] between Afghanistan and Pakistan. Following Pakistan's acceptance of American armament, Daoud decided to open the door of his country for the Soviet Union. He visited the country at the end of the year, the first visit of its kind in the history of Afghan-Soviet relations, where he met premier of the Soviet Union, Bulganin,[14] and the

---

refers here to the designation of the Black Sea as a neutral territory.
[12] A reference to the Anglo-Russian Entente of 1907 with which Tsarist Russia and Britain agreed the division of Iran into three zones.
[13] The Pakhtusa crisis refers here to the attempts of Afghan Prime Minister Muhammad Daoud Khan to reunite the Pashtuns of Pakistan with Afghanistan by extending the Durand Line between the two countries, effectively attempting to annex Pakistani territory.
[14] Nikolaj Aleksandrovitsj Bulganin (1895–1975), premier of the Soviet Union from 1955 until 1958.

party secretary, Khrushchev. That visit resulted in the signing of several documents, treatises, and financial loan agreements, and it ensured that Russia could easily expel the creeping American influence in Afghanistan and link itself tightly to the country. With the arrival of the Russian pipeline to Afghanistan, the Afghans' confidence in Russia increased, and several delegations travelled to the Soviet Union to study or to be trained, which had a significant impact on the emergence of Afghan Marxist parties in a manner that was unspoken of in the mid-1960s.

In July 1973, and after approximately forty years, Muhammad Zahir Shah's rule ended. Muhammad Daoud—with the assistance of some Marxists—managed to seize power and to declare a republican system. Since then, and until April 1978, this period witnessed a sharp escalation of the activity of the Marxist parties, on the one hand, and the spark of the Islamic opposition, on the other. The latter was represented by the existing Islamic groups' declaration of jihad against the existing regime in addition to several other groups.

It seems that Muhammad Daoud, who remained head of ministry for nearly twenty years, was not particularly good at calculating… as he did not realize that he would not be anything more than a bridge to be crossed over by his comrades. Thus, on March 17, 1978, it was his turn to be sacrificed by his comrades on the international altar when Nur Muhammad Taraki[15]—leader of the People's Democratic Party of Afghanistan (Khalq)[16]—seized power after a coup d'état in which Muhammad Daoud himself and forty in his family were killed in a horrendous and barbaric massacre on the Marxist road. Marxist elements had complete control of power from that day in order for a new stage of revolutionary corrosion on the inside to begin.

The coup d'état of Taraki lasted for only five months, however. As he returned from Havana through Moscow, he arrived in Kabul to find death waiting for him at the hands of comrades and by the sharp Soviet bayonets that had escorted him to the throne in a rotten struggle for power and the settling of old accounts.

Hafizullah Amin[17] seems to have displayed a note to his country in the understanding of Russian signals, however, so he had to be replaced by someone with a greater ability to do so… Thus came Babrak Karmal, leader of the People's Democratic Party of Afghanistan (Parcham), through the barrel of the Soviet guns, with whom Russia expressed its historical dreams of reaching the ocean, conceived as a solution to the

---

[15] Nur Muhammad Taraki (1917-79), founding member of the People's Democratic Party of Afghanistan and president from 1978 until his assassination in 1979.

[16] Khalq was a faction of the People's Democratic Party of Afghanistan led by Taraki and Hafizullah Amin. Primarily consisting of Afghan Pashtuns, Khalq has been described as far more tribal than its rival faction Parcham, which was more urban and relied on the Afghan middle class. While Khalq adhered to the vision of a strictly organized and disciplined Marxist-Leninist party, Parcham believed Afghanistan was too underdeveloped and thus proposed a broader popular front with a gradual transition to socialism. After the Saur Revolution (1978), which al-Shiqaqi refers to, Khalq implemented reforms and suppressed opposition, eventually leading to the formation of the Mujahideen.

[17] Hafizullah Amin (1929-79), though being member of the Khalq faction, he came to power in a coup d'état that deposed, and subsequently executed, Taraki. Though attempting to appease the demonstrations and protest against the Taraki government and its brutal oppression, Amin was unsuccessful. The Soviet Union assassinated Amin in 1979 as a part of its invasion of Afghanistan.

potential oil crisis in the 1980s... In addition to the Islamic giant crouching on its border in Iran. All of this under the defiled reconciliation policy...

☪

The Islamic Homeland and the International Laws

No nation in modern and contemporary history has suffered as our umma has suffered, and the greatest calamities of our umma are the majority of its rulers. The recent tragedy of Afghanistan has dissipated all farces of these rulers and all the tragedies of their history. A handful of communists dominates the Afghan Muslim people and sheds their blood in the streets, and no one moves. Russian experts, followed by Russian tanks and thousands of soldiers, then burn the spirit of our Muslim people and pursue them outside of their homeland, and no one batters an eye. They are too busy with the Iranian threat that came from the Muslim people's revolution in Iran against their tyrants!

America then begins its play against the Russians as Carter accuses Brezhnev of lying because he did not tell him the truth about the Russian invasion of Afghanistan beforehand..! Immediately, the American presidential candidate, Mr. Kennedy,[18] goes out to give the play its comedic character, accusing President Carter of also lying because he knew the reality of Russian intentions against Afghanistan and the size of the intervention from its outset, yet did not confront it.

Our own rulers are all moving here: some of them support America—and not the Afghan people—against Russia, believing its sincerity in the conflict against Russian expansion and defending parts of the Islamic homeland, especially the regions of its wealth in the Gulf. Some of these rulers move in defense of the Russian invasion of Afghanistan because this invasion and oppression support the nationalist liberation movement in the Third World against the ambitions of capitalism. As if there is still a place for ideologies between the superpowers, or as if the peoples of our Islamic homeland one day have known—and for more than a century—the taste of freedom or its smell.

What wondrous mystery do these rulers live in? Giving them this calm and peace in the face of our umma's destruction and oppression, while their people flare up for their brothers in Afghanistan, Iran, Eritrea, and Palestine! What deep awareness comprises their enlightened minds as they led our umma to dependence and to the fields of exploitation by the superpowers: once in the name of international law and custom, once in the name of maintaining world peace in shade of the reconciliation conspiracy, and numerously in the name of friendship and cooperation treaties with the great ones.

The Islamic umma must realize the truth about its situation in the world. It must realize what deflection it has taken, with the loss of its independence and wealth. It must today put the lives and future of its people together.

---

[18] Ted Kennedy (1932–2009), American Democratic politician and senator from Massachusetts.

1. We, and the Lies of International Law and Custom

Last year, when the Somali people moved to recover their occupied land under the control of the Ethiopian government, the Russians stood with Colonel Mengistu[19] against the rights of the Somalis. While the Americans did not like all of Siad Barre's[20] supplication attempts to make them help him, they argued that international law and custom did not permit the forcible modification of a state's border. Indeed, the hopes of the Somalis have been crushed in light of reconciliation.

It was the same law that gave Israel the right to expel all of the Palestinians in 1948. It was the same law that gave Israel the right to modify the borders of the neighboring countries with its invasion of 1967, which also occurred under the nose of Russia and America—lest we have not mentioned their primary role in recognizing Israel, and supporting it morally and materially since its establishment. It was also this law that allowed India—with Soviet support—to alter the geography of Pakistan completely, and shatter the Muslim Pakistani people into two with one of them called Bangladesh, also under the nose of America.

Today, while international law does not permit Iran to recover and prosecute the criminal Shah, it allows the Russians to annihilate the Muslim Afghan people and to threaten the neighboring Muslim peoples, just as they were allowed—with American assistance—in their attempt to invade Zaire two years ago. So what international law is this when only the Muslim peoples and the oppressed nations in the world lose? Why are our dreams confiscated and our wealth stolen, while they advance and their people thrive? Is this law not a Western law?

In the mid-seventeenth century and before the advance of the Ottoman Empire in Europe, the Westphalia Conference[21] was held by the European states. It established the first traditional rules of international law governing the relationship between the governments of Europe—in the beginning—and made them devote themselves and join forces against the advance of Islam. In the Ottoman Empire's period of weakness—especially when the secular elements began to take over some of the jurisdictions in its systems—this empire attempted to enter the international community in 1856 and the Europeans agreed: the impermissibility of Islamic law in international issues, and the introduction of some European laws into its governing bodies.

Faced with the advancing phenomenon of European colonization of the world, international custom was based on two principles: the idea of international balance and the non-intervention of one country in the colonies of another. The other principle was the phenomenon of international conferences to solve problems between the great nations dominating the world through negotiations and mutual understanding. The

---

[19] Mengistu Haile Mariam (1937–present), chairman of the Ethiopian military junta and head of the Ethiopian state from 1977 until 1991.
[20] Jaale Mohamed Siad Barre (1919–95), president of Somalia from 1969 until 1991.
[21] The Peace of Westphalia (1648), a series of peace treaties ending the religious wars in Europe. Al-Shiqaqi refers here to the principles the treaties established, including the principle of inter-state aggression held in check by a balance of power, the principle of non-interference in other states' domestic affairs, and the principle of peaceful coexistence.

Vienna Conference[22] was thus convened in 1815 to discuss the impact of the French Revolution, and the Treaty of Aix-la-Chapelle[23] was signed in 1818 to ensure Russia, England, Prussia, Austria, and France the provisions of the Vienna convention, agreeing on armed intervention for the protection of international colonial stability. International law consequently permitted France, England, and Russia to intervene against the Egypt of Muhammad Ali[24] in 1840 when he attempted to build an empire for himself and advanced to the north.

In the wake of the First World War, the international customs shifted from international conferences to international organizations. Thus, the colonial governments—namely Russia, England, and France at the time—established the League of Nations to create a legal framework to control the region of the Islamic homeland, its people, and its wealth after destroying the Islamic state and overthrowing the Caliphate. Hence, a new term was introduced to the world, "mandate," in order to give the phenomenon of western colonialism a modern appearance.

The United Nations emerged as a western idea and entity after the Second World War to ensure the continuation of the western plunder of the world in the contemporary era after the oppressed people were transformed from colonial entities to subordinate entities governed by powers loyal to either the Soviet West, or the European or American West. The borders of the oppressed countries were drawn by the great powers in order to secure their interests. Even the international maritime laws—such as the movement laws in the Suez Canal—were decided by the same countries to contain the possibilities of the oppressed people. The freedom of man is in the end the freedom of western man. The eradication of the Muslim man, and destroying the vision of the oppressed nation's children, by any tool, has nothing to do with freedom.

Indeed, international law and customs were made to confront Islam advancing in Europe and the developments that first took place on the land of the Islamic homeland after the defeat of the Ottoman Empire, the destruction of the Caliphate, and the division of the Islamic homeland. It was so the second time when the people's movements for liberation in the 1940s commenced in the Islamic homeland. This law has always been in the service of the West and its interests. Our umma was, and still is, the loser under the banner of this law: Somalia is wrong, and the Soviets and Ethiopians are right. The Palestinians are criminals, and Israel is the rights holder. The petrol states are savages who do not care about the interests of humanity and the international economy, while Europe and America are moral humanists who embezzle their capital and cheat them in the money market to subvert the true values of oil. Islamic Iran surges with emotions and feelings, while the Shah and America are innocent of all sins.

---

[22] The Vienna Congress, held from October 1814 until June 1815 with the goal of resizing the great European powers in order for European peace to be sustained following the Napoleonic Wars.

[23] Treaty of Aix-la-Chapelle, al-Shiqaqi refers here to the Congress of Aix-la-Chapelle (1818), a diplomatic meeting between France and Britain, Austria, Prussia, and Russia, which effectively ended the great wars of 1792–1815 (the French Revolutionary Wars, 1792–97, and the Napoleonic Wars, 1803–15).

[24] Muhammad Ali Pasha (1769–1849), Ottoman governor of Egypt, subsequently viceroy and Pasha. Ali Pasha is considered the founder of modern Egypt and its ruling dynasty, which lasted until the Egyptian Revolution of 1952.

Finally, under the roof of international law, the Afghan martyrs of women, children, and youth are classified as reactionary clients, while the Soviet colonial army that sheds the blood of the Muslim people stands with the progress and freedom of man!

Is the world not in need of a new law and a new custom? Does not what is mentioned above require the advancing Islamic tide in the world to make its own particular law? And this is just the beginning!!

2. The Conspiracy of Reconciliation and World Peace

The superpowers act on the basis that they have the right to deplete the world. The white man has since the beginning of the renaissance had a strange sense—there is no space here to analyze and study it—that his own well-being and social prosperity are the most important things in this world, and that there is no importance for the reality of man and his future in the oppressed nations outside the West. This was while Islam built its great state that stood with the freedom, progress, and justice of man regardless of race, color, or creed.

The European states agreed in the previous century to preserve the sick man—the Ottoman Empire—until he was exhausted and divided. In the beginning of this century, the English and French agreed without dispute to divide their interests in Africa. The hand of France grasped its north—in exchange for Egypt, the Gulf, and India to remain with England. The Russians and English also agreed to divide their influence in Iran. England and France divided the Islamic homeland between themselves after the First World War, and they gave Palestine to the Jewish movement after the collapse of the Ottoman Empire.

Stalin, Churchill, and Roosevelt met after the Second World War at the Yalta Conference, and divided the world into areas of influence between the East and the West. America took leadership of the capitalist camp, while the Soviet Union became the head of the communist camp. The phase was marked by the Cold War through the attempt of all sides to extend their influence and to tighten their control over all new parts of the world. The Soviet Union appeared with its ideological papers for the people as a supporter of the liberation movements at a time when the capitalist camp had been completely exposed by the peoples and had become a sign of oppression and exploitation.

Kennedy and Khrushchev met in Vienna in June 1961 and put down new rules for the relationship between the two camps—the stage of peaceful coexistence.[25] The areas of influence were then redivided in exchange for concessions from both sides—particularly in the field of nuclear armament for the capitalist camp and in the field of ideological struggle for the communist camp. This caused differences to commence between China and Russia as the Chinese accused their comrades in Moscow of abandoning the working class in Europe and in the world, with Soviet interests being of a colonial nature only. A small example of this concession was the dissolution of the

---

[25] The Vienna Summit (June 4, 1961), summit meeting between US President John F. Kennedy and Soviet Premier Nikita Khrushchev.

Egyptian Communist Party and its integration into the Arab Socialist Union in the early 1960s.

After the important shifts in the international economic standards, there was the so-called oil crisis and the disruption of international law in Southeast Asia and Africa. There was also the emergence of what they call the Middle East crisis, which we call "the problem of the Islamic homeland". After all this, new rules of relations between the two camps were required, so Nixon visited the Soviet Union in May 1973 with the establishment of the so-called "International Accord."[26] The world was divided into Soviet regions of influence, American regions of influence, and grey zones with the right of both to compete without igniting a war between the two, with the oppressed being allowed to slay each other whenever necessary.

We thus noticed new features beginning to appear in the world. The Simla Agreement[27] was signed by India and the secular government of Ali Bhutto[28] in Pakistan, and the government of Pakistan recognized dividing its people in two. The Marxist Aden government remained stable although its neighbors could overthrow it in hours if they wanted to. The former Shah stopped his aid to the Kurds in order to stop Iraq's aid to the Marxists in the Gulf and opening Iraq's doors to western investments—following the Algiers Accord[29] between Saddam and Pahlavi. The regime of Ethiopia transformed into a Marxist military regime, while the American petrol company Gulf Oil continued its petrol investments in Marxist Mozambique. There are many more examples, but they all indicate the same thing: the superpowers have agreed to invest in and divide the oppressed peoples between them. It is not possible—not in the least—for conflict between them on account of the lie of the small peoples' independence.

This is the history of the superpowers' relationship with the oppressed peoples. The wars between the superpowers were only exceptional cases, most of which were a disruption of the rules of international security within Europe itself, while everything is subject to negotiations, mutual understanding, and division outside Europe—outside their world. How can we believe that what is now happening in Afghanistan is not a part of their agreement? The events of Afghanistan today have fully exposed the colonial face of the Soviet Union, while the American colonial face was already well known.

The agreement of the superpowers and their treatises do not cancel the role of the peoples for good, if the peoples are able to discover their own particular way for international influence. This is the second question!

In light of our previous discernment of the relationships between the states, how can we then define the nature of friendship and cooperation between the superpowers and the oppressed countries considered to belong to them? What type of friendship

---

[26] Al-Shiqaqi is here referring to the Moscow Summit in which US President Richard Nixon met Soviet General Secretary Leonid Brezhnev, May 22–30, 1972.
[27] The Simla Agreement (1972), signed between India and Pakistan leading to diplomatic recognition of Bangladesh and the normalization of the two countries' relationship.
[28] Zulfiqar Ali Bhutto (1928–79), president of Pakistan from 1971 until 1973, and prime minister from 1973 until 1977. He was executed after the military coup d'état by General Zia-ul-Haq.
[29] The 1975 Algiers Agreement, agreement between Iraq and Iran, partly to settle border disputes at Shatt al-Arab and Khuzestan.

is there between Yemen, for example, and the Soviet Union or America? Indeed, the friendship between Egypt and the West in the previous century led to the occupation of Egypt. The friendship of Turkey and the United States led to the destruction of the Turkish economy and the remaining Islamic values and manners in Turkish society. It thus dragged Turkey into a general decay and to a comprehensive dependency on the West. There is no need to recall America's Point Four Program and its assistance programs in the 1950s.[30]

Everyone knows what the Egyptian-Soviet friendship means: not attacking Israel and giving us the cotton and strategic facilities. Indeed, the Somali-Soviet friendship ended with the destruction of the Somalians dreams when the Soviet interests turned to Ethiopia. The Soviets cut the roads in Afghanistan in the days of the previous king, and this is not a pure friendship and cooperation with the poor Afghan people, but, rather, the implementation of their future strategic plan directed southwards—as has now been confirmed.

Today, and under the pretext of the Soviet threat, some of the ruling powers in some parts of the Islamic homeland are trying to drag their people into new treaties with America… This is what we saw with the attempts of General Zia-ul-Haq[31] in Pakistan in his latest negotiations with the Americans. Pakistan now declares multiple calls for cooperation with this or that superpower.

There is only one way to preserve the independence and protection of the umma, and it is not friendship treaties and cooperation between the oppressed nations and the great nations. The sons of the Islamic tide in the Islamic homeland must know this and determine this way… and this is the next question.

There are two ways of life between the domination and agreement of the superpowers: the first way is to ensure the interests of one of these states on the land of the small state, which leads to the prominence of its importance in the world. Yet, it also makes it a dependent and stolen state, losing its identity… This is what we should reject. The second way is to threaten its interests. The great state must feel that there is no place for it here, that our independence is a true independence, that its law and customs are not our law or our customs, and that we are the possessors of an independent identity.

This can be done only under four conditions: Internal organization. Possibilities for a true defense, which is neither artificial nor dependent. The way of increased material and technological progress. Last, and most important, a specific and authentic identity, in addition to a historical sense of the conscience of the umma and the principles it brings to humanity in order to overthrow their situations and upset the inhuman laws that now dominate and rule.

Can this lead us to answer the three previous questions and solve the problems of our loss, degradation, dependence, and exploitation? Surely this is not the fourth question!!

---

[30] The Point Four Program was announced by US president Harry S. Truman on January 20, 1949, with the aim of providing technical assistance to "developing countries."

[31] Muhammad Zia-ul-Haq (1924–88), president of Pakistan from 1978 until 1988 following his military coup d'état in 1977 against the government of Zulfiqar Ali Bhutto.

Afghanistan... The Roots of the Conflict

Is the communist West an alternative to the capitalist West against the Islamic awakening?

The West must maintain its growth rates, and economic and social prosperity, which means keeping the North rich and the South poor. The goods of this Earth are sufficient for all humankind to live in real prosperity, but with a slight difference between nations, and not with this dreadful disparity between the lives of the person in the North and the hunger of the person in the South. The West—both the capitalist and the communist—realizes that the greatest danger capable of confronting its domination over the world is the rise of a true humanist ideology, leading the people against the West through their revolution. New values will shine positively on humanity when it is capable of maintaining the progress of civilized humanity and its development, while at the same time achieving human balance, freedom, and justice through it. In particular, the greatest threat to the West and its domination is the Islamic awakening, which is now moving to give the world new features.

Hence, the West sensed that both its parts (capitalist and communist) had to ally themselves in order to confront the next Islamic threat and to maintain its domination over the world. This was only possible, of course, after securing the future of the capitalist entities from the communist ideological threat. The British Labor politician, Cristopher Mayhew,[32] once said: "Ideological coexistence is a condition for peaceful coexistence." He meant that the communists must realize the impossibility of fulfilling the Marxist idea in which it is an inevitability for the communist camp to triumph over the capitalist systems with their transformation into Marxist socialist states.

In return, one of the Russian comrades—Khrushchev—declared in 1956 that "[i]t is our duty to strengthen the working class with material stimulus." He meant an important concession in Marxist ideology to converge with the Western system halfway. This was in addition to the other true concessions approached by the group of Brezhnev on the path of meeting the West. The Western intellectuals see that "the era of the technological revolution will crush the ideological efforts." That is, technological progress will give prosperity to all and eliminate the potential for conflict between the working class and the employers in capitalist countries. Thus, it seems that the intellectual trend dominating the European minds sees a possibility of complete mutual understanding with the socialist camp in order to secure the interests of everyone in the world after the danger of socialist revolution ended in Europe. The Helsinki Conference,[33] convened as a public meeting between the systems of the two camps, was an indication of this assessment, where both camps gave important concessions for an important mutual understanding.

There is consequently a danger that threatens Western interests, which is the danger of the Islamic religion and the awakening of its people—this religion, which was always the barrier against the advancement of the West and its domination throughout the

---

[32] Cristopher Mayhew (1915-97), British Labor politician before joining the Liberals in 1974.
[33] The Helsinki Accords (1975), European congress partly conducted to normalize relations between western and eastern states based on the principles of non-interference and respect for human rights.

previous historical stages from the beginning of the colonial era until its peak, which was accompanied by the fall of the Ottoman Empire.

There is also a possibility of a long and comprehensive coalition between the communist camp and the capitalist camp. Why, then, do the Soviets—representing the largest bloc in the socialist camp—bear the burden of confronting the Islamic tide and the awakening of the Islamic masses? All people of the world have understood the reality of the capitalist states' ugly face with their long colonial history, and there has been enough hostility against Europe and America for these people to fight them until death. Things are no longer coherent in the capitalist camp, as violent social problems resulting from the material and technological progress have erupted. The cohesion of the Western capitalist people is no longer what it was a quarter of a century or half a century ago, for example. Just as the comprehensive Islamic religion required a comprehensive ideology, so is this available in Marxist theory.

For all of these reasons, capitalist Europe—in addition to America—has become convinced that there is a possibility for the Communist West to become an alternative for them in confronting the coming Islamic tide… Particularly since Europe and America with its Christian remnants have realized that "communism is unstable," as the Islamic intellectual Malik Bennabi[34] said—God rest his soul. Communism orders human nature completely, and it will therefore give up its ideological components in the end to distribute all the benefits to the West.

This seems quite logical when we see the Marxist elements continuing to oppose Islam in Iran and standing against the religion of the Arab masses… as is evident from this violent Soviet invasion of Afghanistan, shedding the blood of our Muslim masses. As a start, perhaps, as the Communist West replaces the capitalist West in its attack and response to the next Islamic tide. We must certainly be aware of this new change in the conflict between Islam and its enemies.

---

[34] Malik Bennabi (1905–73), Algerian author and intellectual focusing on the causes of Islamic civilization's fall.

8

The Centrality of Palestine and the Contemporary Islamic Project

Published as a booklet by Fathi al-Shiqaqi, and circulated by the publisher Bayt al-Maqdis, Beirut, June 1989.

The developing ideology of PIJ delineated three dimensions of the Palestinian cause. According to al-Shiqaqi, it had a historical, a de facto, and a Qur'anic dimension which signified its totality. While the historical dimension pertained to the developing relationship and tensions between Western colonialism and the Global South, the de facto dimension delineated the occupation and the oppressive policies of Israel today. By analyzing these two dimensions, PIJ asserted that the State of Israel was the embodiment of Western colonial interests in the region and that a precondition for anti-colonial victory was to erase Israel.

The Qur'anic dimension, however, was different. Although al-Shiqaqi never bothered to develop it at length, and only bits and pieces exist in his oeuvre, the Qur'anic dimension is nonetheless important if one wishes to understand the ideology of PIJ—mainly because it is a sort of an anomaly. While the historical and de facto dimensions provide an analysis of a linear historical development, the Qur'anic dimension has certain cyclical elements. While the historical and de facto dimensions provide a largely secular analysis of the Palestinian struggle and of the Palestinians' predicament, the Qur'anic dimension relies on Qur'anic verses and the sunna.

According to al-Shiqaqi, the Qur'anic dimension of the Palestinian cause showed that the current conflict with the Israelis had been predestined by God. As the Israelites had risen in power and arrogance in the time of the Prophet, they were defeated by true Muslims. However, just as the Jews had risen before, they would do so again. For al-Shiqaqi, Israel was the manifestation of this second rise. Because the conflict was predestined by religion, al-Shiqaqi was certain that Islamic victory was inevitable in the end—if one just returned to religion as ordained by God.

This text matters for three reasons. First, this is one of the most elaborate text by al-Shiqaqi on the Qur'anic dimension. Here, al-Shiqaqi provides numerous references to the Qur'anic verses, interlaced with quotations by, and references to, Islamic theoreticians. The following piece also matters because it is one of the best demonstrations of how al-Shiqaqi combined secular and religious analysis in order to understand the battle in which the Palestinians were engaged. Last, because Israel was the precondition for the continued oppression of the downtrodden in the Global

South, this text highlights how al-Shiqaqi analyzed the Palestinian resistance in relation to other liberation struggles. As he writes below: *"This danger [of Israel] extends until it reaches all the oppressed in the world, [...which] affirms the danger it constitutes against the future of the oppressed in the world as well as Muslims."*

Preface

The Palestinian cause is undoubtedly the most important one of all the Islamic homeland's causes at this stage in its history. Its influence has affected all Arab and Islamic arenas near and far over four full centuries—all up until today. What has happened in Palestine across four full decades is a source of great pain for every Muslim in the world and a source of emotional storm for them. The liberation of Jerusalem remains a shared dream for a billion Muslims despite the difference of geography and thought, and despite the differences in language and ethnicity. Many rulers have ascended or fallen over the four decades of dealing with Palestine. Systems and domination over intellectual or partisan currents have changed or receded, just as hundreds of thousands of martyrs have fallen and the wealth of the umma has been wasted in the name of Palestine, or just as our resources were once deposited to the communist West and numerously to the capitalist West. Parts of the Islamic homeland have been attached to this ally or that axis, while the best sons of the umma have been pushed into the prisons and detention centers or hanged from the gallows.

The Palestinian cause is the most important of the Muslims' causes today. How can they deal with it and yield their vision to it? How can they make it a real concern for them? How can they understand it, perceive its dimensions, and answer the hot questions over its arena? Was it, for example, in vain that the West presented the Balfour Declaration at a time when the West was destroying the structures of the Ottoman Empire and struck the region militarily following the First World War, after more than a century of continuous Westernization and colonial plundering? Was it in vain that those who stabbed the Caliphate State from the back and who in the service of Britain and France worked to overthrow it were the same who continued to rule the Islamic homeland with the logic of fragmentation within the borders of Sykes-Picot? Who were the same who established Israel on their shoulders and in front of their eyes, and who did nothing but escape before thousands of Jews in 1948? Was it in vain that the progressive revolutionary regimes lost Jerusalem, and led Israel to the bank of Jordan and the coast of Suez, not far from Damascus? Who attempted to crush the creed of the umma and dismantle its creedal and historical-civilizational belonging between the two nakbas (1948–67)? Just as they were the same systems from which the leaders of the largest Arab capitals came to kneel before Israel—trading the faith, history, and land?

The Palestinian cause has over the past decades been a field of study and investigation for all the Islamic ideologies in the region. The Islamic attempts at awareness of the cause, and realizing its dimensions, have meanwhile remained emotional and simple. They were stirred by the wonderful and tragic link between Palestine and the al-Aqsa Mosque without realizing the divine dimensions carried by that link, which gives

Palestine its particularity, and which distinguished and characterized it. We rarely find—specifically, we never find—a serious and comprehensive historical study of Palestine from an Islamic viewpoint in the Islamic library. Nothing in our hands now exceeds the field of preaching and sermons about our right to Palestine (the waqf[1] of Muslims and their usurped land) and the need to liberate it. What we notice in the Islamic studies—which finally began to appear, and despite the good things they preach—is that they remain fragmented and do not fulfill the required purpose, which must require Islamic efforts and potentials. It is the beginning of the effort, and perhaps its importance lies in transforming the Palestinian question into an internal concern for the Islamic movement, which it practices, lives, and experiences in its daily life so that the Muslims do not stand by while the Earth, time, and history revolve.

Transforming the Palestinian question into an internal Islamic concern is extremely important and critical, both for the future of Palestine and for the future of the Islamic movement. Our conviction—as regards its importance and gravity—is that it needs nothing but a political decision!! A decision to turn the concerns of the Islamic movement's cadres and its bases to the real battlefield instead of imaginary fields, exhausting efforts and energy. We are convinced that the objective conditions are sufficiently ripe to deal with such a decision, and to achieve a great leap and an important shift in the history of the Islamic movement. The study in our hands is an attempt to put the Palestinian tragedy in its natural place in the march of the Islamic movement by turning it into a real concern driven by the Qur'an, history, and reality—a simple deed that will not replace further study and analysis.

The Centrality of the Palestinian Cause

The Western colonial crusades advanced toward the Islamic homeland, for the Western Industrial Revolution had achieved remarkable scientific and material results that were ascending toward their peak, and the old crusader hatred did not depart from its heart and it did not leave from its blood. The West thus advanced through violence, which was necessary and essential for achieving its goals.

This was not all in the West's process of invading the abode of Islam, however. The military, political, and economic control was not able to end the battle. The civilizational and cultural dimensions have remained the decisive role and the final word. They did so because the salvation of these dimensions, and their liberation, from the colonizer's influence makes us capable of reviving and foiling all other forms of control – whether militarily, politically, or economically. The West thus intended to wage a "total war" against the Islamic homeland, to consecrate the "susceptibility to colonialism" in our minds, and to destroy the sources of our internal strength. It did so by ravaging the creedal, intellectual, and civilizational components of the Islamic society, and by changing the ways of life and production in it, in order to serve its interests and achieve subordination to it.

It was a total war, a fierce battle, in which its armies advanced through two axes:

---

[1] *Waqf* is generally meant as a charitable endowment of certain property.

The First Axis: Including Three Stages

1. Overthrowing the Islamic political system and the dissolution of the Caliphate. After more than a century of Western colonial presence in the region, and with the French offensive forming its vanguard, the Western attack succeeded in overthrowing the Ottoman Empire—the last Islamic state and the symbol of Islamic unity for several decades.
2. Destroying the existing Islamic institutions, whether remnants inherited from the apparatuses of the Ottoman state or Islamic associations or institutions… those institutions that could have been lifeboats by developing into a bloc for the restoration of the Caliphate. The West and its pupils did not desist from attacking the Islamic homeland in such a way, but they also worked to create parallel and hostile institutions, which were nothing but perverted and defective imitations of the West's institutions.
3. Attempting to destroy the sound mind and to fill it with the West's concepts in order to cut all the way through the thinking process of restoring Caliphate. The simple reason for the destruction of the Islamic institutions was that the survival of the vigilant Islamic mind would attempt starting over and ensure the success of the Islamic institutions and the Islamic organization anew.

The Second Axis: Including Three Stages Paralleling the Previous Ones as They Complement Each Other Simultaneously

1. **Fragmentation:**
   The one Islamic homeland was fragmented into dozens of regions and nationalities to the point that the borders of Sykes-Picot became the legitimate borders maintained by each province, and this justified a new flag and a new national anthem for each country. Although the dreams of unity subsequently spread, the transition to devastating national, regional, and border conflicts nevertheless became a routine phenomenon. Thus, a quarter of a century before its establishment and foundation (after its separation from India), Pakistan was split into two independent parts after a brutal and devastating war. Algeria was in a border conflict with Morocco since its independence, Chad with Libya, northern Sudan with its south, and North Yemen with its south. It was also the case within a single capital, such as Beirut, with a bloody conflict between its east and west… and so on.

2. **Westernization:**
   It began from the first day of the French offensive, which was clear in the cunning letter Napoleon Bonaparte sent to the Egyptians. It swept everything away by dispatching intellectuals and politicians, who were embezzled in favor of the West, and who were raised in its nurseries to in the end be devoted to the West.

3. **Establishing the State of Israel:**
   It is considered the most important, most dangerous, and most violent expression of the total war. Through the establishment of the State of Israel and its continued presence in the heart of the Islamic homeland, the Western attack executed the most important and dangerous of its tasks. We are thus not merely facing a military or intellectual challenge here, but also an aggressive settler formation in an important and sensitive place in the Islamic homeland, which gives the conflict all its historical, civilizational, ideological and intellectual dimensions, in addition to the military, political, and economic ones. The establishment of Israel threatens not only the culture of the umma, but also its entire existence. The establishment of Israel also means to conform the dedication to the previous stages: the continued absence of the Islamic political system, the destruction of the Islamic institutions, the continued attempts to destroy the Muslim mind, and fragmentation and Westernization.

All this gives the conflict with Israel that particularity in the thought of the contemporary Islamic movement and in its practice. Or, what we call "the centrality of the Palestinian cause to the contemporary Islamic movement." This is not a voluntary slogan picked up from among several options. It is not raised for immediate or interim objectives. Rather, the strategic slogan was imposed by the confluence of our modern and contemporary history with the Qur'anic Absolute (as we shall see in detail).

The tasks of the contemporary Islamic movement were thus determined by the transformations of our history to confront the results of the modern Western challenge with Westernization, fragmentation, and the establishment of the Zionist entity. The Zionist entity and its persistence have thus come to represent the center of the challenge, the center of the Western attack, and the guarantor for its continued dominance over the reality of division, dependence, and backwardness. All flanks of the Islamic movement, and the millions of the umma's masses everywhere, must therefore make a straight line from the heart of its advanced frontline in the renaissance battle, and in every region of the Islamic homeland, toward the center... toward Jerusalem. The masses of the umma carry within themselves a special ache for Palestine. It is because their historical and creedal sense tells them that it is there... on that tiny strip by the eastern Mediterranean... there lies the central clashing point... there, the battle of our contemporary history will be decided.

The unity of Palestine is the unity coming from the awareness that the persistence of the Zionist entity means the failure of all renaissance projects. Therefore, the debate about what comes first: confronting dependency, Westernization, and fragmentation, or confronting the Zionist entity is a theoretical debate governed by calculations of immediate gains and loss, instead of a serious endeavor to build an integrated and coherent strategy for the contemporary Islamic renaissance's project. The unity around Palestine is the unity of history with the Qur'an, and it is the return of the advancing millions toward their fate... It is the unity of the renaissance project in its entirety. In Jerusalem—the essence and center of the universal conflict today—the features of the decisive battle are determined between the worshippers of God carrying the banner of revelation and the values of unity, on the one hand, and those carrying the values of the conflict philosophy, on the other. It is determined between those eager for the sake of God, and who seek Him, on the one hand, and those who rebel against God, and who have established the vilest civilizational model in human history on Earth, on the other.

The debate continues about what is first. We affirm that this particularity and centrality of the Palestinian cause will never mean to underestimate the importance of other objectives and tasks of the contemporary Islamic movement—such as the establishment of the Islamic state, the unity of the Islamic movement, and the victory of the global Islamic revolution. On the contrary (as we will see in this study), dealing with the cause from this perspective is what will push us to achieve these goals. A reciprocal (dialectic) relationship is clearly and surely that which connects the Palestinian cause with those goals and tasks.

Today, the Islamic movement is accountable for giving Palestine its (forgotten) particularity and for emphasizing its centrality in theory and application (in its thought and practice). It does not forget for a moment that it is Islamic and pertaining to God, and it thus makes the pleasing of God its ultimate goal and "the commencement of the Islamic renaissance everywhere" its minimal goal. Just as it is making its long-term goal that of overcoming the crisis of the modern Western challenge and solving the problems that Muslims are facing—a solution consistent with the creed of Islam and its code. Its short-term goal remains the restoration of the Islamic political system by establishing the Islamic state. In its emphasis upon this particularity and centrality, the Islamic movement is not governed by a regional mood or simply by societal or national interests. Rather, it is governed by the "comprehensive Qur'anic, historical, and de facto" reasons, which are wider and beyond any geographical borders… reasons imposed on this movement to make Palestine an axis for its daily political activity by considering it the meeting point between the approach of Islam and that of the West, toward achieving the aforementioned goals and objectives.

The Qur'anic Dimension

In the blessed Qur'an and in the Prophet's hadith, in the Islamic heritage and history, Palestine and Jerusalem represent a prominent place of special importance, which is not concealed to any reader of these sources. It raises an interest, and perhaps even surprise, when we see the Qur'anic devotion to this sacred land, even many years before the feet of the Muslim mujahidin marched on it. From the early years of the Islamic call—the years of vulnerability and persecution—the master of humankind and the leader of the umma, Muhammad—peace and blessings be upon him—felt the greatest human pain possible, tormented alone while the men of Ta'if split his pure head and bloodied his feet with their stones. So he raised his hands toward the sky—exhausted, wounded, and disillusioned by his disappointment with the people of Ta'if, who were crude and shameless. He raised his hands toward the sky in a cry haunted by human grief to call:

> O God, to You I complain of my weakness, lack of resources and humiliation before these people. You are the Most Merciful, the Lord of the weak and my Master. To

whom will You consign me? To one estranged, bearing ill will, or an enemy given power over me? If You do not assign me any worth, I care not, for Your favor is abundant upon me. I seek refuge in the light of Your countenance by which all darkness is dispelled and every affair of this world and the next is set right, lest Your anger should descend upon me or Your displeasure light upon me. I need only Your pleasure and satisfaction for only You enable me to do good and evade evil. There is no power and no might but You.

When Muhammad—peace and blessings be upon him—arrived at this moment of human grief and weakness, it was truly for God to host and bestow honor upon him, assuring him that the Almighty had not abandoned him and was not angry with him. So the Almighty carried him to Palestine in a sublime, glorious, and miraculous journey, which confirms the universality of this religion through this unique exodus and the miraculous link between Mecca and Jerusalem, between the Great Mosque of Mecca (which had not yet become a mosque) and the al-Aqsa Mosque, which was also yet to be built… this link, which was to be confirmed in the next centuries.

All of this was after the journey of the weakened man, and the journey to Jerusalem was powerful and overwhelming in order to give Muhammad—peace be upon him—the transparency, power, and exaltedness that no person or king ever received. It was a night capturing the spirit of time, which gave the valiant Muslim mujahidin the resolve and pushed them toward Jerusalem after years—and after that for centuries until today—and it gave them a momentum and a morale that cannot be contained. On that night, the universality of this religion was affirmed, carried by that weakened man, whose feet had been bloodied and whose head had been split by the people of Ta'if… On that night, the unity of the message of Truth was affirmed as was the Prophet of Truth, who prayed for the other prophets… On that sacred night, prayer was imposed as a pillar of the religion and as the most important manifestation of Muslim unity, and the divine command of turning one's face toward Jerusalem in prayer was far from the influence of local or regional elements. Therefore, it was not, and never will be, in vain for Islam to give Palestine and Jerusalem this particularity from the years of its first call, and even before the establishment of Islam's state in the city.

This is also evident in numerous Qur'anic verses in which God Almighty bestowed the land of Palestine with blessings:

> And We caused the people who had been oppressed to inherit the eastern regions of the land and the Western ones, which We had blessed.[2]

> Exalted is He who took His Servant by night from the Great Mosque of Mecca to the al-Aqsa Mosque, whose surroundings We have blessed, to show him of Our signs. Indeed, He is the Hearing, the Seeing.[3]

---

[2] See sūrat al-aʿrāf: 117.
[3] See sūrat al-isrāʾ: 1.

And We delivered him and Lot to the land which We had blessed for the worlds.[4]

And to Solomon [We subjected] the wind, blowing forcefully, proceeding by his command toward the land which We had blessed. And We are ever, of all things, Knowing.[5]

And We placed between them and the cities which We had blessed [many] visible cities. And We determined between them the [distances of] journey, [saying], "Travel between them by night or day in safety."[6]

O my people, enter the Holy Land which God has assigned to you and do not turn back [from fighting in God's cause] and [thus] become losers.[7]

In the exegesis "The Fig, The Olive and Mount Sinai" by Abu Hurayra[8]—may God be pleased with him—he writes: "God swore by the four mountains, saying: 'the fig, the olive, Mount Sinai, and this virtuous country.'" And the Prophet said (as narrated by Hurayra): "The fig is the Mount of Olives." In one narration: The olive is the Mount of Olives. Qatada states: "The olive is a mountain under Jerusalem." In the hadith about Aisha[9]—may God be pleased with her—which confirms this blessing and particularity, the Prophet said: "Mecca is a glorious city. God exalted the city and its sanctities, and encircled it with angels. Before creating everything on Earth that day, it took a thousand years. He interlocked Mecca with Medina, and He interlocked Medina with Jerusalem."

- Makhul bin Maymuna (the wife of the prophet)[10] asked the Messenger of God about Jerusalem, and he said: "Indeed, the abode is Jerusalem and a prayer there equals thousands of prayers elsewhere." In the Musnad[11] of Imam Ahmad bin Hanbal,[12] Maymouna asked: "O Messenger of God, explain Jerusalem to us." So he answered, "To pray in the Land of Assembly and Resurrection[13] is like praying a thousand times elsewhere." In the Prophet's hadith, too: "Do not undertake a journey [for worship] but to these three mosques: The Great Mosque of Mecca, this mosque of mine, and the al-Aqsa Mosque."

---

[4] See sūrat al-anbiyāʾ: 71.
[5] See sūrat al-anbiyāʾ: 81.
[6] See sūrat al-sabaʾ: 18.
[7] See sūrat al-māʾida: 21.
[8] Abd al-Rahman ibn Sakhr al-Dawsi (603–81), one of Prophet Muhammad's companions and the most prolific narrator of the hadith.
[9] Aisha bint Abi Bakr (613/14–78), Prophet Muhammad's third wife.
[10] Al-Shiqaqi refers to Makhul bin Maymuna as the "lady" or "mistress" (*mawlāt al-rasūl*) of the Prophet, and presumably refers to his last wife, Maymuna bint al-Harith.
[11] A Musnad is a collection of hadiths, which are traceable in an uninterrupted transcending order. See Oxford Islamic Studies, "Musnad," http://www.oxfordislamicstudies.com/article/opr/t125/e1654 [accessed: August 26, 2019].
[12] Ahmad ibn Hanbal (780–855), Muslim jurist and theologian, and founder of the Hanbali school of Islamic jurisprudence.
[13] Land of Assembly and Resurrection (*arḍ al-maḥshar wa-l-manshar*), a reference to the hadith in which Palestine is designated as the place where all people will be gathered and resurrected on the Day of Judgment.

- In the Musnad of Imam Ahmad bin Hanbal, the Messenger of God said: "A sect of my umma will remain dominant over their subjugating enemy in matters of religion. They will not be hurt by those who differ with them and they will not be afflicted until the command of God comes and they will be victorious." So they asked: "O Messenger of God, where will they be?" So he answered: "In Jerusalem and in Palestine."
- The good Lord, he said to Jerusalem: "You are my garden, my sanctity, and the best of my communities. Those who inhabit you have my blessing, and those who leave you will face my wrath."
- It was narrated in the Musnad of Imran ibn Husayn:[14] "She asked: 'O Messenger of God, what is the greatest city?' So he responded: 'How can you ask if you have seen Jerusalem?' So she asked: 'So it is greater?' And he said: 'How could it not be? All of that which belongs to it is visited, but it does not visit. All spirits are led there, but the spirit of Jerusalem is not led anywhere else.'"[15]

In our Islamic heritage, there are countless remarks mentioning Jerusalem, including the piece of writing by Imam Ali[16]—may God be pleased with him—"Yes, the one who remains steadfast in Jerusalem will be considered a mujahid in the path of God. For a time will come upon the people when one of them will say: O, how I wish I were a blade of straw between the bricks of Jerusalem."

The Islamic history appears for fourteen centuries (before Jerusalem handed over its keys to a new Islamic civilizational cycle, just as its keys were handed over to Umar ibn al-Khattab[17]—may God be pleased with him). Fourteen centuries of Islam's dominion in alternating and successive centers from Damascus to Baghdad, and from Cairo to Istanbul, before its leadership disappeared and the sun of the Caliphate faded. God restored the return of the Tribe of Israel due to the worship of Muslims with all of that which they had perpetrated of offense, sin, abandoning the path of God, and arbitration with man-made alternatives.

God sent us into the heart of the Arabian Peninsula at the beginning of our rise to confront the corruption and rise of the Israelites. So we probed their homes and achieved our victory, our state, and our civilization. We were handed the keys to Jerusalem, and we entered its mosque for the first time… God Almighty restored their return upon us after fourteen centuries, however, erupting from Jerusalem to

---

[14] Imran ibn Husayn (d. 673), one of the companions of Prophet Muhammad and narrator of the hadith.

[15] The latter part is presumably a reference to the Well of Spirits (*bi'r al-arwāḥ*), a cave located under the Dome of the Rock in Jerusalem. It was from the Well of Spirits that Prophet Muhammad ascended to heaven with Archangel Gabriel, and, according to an Islamic medieval legend, it is in this cave that the spirits of the dead await the Day of Judgment. The first part, "visit," is also presumably a reference to the Day of Judgment during which the Kaaba, according to one tradition, shall visit Jerusalem and then both will ascend to Heaven with their inhabitants. See Ofer Livne-Kafri, "Jerusalem in Early Islam: The Eschatological Aspect," *Arabica* 53 (2006): 382–403.

[16] Ali ibn Abi Talib (601–61), fourth Caliph, whose reign lasted from 656 until 661. Although Ali is revered by both Shiites and Sunnis, only Shiites consider Ali as the first Imam after Prophet Muhammad.

[17] Umar ibn Khattab (581–644), companion of Prophet Muhammad and the second caliph following Caliph Abu Bakr.

temporarily bestow superiority and corruption upon them until we wake up from our sleep and return to the approach leading to that which is most suitable and gives good tidings to the believers.[18] After we have crushed the weak man-made alternatives, and we irrevocably dispose of them, God will grant us a solid victory by defeating them, saddening their faces, and entering the al-Aqsa Mosque as we entered it the first time:

> And We conveyed to the Children of Israel in the Scripture that "You will surely cause corruption on the earth twice, and you will surely reach [a degree of] great haughtiness." So when the [time of] promise came for the first of them, We sent against you servants of Ours—those of great military might, and they probed [even] into the homes, and it was a promise fulfilled. Then We gave back to you a return victory over them. And We reinforced you with wealth and sons and made you more numerous in manpower [And said], "If you do good, you do good for yourselves; and if you do evil, [you do it] to yourselves." Then when the final promise came, [We sent your enemies] to sadden your faces and to enter the temple in Jerusalem, as they entered it the first time, and to destroy what they had taken over with [total] destruction.[19]

Our commentators differ greatly in their exegesis of these verses. Some of them state that God set Goliath and his soldiers against the Tribe of Israel. Then there are others who state that He set Nebuchadnezzar, the Amalekites,[20] Sennacherib,[21] the people of Persia, or the Romans on them. Some say that it was the Arabs. Ibn al-Jawzi[22] states in *The Virtues of Jerusalem*: "In the end, God sent Muhammad, thus leaving them with jizya as punishment."[23] Al-Tabari states in his commentary: "In the end, God sent them this tribe of Arabs, who punished them until the Day of Judgement. So they paid jizya and were subdued."

It appears for many of the commentators that the Jews were first corrupted by their killing of their prophets (Isaiah),[24] that Nebuchadnezzar II[25] was the one who put an end to their first rise and corruption, and that they countered their second rise and corruption. A closer look at the verses and the reality of the Jews' history before and after Islam, and at the history of the conflict between them and the Muslims, confirms

---

[18] A reference to sūrat al-isrā': 9. "Indeed, this Qur'an guides to that which is most suitable and gives good tidings to the believers who do righteous deeds that they will have a great reward."
[19] See sūrat al-isrā': 4–7.
[20] The Amalek are referred to as the enemies of the Israelites in the Hebrew Bible and were allegedly a tribe residing in present-day southern Palestine and in the Sinai Peninsula.
[21] Sennacherib (740–681BC), king of Assyria from 705–681BC.
[22] Ibn al-Jawzi (510–97), Islamic jurisconsult who played a significant role in the spread of Hanbalism in Baghdad in present-day Iraq.
[23] *Jizya*, yearly per capita tax paid by non-Muslims in the Caliphate in return for the protection of the state.
[24] Although the Qur'an does not refer to the killing of any particular prophet, it reports that the Israelites killed the prophets sent to them, which allegedly explains the corruption and abasement of the Jews. For an analysis, see Gabriel Said Reynolds, "On the Qur'an and the Theme of Jews as 'Killers of the Prophets,'" *al-Bayān* 10, no. 2 (2012): 9–32.
[25] Nebuchadnezzar II (605–562BC), King of Babylon and he is referred to in the Bible as the destroyer of Solomon's temple.

the weakness of the previous accounts, as none of them referred to the Prophet. We may find a great excuse for those distinguished scholars and commentators as they lived in the shadow of a great Islamic state in which the Jews were no more than weakened and dispersed dhimmis.[26] Indeed, it would not have occurred to the commentators that the Jews would weaken Islam's authority and erase the caliphate from the land in which a time would come for the Tribe of Israel (and, indeed, they were very few) to rise, to corrupt, and to reign over the Muslims.

Yet, we find great wisdom in the old commentators' lack of awareness of the precise meaning and significance behind the verses. We do so because realizing the second rise and corruption before it occurred (as if the distinguished commentators paid attention to it) meant that the Muslims would stand in front of the attack on Palestine and the Islamic homeland by the West and the Jews as if they were standing before a divine destiny. They would have no strength, and they would have no power when confronting the attack—and there would be nothing for them but surrender and capitulation until the cycle of the Jews had expired!! This was sufficient to eliminate the spirit of jihad and the required Islamic resistance to continue the repulsion and the conflict between the Muslims and the Jews… Even if the Jews won, the Islamic impulse and the spirit of resistance would continue like embers under the ashes until the umma realized and understood the true meaning of the verses, giving it this new force and higher trust in its Lord, its religion, and itself—advancing to achieve the divine promise desired.

Sheikh Sa'id Hawwa[27] states in his book, *Soldier of God*: "We can now understand these verses differently than how the old commentators did. The commentators did not face our contemporary reality with the rise of the Tribe of Israel on the land, their corruption, and their annexation of Jerusalem. So they interpreted the verses as having already occurred." Yet, before talking about what we conclude from the beginning of surat al-isra', we point to the opinion piece of the magazine *al-Azhar*, quoting the book of Abd al-Hamid Kishk,[28] *Excerpts from Islamic Studies*:

> It is established that the Night Journey happened for the Messenger of God when he was in Mecca before the emigration. Surat al-isra' was revealed in Mecca as well, so it is a Meccan verse… The Muslims in Mecca were at that time few and oppressed on the land, who feared being swept away by the people there. The Tribe of Israel had no concerns about the Muslims at that time as they had no influence in Mecca. So there was no importance when it was necessary for God to speak of them in such detail in a Meccan verse. What is the secret God informed His messenger of in one verse about his Night Journey—the first verse—after which He ceased talking about it from one sentence to another and instead began talking

---

[26] Dhimmi ("protected person"), term referring to non-Muslims living under legal protection in the Caliphate. In principle, through loyalty to the state and payment of *jizya*, the dhimmi had his life, property, and freedom of religion protected.
[27] Sa'id Hawwa (1935–88), a leading member and cadre of the Syrian Muslim Brotherhood.
[28] Abd al-Hamid Kishk (1933–96), Egyptian preacher and Islamic scholar famous for his use of humor in his sermons. A dissident under the Nasserist state, and boycotted by Egyptian media under the reign of Anwar Sadat, his cassette tapes were nonetheless widely disseminated in the Egyptian public.

about the Tribe of Israel, what He had bestowed upon them and covenanted with them, and of the significant role it would have?? What is the principle of correlation between these verses and the actual events?? The secret is that God Almighty speaks of the Night Journey as a divine decree as He brings glad tidings to his Prophet and the oppressed Muslims, the wretched of the Earth, that their power will rise and spread imminently until the capital of the people of the book and that of polytheism yield to them. As the Almighty states: "Exalted is He who took His Servant by night from the Great Mosque of Mecca to the al-Aqsa Mosque."[29] He did not say from Mecca to Jerusalem as it is, as the Kaaba[30] was not a mosque at that time, but, rather, a house surrounded by idols and with returnees [to disbelief] and polytheists walking around it. Moreover, the Temple of David and Solomon in the "Jewish state" or "Israel" was not yet a mosque. Rather, it was only a house around which the Tribe of Israel engaged in usurious interests and caused corruption. However, God Almighty spoke about this Night Journey as a transition from mosque to mosque, bringing glad tidings to the Muslims that their power will rise so that the country where they were treated arrogantly and were humiliated, and where their sanctities were, would become a holy mosque and an abode of peace and safety.

The editorial of *al-Azhar* then continues by citing Sheikh Kishk to affirm the interpretation of the verse: "So when the [time of] promise came for the first of them, We sent against you servants of Ours,"[31] writing: "It does not remain fully applicable this time, except for the role they played in the era of the Prophet and his companions, and that which God imposed on them." Then it states: "Indeed, this is the first time their description only applies to the followers of God's messenger."

1. They deserve the honor of this attribution, "our servants," for they are Muslims following "His servant," who was taken to heaven by God. As for the followers of Nebuchadnezzar II, Shapur,[32] or Sennacherib, and so on, there were disagreements among the commentators for they were idol worshippers unworthy of God's honor in his saying "ours."
2. They are the ones whom God describes in his Book as "stern against the infidels, and merciful among themselves."
3. For they are the ones who were not assigned to punish the Jews but for the "searching through the homes." As for the followers of Nebuchadnezzar II, they stated that he himself killed 70,000 people to avenge the blood of Zachariah,[33]

---

[29] See sūrat al-isrāʾ: 1.
[30] The Kaaba ("the cube," *al-kaʿba*), the most sacred site in Islam at the center of the Great Mosque of Mecca.
[31] See sūrat al-isrāʾ: 5.
[32] Shapur I (240–270), second king of the Sasanian Empire.
[33] Al-Shiqaqi is here referring to the killing of Zachariah ben Jehoida, a priest who was killed by Jehoash of Judah. As the captain of Nebuchadnezzar, Nebuzar-adan, came to destroy the Temple, he saw Zachariah's blood boil on the ground. Wishing to appease his blood, Nebuzar-adan commenced killing the priests and schoolchildren. See Jewish Encyclopedia, "Zechariah ben Jehoiada," http://www.jewishencyclopedia.com/articles/15201-zechariah-ben-jehoiada [accessed August 31, 2019].

and that he entered Jerusalem with his people and robbed its ornaments. So he "invaded" and did not "search." The editorial of *al-Azhar* continues along the same lines to confirm that the title of the article "surat al-isra' determines the end of Israel."

Now, with a Careful Look, We See What the Verses Refer To

1. The Tribe of Israel rises twice on earth accompanied by corruption. The rise under which some of their prophets lived certainly does not make them companions of corruption.
2. This rise and corruption will bring forth conflict, destruction, and ruin. While the Qur'an places the Tribe of Israel as a clear and certain party twice, it also affirms the existence of another party repeating itself twice, just like the Tribe of Israel.

    The Holy Qur'an referred to this party once by its name in the first verses ("servants of Ours"),[34] and then continues referring to it in the third person in another context assuring that it is the same party that faced the Tribe of Israel the first time. Thus, after "We sent against you servants of Ours," comes the verb "they probed," "Then We gave back to you a return victory over them," and "made you more numerous in manpower."[35] Indeed, there are many more of them: "to sadden…", "to enter…", "to destroy…". So the pronouns of all verbs (active or passive) refer to "servants of Ours," which in both cases start with the battle between two parties only… the same parties, the Muslims and the Jews.
3. It is clear that the other commentaries refer to the confrontation of the Tribe of Israel with more than one people. Once with Nebuchadnezzar, once with Sennacherib, once with the Romans, once with the Persians, and even one time with the Arabs. This contradicts, then, what the verses claimed about the confrontation between the two repeating parties. That is, if the first conflict was with the Persians, then the second (the final) conflict must also be with them.
4. God did not promise the return of the Jews against Nebuchadnezzar, Sennacherib, the Persians, or the Romans. God did not increase their numbers. Sheikh Sa'id Hawwa notes: "The verses allude that the Jews will become greater in number as the Jews were fewer than the Persians. Yet, now, they are able to call upon all nations on Earth." The editorial of *al-Azhar* reads: "The Jews were not greater in number and they had no more support than they have today. At no time in their history or in any other place did the Jews enjoy so much support and so many soldiers as they do now."
5. God brought back the Tribe of Israel against the Muslims (the Arabs) as has been evident since the downfall of Jerusalem, the establishment of their state, and the continuation of their rise and corruption.

---

[34] See sūrat al-isrā': 5.
[35] See sūrat al-isrā': 5–6.

6. The restoration of the Jews' victory does not last long—although it came after the first corruption was eliminated as in "then," the conjunction that signifies temporal inaction. It is as the "Then" signifies in "[then] when the final promise came," which is again signified by the "sequence and succession."[36] Or, when they reach the peak of their rise and corruption after the restoration of victory, it is also the declaration of ending this rise and corruption by the same servants, "servants of Ours," in the way prescribed by the Qur'an. By humiliating them and entering the mosque as these servants entered it the first time, and as happened during the reign of Umar ibn al-Khattab, the commander of the faithful—may God be pleased with him. This way of victory as prescribed by the Qur'an differs from the way of the first victory in which the servants of great military might probed through the homes.

    The "Then" that preceded "[then] we gave back," and the "Then" that preceded "[then] when the final promise came" thus refer to the tangible reality—that is, the great temporal distance between the end of their first rise and corruption in the Arabian Peninsula and their subsequent appearance and ascendancy, which is their second rise and corruption. They equally refer to the short time span in which their second rise and corruption continues until the final promise of ending them arrives.

7. The verb "sending" mentioned in the early verses carries meanings, implications, and signs that ought to be studied. The verb here implies satisfaction, and it is not God's satisfaction with the idolaters and polytheists, but with the believers. The words "we sent" appear seven times in the Holy Qur'an, with God always as the subject, and the prophets and the pious believers as the object i.e., those who were sent).
    - "and We sent from among them twelve leaders."[37]
    - "Then We sent after them Moses with Our signs to Pharaoh and his establishment."[38]
    - "Then We sent after him messengers to their peoples, and they came to them with clear proofs."[39]
    - "Then We sent after them Moses and Aaron to Pharaoh and his establishment with Our signs."[40]
    - "So when the [time of] promise came for the first of them, We sent against you servants of Ours."[41]
    - "And if We had willed, We could have sent into every city a warner."[42]

---

[36] Sequence (*tartīb*) and succession (*taʿqīb*) refer to syntactic discussions in Islamic jurisprudence (*fiqh*) and pertain to how the Qur'anic verses are to be read and understood.
[37] See sūrat al-māʾida: 12.
[38] See sūrat al-aʿrāf: 103.
[39] See sūrat Yūnus: 74.
[40] See sūrat Yūsuf: 75.
[41] See sūrat al-isrāʾ: 5.
[42] See sūrat al-furqān: 51.

It is clear in all of the previous verses how the words "We sent" were mentioned in context of satisfying, praising, and extolling, which was not the case for Nebuchadnezzar, the Romans, or anyone else of the unbelievers. Thus, the verb "to send" is employed seven times in the Qur'an with the same meaning: satisfying and praising. "Mankind was [of] one religion [before their deviation]; then God sent the prophets as bringers of good tidings and warners."[43] And their prophet said to them, "Indeed, God has sent to you Saul as a king."[44] "Certainly did God confer [great] favor upon the believers when He sent among them a Messenger from themselves."[45] "Then God sent a crow searching in the ground to show him how to hide the disgrace of his brother."[46] "Has God sent a human messenger?"[47] "Is this the one whom God has sent as a messenger?"[48] "It is He who has sent among the unlettered a Messenger from themselves reciting to them His verses."[49]

8. The manner in which the Prophet—peace be upon him—and his esteemed companions dealt with the Tribe of Israel in Medina and in the Arabian Peninsula applies fully to the following words: "We sent against you servants of Ours—those of great military might, and they probed [even] into the homes."[50] It also applies to the attributes of the companions—may God be pleased with them—with their military might and manner of fighting in the homes of the Jews. It was the first clash with the Tribe of Qaynuqa'[51] who mocked the Prophet when he called them to Islam: "O Muhammad, you seem to think that we are your people. Do not deceive yourself to think you have found a people unbeknown to war. For, by God, if you fight us, you will see what kind of men we are." They were the corrupted, who attempted to disgracefully unveil the Muslim woman and abuse her, and they killed the Muslim man who came to her rescue. So the Messenger of God besieged them and he wanted to kill four hundred unarmed and three hundred armed, if Abdallah bin Abu Salul had not intervened.[52] Abu Salul attempted hard to avert them from this fate until the Prophet became infuriated. The Prophet then ordered them to be expelled from Medina, never to return. So they went to Daraa in the Levant, and most of them perished there, and this was in the second year of the migration. In

---

[43] See sūrat al-baqara: 213.
[44] See sūrat al-baqara: 247.
[45] See sūrat āl ʿimrān: 164.
[46] See sūrat al-māʾida: 31.
[47] See sūrat al-isrāʾ: 94.
[48] See sūrat al-furqān: 41.
[49] See sūrat al-jumʿa: 2.
[50] See sūrat al-isrāʾ: 5.
[51] The Tribe of Qaynuqaʿ was one of the three great Jewish tribes in Medina in present-day Saudi Arabia. Breaking the Constitution of Medina, they were expelled by Prophet Muhammad and his companions and subsequently settled in Daraa in present-day Syria.
[52] Abdallah bin Ubayy (d. 631), also known as ibn Salul, was chief of the Tribe of Khazraj. Ibn Salul converted to Islam with the arrival of Prophet Muhammad in Medina. He is referred to as a "hypocrite" (munāfiq), however, due to his many conflicts with the Prophet. In modern usage, ibn Salul is employed as a pejorative designation. The Islamic State (IS), for example, referred to the Saudi royal family as the Al Salul (the House of Salul). See Cole Bunzel, "The Kingdom and the Caliphate: Duel of the Islamic States" (Massachusetts: Carnegie Endowment for International Peace, 2016), 4.

the fourth year of the migration, the Tribe of Nadir[53] betrayed the Messenger of God, flinging a stone to kill him. So he fought against them, and they fortified their fortresses with arrows and stones until the Muslims believed they could not expel them. God cast terror into their hearts, however, so the Muslims entered and drove them out of their homes. They then cut down their palm trees and destroyed their fortresses: "Whatever you have cut down of [their] palm trees or left standing on their trunks—it was by permission of God and so He would disgrace the defiantly disobedient."[54]

The Jews called upon the parties and they returned with three thousand men. Yet, God drove them back depraved and the Messenger of God returned to Medina. Archangel Gabriel came to him, commanding the Prophet to return to the Tribe of Qurayza[55] who betrayed the pact and rallied the parties. So he went to them as they were fortified in their fortresses, and he besieged them for fifteen days until the siege wore them out and they yielded to the Prophet who drove them to the trenches of Medina where he killed all of their fighters and took their possessions. In the seventh year of the migration, the Prophet headed for Khaybar, which was a great city lying 100 miles north of Medina. So he probed into their homes and conquered their impenetrable fortresses one by one, except for two, which were besieged for twenty nights until those inside became certain of destruction.[56] So they submitted to his verdict of exile and withdrawal. Yet, they asked the Prophet—peace be upon him—to remain in Khaybar and cultivate it as they had a part that could be divided, so he agreed: "If we wanted to expel you, we would have done so." They remained there so, killing one of the Prophet's followers and assaulting Abdallah ibn Umar[57] during the reign of the commander of the faithful, Umar ibn al-Khattab—may God be pleased with him—so they were all expelled from the Arabian Peninsula.

9. The verses have since the beginning referred to the party confronting the Tribe of Israel as "servants of Ours." And "servants of Ours" do to not refer to the Persians' idolatrous armies or anyone else, but, rather, to the armies of faith. It is thus unlikely that God would link himself with the Assyrian pagan. In the beginning of surat al-isra', He wanted to honor Muhammad, so he linked him to Himself: "Exalted is He who took His servant."[58] Sheikh Sa'id Hawwa says: "The verses referred to the servants of God and a mosque. So the first thing for us to understand by that is the particular worship connected to the mosque, and this was not something referring to the idolatrous Persians who ruled over the Jews more than once."

---

[53] Tribe of Nadir, Jewish tribe living by the oasis of Medina. Challenging Prophet Muhammad as leader, they were expelled from Medina, and later participated in the Battle of Khaybar.
[54] See sūrat al-ḥashr: 5.
[55] The Tribe of Qurayza was a Jewish tribe by the Oasis of Yathrib, present-day Medina. After allegedly breaching their pact with Prophet Muhammad, the tribe surrendered, and its men were beheaded after the forces of the Prophet besieged them.
[56] A reference to the Battle of Khaybar in 628 between Prophet Muhammad and his followers, and the Jews of the oasis Khaybar in the north-westerrn Arabian Peninsula.
[57] Abdallah ibn Umar (610–93), son of Caliph Umar and brother-in-law of Prophet Muhammad.
[58] See sūrat al-isrā': 1.

The words "of Ours" referred to in the Qur'an meant the believers or the Arabs. If attributed to God, then it in most cases meant the believers. So if the attribution came in the context of God Almighty speaking about himself ("servants of Ours… that is, My servants") then it meant the believers. The word "servants" appeared in the heart of surat al-isra' as an attribution to God by virtue of the "of [Ours]" in "servants of Ours," thus strongly suggesting this link and particularity. This is a clear reference to the faith and goodness of those servants.

10. When God restores victory for the Tribe of Israel over His servants, He supplies them with wealth and sons. Every observer sees that He does so without this assistance of wealth for us. The Zionist entity does not thus rely on itself economically despite its relative scientific and technological progress, and it would be incapable of remaining steadfast and staying on its feet without its billion dollars' support every year. If the foreign aid—the supply—is necessary for the continuation and survival of the Jewish state, then the supply of sons is also very important. The foundation of the Zionist project was from the end of the nineteenth century via the establishment of their state until now to bring Jewish immigrants (sons) to Palestine. Thus, they prepared institutions and funds, supported strong governments, and entered conflicts to secure this supply coming to them from everywhere. Even if the Arabs and Muslims had their wealth and people like the Jews have, then God still favored the Jews above the Muslims—this time—with greater numbers, and everyone sees and knows how many they are… For they are more capable of mobilizing arms, employing power, and calling upon the world of the powerful to stand beside them against the Muslims. Their voice is stronger than that of the Muslims, their propaganda is more effective, and the international press and media are in their hands… When they ask for weapons, they find them of every kind and in all numbers.

11. Surat al-isra' has another name, which is "the Tribe of Israel," for it does not talk about the Night Journey except in one verse after which it continues to elaborate on the Tribe of Israel. So it talks about their rise and corruption in the beginning (from the third to the seventh verse). Before its end (in verse 104), God addresses the Tribe of Israel: "and when there comes the promise of the Hereafter, We will bring you forth in [one] gathering."[59] This is a fact worthy of reflection. The Jews, who have been far from Palestine for thousands of years, are now returning after these long centuries, and they come as a mixed crowd—in groups—from all countries on Earth in order to fulfill the final promise and that which has been decreed.

12. Observing the verbs in the verses that talk about the conflict between the Muslims and the Tribe of Israel, one notices the declaration of fulfilling the first promise in the past tense: "We sent against you servants of Ours." Yet, the Qur'an talks about fulfilling the victory of the Muslims the second time in the present tense: "Then when the final promise came, [We sent your enemies] to sadden your faces and to enter the temple in Jerusalem, as they entered it the first

---

[59] See sūrat al-isrā': 104.

time, and to destroy what they had taken over with [total] destruction."⁶⁰ This is a graceful Qur'anic implication that can be added to the rest of the evidence indicating the fulfillment of the victory of God's worshippers over the Tribe of Israel—the second time—in the near future, which is a direct extension of the present.

13. For those who think that the Jews in the Arabian Peninsula did not reach a level of strength in the era of the Prophet, leading to their rise and corruption, we only need to remind them of the beginning of surat al-hashr: "Whatever is in the heavens and whatever is on the earth exalts God, and He is the Exalted in Might, the Wise. It is He who expelled the ones who disbelieved among the People of the Scripture from their homes at the first gathering. You did not think they would leave, and they thought that their fortresses would protect them from God ; but [the decree of] God came upon them from where they had not expected, and He cast terror into their hearts [so] they destroyed their houses by their [own] hands and the hands of the believers. So take warning, O people of vision."⁶¹

    The Muslims thus believed, including the Messenger of God, that the Jews in the Tribe of Nadir had such a strength that they could not expel them… The Jews themselves thought that no one was capable of expelling them because of the impregnability of their forts, their confidence, and their arrogance. It was in the end God's will to throw fear into their hearts in preparation for striking them and defeating them.

    The history of the Jews in the Arabian Peninsula confirms that they lived in Yathrib (Medina), and their great economic, political, cultural, religious, and military power was the greatest in the peninsula. It confirms that they grew at the expense of the Arabs, that they fostered conflicts with the al-Aws⁶² and Khazraj,⁶³ and that they controlled the markets in the region while the Arabs remained consumers and wage earners for them, for they had gold, silver, vineyards, orchards, and farms, just as they looked down upon the Arabs as they were people of the Book⁶⁴ and the people of knowledge and culture. All of this turned them into an arrogant tool for corruption, so they rejected the message of Muhammad—peace be upon him—despite their certainty of it, and they attempted to assassinate him. They were a source of support and assistance for the polytheists of Quraysh in their war against Islam, just like the Tribe of Nadir that attempted to kill him and then repeated the attempt on the day of Khaybar, while the Tribe of Qurayza violated its pact with the Prophet.

14. The Holy Qur'an referred so clearly to a great epic in Jerusalem leading to the victory of God's servants, the Muslims, and the disappearance of the Tribe of Israel's polytheism, might, and corruption. The prophetic sunna, complemented

---

⁶⁰ See sūrat al-isrā': 7.
⁶¹ See sūrat al-ḥashr: 1–2.
⁶² The Tribe of Aws, one of the main tribes in Medina; its members were known as followers of Prophet Muhammad. Al-Shiqaqi is most likely referring to the conflict that prevailed between al-Aws and the Tribe of Khazraj in 617 when he states that the Tribe of Israel fostered conflict between them.
⁶³ The Tribe of Khazraj, one of the main tribes of Medina.
⁶⁴ People of the Book (*ahl al-kitāb*) is a reference to Jews, Christians, and Sabians.

and commented, affirms this signification… For it speaks about the persistence of conflict, about the presence of a group of the rightful mujahidin in Palestine, and about Palestine. So al-Bukhari,[65] Muslim,[66] and others narrate that the Messenger of God said: "A sect of my umma will remain triumphant upon truth over their subjugating enemy. They will not be opposed or harmed by those who differ with them and they will not be afflicted by misfortune until the command of God comes and they will be victorious." So they asked him: "Where will they be?" So he answered: "In Jerusalem and in Palestine."

It subsequently talks about the Muslims' confrontation with the Jews, and it says: "The Day of Judgment will not come about before the Muslims fight the Jews. So the Muslims kill them until the Jew hides behind the tree and the rock, so the tree and the rock say: 'O Muslim, O servant of God, this Jew is behind me, so come and slay him.'" In another narration: "You will fight the Jews while you are east of the river and they are to its West," and it was said to be the River Jordan. In other narrations, the Messenger of God—peace be upon him—speaks of black banners emanating in Khurasan, and which will not be stopped by anything until they are planted in Jerusalem."

Consequently, all of this confirms the Qur'anic dimension of the Palestinian cause, the particularity of this land—Palestine—and the particularity of this cause beyond any doubt, and therefore their centrality in the thought and practice of the Islamic movement.

The Muslims departed from the heart of the Arabian Peninsula toward the basin of civilizations. They managed to establish a magnificent and vast state in record time, and to establish the greatest and most influential of civilizations in the history of humankind. This civilization persisted for more than thirteen centuries with alternating and successive centers. From Medina to Damascus, and from Baghdad via Cairo to Istanbul, it represented the Qur'anic spirit arising from the encounter between the Heavens and Earth that started from Hira,[67] and arising from the monotheistic approach. It represented the driving force of the Muslims' movement, their triumphs, and their marvelous achievements throughout several centuries. Islam was from early on subjected to great strife after its appearance, which was sufficient to destroy the most powerful nations. Yet, the tremendous and inherent energy of Islam's monotheistic approach gave the Islamic civilization, beyond the long life, a force and greatness. It thus exceeded the strife under which the greatest mountains, nations, and civilizations are overwhelmed.

The remarkable influence of the Qur'anic spirit and impetus has continued for many centuries, despite the negative influence of consecutive strife and conflicts against that

---

[65] Muhammad al-Bukhari (810–70), a Persian Islamic scholar and the author of the hadith collection ṣaḥīḥ al-bukhārī, regarded by Sunni Muslims as one of the most trusted ones.
[66] Muslim ibn al-Hajjaj (815–75), an Islamic scholar and hadith collector. His collection ṣaḥīḥ Muslim is one of the six great hadith collections.
[67] The Cave of Hira resides in Jabal al-Nur ("the Mountain of Light") near Mecca. The Cave of Hira has a great significance for Muslims at is believed it was there that Prophet Muhammad received his first revelation from God.

very spirit and impetus. Necessarily, it left a negative impact over time on the march of the Muslims and at times left them at risk, but only for a time. The crusader campaigns that the Islamic homeland was subjected to approximately eight centuries ago were the greatest threat the Muslims had ever faced. Yet, the Qur'anic impetus was still able to influence the Islamic body to a point in which the latter could finally absorb and respond to the attacks…

This did not last longer, however, as the process of regression continued within the structures of the Islamic homeland. Once the eighteenth century came, and with it the armies of the West, the encounter was even more difficult and tragic, for the West had accomplished important achievements after its industrial revolution while building its material, civilizational renaissance. So it had become sufficiently strong and vigorous. The Qur'anic impulse, on the other hand, faded away in the Islamic body and left it weakened and vulnerable to harm. Thus came the French campaign in the eighteenth century, which was immeasurably smaller than those crusader wars… Yet, it left tremendous impacts on the exhausted body with consequences with which we are still living.

Although the French campaign left a few years later, the structures of the weak umma were nevertheless disrupted by Westernization, which at the onset commenced innocently and inconspicuously as was the case with Rifa'at al-Tahtawi…[68] He was the sheikh and teacher who travelled with the educational delegation dispatched to Paris by Muhammad Ali, to lead them in prayer and serve as guidance. The sheikh thus returned, left breathlessly by the progress of France, the development of its laws, and its constitution… The social relations, the order in the streets, and the cars driving on them left him equally breathless. However, the Westernization current became increasingly visible over time as with the Turkish intellectuals in the Young Turks, subsequently known as the Party of Union and Progress. The same applies to the Arab intellectuals in the secret Arab societies in the Ottoman Empire, such as the Beirut Reform Society, the al-Qahtaniya Society,[69] the Young Arab Society, and the Covenant Society, as well as the officialdom of Naser al-Din Shah[70] in Iran and the rest of the Qajari dynasty.[71]

The West (the modern Western challenge) was moving toward the Islamic homeland in the nineteenth century with all of its long-standing crusader hatred in addition to the weight of economic and political factors… For it sought raw materials as well, and it wanted to sell its products and goods, always desiring areas of influence. The West collided with the Islamic wall, however, thus pushing it in the attempt to destroy it—beginning by expanding the base of the Westernization current among the people and intellectuals of our umma, by establishing missionary schools through embassies

---

[68] Rifa'at al-Tahtawi (1801–73), Islamic scholar and lecturer at al-Azhar before becoming a preacher in one of the new government infantry divisions in 1824. In 1826, al-Tahtawi travelled to Paris in the first major educational mission to Europe sent by Muhammad Ali. See Eugene Rogan, *The Arabs: A History* (London and New York: Penguin Books, 2011), Chapter 4.

[69] The Qahtaniya Society, a secret society established in 1909 in order to turn the Ottoman Empire into a dual monarchy. The Arab provinces were to be a single kingdom with its own parliament and government, with the kingdom being part of a Turco-Arab empire.

[70] Naser al-Din Shah (1831–96), King of Persia from 1848 until 1896.

[71] The Qajari dynasty, of the Qajar tribe, the Iranian royal dynasty from 1789 until 1925.

and consulates, and through the translation of Western literature, philosophy, and arts (instead of applied sciences and study expeditions).

This colonial project had in the end nothing in front of itself but the use of violence in order to bring down the great Islamic wall, and violence was the West's main feature in all stages of its conflict with Islam. What is important is that the West was not alone this time, as it had concluded an alliance with the Zionist government, which at the end of the nineteenth century represented the political framework of the false Jewish religious thesis of a homeland for God's chosen people: Jews in God's holy land (Palestine). Everyone made an alliance to overthrow the Ottoman Empire: the Jews and the West, on the one hand, and the Westernization current, on the other. They thus tilted the power balance and altered the political and intellectual map of the region. The regional scenery accordingly revealed Mustafa Kemal Atatürk[72] in Turkey, Reza Shah[73] in Iran, the sons of al-Sharif Hussein in the Levant, and the school of the Wafd Party[74] in Egypt.

These were difficult years, those covering the first quarter of the twentieth century, while the colonial project took shape more clearly. The Jewish project was the central component of this project and of every Western attack. Consequently, those who overthrew the Caliphal state in service of the West were those who ruled the region on the basis of Sykes-Picot. They were themselves the ones who established the Jewish state on their shoulders and in front of their eyes. They were constantly attempting to destroy the religion of the umma, the true and complete antithesis of the Western attack. The project of establishing Israel was thus implemented, not just as the Western attack's main objective, but also as a comprehensive incarnation of its tyranny and continuing presence in the region.

So came Israel, because the decision makers in the colonial project realized that the Westernized Arab elites were too weak to ensure their interests and to continue the battle against the heart and creed of the Islamic umma and against the fourteen centuries of the glorious Islamic history. They inserted this alien entity into the heart of the Islamic homeland in order to ensure the state of Western hegemony and to establish subordination and dependency. So when the Muslim masses were surprised by the trap set up in Palestine, they understood the conspiracy, as the dimensions of the nakba were revealed. However, colonialism was quicker to realize the new problem of the masses, so it rushed to alter the regimes and to steal the umma's slogans, dreams of change, and renaissance.

A new pattern thus appeared on the scene with the coup d'états of the Syrian and Iraqi militaries, Cemal Gürsel[75] in Turkey, Ahmed Sukarno[76] in Indonesia, and Ayub

---

[72] Mustafa Kemal Atatürk (1881–1938), the founder of the Republic of Turkey and the leading proponent of modernizing and liberalizing reforms based on secular and nationalist policies.
[73] Reza Shah Pahlavi (1878–1944), Shah of Iran from 1925 until 1941 who aimed to modernize Iran by implementing infrastructural and agricultural reforms.
[74] The Wafd Party, Egyptian nationalist and liberal party, whose role in the 1923 constitution was decisive. The party was dissolved following the revolution of 1952.
[75] Cemal Gürsel (1895–1966), fourth president of Turkey following the 1960 Turkish coup d'état.
[76] Sukarno (1901–70), the first president of Indonesia from 1945 until 1967. Al-Shiqaqi is presumably referring to Sukarno's disbanding of the Islamic party Masyumi and the imprisonment of Islamic politicians such as Mohammad Natsir and Hamka in 1960.

Khan[77] in Pakistan. All of them were links in one approach, and the goal became the final liquidation of Islam in order to implement the objectives and tasks of the West by the hands of the Islamic homeland's sons themselves. The nakba of 1967 thus took place, when Jerusalem fell with even more of the geography and the history. More land of faith was subjected to the menace because of the imbalance of the Arab person, brought forth by the epidemical Western ideas, placing the Islamic historical belonging and the Islamic creedal awareness in unending controversy, which could bear no other fruit but sterility. In short, the colonial project spanning across two centuries, which tried its best to sever the historical and civilizational continuity of the Islamic umma, succeeded in establishing Israel after a century and a half of its presence in the region—the most important, effective, and significant tool in severing the historical and civilizational continuity of the umma… The historical analysis thus confirms that which has already been confirmed by the Qur'anic analysis of the danger of the Jewish project in Palestine.

The historical analysis considers the Jewish project as the central component of the Western attack and of the Western modern challenge, and as the most important difficulties of the Islamic homeland. This is a reaffirmation of the uniqueness, particularity, and centrality of the Palestinian cause… a reaffirmation making it difficult for the contemporary Islamic movement to achieve its objectives in the confrontation with the effects and consequences of the Western attack in our countries, causing fragmentation, Westernization, dependency, and annexation, without confronting the heart of this attack and without confronting its continued domination in Palestine.

Before we proceed to the de facto dimension, however, we must point out that while we speak of Israel as a part of the colonial project, we have no illusion that "Israel is nothing more than a political tool in the hands of the West," for the Zionist movement is not a tool in the narrow sense, but it is also a true ally. There are shared objectives for the two parties (the Zionists and the West) making Israel appear as if it is a tool for the West. It is the advanced tool of the alliance of the West and the Zionist movement as Israel remains the most important and visible component of the Zionist and Jewish movement's extended body in the world in general and the Western world in particular.

The fact that Israel is the central component of the continuing Western attack against the Islamic homeland means that Israel must play a central role in the work to achieve the objectives of this very attack. It includes isolating Islam far from life and governance, continuing to destroy it at all levels, and constantly moving toward preserving the Westernized, dominant, and powerful symbolic figures in the Islamic homeland, including the preservation of all the West's interests in the region. It is from this perspective that we must understand Israel's extraordinary role and the comprehensive dimensions of the Israeli threat. The most prominent manifestations of this danger are as follows:

---

[77] Ayub Khan (1907–74), second president of Pakistan after the first coup d'état in Pakistan's history. Once in power, Khan reformed the constitution in which Islam was respected, yet not declared as a religion of state.

1. Israel realistically embodies the peak of the man-made, conflicting approach against Islam… the religion of peace, Truth, and dignity, which respects man and gives him a distinctive value emanating from God. Israel embodies a persisting escalation of the conflict and of falsehood in terms of being the state of the false Jewish dream, as the homeland of God's chosen people, and the fact that these chosen people are distinguished and separate from the rest of mankind. This aspect followed the Jews over the centuries, and it was the cause of their rise and corruption, as well as their isolation and the destruction of their homes. They were the ones who said: "There is no blame upon us concerning the unlearned."[78] They were the ones who created the usury systems, the foundation of capitalism, exploitation, and monopoly.
2. Israel represents a direct and daily threat to the Palestinian people, whose land it usurped. It drives away an important part of the Palestinian people—generation after generation, and from exile to exile. Those who remained within the framework of occupation are suffering daily from the persisting oppression of the security forces, soldiers, settlers, and the employer. They suffer at all levels of authority, which determine the amount of water the Palestinian citizen can drink and use for irrigating his crops (if there are any, and if they are not yet confiscated). They determine the amount of electricity that will pass through the Palestinian's village or home—thus affecting him at the level of breakfast, lunch, and dinner, and sometimes at the level of the education he could possibly get!! As for the attempts by the occupation authority at moral, intellectual, security, and political destruction, it does not stop there. In short, the Palestinian citizen is besieged by the direct and daily Zionist threat, which holds his freedom against him and by force prevents him from having a dignified life.
3. The borders of Israel's influence extend beyond the Palestinian Muslim to all Muslims and Arabs around Palestine—from the anti-Islamic and brutal bombings of defenseless villages to the invasion and occupation of Beirut in 1982 with the continuing occupation of southern Lebanon. Regarding Jordan, the specter of Israel influences it militarily, politically, and economically like no other existing factor. Indeed, the Jordanian king lost half his kingdom and conspicuously gave it to Israel in 1967. The Jordanians then suffered at the hands of Israel directly for three consecutive years, as they had earlier, and are still suffering.

   In Egypt, Israel entered every home… Once through war, and at another time through the desecrated peace. The Egyptian people suffered in all villages and hamlets—in Abu Zaabal and in Bahr al-Baqar,[79] as tens of thousands of Egyptian soldiers suffered from the harshest exhaustion, fatigue, and degradation in the desert of hunger and thirst… In Sinai… They must today smile in the presence of

---

[78] See sūrat āl ʿimrān: 75.
[79] Al-Shiqaqi is presumably referring to the Abu Zaabal bombing and the Bahr al-Baqar primary school bombing. On February 13, 1970, the Israeli Air Forces dropped napalm on an industrial plant by the settlement, killing eighty civilian Egyptian workers. The second occurred on April 8, 1970, when the Israeli Air Force bombed the Bahr al-Baqar primary school, killing forty-six children.

their killers and receive them with a welcome—a forced one—and rely on them and follow them.

4. Israel constitutes a real danger to all the people of the Islamic umma—from Tangiers to Jakarta, from Istanbul to Lagos, and from the far East to the far West. This is because of the Jews' awareness of Islam as the essential and complete antithesis to them, leading them to pursue Muslims everywhere. One of the State of Israel's ministers said: "If it was my decision, I would have ridden my tank from Jerusalem, and I would not stop before reaching Karachi." The Israeli part in pursuing Muslims does not stop at its borders, but goes from Eritrea to the Philippines, to Thailand, to India, to Southern Sudan, and to all of Africa.

5. This danger extends until it reaches all the oppressed in the world, so Israel's close relationship with the forces of international arrogance and its assistance to the racist governments and dictatorial regimes in Africa and elsewhere affirms the danger it constitutes against the future of the oppressed in the world as well as Muslims.

6. Israel constitutes an integral component of the Western attack and the nucleus of the great Jewish dream in consecrating the reality of fragmentation taking place in the Islamic homeland and ensuring it, by pushing toward further fragmentation at the Arab regional, national, and doctrinal levels. The leadership and researchers in Israel speak of the doctrinal differences in the Middle East, and they try to increase it (like the Baháʾí),[80] for example by stressing racial differences (like the Kurdish issue). They simultaneously resist attempts at unity. We can thus talk about an integral Israeli theory employing a mosaic as a transition through which the region passes in preparation for Jewish domination on sectarian grounds, such as the establishment of a Maronite state and another for the Kurds, a Christian state, and a Druze one… It will transform the region into dozens of small, conflicting states.

7. As the cornerstone of the Western attack, Israel also represents a tool for the continuation of this Western onslaught and for achieving its desired results. The most important means of the Western attack comes from destroying the ideological dimension of the Muslim man.

    The Israeli culture that Israel attempts to infuse into the people of the Islamic umma, inside of Palestine, is regarded the most important instrument for the Westernization and destruction of Islamic belonging: unrestricted sex and sexual freedom, the overthrow of values associated with religion, the destruction of the family and the intensification of generational conflict, and the promotion of the consumer society among Muslims, and so on. Together, they all comprise several steps toward the destruction of the Islamic self and producing the Westernized self, which carries all the dimensions of colonialism within itself.

8. On the economic level, Israel persists as a guardian of the interests of colonialism and the global arrogance led by the United States of America. It employs its military instrument and its political threats to continue the economic plundering of the Islamic homeland's wealth and raw materials, such as oil and agricultural products.

---

[80] The Baháʾí, a religious faith that emanated in Persia in 1863.

Reality thus confirms the danger of Israel on all levels, which employs all the means and events possible in order to destroy the umma and liquidate it... It is a cancerous danger that grows and expands at the expense of the Muslims everywhere as it departs from Palestine. Reality consequently confirms the particularity of the Zionist menace, whose threat and centrality are unparalleled in the reality of the Muslims. It pushes them to the wall with endless cruelty, but it also pushes them to the necessity of being alert to this particularity. Focusing on the particularity of the Palestinian cause is not merely to focus on the cultural dimension for them… for it is the particularity of a conflict that targets all forms of our existence.

Palestine Is on a Collision Course with the Western Colonial Project

August 1989, interview with Fathi al-Shiqaqi published in the newspaper al-Khalij, pages unknown.

Al-Shiqaqi never devoted much time to the Qur'anic dimension of the Palestinian cause and was always more interested in history than religious exegesis. Yet, the following interview with al-Shiqaqi is one of few publications in which he elaborates on its significance and meaning. The following text is thus a direct continuation of "The Centrality of Palestine and the Contemporary Islamic Project." Relying far less on the many Qur'anic references, this interview is a more straightforward explanation of the Palestinian cause's religious dimension. Here al-Shiqaqi connects the three dimensions by explaining how the Western colonial project is confirmed by the Qur'anic verses, and how history and religion meet on Palestinian lands to confirm the blessedness of Palestine.

Presumably, the Qur'anic dimension was a product of its time. As the founding fathers of PIJ struggled to convince the leaders of the Palestinian Muslim Brotherhood to commence armed struggle, the Qur'anic dimension was an iron gauntlet flung at their faces. Not only did the PIJ cadres' interpretation of religion suggest that it was a duty for all Palestinians to participate in the armed struggle, their future victory was also predestined by God.[1] This was of utmost importance because, as al-Shiqaqi suggests below, "[the alliance with the Western colonial project] is a distinct component of the Zionist colonial alliance targeting the wealth and future of the region. This alliance is a universal threat to Arabs and Muslims, so as long as Israel continues to exist, our dependence on the West will persist on all the intellectual, political, economic, and military levels."

The following piece matters for three reasons. First, as noted, this is a much-needed elaboration on the Qur'anic dimension given the few PIJ texts that exist on the topic. Second, the document matters because al-Shiqaqi also discusses the emergence of Hamas and how PIJ's understanding of the Palestinian cause sets it apart from the other Palestinian resistance movements. As al-Shiqaqi stresses, the conflict with the Palestinian Muslim Brotherhood was allegedly not just about armed struggle, but equally about allotting sufficient importance to the Palestinian cause. After all, the

---

[1] For an analysis of the ideology of Palestinian Islamic Jihad, see Skare, *A History of Palestinian Islamic Jihad: Faith, Awareness, and Revolution in the Middle East*.

Palestinian cause was not merely one of many causes, but the most important one. Last, the document matters because it implies some of the more pragmatic traits of PIJ. Al-Shiqaqi is, for example, asked about the cooperation between his movement and the other Palestinian factions, and he declares the willingness to cooperate with anyone sharing their goals. As we have seen throughout the years, the issue has always been armed struggle. PIJ has thus traditionally cooperated with a wide range of actors—from the Islamic (Hamas) to the Marxist (Popular Front for the Liberation of Palestine).

℃

You mentioned that the beginning was your distinct understanding of Islam and of the Qur'anic approach, which led you to realize the centrality of Palestine for Islam and the Islamic movement. So what is this distinctive understanding of the Qur'an and of Islam in general for the Palestinian cause?

In fact, we are all—as Muslims—reading the Qur'an. By having the correct method, however, we are able to understand the Qur'an, the Islamic sciences, reality, and the world within one complete structure, without which we would never have understood or realized this power. The method thus led us to discover Palestine in the heart of the Qur'an. Our understanding of history and of its dimensions helped us to discover a high degree of concurrence between history and the Absolute in the Qur'an. It was the encounter of history with the Absolute on the land of Palestine.

History affirms to us that we have been living in a violent conflict with the colonial project for two centuries, which laid the foundation of Westernization in the region, established Sykes-Picot, and partitioned the Arab and Islamic homeland. This project is implemented through the establishment of Israel in the heart of the Arab-Islamic homeland. It is right here that this historical reality encountered the absolute conclusion of the Qur'an, which makes Palestine a verse of the Book when it numerously refers to the sanctity of Palestine. There is no land blessed so numerously as Palestine. There are distinct verses on the nature of the conflict between the Tribe of Israel—as a corrupt and exploitative force—and Islam and the Islamic phenomenon.

The account of the conflict moved from the dawn of Islam to the present era, moving from Mecca and Medina in the seventh century to Jerusalem in the twenty-first[2] so that we witnessed the Islamic history extending between two axes: between Mecca and Medina, and Jerusalem; between Jara' and Camp David; between the Tribe of Qurayza and Likud; and between the Qur'anic sayings "we sent" and "we gave back to you a return victory." Between "they probed [even] into the homes" and "then We gave back to you a return victory over them,"[3] as if history extends from the Qur'an to the Qur'an, and, as we have pointed out, our understanding of history meets that of the Absolute in the Qur'an—the two encountered each other on the land of Palestine.

---

[2] Al-Shiqaqi dates the move from Mecca and Medina to Jerusalem as the first and the fourteenth Hijri centuries (the Islamic calendar), which corresponds to the seventh and twenty-first centuries in the Gregorian calendar.

[3] See sūrat al-isrā': 5 and 6 for all four sayings.

It was here that our distinct awareness was shaped; a distinct awareness of Palestine's particularity in the Qur'an, in our Arab and Islamic history, and in our struggle with the colonial phenomenon embodied in the vilest, that is, the Zionist, entity.

With this distinct understanding of Palestine in the Qur'an, have you obtained a distinct vision of the conflict's particularity now taking place in Palestine and of its future?

Through this understanding, we concluded that the essence of the conflict in the region is the conflict between the colonial project and the Islamic project, between the Western-Zionist alliance and the Arab and Islamic umma, and that this essence now lies, and is concentrated, in Palestine, where it constitutes a danger for the entire Arab and Islamic umma. Therefore, if we want to confront the colonial project, then we have to commence from here, from Palestine. We have to do so because Palestine is the vulnerable spot of the colonialist project, as Israel is the heart of this project.

In the event of persisting Israeli presence, true independence, freedom, and renaissance will never be achieved for the umma. These goals and slogans will remain devoid of any real content as long as Israel continues to exist in this region. In our view, all theses that have attempted to understand this conflict far from its Islamic prospects, on the one hand, and its comprehensive colonial dimensions, on the other, will remain incapable of continuing this conflict until the end. They will fall on the road due to the deficiency of their visions and realizations of the conflict's reality.

Because "Israel" is not only a US aircraft carrier, nor is it simply an economic representative of the West. Before all this, it is a distinct component of the Zionist colonial alliance targeting the wealth and future of the region. This alliance is a universal threat to Arabs and Muslims, so as long as Israel continues to exist, our dependence on the West will persist on all the intellectual, political, economic, and military levels. We will never be able to start our own project. The conflict is therefore without any doubt a decisive conflict, and it is a conflict of existence between the Zionist project and the Islamic project.

According to this understanding, we have affirmed that this dear, sacred, little homeland, "Palestine," cannot in any way have enough room for more than one people, the people of Palestine. There is no room for more than one sovereignty, namely a Palestinian sovereignty. There is no racist tendency against Jews in this because Jews lived under Islam without injustice and without discrimination. However, we believe that the political power in Palestine cannot be divided into two powers. The conflict must be resolved in favor of one people and one sovereignty.

What are the differences between your vision of this conflict as Palestinian Islamic Jihad and the vision of The Islamic Resistance Movement, Hamas, which began to practice a significant role on the political and struggling level in Palestine?

Before we talk about the differences between our vision of the conflict and that of Hamas, we must talk about the differences between the traditional Islamic movement and us. I mean the Muslim Brotherhood because Hamas appeared recently after the outbreak of the intifada, and it is an intellectual expression, and an extension, of the Muslim Brotherhood line.

For the traditional Islamic movement, the Palestinian issue was a sub-issue on par with any other problem experienced by the Islamic homeland. So they could not find any distinction between the Palestinian cause and any other cause, such as the cause of the Muslims in the Philippines, in Kashmir, or in Eritrea. They believed that the Palestinian problem would never be solved before the establishment of the Islamic state outside of Palestine. This Islamic state—if established—is that which will take the responsibility upon its shoulders, raise the banner of jihad, and move forward for the liberation of Palestine as an Islamic land just like the rest of the colonized or occupied Islamic lands.

This is the understanding with which we disagree because we consider that Palestine stands out in more than one way. It is distinct based on the historical understanding of the region's conflicts, and it is distinct based on its existence in the heart of the Qur'an. Palestine is therefore the most important cause that Muslims must experience. It cannot be compared to any other cause or problem the Islamic world is facing. It cannot be so because the danger of any other cause is confined to those who suffer from it directly, while the Palestinian cause is the meeting point, and its threat extends to every Palestinian, every Arab, every Muslim, and everyone who is oppressed. So this is the first point of difference.

The second point of difference is that we refuse to wait for the establishment of an Islamic state to commence the liberation of Palestine, and we consider this talk to be a kind of fallacy. We support the establishment of an Islamic state on all Islamic lands and everywhere, and we call for the establishment of an Islamic state raising the banner of Islam. However, it is not permissible to argue for the postponement of jihad for the liberation of Palestine without the establishment of that state.

We argue for the opposite. We argue that the more we move toward Palestine, and the more we exercise our jihad as Islamists in Palestine, the more the Islamic role in the region and in the world will be strengthened. We also believe that the more the Islamic movements distinguish the cause of Palestine, and the more they draw the people around this cause, the more these movements will be strengthened in their countries, and the more legitimacy they will achieve. Yet, to argue that there must first be a great Imam holding the banner of jihad, and that one must wait for him from Egypt, Jordan, Syria, or any other place to commence the liberation of Palestine is unacceptable to us. We consequently disagreed with the theses of the traditional Islamic movement as represented by the Muslim Brotherhood.

Do you think that this traditional Islamic vision assumed by the Muslim Brotherhood is just an excuse to evade jihad for Palestine, or is it a vision that stems from the role assigned to this movement?

Truly, I do not want to misrepresent the traditional Islamic current. I want to add that we look to our jihad in Palestine as a renaissance project for the Arab and Islamic umma as well. Regarding the positions of Hamas, I say that Hamas' participation in the intifada with force, diligence, and momentum has made the difference between us smaller. There may still be some different analyses between them and us, just as we have a clearer methodology for the conflict than they do. However, their participation in the intifada has made the distance smaller on the Palestinian national level. Their adoption of the call for continued armed jihad against the enemy until the end will make—in the case of stability—the distance smaller and smaller.

What are your differences with the other Palestinian national organization and movements?

The disagreement between them and us is more intellectual and political. On the level of intellectual disagreement, we believe in the role of Islam in the battle and the role of Islam in the peoples' liberation movements. We believe that the creed and the faith in God Almighty and treating Islam as an ideology are our most important weapons in the resistance against colonialism and for achieving independence and renaissance. The nationalist forces split into two because of the Islamic phenomenon throughout the 1950s and 1960s—the first section believed that religion was a personal issue and that everyone was free to practice or not to practice his religious rites, and this had nothing to do with the issue of struggle. Any dealing with religion was only as a slogan and as a bond between man and his Lord. The second section, on the other hand, refused to have anything to do with religion because religion had disintegrated the national front against colonialism, and therefore its role had to be abolished.

On the level of political disagreement, then, there is no doubt that we agreed on the necessity of liberating all Palestinian national territory in the beginning. However, the ideological and intellectual bacteria in the Palestinian national movement finally made it concur with the official Arab position and make baffling and surprising concessions in a period exceeding not even twenty years. It forced us to enter sharp disputes with them, with the emergence of the Palestinian line calling for recognition of the Zionist entity and promoting the possibility of dividing Palestine between the Palestinian people and the Israeli people.

It is difficult to generalize this assessment to all Palestinian forces. Perhaps this may be true for movements and organizations with a narrow national horizon. That is, organizations dealing with the Palestinian cause from a perspective of territory. Like all other Arab governing authorities, they finally met with them on the issue of recognizing the enemy and the question of establishing two states. Yet, the issue is very different for the Palestinian national forces. In Palestine, for example, there is an important and extensive national current among the Palestinian people. Abroad, they are committed to the national vision of the conflict, which considers Israel as the heart of the Western colonial project, or the conflict in Palestine as a conflict between the Zionist colonial project and the Arab national project. Alternatively, regarding the view of Palestine as a purely Arab land, they will not accept any division or fragmentation because it is a conflict of existence and not a conflict over borders. How do you see the danger of this logic?

There is no doubt that the bacteria in the national logic weakened its strength and brought it to these projects. We imagine that in the face of a very unjust power balance in favor of America and Israel, which has been ongoing for decades in the region, there will be no possibility of resistance except for the "venerable." Only the venerable are capable of confrontation. If the national trend possessed this, then it would have been able to resist and to continue the conflict. Yet, if one lacks that, then one may be in the same problems as those in the national current.

You are now bringing us to a maliciously and deliberately fabricated issue. That is, the issue of separating Arabism and Islam. For we believe in the inextricable link between Arabism and Islam, and the two are what the umma holds dearest for its own salvation. We believe that those who call for the separation between Arabism and Islam are enemies of both Arabism and Islam, either intentionally, in service of hostile objectives and schemes, or by the ignorance and blindness of these schemes. How does Palestinian Islamic Jihad view that cause, the cause of Arabism and Islam?

We do not believe there is any contradiction between Arabism and Islam. However, those who create this contradiction are the same who harbor Arabism with implications contradicting it and Islam. So there will be no conflict or any issues between them, but there will be affinity, harmony, and unity, and we are certain that the problem of Islam is not with Arabism. The problem of Islam is not with any Arabist proposal, but with the contents of its struggling, its resistance, and it differs with its basic premises.

The problem of Arabism is with the enemies of Islam and the cause is therefore one and so is the goal.

Since our inception in Palestine we decided that we have one single and fundamental enemy, and that enemy is the Zionist enemy. The conflict is with this enemy only, and what remain are merely intellectual or political differences with the Palestinian forces on the scene. These intellectual and political differences are resolved through an ongoing dialogue and not through any other method. Violence is only directed toward one side, and that is the Israeli enemy. As for the Palestinian parties we disagree with, we can never enter into conflict or a clash with them. If I talk and discuss calmly and objectively, it does not then produce any provocation and it does not drag us into any battle.

How has this vision reflected on the alliances and relations between you and the other Palestinian forces?

In theory, we believed in the need to establish alliances with any party wanting to fight the enemy, but the practical reasons are beyond our control. The same applies to the historical circumstances experienced by everyone, and we have not been able to achieve this alliance on the ground. All we could achieve was to reach an understanding on several issues and to agree on common visions on some partial issues. We have not discussed entering a front with any other force, however, and we have not considered any coordination in the political sense of the word with any other party.

For the Intifada, all the forces are involved as all the Palestinian groups are involved, so there is coordination that happens automatically. There were dialogues about the participation of Palestinian Islamic Jihad in the Unified National Leadership of the Intifada (UNLU)⁴ at the beginning of the intifada, but these dialogues did not bear fruit. Therefore, Palestinian Islamic Jihad did not participate in UNLU. Actual coordination on the ground was established, however, and we agreed that cooperation is the basis and rejected any possibility of infighting. We determined that the stone has one path and one goal: the chest of the occupying enemy. We do not deny our political differences, but these differences must not affect the intensity of our strikes against the enemy.

☾

---

[4] The Unified Leadership of the Uprising (*al-qiyāda al-waṭaniyya al-muwaḥḥada*), a coalition of the local Palestinian leadership in the Occupied Palestinian Territories during the First Intifada. Catching the PLO by surprise, the UNLU signified how a new Palestinian leadership had emerged in the Occupied Territories and new leaders with it who had grown restless with twenty years of seemingly unending occupation. See Jacob Høigilt, "The Palestinian Spring That Was Not: The Youth and Political Activism in the Occupied Palestinian Territories," *Arab Studies Quarterly* 35, no. 4 (Fall 2013): 343–59.

Part III

Iran and the Shiites

10

Excerpts from *Khomeini*

The Islamic Solution and Alternative

1979, published by al-Mukhtar al-Islami Publishers in Cairo.

When the PIJ founding fathers returned to the Gaza Strip in 1981, they undoubtedly sensed that anything was now possible. The Egyptian autocrat, Anwar al-Sadat, had been slayed at the hands of Khalid al-Islambouli and EIJ. The Iranian revolution oversaw the end of a regime allied with Israel and supported by the United States. If the Egyptians and Iranians had done the "impossible," then certainly the Palestinians could do that which no one before them had accomplished: liberating Palestine.

The booklet Khomeini: The Islamic Solution and Alternative *was written by al-Shiqaqi shortly after the overthrow of the shah. Allegedly, it was the first "book" in Arabic about Ayatollah Khomeini and the revolution, and Egyptian authorities arrested al-Shiqaqi twice for writing it: first when it was published, and then once again when it was sold out and republished. As the booklet was written in a period of energetic debates with leftist and Marxist student groups about the way forward, this booklet was in many ways attempting to show what a return to religion could achieve. Here, the Iranian revolution is hailed for its strike against Western colonialism and for showing the true transformative power of the Islamic creed.*

This document matters for four reasons. First, this booklet is the most elaborate text by anyone in PIJ on the Iranian Revolution and what it signified—for the region, for the religion, and for the Palestinian cause. Second, the Iranian revolution was undoubtedly an inspiration for the young Palestinian students in Cairo, and this document highlights why. Third, the Iranian revolution has in many ways defined PIJ. Its founding fathers were, for example, accused of being Shiites in disguise in the 1980s (an allegation which the movement has never managed to fully escape despite it being factually wrong), and Iran became the main patron of the movement from the late 1980s. Fourth, contrary to belief, this document shows that the leitmotif in al-Shiqaqi's writings always was Western colonialism. Commencing with Napoleon Bonaparte at the end of the eighteenth century via the Westernization of Arab-Islamic thought to the Zionist movement, the Islamic world is weak because of the control, domination, and exploitation of the Western colonial project. The Iranian revolution was thus not important simply because a people had managed to topple a regime allied with the West and Israel, but because they had done so while basing their revolution on the Islamic creed and religion as a revolutionary ideology. It thus proved that the success of the masses could be achieved only through the return to religion.

We move with the logic in Islam, so if we are killed, then we will be in paradise... If we are defeated, then we will be in paradise, and if we defeat the enemies of Islam, then we will also be in paradise. Therefore, we do not fear defeat. Indeed, we do not fear anything as the Prophet, peace and blessings be upon him, was defeated in some invasions. For we are fighting with the sword of God and the movement will persist.

Ayatollah[1] Khomeini

Dedications:
For the two men of the century:
To the martyr imam Hassan al-Banna
To the revolutionary imam Ayatollah Khomeini

Preface

The objective conditions for revolution had matured by the end of 1977. They did so locally with the massive corruption. The objective conditions also matured religiously with a growing awareness and a highly scientific, intellectual, and political experiment in the framework of modern Shiite theses—which approached the Sunnis—in one of the most intellectually active periods in their history. Last, they matured internationally with Western dissatisfaction.

Thus came the winter of 1978, which was not a very cold one... So spring came early to Iran... A spring of revolution that spread with a historical splendor never registered before... clever steps... characterized by a modern awareness and the beauty of a lover... The black turbans have a role in the last quarter of the twentieth century... So do the black veils...

The world stood baffled, watching the Iranian lady as she descended from the mountains of Qom, Shiraz, and Tabriz to the streets of Teheran... Raising her hand in the face of the military, the oil cranes, and the monopolies of the great powers... The early movement's logic of Islam reappears, and the Western media and its disciples stand confused and floundering... They dip their pens in the ink of Satan to write about the ayatollah whom millions of the masses turned to—hungry for freedom and the return to God—while every day they search for a new excuse for this mad pastor, James Jones, perpetrator of the American Guyana massacre.[2] The American computer

---

[1] Ayatollah, honorific title in Shiite Islam assigned to outstanding legal scholars who are fully qualified mujtahidin and serve as marja' al-taqlid.
[2] James Jones (1931–78), American preacher and cult leader. Setting up the religious community Jonestown in Guyana, Jones planned and executed mass suicide and murder of its inhabitants. More than 900 of its inhabitants were killed by cyanide poisoning.

was unable to understand the relationship between al-Husayn's martyrdom more than 1,300 years ago and the fall of a regime considered as the most modern and stable in West Asia.

With the continuation of the revolution and its advance, new concepts appear while old ones dissolve…

- The constant terror in the sick minds of the great powers and their domination, violence, and its representation as a sword hanging over Islam and its future… This terror is now falling down, and these fantasies are collapsing; so the great powers, like all beings on Earth, can miscalculate—even with a computer!
- This is the stage of Islam, and so the masses came out from under its shadow… If it were not its stage, then the masses would not have come out for its sake like this… All prospects collapsed in front of the peoples of the region… and the painstaking experiments with liberalism and socialism now declare their failure and fall.
- The coming battle will be between Islam and communism. So global capitalism does no longer protect anyone, and the theses of liquefaction, hesitation, and vagueness no longer produce real development, real people, or real power, and it no longer protects our looted wealth. Generations are now formed in this region with a greater awareness of the realities of things. They approach Islam under the next communist threat, and we should not forget here the Jewish relationship with the communist movement… We should also seriously consider the possibility of the Israeli-American alliance becoming an Israeli-Soviet alliance (particularly after the lessons of Vietnam, Formosa,[3] and Iran).

The last question remains… The possibility that the Islamic movement does not take power… It would be difficult for us at that point to suggest that they were not defeated in the battle… Indeed, the termination of the revolution in Iran in any form or by any means would mean that the Islamic movement in the world would receive its harshest blows since 1954…[4] This does not mean that the eastern question is over, however. For in addition to the new emerging concepts to which we have referred, Islam remains capable of moving the masses, restoring the realities of force in the world to other situations, coming closer to power, and—perhaps—even seizing it… The most serious issue is not only the appearance of a coherent creedal entity in defiance of a series of materialistic doctrines cast down before man… But also that the Islamic homeland has become more important strategically and economically in the so-called era of economy.

If that should happen—God forbid—the Muslim would still not know defeat, and we repeat with Imam Khomeini:

---

[3] Al-Shiqaqi is presumably referring to Taiwan, historically known as Formosa, and the American Formosa Resolution of 1955, which pledged to defend Taiwan against invasion from China.

[4] Al-Shiqaqi refers to the mass incarceration and political suppression carried out by Egyptian authorities against the Muslim Brotherhood after the attempted assassination against Gamal Abdel Nasser in 1954.

We know that all the political forces in the world want to destroy our movement. Yet, we know at the same time that our Islamic responsibility and the divine decree imposes on us not to be too worried. For we move with the logic in Islam, so if we are killed, then we will be in paradise. If we are defeated, then we will be in paradise. If we defeat the enemies of Islam, then we will also be in paradise. Therefore, we do not fear defeat. Indeed, we do not fear anything as the Prophet, peace and blessings be upon him, was defeated in some invasions. For we are fighting with the sword of God and the movement will persist.

In the name of God, the Most Gracious, the Most Merciful

"The example of those who take allies other than God is like that of the spider who takes a home. And indeed, the weakest of homes is the home of the spider, if they only knew."[5] **God Almighty Speaks the Truth.**

"Certainly, the mill of Islam is turning, so turn with Islam where it turns. The Book and power will be separated, so be with the Book. Emirs will rule over you, who will degrade you if you obey them, and kill you if you disobey. So they asked: "What should we do, O Messenger of God?" He replied: "Be like the companions of Isa, who were hacked with saws and loaded on to timber, for by Him in Whose hand Muhammad's soul is ... For death because of obedience to God is better than a life sinning against Him." **The Messenger of God, peace and blessings be upon him, speaks the Truth.**

* * *

Chapter 1: The Islamic Movement and the Challenge

(1)

Has the era of Lilliputians and castrates ended, who rose to the surface of Arab and Islamic time over a century ago? Has the era ended in which one man called his son "Lahab" until the people called him "Abu Lahab"?[6]

Is it the end of experiments exhausting our umma and paralyzing its forces under the auspices of colonialism in order to create alternatives to Islam... picking them up from the thinking of our enemies? Has the phase of the people ended, in which they, inspired by the apparatuses and clients, step out to shout against their own interests, their own wealth, and their true ideology? Has the phase of soldiers ended, who wear

---

[5] See sūrat al-ʿankabūt: 41.
[6] Abu Lahab (549–624), Muhammad's paternal uncle and Meccan Quraysh leader opposing Muhammad and his followers.

the crowns of emperors and the shoes of the masses? Has the phase of progressive claims and slogans ended, which wasted thousands of our umma's kilometers and its spirit?

To quote the French magazine, *Paris Match*: Has the Islamic war commenced?

(2)

In the late 1940s and early 1950s, Egypt was rippling with a fierce and turbulent commotion. It was the Islamic movement taking its natural place in leading the masses; on the verge of shaking the worn-out throne... Suddenly, Gamal Abdel Nasser jumped to power, and only a few years passed until the national Islamic forces were eliminated in one of the ugliest liquidation processes in modern Islamic history... It happened despite Abdel Nasser's claim—in an interview with the editor of *Lebanese Events*—of the need for an Islamic cultural revolution, saying: "I am the one who will carry out this revolution... I only wish I were a cleric!"

However, the war against the umma's ideology and the only idea capable of mobilizing it in its political and social battle continued... Abdel Nasser departed, leaving thousands of kilometers in the hands of this umma's enemies... Leaving Egypt wailing under the weight of deteriorating economic conditions and debts exceeding $10 billion.

From Egypt to Algeria... Houari Boumédiène[7] replied in 1966 to a question about what made him move against Ben Bella,[8] the symbol of the revolution, saying:

> I only took the responsibility of governance after seeing hundreds of thousands of Algerians marching at the funeral of Bachir El Ibrahimi.[9] As if they wished to declare their unbelief anew, which was brought to them by Ben Bella... A nostalgia for a conservative past overwhelms the people ... and they see what the hand of the revolutionary present does to them.

Therefore... Consequently... Yet, the Algerian reality deceives Boumédiène... and presents another answer. The funeral of Sheikh El Ibrahimi was an opportunity for the masses to express their discontent with the non-Islamic slogans the One Million Martyr Revolution began to propose. The emergence of the masses at the time was a declaration of the determination of this Muslim people to adhere to their authenticity and heritage. These feelings had thus to be aborted. This is why Boumédiène—absent from Algeria for thirteen years—set forth a spiral of programs whose fate was hopeless... Leaving a rich country whose debts have risen to $6 billion.

In Sudan, the cradle of the great Mahdist Revolution,[10] there was a coup d'état on May 25, 1979. The coup brought the military to power, marking the commencement of

---

[7] Houari Boumédiène (1932–78), second Algerian president after his coup d'état against Ahmed Ben Bella in 1965.
[8] Ahmed Ben Bella (1916–2012), first Algerian president from 1963 until 1965.
[9] Mohamed Bachir El Ibrahimi (1889–1965), Algerian Islamic scholar and founder of the Association of Algerian Muslim Ulama.
[10] Mahdist Revolution (1881–98), also known as the Mahdist War, the conflict between the politico-religious Sudanese Mahdiyya Movement led by Muhammad Ahmad bin Abdallah, on the one hand, and Muhammad Ali's Egypt and (subsequently) the British, on the other. Rising up against

a liquidation process on the Nasserite path against the Islamic movement—although the latest developments proved that these attempts were in vain. In addition, the military appeared in Pakistan and Indonesia whenever the Muslim masses were about to take control of their own affairs.

(3)

Throughout all of its crusader battles, colonialism realized the extent to which the creed of Islam penetrated the hearts of its members. It realized the extent to which Muslims around the world have gathered around the banner of the Qur'an and the Islamic political system, which was represented by the Ottoman Empire throughout the last centuries. Crusader colonialism understood equally well that it would never be able to confront this unity and this current, which declared that there was no nationality for Muslims except their religion. It understood that it could not confront it with soldiers or equipment. When Napoleon entered Egypt at the end of the eighteenth century, he prepared a statement addressing the Egyptians in which he said:

> In the name of God, the Most Gracious, the Most Merciful. There is no god but God, and he has neither son nor partner in his dominion. On behalf of the French republic, which is based upon the foundation of liberty and equality, General Bonaparte makes it known that the beys who govern Egypt have for long insulted the French nation and injured its merchants with abuse and infringement. The hour for their punishment has come. For too long, this group of Mamelukes from the lands of Abazi and Circassia have tyrannized the most beautiful part of the world. Yet, God Almighty, on whom all depends, has ordered that their state shall cease.
>
> O Egyptians, you have been told that I only came to this region with the purpose of destroying your religion. This is a blatant lie. Do not believe it, and tell the slanderers that I only came to restore your rights from the hands of the oppressors. Tell them that I worship God Almighty, more than the Mamelukes do, and that I revere the Prophet and the Holy Qur'an. O Sheikhs, judges, imams, and notables of this country, tell your nation that also the French are faithful Muslims (In the French version: We are true friends of the Muslims) and assert that the French descended from the great Romans and destroyed the chair of the pope, who always impelled the Christians to fight Islam. Then they went to Malta and expelled their knights who claimed that God Almighty demanded them to fight the Muslims. We have been friends of his Highness, the Ottoman Sultan, through centuries, and we have been enemies of his enemies. As for the Mamelukes, on the other hand, have they not revolted against the authority of the Sultan, which they even now reject?

At the end of the statement, he says:

> The Sheikhs, scholars, judges, and imams are obligated to do their jobs, and each and every one of the country's people should stay in his comforting home. The prayers

the oppressive rule of the Egyptians, bin Abdallah led his forces after being declared the Mahdi and established an Islamic state following a series of military triumphs.

are to be based in the mosque as usual, and all Egyptians should thank God Almighty for the end of the Mameluke state, saying aloud: May God perpetuate the exaltation of the Ottoman Sultan. May God perpetuate the exaltation of the French army.

Notwithstanding, the French campaign is precisely the phase when we may start dating the process of proposing alternatives to Islam in the region.

The French Revolution destroyed the monarchy and it brought out its new slogans of freedom and equality to conquer the world!! The choice was Egypt due to its geographical and political importance in the region… The French campaign and the appearance of Muhammad Ali were followed by the departure of delegations from Egypt to Europe to receive new information and science. A great confusion occurred then (and still does) between the values of heritage and the values of knowledge, between the impelling values of heritage capable of mobilizing the umma… Capable of responding to the challenge and acting simultaneously… and the values of knowledge linked to the natural sciences and technological progress, which we must learn and in whose development we must participate. Not as an alternative ideology, however, as proposed by some of those who travelled to Europe and were mesmerized by the cleanliness of the streets of London and Paris. They thought that we could not build on Western technology without the structures and institutions based on the Western vision. That is, calling for liberalism as an ideology!

The process of proposing alternatives, and of questioning the Islamic ideology and its ability in surviving and preserving the umma, was the heart of the conflict beginning in the nineteenth century and which has continued until now… This was a prelude to transforming the political conditions, which necessitated the commitment of the Muslim masses to the symbol of their unity in the Ottoman Empire. This attempt did not pass easily. The masses stood up against it under the leadership of the scholars, intellectuals, and revolutionaries of the Muslims. This Urabi revolted against the corruption of Egypt's government and against the English without even thinking of renouncing his obedience to the Caliph or rebelling against him. As the memoirs of Urabi narrate, he showed that his measures derived their authority from the Caliph in everything he was doing.

This is what Imam Muhammad Abduh says during his stay in Beirut in 1886:

> Preserving the Exalted Ottoman State is the third article of faith after the belief in God and His messenger. It alone is the preserver of the rule of religion, it alone is the protector of its survival, and religion has no authority without it. I am with this creed, praise be to God, as we live and die by it.

This is confirmed in an interview with Rashid Rida after the Turks' victory in the Greco-Turkish War[11] in 1897:

> Many Egyptian dignitaries hate the Ottoman Empire and slander it, although most of them love it. I too hate the Sultan. However, no Muslim wants the state to be

---

[11] The Greco-Turkish War (1919–22), the conflict between Greece and the Turkish National Movement following the collapse of the Ottoman Empire when the former sought territorial gains.

worse, so it is a shield. If it fell, then we Muslims would persist as the Jews, but as something lesser. The Jews have something that preserves them and protects their interests and community, which is wealth. We have nothing left, for we have lost everything.

Mustafa Kamil, one of the leaders in the nationalist movement in Egypt, said in his sermon in 1900 that religion and nationalism are inseparable twins. He answered a question from Evelyn Baring[12] about his nationality, saying: "I am an Ottoman-Egyptian." Yet, the process of forcing Muslims to relinquish Islam as an ideology and to abandon the Ottoman Empire as a symbol of Islamic unity continued fiercely. A French writer believes that there is no solution to the Islamic question but annihilating the Muslims and digging up the grave of the Holy Prophet to transfer his bones to the Louvre in Paris.

Gladstone,[13] leader of the British Liberal Party,[14] declared that the English would remain restless until they had burned the Qur'an in the hearts of the Egyptians... He once referred to Sultan Abdul Hamid II[15] as the enemy of the Messiah, and another time as Satan. Moreover, this Englishman, Blunt,[16] writes in his book *The Future of Islam*: "The destruction of the Ottoman Sultanate does not harm the Muslims. Indeed, this Ottoman state is divided into better and more beautiful Arab states." This was the reason for introducing Arabism as an interim alternative to Islam, which was less dangerous for colonialism. Besides, this deduction pierced the idea of Islamic unity and undermined the Ottoman Empire under the guise of Arabism, which made it easier for them to divide the region between them. In addition, it would subsequently limit the Arab movement in Asia, as it was difficult to separate Arabism from Islam in Arab Africa.

In order to achieve this plan, colonialism began educating its students by sending them in delegations to Europe, or through missionaries, preachers, schools, and newspapers funded and supervised by their clients. This activity, and the colonial tide, culminated in the Great Arab Revolt,[17] which was planned by the British and carried out by the hands of the Arabs... This revolution, which was a wedge in the state of Islam's body. Yet, he who laughs last laughs loudest, for the umma will not have mercy on those who raised their enemies' weapons against their brothers, even if they make the same excuse as Prince Ali bin Hussein[18] did when he said:

---

[12] Evelyn Baring, 1st Earl of Cromer (1841–1917), British colonial administrator; British controller-general in Egypt from 1878 until 1879; and first Consul-General of Egypt from 1883 until 1907.
[13] William Ewert Gladstone (1809–98), Liberal politician and prime minister of UK.
[14] Liberal Party, with the Conservative Party constituting one of the main UK political parties in the nineteenth and twentieth centuries.
[15] Abdul Hamid II (1842–1918), the last sultan with de facto control over the disintegrating Ottoman Empire. Abdul Hamid II's reign lasted from 1876 until 1909.
[16] Wilfrid Scawen Blunt (1840–1922), English poet, translator of Arabic poetry, and a leading critic of British imperialism in Africa. See Luisa Villa, "A 'Political Education': Wilfrid Scawen Blunt, the Arabs and the Egyptian Revolution (1881–82)," *Journal of Victorian Culture* 17, no. 1 (2012): 46–63.
[17] The Great Arab Revolt (*al-thawra al-'arabiyya al-kubrā*), Arab military uprising against the Ottoman central power for national independence commencing in 1916.
[18] Ali bin Hussein (1879–1935), also known as Ali of Hijaz, king of Hijaz and Grand Sharif of Mecca from 1924 until 1925.

We are nothing but a simple whim... Before the revolution, we never entered international life, traded with foreigners, or communicated with them from near or far. Indeed, the British came to us in the Hijaz, and not we who went to them. They came to us with a white sheet of paper with an imperial stamp at the bottom. They told us that this is an official document, so write what you want and we are ready to implement and fulfill. So we trusted them, and they betrayed us.

Amin Sa'id also narrates about the leader of the revolution in his book *The Secrets of the Arab Revolution and the Tragedy of al-Sharif Hussein*: "He only lived for a few days after his arrival in Jordan during which he was unconscious, saying and calling out: 'This is the penalty for those who trust the British, who befriend them, and who work with them.'" History will not have mercy, and it will disdain anyone who attempts to pursue a tactic or strategy separated from the ideology of his umma, whether it is al-Sharif Hussein or the row of leaders and commanders who continue taking turns at this umma's leadership, usurping its power.

The Caliphate fell and the crusader armies were stationed in our country. Colonialism, however, which knows that there is no place for its armies in the land of Islam, began dividing the region and giving the parts to its agents and disciples, whom it had created. Fear of the danger of the Islamic revival and the Islamic revolution continued to worry and frighten them as it always remained in their plans and calculations... Despite all their efforts, the masses and the Islamic movements remained the center of gravity in the region with their heroic stances against colonialism, both before and after the overthrow of the Caliphate. It commenced with the Islamic Mahdist Revolution in Sudan—which would have changed the face of Africa and the Arab Mashriq[19] if it had been destined to live—and ended with the latest revolution of Iran under the leadership of the Islamic commander Ayatollah Khomeini. It did so via the rebellious leader Jamal al-Din al-Afghani, who stood on the lookout against colonialism and who chased it everywhere—a spiritual father for many of the intellectuals, preachers, and Islamic movements.

There were also the continuous Islamic revolutions in Algeria under the leadership of Abd al-Qadir al-Jaza'iri,[20] Ben Badis,[21] and the Association of Ulama,[22] which created the Algerian National Charter—which was a secular one. It acknowledged their important role while considering Islam an impregnable fortress, which enabled the Algerians to stand steadfast facing all attempts at undermining their personalities. The Algerian people thus fortified themselves with Islam as a religion of struggle,

---

[19] The Mashriq refers to the eastern part of the Arab world, comprising Oman, Yemen, Saudi Arabia, the United Arab Emirates, Qatar, Bahrain, Kuwait, Iraq, Syria, Lebanon, Jordan, Palestine, Egypt, and Sudan.
[20] Abd al-Qadir ibn Muhieddine, known as Abd al-Qadir al-Jaza'iri (1808–83), religious and military leader, and Islamic scholar renowned for his struggle against French colonialism in the nineteenth century.
[21] Abdelhamid Ben Badis (1889–1940), founder of the Association of Algerian Muslim Ulama and leading figure in the Algerian reform movement.
[22] The Association of Algerian Muslim Ulama (*jam'iyyat al-'ulamā' al-muslimīn al-jazā'iriyyīn*), commonly known as Association of Ulama, a cultural and religious movement in Algeria established by Abdelhamid Ben Badis in 1931.

determination, justice, and equality. They sought refuge in the religion in the darkest era of colonial domination, and they derived moral energy and spiritual strength from it, which kept them from giving in to despair and provided them with reasons for triumph.

There was also Abd al-Karim al-Khattabi[23] in Morocco, who defeated the Spanish Armies and confronted a French army with the participation of the fleet and airplanes on a combat line of 450 miles. The Senussian movement in Libya and the mujahid Umar Mukhtar[24] had an important role in the resistance against the Italians, who came with approximately 100,000 soldiers to exterminate the Libyan Muslim people. Izz al-Din al-Qassam, student of Sheikh Muhammad Abduh, led the revolution against the British in Palestine until he was martyred, so it continued after him without interruption. The Muslim Brotherhood fought valiantly in 1948 and stunned everyone; the seriousness of this believing group against the interests of colonialism and Zionism was revealed.

Yet, colonialism attempted to isolate all of these revolutions and Islamic movements, and it led a counter-campaign with its agents and disciples of the Westernization campaign, which Farah Antun introduced with his book *Averroes and his Philosophy* (1902).[25] This book was merely a distorted copy of the French intellectual Ernest Renan's book, *Averroes and Averroism* (1852).[26] Ali Abdel Raziq[27] followed this up in *Islam and the Principles of Governance* where he demanded the separation of religion and state; following what the Europeans did; and forgetting or ignoring the clash in Europe, which is rejected, and illogical to occur in our Islamic society due to reasons for which there is insufficient room to discuss here… It suffices to note, however, that the arising conflict between the Church—which holds the view of abstaining from life and pursuing personal gains—and the emerging bourgeoisie could never have happened here… For Islam—in addition to being a more comprehensive organization in all aspects of life—only demanded of its followers to be more effective on the worldly side, which is what will sate the desires and fulfill the ambitions of any active and rising power.

---

[23] Muhammad ibn Abd al-Karim al-Khattabi (1882–1963), also known as Abd el-Krim, a Moroccan political and military leader who led a coalition of tribes against French and Spanish colonialism in northern Morocco, leading to the establishment of the Confederate Republic of the Tribes of the Rif (1921–26).

[24] Umar Mukhtar (1858–1931), leader of the Senussi movement and the resistance against Italian colonialism in present-day Libya. Captured by the Italians after twenty years of conflict, Mukhtar was hanged in 1931.

[25] Ibn Rushd (1126–98), also known as Averroes in Latin, a Muslim Andalusian philosopher and follower of Aristotelianism, who became renowned for his commentaries on Aristotle.

[26] Averroism, school of medieval philosophy based on the works of ibn Rushd, also described as a radical form of Aristotelianism, postulating that all human beings share one intellect, that happiness is attainable in this world, and that the Hereafter has no temporal beginning or end. See Routledge Encyclopedia of Philosophy, "Averroism," 1998, doi:10.4324/9780415249126-B012-1 [accessed: November 21, 2019].

[27] Ali Abdel Raziq (1888–1966), Egyptian Islamic scholar at al-Azhar who argued for the separation of state and religion as the Qur'an and Prophetic sunna did not prescribe an Islamic government. See John L. Esposito, *Islam and Politics*, 4th ed. (Syracuse and New York: Syracuse University Press, 1998), 71–3.

Then Ahmad Lutfi al-Sayyid called for the "naturalization" of foreigners in Egypt at a time when they were controlling the economic life—as if he were calling for an extension of this economic influence into the political life too. Taha Hussein, on the other hand, called for the dissolution of the Egyptian nation into the European civilization in his book *The Future of Culture*: "Its goodness and evil. Its sweetness and bitterness. What we love about it and what we hate. What is praised and what is criticized." Finally, there is Louis Awad, who on April 7, 1978, blamed us for having taught our children more about the history of the Hawk of Quraysh[28] and Saladin than what we had taught them about the history of Ali Bey al-Kabir,[29] Muhammad Ali, and Khedive Ismael.[30]

While these liberal ideas made their way among the intellectuals and writers, the other side of the coin was the arrival of the liberal regimes as the first organized alternative to Islam… These regimes—which borrowed nothing from Western liberalism except its form, and which seemed incapable of doing otherwise—quickly declared their inability to continue their claims of saving this umma and consolidating their nationalist march. The defeat of 1948 came to declare the following:

1. The liberal regimes' lack of awareness of the conflict's nature.
2. Their inability to confront the enemy until the end.

3. Their inability to achieve modernization within actual national independence.
4. Their lack of authenticity and sudden intrusion into the Muslim community.

The secularization and Westernization current did not despair after the liberal defeat, however, and attempted to save itself and block the road for a return to the Islamic solution, which loomed on the horizon and suppressed the phenomenon of military coup d'etats, in which the American intelligence services had a key role…

The so-called revolutionary socialism then commenced taking its role as a new alternative. If the liberal regimes practiced their role by putting obstacles in the way of the Islamic movement—sometimes attempting to weaken it through invasion and intellectual oppression and at other times through political isolation—then the military socialist regimes exercised their role through the physical liquidation of the Islamic movement in addition to the intellectual oppression and political isolation. The socialists and anarchists treated the Islamic movement as political opponents and (even much less) as ideological opponents because they—and this is only one of the reasons—realized that the battle about its second face would mean the masks would fall. We are not here, however, to evaluate the socialist experience. It soon came to a defeat in 1967 to declare that which the defeat of 1948 had already declared in the great confrontation between the Arab and Islamic umma, on the one hand, and the new colonialism and Zionism in the tenth crusader campaign, on the other, which commenced in 1948 and whose flame is still burning.

[28] Abd al-Rahman I (731–88), also known as the Hawk of Quraysh (*ṣaqr quraysh*), founder of the Islamic dynasty in Iberia and member of the Umayyad dynasty in Damascus.
[29] Ali Bey al-Kabir (1728–73), Mamluk leader in Egypt who rebelled against the Ottoman rulers.
[30] Isma'il Pasha, also known as Ismail the Magnificent (1830–95), khedive and pasha of Egypt from 1863 until 1879.

The burial has not yet taken place although the death certificate has been signed off for the military socialist, revolutionary, or anarchist regimes (call it what you will), just as it was signed off for its sister in the "liberal" torture current… In a desperate attempt to revive the rotting corpses whose smell blocks the noses. As the year went by for the Shah, who as one of the liberal strongholds attempted to resist the burial, it will be implemented for the others… The era will end when an Arab fighter belonging to a revolutionary organization is fully engaged in the struggle against Zionism, when its Muslim youth is martyred every day while Sadiq Jalal al-Azm[31] writes for us about the plight of Iblis in the Qur'an[32] in his *Criticism of Religious Thought*.

Just as voices like this cacophony issued on the sixth anniversary of the 1967 nakba (perhaps coincidentally) will be refuted. It is shamefully declared in the book *In Religion and Heritage* by the publisher Dar al-Awda of the Iraqi Marxist Hadi al-Alawi:[33] "There is principally no contradiction between Islam and colonialism. So colonialism does not fight religions because, primarily, they [religions] do not fight it. Islam as a creed has nothing to do with colonialism." He cries out once again: "The revolutionary ideology is fundamentally incompatible with religion. Religion, in turn, has no contribution to make in our current struggle against colonialism and imperialism."

Has this "fighter" read the history of his umma!? Or is he not allowed as a revolutionary fighter to look back? If so, then we have an argument against him in our current struggle against colonialism and imperialism.

A Stance with the Islamic Movement and Revolution

At a time when the modern Western challenge crossed the borders of our country, attempting to remove the Islamic ideology from power and to present its alternatives, the Islamic movement emerged as a natural reaction to this invasion and to the overthrow of the Caliphate. Its appearance in the 1920s as an effective social current in Islamic society had a great impact… New serious steps were thus taken on the path of Islamic revival in order to restore the existence and international influence of the Muslim umma anew. The Islamic movement succeeded greatly in restoring the psychological balance of Islamic society. It led its role in the process of cleansing the mind of the individual and of Islamic society to throw off their inferiority complex in front of the coming challenges.

---

[31] Sadiq Jalal al-Azm (1934–2016), Syrian professor of modern European philosophy at the University of Damascus with specialization in Kantianism.

[32] Iblis, figure in the Qur'an who was cast out of heaven after refusing to bow down to Adam. Though often referred to as synonymous with Satan (*shayṭān*), Islamic scholars have debated whether Iblis is an angel or a jinn. See Encyclopædia Britannica, "Iblīs," https://www.britannica.com/topic/Iblis [accessed: November 21, 2019].

[33] Hadi al-Alawi (1932–), Iraqi Marxist scholar and member of the Iraqi Communist Party. Although he left the Iraqi Communist Party, he kept his leftist convictions and worked on his reading of tradition (*turāth*) through the lens of class conflict in order to indigenize the application of Communism. See Mohammed al-Sudairi, "Mao in the Middle East: Hadi al-'Alawi, Scion of the Two Civilizations," *Middle East Report* 270 (Spring 2014): 19–20.

The Islamic intellectual Tawfiq al-Tayyib[34] expressed his hopes for this role in his book *After the two Catastrophes*[35]—published after the 1967 nakba—saying:

> After today, there is no longer any excuse for a Muslim intellectual to be infatuated reading a European book, but instead doing so scholastically and critically. No longer does he stand admiringly in front of a painting he does not understand, but instead doing so contemplatively and as a connoisseur. Nor does he stand impressed in front of a machine, but instead does so educated, controlled, or well-grounded. He will perhaps become a teacher one day, or a witness as the Holy Qur'an wishes for him to be.

The Islamic movement—emerging with the support, and from the center, of the popular masses—has grown in a way that surprised the observers. It confirmed what was stated in the book *Whither Islam*, written by a group of orientalists and edited by the British foreign adviser H.A.R. Gibb:[36]

> The Islamic movements have developed at an incredible and surprising pace... It suddenly burst forth before the observers could discern from its signs what made them suspicious... For the Islamic movements lack nothing but leadership... They lack nothing but the emergence of a Saladin.

A movement such as the Muslim Brotherhood was, for example, capable of becoming the greatest mass collective. It entered the villages of Egypt and its cities, as well as the army and universities. The secret of this mass collective was, in the words of an Egyptian Marxist—without any sense of neutrality or objectivity in an analytical introduction to the translation of Richard Mitchell's book about the Muslim Brotherhood[37]:

> They proceeded from an ideology capable of attracting the widest masses. They then proved their skills through their effective organizing, and applied one of the most important, classical slogans from their traditional opponents—the communists—which was the slogan of the iron organization. The Muslim Brotherhood applied this slogan in practice while it mostly and generally remained just a slogan for others.

---

[34] Tawfiq al-Tayyib, little information about al-Tayyib exists. Azzam Tamimi refers to him as a "Syrian post-graduate student," while Meir Hatina refers to him as a Jordanian Islamist. Nonetheless, his text *The Islamic Solution after the Two Catastrophes* was defining for the founding fathers of PIJ. Tamimi, *Hamas: Unwritten Chapters*, 27; Meir Hatina, "Restoring a Lost Identity: Models of Education in Modern Islamic Thought," *British Journal of Middle Eastern Studies* 33, no. 2 (2006): 188.

[35] *Mā ba'd al-nakbatayn* (*After the two Catastrophes*), al-Shiqaqi is presumably referring to al-Tayyib's paper *al-ḥall al-islāmī wa mā ba'd al-nakbatayn* (*The Islamic Solution after the two Catastrophes*), which was frequently referenced by PIJ in its early years.

[36] Sir Hamilton Alexander Rosskeen Gibb (1895–1971), Scottish historian, orientalist, and Professor of Arabic at Harvard University.

[37] Richard P. Mitchell (1925–83), Professor of History and specialist in the history of the modern Middle East and North Africa. His most famous work was *The Society of the Muslim Brothers* (New York: Oxford University Press, 1969).

In its revival, the Islamic revolution sought to unite the Muslim with his identity and theory. It sought to reject the existing ignorance and the tyrants, who created the contradiction and crisis in the life of the individual and in Islamic society. For it carries an ideology and sees a completely different reality… the reality of injustice and inequality… The process of change in which unification will take place is organized in two cases, which are two sides of the same coin… The ideology as a divine, realistic, ethical, positive, and universal method that includes solutions to all problems of contemporary society. Yet, these solutions will remain the chatter of intellectuals in moments of ecstasy unless the masses arm themselves with them, move to implement them, fight for them, and rush into political conflicts for them.

Some, like the Shah of Iran and others, may imagine that these problems can be solved in the Islamic society once the objective conditions of the solution are met—or only some of them (Western capital and technology)—without taking the subjective conditions into account… These subjective conditions are witnessed in their absorption of the other side, the objective conditions, in order to achieve the renaissance. This subjective condition, which we intend to achieve, is the mobilization of the masses in any battle—whether battles of development or military jihad—through the Islamic revival of the umma; by getting rid of the Westernization currents; and by eliminating the phenomena of duplication, fabrication, and schizophrenia.

Here is the other side of the coin. It is the nature of Islamic thought's revolutionary formulation, the formulation with which, and through which, the Islamic movement is able to establish strong bridges with the Muslim masses. It does so, so that these masses understand the meaning of their connection with the Islamic movement and the role of this connection in preserving their history, heritage, and interests, and so that the Islamic body becomes one body, and if one of the limbs suffers, the whole body responds to it with wakefulness and fever, as the great prophet—peace and blessings be upon him—narrated.

The formulation process—which appears to have been successful in the Islamic movement in Iran, as we will see in the next and subsequent chapters—needs to adopt internal dialogue and criticism. Self-criticism is a first step on the road. The dialogue has so far been impeded by the Islamic movement's excessive sensitivity to criticism. Perhaps the secret lies in the falsehoods and lies spread about the Islamic movement, which were too great to be tolerated without a reaction. Yet, they were of an intensity sufficient to actually isolate this movement from the Muslim masses in particular. There were two important conditions for this atmosphere of lies:

1. The absence of the Islamic movement from the scene and its forced silence as a result of the arrests and liquidations.
2. The Arab and Muslim mind losing the critical sense at the stage of distortion and terrorism… This loss, which struck the social awareness of the umma at its core, hindered a correct vision, although temporarily. Perhaps one of the cheapest and most vicious lies fabricated was that of Refaat El-Saeed[38] in his book about

---

[38] Mohamed Rifat El-Saeed (1932–2017), Egyptian scholar and general-secretary of the Egyptian National Progressive Unionist Party. He was hostile to Islamism in general and the Muslim

the imam Hassan al-Banna (Madbouli Library—1988), which he dedicated to everyone working for a new era of enlightenment in Egypt and warding off the raids of the new Tatars... Especially what he concocted about the words of the martyr imam on the subject of consultation, pointing out succinctly that what he quoted could be found in the letter "Our problems in light of the Islamic system."

Nevertheless, I reiterate that this sensitivity should not prevent the first and most fundamental demand in the movement: namely, internal dialogue and self-criticism. This will surely lead to the creation of an atmosphere advancing scientific and analytical studies of the very reality the movement came to transform... It will also actualize another necessary issue: namely, the creation of an Islamic conception of the Islamic world's main problems, their nature, and their priorities. A unified program for action then starts identifying starting points and means, understanding the dialectical relationship between the two, and subsequently defining the final, direct, and indirect goals of the movement.

Chapter 2: Imam Khomeini: The Fighter and Intellectual

(1)

We will talk about the principles of Shiite thought and how it emerged, in the following chapter. We will also discuss the organizations of the Islamic movement and their role in another chapter. In this chapter, however, we will turn our attention to the thought of the Islamic movement through the thought of its leader, Imam Ayatollah Khomeini... This leader, whose name began to be heard by the Muslims and the world since the early 1960s as a symbol, inspirer, and leader of the Islamic revolution in Iran, which has become a great and unparalleled model in the history of human revolutions... Since the beginning of his life, the imam was an ambitious student of science, characterized by piety, devoutness, and asceticism... He began appearing in public and popular circles from the 1940s through the teaching sessions at the Faydiyya seminary[39] in Qom where thousands of students gathered around him... whom the imam did not manufacture as the dervishes[40] and murids did,[41] but, instead, prepared them as bases for protest and revolution.

Brotherhood in particular. Mohammad Zahid notes that "[El-Saeed's] opposition to political Islam marks much of his academic and scholarly output." Mohammed Zahid, *The Muslim Brotherhood and Egypt's Succession Crisis: The Politics of Liberalisation and Reform in the Middle East* (London: I.B. Tauris, 2012), 172.

[39] Faydiyya School, one of the most important schools of the Seminary of Qom, established in the Safavid era.

[40] Dervish (*Darwīsh*), ascetic Sufis dedicated to a life of prayer, meditation, and fasting in the pursuit of hidden or deeper guidance. See Oxford Islamic Online, "Dervish," http://www.oxfordislamicstudies.com/article/opr/t125/e523 [accessed: November 25, 2019].

[41] Murid (*murīd*), disciple in a Sufi order submitted to the authority of the murshid (Sufi master). See Oxford Islamic Online, "Murid," http://www.oxfordislamicstudies.com/article/opr/t125/e1622 [accessed: November 25, 2019].

Throughout the petrol crisis and the Mossadegh[42] government (1951), Imam Khomeini was close to the great Islamic leader Ayatollah Kashani.[43] Ayatollah Kashani was a man whose voice rang out across the world: "O British dogs... Leave the petrol to us and leave our country." It was he who was the spiritual pillar of Rashid Ali Gaylani's[44] revolution in Iraq in 1941. He, Gaylani, and the mufti of Palestine, al-Hajj Amin al-Husayni, formed a triad governing Baghdad in those days, and Kashani escorted Gaylani and al-Husayni to Iran when the revolution failed.

When a member of the Fada'iyan-e Islam,[45] the Muslim fedayee Khalil Tahmasebi,[46] assassinated the Iranian prime minister,[47] Ayatollah Kashani issued a statement in which he said: "The bullets wanting Razmara[48] dead were blessed and provided with the success granted by God." He then sent a provocative letter to the shah, stating:

He is the Glorified,

O son of Pahlavi

You must apologize to Khalil Tahmabesi for his trouble caused by the arrest. You must release him with honor and dignity within three days. All those responsible for his arrest will otherwise be subjected to the same punishment as that of Razmara. You have to release our holy men within these three days. If you do not, then you approach hell step by step.

It was Kashani who remained behind Mossadegh, who supported him, and even brought him to power. The story of the huge demonstration he led in Iran, when Ayatollah Kashani's house was surrounded by a fence of security personnel one day to prevent him from carrying out the demonstration in support of Mossadegh, is well known. Ayatollah Kashani then looked at his son, Mohammad Kashani, saying: "Bring me the shroud." So they came with the cloth he had prepared for his own coffin, and he then moved among his followers outside the house, surrounded by heavily armed security personnel. Everyone stood astonished and motionless in front of this shroud walking on two feet, and the security personnel forgot their mission before the splendor and solemnity of the scene. Ayatollah Kashani passed through, and the news

---

[42] Mohammad Mossadegh (1882–1967), prime minister of Iran from 1951 until 1953, when he and his government were overthrown in the 1953 Iranian coup d'état.
[43] Abol-Ghasem Kashani (1882–1962), Iraqi politician and Shiite marja' who served as speaker of parliament during Mossadegh, but later turned against him in the coup d'état of 1953 once Mossadegh attempted to dissolve the parliament. He supported and protected the Fada'iyan-e Islam in the 1950s.
[44] Rashid Ali Gaylani (1892–1965), Arab nationalist and prime minister of Iraq in three intermittent periods from 1933 until 1941.
[45] Fada'iyan-e Islam, a Shiite militant group founded in 1946 by Navvab Safavi, which commenced a series of assassinations against intellectuals and politicians to purify society of corrupting elements.
[46] Khalil Tahmasebi (1924–55), member of Fada'iyan-e Islam who assassinated Iranian prime minister Ali Razmara in 1951.
[47] Refers to the assassination of Iranian prime minister Ali Razmara.
[48] Hajj Ali Razmara (1901–51), Iranian prime minister from 1950 until his assassination in 1951.

spread in Teheran for the largest popular demonstration in the history of Iran to date to depart.

Before we again return to Imam Khomeini, we refer to what the American writer Robert Jackson[49] mentioned in his book about Hassan al-Banna:

> If this man, Hassan al-Banna, had lived long, much could have been achieved for this country. Especially if Hassan al-Banna and the Iranian leader, Ayatollah Kashani, had agreed to end the dispute between the Sunnis and the Shiites. The two men met in Hijaz in 1948, and they seemed to have reached an understanding and a key point had it not been for the assassination of al-Banna.

This quote indicates the necessity, importance, and gravity of such a rapprochement between Kashani and al-Banna, and what is required for rapprochement between Khomeini and the rest of the Islamic movements in the world today. One of al-Banna's followers commented on Jackson's words, saying: "What if he had realized al-Banna's role in this field (rapprochement), which there is no sufficient space to mention."

Indeed, Imam Khomeini, from a position near Ayatollah Kashani, watched and participated in all of the important events—prepared for the coming historical tasks... Imam Khomeini resisted the shah with all force and eagerness when the latter announced the White Revolution.[50] Khomeini did so to reveal the falsity of the revolution through his conviction the Iranian authorities were fundamentally linked to colonialism and subordinate to it. The Iranian authorities thus set out to move only according to the orders and directives of colonialism. He led the popular mass uprising on June 5, 1963...[51] in which the Muslim people offered thousands of martyrs who fell by the shah's bullets... The shah then met Khomeini who gave a harsh speech the shah's pride could not endure. Furious, the shah left, asking his security director to take the imam to Turkey where Khomeini stayed for approximately a year. Imam Khomeini then moved to Najaf in Iraq.

(2)

Besides, the Shiite multitude and scholars believe that their supreme leadership is divided between Imam Ayatollah Khomeini—who is followed by most Shiites in Iran,

---

[49] Robert Jackson, little information is available about Jackson, although numerous Islamist sources quote his description of Hassan al-Banna. According to Helbawy, Jackson met al-Banna in 1946 and wrote the book *Hassan Al Banna—The Qur'anic Man* (I have not found further references for this book). It is presumably this book al-Shiqaqi refers to as it was translated into Arabic by Anwar al-Jundi and published by *al-Mukhtār al-Islāmī* in 1977. See Kamal Helbawy, "The Muslim Brotherhood in Egypt: Historical Evolution and Future Prospects," in *Political Islam: Context versus Ideology*, ed. Khaled Hroub (London: Saqi, 2010), 69, ft. 10.

[50] The White Revolution (*Enqelāb-e Sefid*), a series of wide-reaching reforms implemented by the regime of Shah Reza Pahlavi from 1963 until 1979 with the aims of modernizing the economy and obtaining support from the Iranian working class and peasants as a bulwark against an increasingly hostile Iranian middle class.

[51] 1963 demonstrations in Iran, demonstrations on June 5–6, 1963, erupting after Shah Reza Pahlavi's arrest of Ayatollah Khomeini for his denouncement of the shah and of Israel.

Pakistan, India, and Afghanistan—and the religious marja',[52] Abu al-Qasim al-Khoei in Iraq…[53] Imam Khomeini represents the dynamic current, which desires to revive the Islamic religion as an ideology addressing all aspects of life by establishing an Islamic government. Abu al-Qasim al-Khoei, on the other hand, represents the traditional direction, which attempts to stay away from political battles.

Imam Khomeini starts from his understanding of Islam in its revolutionary holistic sense: "Islam is the religion of the mujahidin who strives for Truth and justice. The religion of those who demand freedom and independence, and of those who do not wish to give the unbelievers the upper hand over the believers." He attacks the perception colonialism attempted to incorporate in our country through a process of intellectual and military invasion, and the view that Islam has nothing to do with the organization of life and of society—the perception that Islam pertains only to menstruation and childbirth and that Islam may have an ethic, but that it has nothing to do with life and the organization of society beyond that. It is believed that this perception came through the colonial activity emerging three centuries ago because the greatest thing preventing them from achieving their goals—putting their political plans on the edge of a cliff about to collapse[54]—is Islam with its legal provisions, beliefs, and what people have of faith.

Sarcastically and vehemently, he attacks those he calls "pretenders of simple-minded holiness" among the clerics—those who portray Islam as a spiritual system irrelevant for politics or societal affairs. He asks for them to be considered enemies from within: "For they do not care about what is happening, and they interfere between the true scholars, taking over power, and taking control. They thus direct the greatest blow against Islam." He requests for cleansing the religious centers from the sultan's jurists and preachers as he calls them, and dismisses them saying:

> These ones are not scholars… Some of them have been dressed up with turbans by the security and intelligence services in order to pray for the sultan and to invoke His blessings and mercy upon him. They must be exposed, for they are enemies of Islam. Society must renounce them, for the victory of Islam and the cause of Muslims lie in their renouncement and contempt. Our youth and our sons must grab the turbans from above their heads. I do not say kill them… But at least grab their turbans.

---

[52] Marja', sometimes marja' al-taqlid, highest authority in Twelver Shiism and applied to between four and eight high-ranking jurists. The title was after 1970 held by Ayatollah Khomeini and Ayatollah Abu al-Qasim al-Khoei, mentioning only some. See Oxford Islamic Online, "Marja al-Taqlid," http://www.oxfordislamicstudies.com/article/opr/t125/e1437 [accessed: November 25, 2019].

[53] Abu al-Qasim al-Khoei (1899–1992), Iranian Shiite scholar, and recognized as one of the most influential Twelver marja' and spiritual leader of Shiites until his death in 1992. He was succeeded by Ali al-Sistani.

[54] Al-Shiqaqi uses the expression "'alā shafā jurufin hārin" ("on the edge of a cliff about to collapse"), which presumably refers to sūrat al-tawba: 109. "Then is one who laid the foundation of his building on righteousness [with fear] from God and [seeking] His approval better or one who laid the foundation of his building on the edge of a cliff about to collapse, so it collapsed with him into the fire of Hell? And God does not guide the wrongdoing people."

As Khomeini said in a statement issued on July 27, 1978:[55]

> The esteemed imams of the community must call upon the faithful preachers; those eager for the Islamic movement; and those with lofty goals in order to assume the responsibility of raising the people's awareness. They must strongly avoid the call of the "preachers of the sultans" and of people who protect the interests of the system by knowingly or unbeknownst choose issues that distract the people from the major contemporary causes.

Imam Khomeini assumes a wonderful Islamic and revolutionary position when he stands up to some of the Shiites who sit down waiting for the Mahdi to establish the rule of Islam and fill the land with justice after it having been filled with injustice and oppression. As some of them say: Sin should be spread to usher in the appearance of the Mahdi…[56] Meaning, if vile deeds are not spread, then the Mahdi will never emerge. Khomeini responds, saying:

> The great occultation of our Mahdi Imam has lasted for more than a thousand years, and a thousand more years may pass before the matter demands the arrival of the expected imam… Are the legal provisions of Islam left abandoned? Can people do whatever they want in the meantime? Does that not cause civil disorders and wars? The laws that the Prophet of Islam complied with for twenty-three years, peace and blessings be upon him, and the efforts to spread them, elucidate them, and implement them… was all of that only for a limited time? Did God restrict the age of Islamic law to two hundred years, for example? Should Islam lose everything after the minor occultation? This view is in my opinion worse than believing that Islam is abrogated.[57]

No one believing in God and the Last Day can say that he is not required to defend the homeland or that it is permissible for him to refrain from paying zakat, from the five pillars, or from anything else. He cannot say that the criminal law in Islam is suspended or that restorative justice[58] and financial compensation[59] are frozen.

---

[55] Al-Shiqaqi dates the statement to the "21 sha'ban last year" (Hijri calendar), as this booklet was published in early 1979 (al-Shiqaqi was arrested by Egyptian authorities in February that year because of it), we may assume that the date "21 sha'ban 1398," corresponds to July 27, 1978 (Gregorian calendar).

[56] The occultation, the "hidden" state of the twelfth Shiite Imam; when the twelfth imam disappeared (the minor occultation) it was believed he still communicated with the four subsequent imams. Yet, once it was beyond any doubt that he could not be alive, the Greater Occultation commenced when Shiite jurists were recognized as his agents. See in particular Haider, *Shī'ī Islam: An Introduction*, Chapter 7, "Twelver Shī'ism and the Problem of the Hidden Imām."

[57] "*bi-an al-islām mansūkh*" ("that the religion is abrogated"), derived from *naskh* (abrogation) related to Islamic legal exegesis (*tafsīr*) attempting to solve contradictory rulings of Islamic revelation (the Qur'an and hadith) by superseding or canceling earlier revelations. See Oxford Islamic Online, "Naskh," http://www.oxfordislamicstudies.com/article/opr/t125/e1721 [accessed: November 25, 2019].

[58] Restorative justice (*qiṣāṣ*), prescribed for "murder, voluntary manslaughter, involuntary killing, intentional physical harm, and unintentional physical injury." In cases of voluntary harm (killing or injury), the victim or kin of victim may "waive retribution and exact monetary compensation." See Oxford Islamic Online, "Qisas," http://www.oxfordislamicstudies.com/article/opr/t125/e1931 [accessed: November 25, 2019].

[59] Financial compensation (*diyāt*), payment of blood money in murder cases.

Therefore, anyone who supports the view that there is no need to form Islamic governance also denies the need to implement the Islamic legal provisions. He calls for suspending and freezing them, and therefore denies the completeness and immortality of the true Islamic religion.

Khomeini considers knowledge of law and justice the most important pillars of the imam, and says: "It is the opinion of the Shiites that he who is entitled to lead the people has been known since the death of the Prophet, peace and blessings be upon him, and until the time of the occultation. The Imam is thus the superior legal expert for them in enforcing the legal provisions, laws, and justice, who is fair regardless of the blame of a critic." He then writes on page 19: "The Caliph is not a messenger of laws; nor is he a legislator. Rather, the Caliph is intended for their implementation." Then on page 28: "For the glorious Qur'an and the virtuous sunna contain all legal provisions and regulations that make man happy and predispose him to wholeness."

Regarding Muslim unity, Imam Khomeini sees the necessity of the Islamic country's unity, which colonialism divided and whose people were turned into nations. He thus sees the Ottoman Empire as a united state fought by colonialism: "With the emergence of the Ottoman Empire as a unified state, the colonialists sought to fragment it. So Russia, Britain, and their partners made an alliance and fought the Ottomans. They then shared the spoils, as you know." Although he is more critical of the Ottoman rulers, Imam Khomeini nevertheless believes colonialism feared some reformers' arrival to power: "It dispelled all the hopes of the colonialists and their dreams. It was for this reason they divided the country into several micro-states soon after the First World War ended and made each of them their client."

He believes that the solution then was to impose jihad on all male and female Muslims in defense of the Ottoman Empire when the British armies entered Basra in Iraq... Imam Khomeini believes that the means to unite the umma is the overthrow of the client governments "and subsequently seek to establish our Islamic government. This will in turn be crowned with success the day it is able to destroy the heads of betrayal and smash the idols and tyrants spreading oppression and corruption on earth." The imam discusses at length as he looks for evidence for the necessity of forming the government based on the Qur'an and the sunna, which leads to the prohibition of non-Islamic litigation of the judges of oppression,[60] as he calls them.

When he discusses the Islamic government, he shows that it does not resemble any known forms of governance, for the head of state is not free to rule tyrannically. The form of Islamic government is, instead, constitutional, although not in the traditional sense of the word... which means a parliamentary system or popular councils. Rather, it is in the sense of restricting those responsible with a set of rules and conditions set out in the Qur'an and the sunna. It is, however, the representatives of the people and God who legislate and codify the constitutional systems. For the authority to legislate

---

[60] The people of oppression (*ḥukkām al-jawr*), also described as judges of oppression, often referring to the law of the state (the law of judges) as opposed to sacred law (the law of jurists). See Said Amir Arjomand, *The Shadow of God and the Hidden Imam: Religion, Political Order, and Societal Change in Shi'ite Iran from the Beginning to 1890* (Chicago and London: The University of Chicago Press, 1987), 50–1.

in Islam is exclusively that of God Almighty. No one has the right to legislate and no one has the right to rule by what God has given no power. For this reason, Islam replaced the legislative council with another one for ruling. The government of Islam is a government of law, and the ruler is God alone. It is not a monarchy, a Shahanshahi system,[61] or an empire immersed in opulence and luxury.

Yet, how does one form an Islamic government? It is the path of struggle: "For ideas commence small before they grow. The people then gather around them, gain strength, and then take matters into their own hands." Imam Khomeini thus believes that the Islamic movement should coalesce with the mass bases and work persistently to raise their awareness; to enlighten them; and to expose the methods and ways used to deceive them, absorb their wrath, and make them sell out their causes. We see this in the statement published on September 18[62] to mark the Khurasan earthquake[63] last year:

> O all of our Muslim masses in Iran, beware of the means of the authorities. Do not allow earthquakes, floods, and the like to dissuade you from your path... Do not listen to the propaganda trumpets of the Shah. Continue your Islamic revolution until the overthrow of the authoritarian regime based on the humiliation and oppression of the people. The clergy must—at a time when the Shah exploits the earthquake to make the people ignore their cause—assume their momentous religious responsibility in raising the people's awareness about these despicable methods... The politicians, intellectuals, and academics must fulfill their Islamic mission and not allow the authorities to dissuade them from revolution or extinguish its flame.

When the shah tried to introduce some formal Islamic changes in order to pull the rug from under the clerics' feet through the ministry of Jafar Sharif-Emami,[64] Imam Khomeini exposed it in a statement issued on August 27, 1978, in which he stated:

> As for closing gambling clubs, then it is a matter of no value as it is merely another trick to mislead the wing of clerics... But they close the gambling clubs with respect for Islam! All the while other centers of whoredom remain in their place!! Oppression, murder, and plunder remains normal for the hangmen of the Shah,

---

[61] Shahanshahi, often translated into "imperial." Yet, as the shah described it: "the meaning of the western term Imperial is simply political and geographic, whereas from the Iranian perspective, the term Shahanshahi has more than the normal meaning, it has a spiritual, philosophical, symbolic, and to a great extent, a sentimental aspect, in other words, just as it has a rational and thoughtful relevance, so too it has a moral and emotional dimension." Quoted in Ali M. Ansari, *Modern Iran: The Pahlavis and After*, 2nd ed. (Harlow: Pearson Education lmt., 2007), 238.
[62] Al-Shiqaqi dates the statement to the "15 shawwāl last year" (Hijri calendar). I have consequently interpreted the date as "15 shawwāl 1398," which corresponds to September 18, 1978 (Gregorian calendar).
[63] Al-Shiqaqi presumably refers to the 1978 Tabas earthquake in the South Khorasan Province of Iran, which caused the deaths of approximately 20,000 people.
[64] Jafar Sharif-Emami (1912–98), Iranian prime minister from 1960 until 1961, and in 1978. He also served as the president of the Iranian senate, of the Pahlavi Foundation, and of the Iran chamber of industries and mines under Shah Reza Pahlavi.

despite the laws of Islam and the verses of the Holy Qur'an!! They claim to give you freedom all the while the best and dearest sons of Islam and of Iran remain in the prisons and detention centers under royal torture or live in exile!!

Imam Khomeini succeeded with these methods, and the cassette tapes and his publications became the daily bread for the Muslim masses in Iran. He focused on the Word of God and the call in the role of revival, saying ten years earlier:

> You have neither state nor army today, but you do have the call. For your enemy has not taken away from you the ability [of] inviting others to Islam, guidance, and conveyance of the Message. We must seek to lay the cornerstone of the rightful Islamic state. We thus call, demonstrate our ideas, issue our instructions, and win over supporters and followers. We find waves of conscious direction and coordinated guidance for the masses to get a collective reaction leading to a situation in which the aware crowds of Muslims committed to their religion are fully prepared to carry out the burdens of forming an Islamic government.

The imam calls for focusing on the ranks of academics in the call, for they are the most receptive and with the greatest hostility against despotism, treason, betrayal, and the plundering of wealth and resources… He also calls for taking advantage of the benefits offered by Islam, which are only afforded non-Muslims with great difficulty, such as the congregational prayer,[65] hajj,[66] and Friday prayers:

> We will have to consider these gatherings as a golden opportunity to serve the principle and conviction of publicly explaining the beliefs, legal provisions, and regulations. We must thus take advantage of the hajj season and reap the best fruits in the call for unity and for the arbitration of Islam. We must examine our problems and discover what radical solutions Islam has proposed for them.

Then, on page 125:

> O sons of Islam, be strong and be tough when proclaiming your argument to the people in order to overcome your enemy with all his weapons, military, and guards. Explain the truth to the masses and incite them. Inflame the merchant, the man of the street, the worker, the peasant, and the academic with the spirit of jihad… Everyone will embark upon jihad.

We see a vibrant reality in the streets of Iran from these words of Imam Khomeini ten years ago… we witness it as it has paid off and borne fruit in every citizen…This correspondent from one of the American magazines thus asks a normal citizen why

---

[65] Congregational prayer (*ṣalāt al-jamā'a*), prayer carried out in a congregation composing parallel rows behind the chosen leader of prayer.
[66] Pilgrimage (*ḥajj*), annual pilgrimage to Mecca in Saudi Arabia.

his son does not go to school, so the Muslim citizen replies: "What school is this? Why does he not go to be martyred in the cause of his religion?"

If the martyr imam Sayyid Qutb already called for this revival process and understood how long and arduous it is, he announced: "I know that the distance between the attempt at revival and taking power is vast." Imam Khomeini therefore took this into account when he said: "We do not expect our instructions and efforts to pay off in a short time for cementing the pillars of Islamic governance requires considerable time and tireless effort."

He warns the Muslim youth and masses of the lies of colonialism and its clients when the latter attempt to persuade us that politics is wicked, malicious, and deceptive to distract us from it, so that they can abuse the affairs of the umma as they please. He calls upon the Muslim youth to come out from their seclusion, to complete their study programs, and overcome the difficulties in order to plan for the Islamic governance coming after removing the unjust government, which Imam Khomeini believes will happen after the process of proselytization and revival through

1. Resisting the institutions of the unjust government.
2. Ending cooperation with it.
3. Abstaining from any work benefiting it.
4. Establishing new judicial, financial, economic, political, and cultural institutions.

* * *

There is an important cause remaining in the thought of Imam Khomeini and in the practice of the Islamic movement in Iran, namely the position on the cause of Palestine… This position, from a tactical and strategic awareness, is particularly important and has considerable impact. It is a position that must be reflected upon by the rest of the Islamic movements from which they must take a lesson and example—not just on a theoretical level but also on the level of practice and application… For remaining trapped on the theoretical level is a form of evasion allowing all thought to remain crude and unstructured so that its role remains to perform in an unhealthy manner.

Imam Khomeini has understood the nature and role of colonialism and of the modern Western challenge for Islam and the intellectual invasion that followed… He simultaneously realized that Israel is the de facto embodiment of this challenge. Israel is the very appearance of the challenge in its most extreme form as the Islamic intellectual Tawfiq al-Tayyib says:

> For here we are not confronting the culture of the West in a particular current, but rather confronting it in the Western man himself… We are confronting the modern Western civilization in its thought, ethics, and perception. We are not confronting it in the form of peaceful dialogue, but in the form of a violent clash… For we are not confronting it as a culture, but rather as a human block… As an occupation with which we have established two inevitable possibilities: land or war. And land means here the history and the people.

The Islamic intellectual Tawfiq al-Tayyib then proceeds by stating that "Islam as a creed and the Arabs as a people are facing their fate. The touchstone is Palestine." This is exactly what Imam Khomeini and Professor Abul Ala' al-Mawdudi in Pakistan understood when declaring that Palestine must be the axis of the Islamic movement.

It was here that the relationship between the Islamic movement in Iran and Palestine came into existence... Although this relationship cannot be fully explored in this book, we may perhaps point out some of its various aspects. The Islamic movement has always accused the shah of working for, and supporting, Israel. Imam Khomeini writes in his book *The Islamic Government*: "The Shah's regime... procures Phantom Airplanes whose pilots are to be trained by the Israelis while Israel is in a state of war with the Muslims. Thus, everyone who assists and supports it, is by virtue of his role in a state of war with the Muslims." While some of the Islamic movement's cadres were trained in the camps of the Palestinian revolution with a close cooperation between the two parties, Imam Khomeini declared his support for the armed struggle. He declared in his historical fatwa that working to remove the Zionist entity is an obligation; he stated: "The Islamic countries and the Muslim public must remove the element of corruption—Israel—and not fail in their support of the revolutionaries. They must pay zakat and other alms in this crucial matter."

When colonialism and the separationists in Lebanon attempted to liquidate the Palestinian revolution, Imam Khomeini issued a call in which he revealed the dimensions of the conspiracy and affirmed the necessity of providing support for the resistance... In the October War of 1973[67] he issued two statements impelling the Islamic people and countries to assist the Arab people in the confrontation with the usurping Zionist enemy. He cautioned the leaders of the Islamic countries against the bacteria of Zionist corruption in the heart of the Islamic countries, and he called upon them to cut the oil off from the countries supporting the Zionists in the face of Israel's brutal aggression against their Arab and Muslim brothers. He also urged the Iranian Muslim people against neutrality, and he called on them to strike the American and Israeli interests. Then, in a letter to Yasser Arafat on September 19, 1978, he said: "We always differ with the Shah in his policies and his position on the Palestinian cause, just as we fight Israel and its followers... We meet you in your revolution against them."

Imam Khomeini accused Israel of partaking in the suppression of the Islamic revolution in Iran. In a statement on September 18, 1978, he stated: "Those who mowed down the sons of Islam and the followers of the Holy Qur'an with machine gun fire, as is well known, they mobilized the Israeli commandos to kill the brave and defenseless masses." And then...

This is a glimpse of the thought of Imam Khomeini and the Islamic movement in Iran, and we will talk about the Islamic organization itself in a subsequent chapter. Before ending this chapter, I would like to point out that the Islamic revolution in Iran is an Islamic revolution in the broad Qur'anic sense of the term... It is not a revolution of one sect without the other. The commonalities between the Sunni and Shiite

---

[67] The Yom Kippur War, also known as the Arab-Israeli War of 1973, fought from October 6–25 between the State of Israel and a coalition of Arab states following a joint surprise attack by the latter.

Muslims are almost—indeed, they are—the body of this revolution, commencing with its starting points, objectives, means, and motivations… The contentious disputes between the Sunnis and the Shiites about the imamate of the Twelver Shiites, and the infallibility[68] of the imams, do not constitute—neither positively nor negatively—any impact on the nature and course of the revolution.

☪

---

[68] Moral infallibility (*'iṣma*), a characteristic of prophets and imams in Shiite theology. Sunnis interpret the concept of *'iṣma* as the moral infallibility of Prophets before or after receiving God's revelation, as they are unable to intentionally commit a sin. See Norah Sonya Elamir, "The Theological Concept of *'Iṣma* from the Early to Modern Period of Islam" (Master's thesis, The University of Texas at Austin, 2016).

11

The Sunni and the Shiite

A Fabricated and Regrettable Pandemonium

Published in al-Ṭalīʿa al-Islāmiyya *(The Islamic Vanguard), no. 0, December 1982 (pages unknown), written by Fathi al-Shiqaqi.*

PIJ is in many ways perceived as one of the least compromising Palestinian factions. No negotiations, no two-state solution, no compromises, and only armed struggle can liberate Palestine from the river to the sea. Yet, the movement is also perceived by many in the Occupied Palestinian Territories as a moderate player, as it stresses the need for intra-Palestinian dialogue, in times of conflict and the necessity of avoiding strife, and with its calls for conciliation between Sunnis and Shiites.

This piece was, as so many others, written in times of bitter conflict with the Palestinian Muslim Brotherhood. It is far from the most innovative work of al-Shiqaqi, as he largely relies on the work of others—particularly on Muslim Brotherhood intellectuals. Indeed, al-Shiqaqi often provides mere sentences and bridges between quotations. Yet, these references are all but coincidental. As the PIJ founding fathers perceived the Iranian revolution to be one of the first successful strikes against the Western colonial project, they hoped for its revolutionary fervor to spread to the rest of the Islamic lands, which would lead to the eventual liberation and pride of Muslims. It was thus a duty for all to support the revolution so that it would not remain isolated. This support was not given by the Palestinian Brotherhood, however. Feeling threatened by the prospects of the PIJ nucleus pulling the rug from under its feet, the Brotherhood in Gaza accused it of being Shiite in disguise and proclaimed that the Iranian revolution was a non-Islamic one—at least in the narration of Fathi al-Shiqaqi and of PIJ. Consequently, the question that al-Shiqaqi poses between the lines is the following: "If the other branches of the Muslim Brotherhood—as in Egypt—and the other Islamic movements support the Iranian revolution, then why cannot you do the same?"

This document matters for three reasons. First, this is a historical document illustrating the conflict between PIJ and the Muslim Brotherhood in Gaza. Second, the document is important because it adds another facet to the movement's support for the Iranian revolution and the Khomeinist regime. Third, the document matters because it shows the conciliatory features of a movement that is often perceived as one of the most uncompromising factions in the Palestinian resistance. Yet, only strength through unity can defeat colonialism. As al-Shiqaqi writes later: "The umma will realize that the strife [between Sunni and Shiite] is fabricated and that colonialism wishes to isolate the Muslim people, so that they in the end confront their hangmen individually."

The Islamic homeland has been confronted by the modern Western challenge since the beginning of the nineteenth century... The challenge produced by the bourgeois industrial revolution and the old crusader hatred as the French campaign formed its first vanguard. This challenge overthrew our political system as represented in the Caliphate, occupied our land, and continued invading us morally, intellectually, and spiritually—proposing its emaciated secular alternatives... More than thirty years ago, this challenge achieved one of its most significant tasks when the Jewish state was established in the heart of the Islamic homeland, on the one hand, and when it brought its clients and apprentices to the power it had usurped, on the other.

This was formed through a dialectical, foul system... Consecrating the challenge could therefore be achieved only by establishing Israel. The establishment of the latter required the overthrow of the Caliphate, and its continuation required governing systems in the Islamic homeland that were clients and followers of colonialism. They are thus colonialism's natural and logical product, and they are the one face of the evil deed, while Israel is the other.

Thus commenced these matters and the Western challenge thought until just a few years ago that it had delivered its final, lethal blows to the collapsed (!) Islamic civilization... until the Islamic revolution in Iran aimed its first arrows at the West and achieved the first victory for Islam in the modern era. Life returned to this body, which they presumed had become a stiff corpse... Yet here it awakens anew and rises gloriously and youthfully... From where? From where their Satanic influence was the firmest, strongest, and fiercest that was... We have discovered ourselves and here we rise after two centuries of degradation and humiliation—after two centuries of backwardness and ignorance.

Here the Islamic revolution moves forward to outline several concepts, which are as follows:

1. The fright of the great states and powers vanished from everyone's minds—particularly the Muslims and oppressed of the world.
2. The revolution presented a new civilizational model and design for humanity after the Western model was put in the dock. The famous French thinker Roger Garaudy[1] says: "Khomeini put the growth model of the West in the dock." He then notes: "Khomeini gave meaning to the lives of the Iranians."
3. It affirmed the historical role that revolutionary Islam will play in the lives of the region's people after more than a century of trying to remove Islam from power and influence.

However, do the West and its collaborators leave the revolution to continue its course... as it throws obstacles in its way and destroys its power? Will they keep silent about the

---

[1] Roger Garaudy (1913–2012), French communist philosopher who converted to Islam in 1982.

joy that inhabited the umma as if it were rain finally befalling the barren land? Will they allow this Islamic aspiration, ignited by the revolution, to spread?

The uprising of this Muslim people and their impossible revolution struck them with terror. So they tried hard to stand between the revolutionary Islamists and their attainment of power, and they moved on several different and interlocking axes when they failed:

1. They commenced stirring up different minorities—taking advantage of what they called the stage of chaos, which the revolution experienced.
2. Supporting the Iranian opposition groups… both remnants of the royal family and the SAVAK,[2] or some of the secular organizations carrying arms to fight the revolution.
3. Carrying out the economic and political siege, led by America and western Europe, as clearly demonstrated during the spy hostage crisis.[3]
4. Launching an external invasion by using Saddam Hussein and the Iraqi army, subjugated under its command.
5. Stirring strife between the wings of the Muslim umma—Sunnis and Shiites—in a last attempt to besiege the revolutionary tide and to prevent its influence from reaching Sunni areas, whether those rich with oil, or those facing Israel.

The plots continued… While the minorities' rebellion was crushed with firmness; while the fragments of the royalists and miserable remnants of the secular opposition were eliminated; and while the revolution faced a blockade to the extent that the imam regarded it as auspicious, and he told the students walking his path: "We did not embark upon the revolution to fill our stomachs." This is why they will never succeed in silencing us when they threaten to impose famine upon us. We have risen for Islam as Muhammad—peace be upon him—did at the beginning of the first movement. We have not yet suffered anything compared to what the Prophet—peace be upon him—suffered and faced as he then said: "As long as you are not isolated, your heads will not work."

Regarding the foreign invasion, then, pain, distress, and crushing defeat has returned to the hearts of its perpetrators. Yet, it must be acknowledged that the plot's fifth axis has achieved some success in fomenting strife between Sunnis and Shiites despite all of this, although only for a while, as the umma will quickly notice any Satan breathing into the fire of strife. The umma will realize that the strife is fabricated, and that colonialism wishes to isolate the Muslim people, so that they in the end confront their hangmen individually.

Some of them have launched a suspicious and surprising campaign against the Islamic revolution, which they finally discovered was a "Shiite revolution"; that "the Shiites are a sect astray or infidel"; and that Ayatollah Khomeini, who they say shook

---

[2] SAVAK (National Organization for Security and Intelligence), secret police during the reign of the Iranian Pahlavi dynasty until the Iranian revolution in 1979.
[3] The Iran hostage crisis (November 4, 1979–January 20, 1981) developed as fifty-two American diplomats and citizens were kept hostage at the American embassy in Teheran for 444 days following the Iranian revolution.

the throne while sitting on his rug, has become a "misguided infidel," too (!). The sight of the young Muslim (!) who carries a Saudi book full of fallacies and fabrications began being repeated in front of us. He carries it from mosque to mosque explaining to people and preaching his delusions… I realize that some of these young men are moving in good faith, though delusional, believing that they work for God just as it is understood that the road to hell is paved with such good intentions… So when will those young men realize that they in good faith are carrying out colonial plans, and that they must save themselves before it is too late. The position of some of the Islamists against the revolution obliges the umma to oppose the position of doubt and suspicion among them… from their starting points, their motives, and purposes.

Their peculiar stance even puts the Islamic movement in a serious predicament it had never experienced before as the performance of the revolution in the ranks of the Islamic movement deprives them of their justification for existence, and the real movement has no choice but to expel them eventually.

Those who want to kill the illustrious Iranian model in the Muslim personality and in this occupied homeland in particular are only killing themselves. For they stand in front of the trajectory of advancing history and confront an Islamic revolution led by an imam who is "the pride of Islam and of the Muslims" as stated in one of the declarations of the International Organization of the Muslim Brotherhood.

I do not know if it was strange or not what a young Muslim told me, who had visited more than one Islamic country. For he said he could not find anything uglier than this attack against the revolution as that by some "Islamists" in this occupied homeland, while he could not find anyone more welcoming and enthusiastic about the revolution than the Palestinian people.

After the introduction of this study, I seek to present some important facts for the Muslims in general and the bases of the Islamic movement in particular. I will not try to formulate an independent judgment in a legal or theological question in order to say that Shiites and Sunnis are brothers in Islam, that their differing interpretations of the Qur'an and the sunna do not affect their brothers, and that one of them, in the eyes of the other, does not depart from Islam. I will also not attempt to cite the legal evidence,[4] which is not concluded with the sincerity of this clear and definite written statement—for this is another area of research to which we are obliged in this time in which ignorance and hateful partisan intolerance prevail… I will, however, address the issue from another angle, and it is an attempt to present the positions and opinions of the Muslim leaders, intellectuals, and scholars, many of whom the Islamic movements agree with and consider leaders.

I understand very well that the position of some of the Islamic movement's bases against the revolution and the fabricated pandemonium about the Sunnis and Shiites is not a radical and genuine position, but a sudden position imposed by others (!) on this faithful and pure youth after being put in a spiral of doubt and despair. Finally, he

---

[4] Al-Shiqaqi's point in this paragraph is to emphasize that he is not engaging in independent reasoning (*ijtihād*) when delving into the issue of strife between the Sunnis and Shiites because, essentially, he is not a *mujtahid* (someone exercising independent reasoning, and who must have training in the schools of Islamic law). While "legal evidence" (*al-adilla al-shar'iyya*) is an appropriate translation, it also refers to the four Sunni schools of jurisprudence (*madhhab*).

discovers that the revolution that ignited his hopes is not an Islamic revolution but a Shiite one, that the Shiites are "infidels"... This is Muhibb al-Din al-Khatib, the author of the infamous Saudi book, which was reprinted in this country with "5000 copies"!!!⁵ Here he presents proof after proof of their infidelity, straying from the right path, and their deviation from Islam: "They have a Qur'an other than the one in our hands," and other delusions and nonsense.

Mr. Khatib, whose fallacious and misguided ideas some propagate while neglecting the ideas contradicting the leading Islamic authorities in their own movements... He who fought the Islamic Caliphate, so he worked with one of the Arab nationalist movements—the Vanguard of Arab Youth—and when his plot was detected in 1905 when he was in Astana for his education, al-Khatib fled to Yemen.⁶ When al-Sharif Hussein announced the Arab revolution, he joined it, and the Caliphate subsequently sentenced him to death. Al-Khatib did not return to Damascus except before the Turkish defeat and the entry of the Arab (!) army into the city, where he took management of their first Arabic newspaper, *The Capital*.⁷

We now return to the attempt at reviewing the positions and opinions of the Islamic movements and the Islamic intellectuals on this unlawful strife and this fabricated and regrettable pandemonium.

The martyr imam Hassan al-Banna... pioneer of the contemporary Islamic movement, he is one of the pioneers who embodied the idea of reconciliation between the Shiites and the Sunnis. He was thus one of the contributors in the work of the Group of Reconciliation between the Islamic Legal Schools, which some perceived as impossible.⁸ Al-Banna, a group of Islamic leaders, and its great sheikhs, on the other hand, thought this was possible. They agreed that all Muslims (Sunnis and Shiites) would meet around the agreed beliefs and principles, and that they would tolerate each other in matters beyond that, which were not a condition of faith, a pillar of the religion, or that which was not denied as required by the religion.

---

5   Muhibb al-Din al-Khatib (1886–1969), Syrian Salafi intellectual, infamous for his anti-Shiite positions. Indeed, it is plausible that the book al-Shiqaqi refers to is his *al-khuṭūṭ al-ʿarīḍa* (*Broad Outlines*), a pamphlet described as "seething with hatred, in which he describes the Shiʿa as another religion (*din*)." Werner Ende, "Sunni Polemical Writings on the Shiʿa and the Iranian Revolution," in *The Iranian Revolution and the Muslim World*, ed. David Menashri (Boulder: Westview Press, 1990), 227.

6   Here, al-Shiqaqi seems to confuse the biographical entries of Muhibb al-Din al-Khatib. For example, al-Khatib did not cooperate with, or form, an organization called the Vanguard of Arab Youth (*ṭalāʾiʿ al-shabāb al-ʿarabī*), but he *did* form a secret society called the Arab Renaissance Society (*jamʿiyyat al-nahḍa al-ʿarabiyya*). Further, he *was* put under surveillance by Ottoman authorities, but al-Khatib was at that time in Istanbul, which made him leave the city. Yet, he only did so in October 1907, and he left for Damascus. As Damascus proved to be equally dangerous for al-Khatib, he went to Yemen, where he accepted the post of translator at the British consulate in Hudayda. See Sayyid Muhammad Rizvi, "Muhibb al-Din al-Khatib: A Portrait of a Salafi-Arabist" (Master's thesis, Simon Fraser University, 1991), 22–24.

7   *The Capital* (*al-ʿāṣima*) was an official biweekly newspaper, published in Damascus one year after the end of the First World War.

8   The Group of Reconciliation between the Islamic Legal Schools (*jamāʿat al-taqrīb bayn al-madhāhib al-islāmiyya*), a group organized in Cairo in 1947.

Abd al-Karim al-Shirazi writes about the Group of Reconciliation in the book *Islamic Unity*—consisting of articles of both Shiite and Sunni scholars published in the magazine *Islam's Message*, issued by al-Azhar:

> They agreed that a Muslim is he who believes in God as the Lord, and Muhammad as a prophet and a messenger, and that there was neither a prophet nor a messenger after him. He is a Muslim, he who believes in the Qur'an as the Book, the kaaba as a *qibla* and a veiled abode, and in the five determined pillars. He is a Muslim, he who has faith in resurrection, and in the knowledge of what is required in religion.

It was these five pillars, which we mentioned exclusively, that were the locus of agreement between the two groups, representatives of the Sunnis with their four established Islamic legal schools, and representatives of the Shiites with their two Islamic legal schools, Zaydism[9] and Twelver Shiism.[10] The sheikh of al-Azhar and the high reference for fatwas at the time participated in this group—the grand imam Abd al-Majid Salim,[11] the imam Mustafa Abd al-Raziq,[12] and Sheikh Mahmud Shaltut.[13]

We do not have accurate information about the particular role assigned to the martyr imam al-Banna in this affair. Yet, one of the intellectuals in the Muslim Brotherhood, Professor Salim al-Bahnasawi,[14] suggests in his book *The Tradition Being Falsified*: "Cooperation existed between the Muslim Brotherhood and the Shiites from the foundation of the Group of Reconciliation between the Islamic Legal Schools, in which imam al-Banna and imam al-Qomi partook. This led to the visit of imam Navvab Safavi to Cairo in 1954."[15] Al-Bahnasawi writes subsequently on the same page: "This is no wonder as the programs of the two groups led to this cooperation."

It is well known that imam al-Banna met the Shiite cleric Ayatollah Kashani during hajj in 1948, and an agreement was reached between them. One of the most important Muslim Brotherhood figures today and a student of the martyr imam referred to this.

---

[9] Zaydism, one of the main Shiite sects emerging in the eighth century, and the second largest after Twelver Shiism, mainly found in Yemen. Named after Zayd ibn Ali, grandson of Husayn ibn Ali, Zaydism does not promote the infallibility (*'iṣma*) of the imams and has several traces of Ibadism and Mu'tazilism.

[10] Twelver Shiism, largest branch of Shiism. The name refers to the twelve imams as the successors of Prophet Muhammad, and that the last imam, Muhammad al-Mahdi, lives in occultation in order to reappear as the mahdi. Believing in the infallibility (*'iṣma*) of the imams, they do not merely rule with justice, but have the capability of interpreting Islamic law and the meaning of the Qur'an.

[11] Abd al-Majid Salim (1882–1954), Mufti of Egypt and subsequently appointed to the Fatwa Council of al-Azhar. Salim was one of the leading forces behind the Group of Reconciliation between the Islamic Legal Schools. See Jakob Skovgaard-Petersen, *Defining Islam for the Egyptian State: Muftis and Fatwas of the Dār al-Iftā* (Leiden: Brill, 1997), 160–3.

[12] Mustafa Abd al-Raziq (1885–1947), Egyptian Islamic philosopher, follower of Muhammad Abduh, and rector of al-Azhar.

[13] Mahmud Shaltut (1893–1963), Egyptian Sunni religious scholar and disciple of Muhammad Abduh. Shaltut became Grand Imam of al-Azhar from 1958 until 1963.

[14] Salim al-Bahnasawi (d. 2006), Egyptian jurist and Muslim Brotherhood intellectual.

[15] Navvab Safavi (1924–56), Iranian Shiite cleric and founder of Fada'iyan-e Islam (Fedayeen of Islam). Taking part in assassinations, including those of Abdolhossein Hazhir, Haj Ali Razmara, and Ahmad Kasravi, Safavi was arrested and executed after the failed attempt to kill Iranian prime minister Hosein Ala'.

He is professor Abd al-Muta'al al-Jabri, who writes in his book *Why Hassan al-Banna Was Assassinated*, quoting Robert Jackson:

> If the life of this man (he means Hassan al-Banna) had been longer it would have been possible to gain many benefits for this land, especially in the agreement between al-Banna and Ayatollah Kashani, the Iranian leader, to uproot the discord between the Sunnis and Shiites... The two men met in Hijaz in 1948, and it appears that they conferred with each other and reached a basic understanding, but Hasan al-Banna was quickly assassinated.

Professor al-Jabri comments on this, saying: "Jackson believed, and perceived with his political sense, the efforts of the imam [al-Banna] in bringing together the various Islamic schools of law. So what if he had realized his stupendous role in this field...but there is no room here for it all."

We conclude the following from these important facts:

1. Both Sunnis and Shiites view each other as Muslims.
2. The meeting and understanding between the two and the transcendence of the possible and required differences, and this is the responsibility of the conscious and committed Islamic movement.
3. The martyr imam Hassan al-Banna made a great effort on this path.

Dr. Ishaq Musa al-Husayni[16] narrates in his book *The Muslim Brotherhood: The Greatest Modern Islamic Movement* how some of the students studying in Egypt joined this group.

It is known that the ranks of the Muslim Brotherhood in Iraq were largely composed by Shiites, and when Navvab Safavi visited Syria and met Dr. Mustafa al-Siba'i,[17] the general supervisor of the Muslim Brotherhood there, the latter complained to him that some Shiite youths had joined the secular and Arab-nationalist movements. So Navvab went up on one of the pulpits and said to a crowd of Shiites and Sunnis: "Whoever wants to be a true Ja'fari,[18] join the ranks of the Muslim Brotherhood."

Yet, who is Navvab Safavi? He is the leader of the Shiite organization Fada'iyan-e Islam. Professor Muhammad Ali al-Dinawi quotes Safavi in his book *The Greatest Modern Islamic Movement*:

---

[16] Ishaq Musa al-Husayni (1904–90), Palestinian scholar, critic, philologist, and translator. Al-Husayni was also the first Palestinian academic to specialize in literary studies and is considered a pioneer of literary studies in Palestine. An Arab nationalist, al-Husayni called for Arab unity, and believed in education as a means to those ends.

[17] Mustafa al-Siba'i (1915–64), Syrian politician, activist, dean of the Faculty of Islamic Jurisprudence, and leader of the Syrian branch of the Muslim Brotherhood, the Islamic Socialist Front, from 1945 until 1961.

[18] Ja'fari, the largest Shiite school of jurisprudence.

First: Islam is a comprehensive system for life.
Second: There is no sectarianism between Muslims... Nor is there between Sunnis and Shiites.

Then he quotes him, again: "To work together for Islam and to forget all but our jihad for the sake of Islam's glory. However, is it time for Muslims to understand as they call for division between the Shiite and the Sunni?"

In *The Movement Encyclopedia*, Professor Fathi Yakan[19] talks about Navvab Safavi's visit to Cairo and the intense enthusiasm with which he was met by the Muslim Brotherhood. Then he writes about the death sentence imposed on him by the shah, saying:

> This unjust sentence resonated fiercely in the Islamic countries and it shook the Muslim masses, which valued the heroism of Navvab and his jihad. They revolted against the judgment and thousands of telegrams flew from across the Islamic world, condemning the sentence on the believing and heroic mujahid, whose execution was a great loss in the modern era.

Thus became a Shiite Muslim one of the greatest Brotherhood martyrs in the opinion of Professor Fathi Yakan. Indeed, he considers Navvab and his companions as having joined the caravan of immortal martyrs, through their martyrdom, whose pure blood will be the flame illuminating the path of freedom and redemption for future generations... and that is what was...

So times have changed until the Islamic revolution in Iran was fulfilled. And the revolution destroyed the throne of the tyrant (the shah), who was displaced in the horizons and Truth of God Almighty, when He says: "And Our word has already preceded for Our servants, the messengers, [that] indeed, they would be those given victory, and [that] indeed, Our soldiers will be those to overcome."[20]

In his book *Islam Is an Idea, a Movement, and a Revolution*, Professor Fathi Yakan says that after the shah's Iran recognized Israel: "The Arabs must search in Iran for a Navvab and his brothers... The Arab countries, however, have not yet realized this... They do not know that only the Islamic movement supports his causes outside the Arab world... So does Iran have a Navvab today?" So if Professor Yakan awaits a Navvab, then why—by God—did the noses swell and redden when Navvab came? For who is greater than Navvab?

The magazine *The Muslims*, which the Muslim Brotherhood issued... It states in its first issue of the fifth volume published in April 1956 under the title "With Navvab Safavi" that: "The dear martyr—may God make the memory of him flourish—was close to *The Muslims*, and he came as a guest in its house in Cairo during his visit to

---

[19] Fathi Yakan (1933–2009), Lebanese Islamic cleric and head of the Lebanese Islamic Front. He is regarded as the leading ideologue of the Islamic Group, the Lebanese branch of the Muslim Brotherhood.
[20] See sūrat al-ṣaffāt: 171–3.

Egypt in January 1954." Then the magazine goes on to quote the opinion of Navvab about the arrest of the Brethren:

> It is when the tyrant oppresses the men of religion everywhere that Muslims transcend doctrinal differences and share the pain and sorrows of their persecuted brothers equally. There is no doubt that we in our constructive Islamic struggle can foil the enemies' plans, who aim for division among Muslims since there is no harm in doctrinal differences and we cannot abolish them... What we must work to stop and to prevent is for this situation to be exploited in favor of those guided by personal interests.

The magazine quotes Navvab at the end of the article, when he says: "We are certain that we will be killed. If not today, then tomorrow. Our blood and sacrifices will give new life to Islam, however, and induce it to revive. Islam needs this blood and sacrifice today, and it will never revive without it."

Before we leave this aspect in the relationship of the Muslim Brotherhood with the Shiites, we refer to the General Supervisor of the Muslim Brotherhood in North Yemen until just two years ago, Professor Abd al-Majid al-Zindani, who was a Shiite.[21] We also note that a great number of the Brethren in North Yemen were Shiites.

We now return anew to the issue of the Group of Reconciliation in order to listen to a prominent member in the group, who is Grand Imam Muhammad Shaltut and Sheikh of the al-Azhar Mosque, who says: "I believed in the idea of reconciliation as a valid approach, and I have contributed in the group from the first day." Then he writes: "Here, honorable al-Azhar complies with the ruling on the principle of reconciliation between the masters of the different legal schools. Thus, it decides to examine the jurisprudence of the Sunni and Shiite Islamic legal schools of law, which relies on evidence and proof, devoid of intolerance against so and so." He then continues:

> I would like to talk about the meetings in the house of the Group of Reconciliation, where the Egyptian sat next to the Iranian, the Lebanese, the Iraqi, the Pakistani; or next to anyone else from various Islamic people. Where the Hanafi, the Maliki, the Shafi'i, and the Hanbali sat next to the Twelver and the Zaydi around one table, with voices of science, mysticism, and jurisprudence reverberating. All in the spirit of brotherhood, with a sense of love and affection, in a fellowship of science and knowledge.

Sheikh Shaltut points out that those who fought the idea of reconciliation thought that the group wished to abolish the Islamic legal schools of law, or to integrate some of them into the others... Thus he states:

> This idea was fought by the narrow-minded, and also by another category consisting of those with special and negative interests... No nation is devoid of

---

[21] Abd al-Majid al-Zindani (1942–present), founder and head of the Yemeni branch of the Muslim Brotherhood.

this type of people, and those who found a guarantee for their subsistence and living in division fought the idea. It was fought by sick souls, by sectarians, and by particular tendencies… These people, and those lending their pens for policies of division, have direct and indirect methods to resist any reform movement. The stance for the sake of any work involves including all Muslims and gathering all their weight.

Before leaving al-Azhar, we will lend our ears to the fatwa concerning the Shiite school of law. One part of it states: "The Ja'fari doctrine, known as the Twelver Shiite doctrine, may be worshipped legally like all doctrines of the Sunnis. Thus, all Muslims must know that, and get rid of any unjust partisanship against certain doctrines… What the religion of God and his code were regarding following a particular doctrine or being confined to a doctrine… everyone is a mujtahid accepted by God."

From the Group of Reconciliation to an unending convoy of Islamic intellectuals, we commence with Sheikh Muhammad al-Ghazali,[22] who in his book *How Do We Understand Islam*, writes:

> The creeds have not been spared the consequence of the disruption befalling governance, as the greed of superiority and exclusive power dragged into it what was not of it… Then the Muslims are two large Sunni and Shiite divisions, although both believe in God alone and the prophecy of Muhammad, peace be upon him. None of the two summon the elements of belief suitable to the religion and seeks salvation more than the other does.

Then he writes on the same page: "Although I follow doctrines other than those of the Shiites in many of my rulings, I am not considering my opinion as a religion accusing anyone opposing it to be a sinner; the same applies to my position regarding some common jurisprudential views among the Sunnis."

He writes:

> Ultimately, the discord between the Shiites and the Sunnis was connected to the principles of the creed! To tear the one religion apart and to divide the umma into two people, both lying in wait for the other, but the only thing awaiting is misfortune! Each person will be appointed to this sect by a statement, which is mentioned in the verse: "Indeed, those who have divided their religion and become sects—you, [O Muhammad], are not [associated] with them in anything. Their affair is only [left] to God; then He will inform them about what they used to do."[23] I know that undertaking excommunication is available in an argument, and that intimidating the opponent with disbelief because of his opinion is easy in the heat of the debate.

---

[22] Muhammad al-Ghazali (1917–96), Egyptian Islamic scholar who attempted to interpret the Qur'an in a modern framework. He is widely credited with contributing to the religious revival in Egypt. As Fathi al-Shiqaqi turned to religion, al-Ghazali's *How Do We Understand Islam* was allegedly the first book that he read to reorient himself.

[23] See sūrat al-an'ām: 159.

Then Sheikh al-Ghazali says: "The two groups assess their bond to Islam on the faith in the book of God and in the tradition of the Prophet, and they agree fully on the universal principles in this religion. If opinions then subsequently argue on sections of jurisprudence and legislation, then the Muslims' schools of law are all the same in that the mujtahid receives his reward no matter if he is right or wrong." He then proceeds, saying:

> When we enter the field of comparative jurisprudence—and we experience hardship caused by jurisprudential difference between opinions or between authenticating a hadith or weakening it—we see that the distance between the Sunni and the Shiite is like that between the legal school of Abu Hanifa, the school of Maliki, or that of al-Shafi'i… We see that everyone seeks the truth albeit with different methods.

In Sheikh Ghazali's book *Reflections in the Qur'an*, we find him quoting the words of one of the Shiite scholars in a footnote. He writes: "He is one of the Shiite scholars and their literati. We have deliberately transmitted all of his words because some ignorant believe that the Shiites are strangers to Islam who deviate from its path. We will say more about how we understand this term in the chapter on the Qur'an's inimitability." He then writes in a footnote on page 158 when presenting another scholar, Hibat al-Din al-Husayni: "From the revered Shiite scholars. We have deliberately published the full compendium to show the Muslim reader this scholar's extent of jurisprudence, and thus the extent the Shiites revere the Book of God."

Thus speaks Sheikh al-Ghazali—one of the most important intellectuals of the Muslim Brotherhood—of the Shiites, expelling all simplistic delusions in order to dispel the darkness of ignorance, hatred, and selfish interests with the light of truth. Dr. Subhi al-Salih says in his book *Milestones of Islamic Law*: "In the hadiths of the Shiites, they too do not narrate anything that does not correspond to the sunna, the greatest authority following the Book of God among the 283 prophetic sources." He then writes: "It is their legislation, just as it is for the Sunnis."

Professor Sa'id Hawwa writes in his book *Islam* about the administrative divisions in the abode of Islam as they expanded. He writes:

> The practical reality of the Islamic world is that it is composed of jurisprudential Islamic legal schools, and each one predominates [in] some place… Facing this reality, is there a legal obstacle preventing these meanings from being noted in the administrative divisions? Thus, the region with one language has one jurisdiction, the Shiite region has another, and the region with one legal school of law has one jurisdiction, and each jurisdiction has its own governor subjected to the central authority as represented by the Caliph.

This is a clear and evident recognition by one of the Muslim Brotherhood's authorities today that the variety of legal schools—including the Shiites—does not violate the religion of the people or their creed, and the Shiites have an emir chosen from them under the abode of Islam.

In the book *Islam without Legal Schools*, the Islamic researcher Dr. Mustafa al-Shak'a writes:

> The Twelver Shiites are the majority of those living among us today, and they are linked with us, the Sunnis, through bonds of tolerance and of seeking reconciliation of the legal schools. They are so because the essence of the religion is one, it has an origin, and it does not allow discord.

Later, he writes about this sect, which comprises most of Iran's people today, and about their reasonableness: "They got rid of the treatises derived from some sects, which they considered impermissible and erroneous."

The Grand Imam, Sheikh Muhammad Abu Zahra,[24] writes in his book, *The History of the Islamic Legal Schools*:

> The Shiites are undoubtedly an Islamic sect, given that we exclude the Saba'iyyans,[25] who deified Ali—it is well known that they are infidels in the eyes of the Shiites. [There] is also no doubt that all they say is related to the Qur'anic texts and the hadiths attributed to the Prophet. They show love and affection to those who are close to them among the Sunnis and they do not disagree with them.

Dr. Abd al-Karim Zaydan,[26] one of the most important Muslim Brothers in Iraq, says in the book *Introduction to Islamic Law*:

> There is the Ja'fari legal school in Iran, Iraq, India, Pakistan, and Lebanon, and it has followers in the Levant and in other countries, too. There are no greater differences between the Ja'fari jurisprudence and the other legal schools than there are among the other legal schools themselves.

Dr. Salim al-Bahnasawi, one of the Brotherhood intellectuals who turned their attention to this subject, answers those who claim the Shiites have a different Qur'an than ours in his important book *The Tradition being Falsified*: "The Qur'an of the Sunnis is the same as that in the mosques and homes of the Shiites." He then states: "The Ja'fari Shiites assesses disbelief from the letters of the Qur'an, upon which the umma has agreed since the dawn of Islam." Al-Bahnasawi then continues to comment, in his response

---

[24] Muhammad Abu Zahra (1898–1974), Egyptian Hanafi jurist, lecturer of Islamic law at the al-Azhar University, and professor at Cairo University.
[25] The saba'iyya, known as one of the first sects in Islam, and referred to as one of the earliest manifestations of Shiite extremism. Named after Abdallah ibn Saba', ibn Saba' was allegedly a Jewish convert and subsequently one of Ali's military leaders. Yet, ibn Saba' did not acknowledge Ali's death and, instead, believed he would return as the mahdi, thus deifying Ali. See Sean W. Anthony, *The Caliph and the Heretic: Ibn Saba' and the Origins of Shi'ism* (Leiden and Boston: Brill, 2012).
[26] Abd al-Karim Zaydan (1917–2014), professor and dean at the Faculty of Islamic Law at the University of Baghdad, but he migrated to Yemen in the early 1990s due to persecution by the Baathist regime of Saddam Hussein.

to Muhibb al-Din al-Khatib and Ihsan Zahir,[27] on the issue of distorting the Qur'an, so he presents the opinions of numerous Shiite scholars and mujtahidin about these allegations on pages 67 to 75. He thus quotes Imam Sayyid Abu al-Qasim al-Khoei: "It is well-known among Muslims that distortion of the Qur'an does not occur, and that which is in our hands is the Qur'an in its entirety as revealed to the great Prophet from heaven, peace be upon him." He also quotes Sheikh Muhammad Rida Muzzafar:[28]

> That which is in our hands and from which we recite is the same Qur'an as revealed to the Prophet from heaven. He who claims otherwise is an inciter, fallacious, or dubious—all of them adrift. For the words of God are: "Falsehood cannot approach it from before it or from behind it."[29]

He then cites the words of Imam Kashaf al-Ghata': "There is no omission from, distortion of, or addition to the Qur'an, and there is a consensus on it."

There are many opinions to consult about the aforementioned pages. The false accounts on which some rely are then condemned and rejected. There is a parallel among the Sunnis that is also condemned and rejected. On page 61, Professor al-Bahnasawi discusses the issue of moral infallibility, and he writes:

> In the concept of moral infallibility, which the Sunnis deny if the Shiite and Sunnis are to understand it as the Twelvers do, one would still not find anything leading the one to excommunicate the other… For the Twelvers, this does not equal a departure from Islam in the beliefs of the Sunnis. Acknowledgment of moral infallibility, which the Sunnis deny, is merely theoretical, as it does not appear in the Qur'anic texts believed to be valid. It is well known that infidelity is the consequence of constant denial of the Qur'an and the sunna with the knowledge that doing so is forbidden. Ignorance or believing in the invalidity of a narration is not infidelity if it is not based on legal evidence.

Then from Professor al-Bahnasawi to Professor Anwar al-Jundi[30] and his book *Islam and the Trajectory of History*, where the latter writes:

> Islam's history was filled with differences, intellectual debates, and political conflict between the Sunnis and the Shiites… The external invasion extended since the crusader wars nourished this dispute and deepened its effects as to not rally unity in the world of Islam. The westernization movement was behind the tumbling between the Sunnis and the Shiites, split their words, and fueled their rivalry. Both

---

[27] Ihsan Ilahi Zahir (1945–87), Pakistani Islamic cleric and leader of the Pakistani Ahl-e-Hadith movement. Zahir wrote the book *Shiites and Shiism: Their Genesis and Evolution* in 1980 in which he accused the Shiites of heresy and of being Zionist agents in the region.
[28] Muhammad Rida Muzzafar (1904–64), Shiite scholar and jurist.
[29] See sūrat al-fuṣṣilat: 42.
[30] Anwar al-Jundi (1917–2002), Egyptian journalist and literary critic known for his polemical texts against western cultural influence in the Arab world. See Werner Ende, "al-Jundī, Anwar," in *Encyclopedia of Islam* III, ed. Kate Fleet, Gudrun Krämer, Denis Matringe, John Newas, and Everett Rowson, http://dx.doi.org/10.1163/1573-3912_ei3_COM_32879 [accessed: October 3, 2019].

Sunnis and the Shiites became aware of these conspiracies and worked to narrow the gap of difference.

So have we understood who provokes this unlawful strife? Have we understood who benefits from it? Have we understood that it is Satan who induces our division, and that we are excommunicating each other while the difference is so much smaller than some who fell in love with this Satan imagine? Professor al-Jundi writes: "The truth is that the difference between the Sunnis and the Shiites is no greater than that between the four Islamic schools of law." So we read al-Jundi so that we do not fall to the illusions that Sunnis and Shiites is one thing, or that there have been no fanatics in their history: "It is true that the researcher must be observant in distinguishing between the Shiites and the fanatics, those whom the Shiites' imams themselves warn against."

Professor Samih Atif Zayn, author of *Islam and Human Culture*, wrote a book called *The Muslims . . . Who Are They?* in which he discusses the issue of the Sunnis and the Shiites. He writes in the preface:

> Distinguished reader, it is no secret that the blind division in our society today is what induced us to write this book, particularly the division between the Shiite and Sunni Muslim, which must be evaporated alongside ignorance. Yet, unfortunately, the division still has some roots in sick minds because its insertion was firm, ruling the Islamic world on basis of division and who were enemies of the religion. They were beneficiaries refusing to live, except as parasites living on the blood of others. O Shiite brother, O Sunni brother, I will in this book present the most important facts of differences on the understanding the Qur'an, the Sunni, and the Shiite, which never was a difference about the Qur'an or the sunna, but about a different understanding of them.

Sami Atif Zayn writes at the end of the book:

> Now, after we have disclosed the most important causes for what shook this umma thoroughly, we conclude this book by noting: It is incumbent upon us as Muslims—and particularly in this age of ours—to respond to the deviation of those who have taken the Islamic legal schools as a means to mislead, play with minds, and increase doubt. We must erase the hateful spirit of sectarianism, and intercept those who spread feud in religion, until Muslims return as they once were, a cooperating and harmonious group, instead of being numerous, feuding, and conflicting groups. They must thus follow the example of the four first caliphs of tolerance and cooperation.

Abul Hasan Nadwi[31] hoped for the rapprochement of Sunnis and Shiites, and he told the Egyptian Islamic magazine *Adherence*: "If this is fulfilled—reconciliation—an unprecedented revolution will occur in the history of the renewal of Islamic thought." Professor Sabir Ta'ima writes in the book *Challenges facing Arabism and Islam*:

---

[31] Abul Hasan Ali Hasani Nadwi (1914–99), Indian Islamic scholar.

It is true what is said that there is no difference between Shiites and Sunnis in the general principles, as all agree on the oneness of God but with disagreements in the branches of Islam… It is a difference similar to that between the Sunni Islamic legal schools themselves (the Shafi'i and Hanbali), as they believe in the principles of the religion as they appear in the Qur'an and sunna. Just as they believe in everything required by faith, and Islam necessarily invalidates departing from it in the rulings on the necessary components of the faith. It is true that the Sunnis and Shiites are two of Islam's legal schools derived from the book of God and the sunna of His messenger.

The scholars of the principles of jurisprudence consider that there cannot be a consensus if the mujtahidin of the Shiites do not fully agree, just as there can be no consensus if the mujtahidin of the Sunnis do not agree. Abd al-Wahhab Khalaf[32] writes in the book *The Science of the Principles of Jurisprudence*:

Consensus has four pillars and it is not legally concluded unless these four are realized:
All mujtahidin of the Muslims must agree on the legal ruling on the case at the time it occurs, irrespective of their country, ethnicity, or sect. If only the mujtahidin of the Two Holy Mosques agree on the legal ruling, or just the mujtahidin of the Al al-Bayt, or the mujtahidin of the Sunnis without those of the Shiites, then there is no general agreement between all the mujtahidin in the Islamic world, not including the non-mujtahidin.

So if the consent of the Shiites is required for the consensus of Muslims, do they still remain a sect astray and in hell!!?

Professor Ahmad Ibrahim Bakk,[33] in his book *The Principles of Jurisprudence's Science and the History of Islamic Legislation*, writes in a particular section on legislation's history: "The Twelvers are Muslims who believe in God, His messenger, the Qur'an, and everything that was revealed to Muhammad, peace be upon him, and their legal school is dominant in the Persian country." He then writes: "There have come from the Twelvers, both old and new, great jurists and scholars of all arts and sciences, and there are many of them." He writes in a footnote on the same page: "There are certainly fanatics among the Shiites who deviated from Islam with their creed, but they are not heeded by the majority of Twelver Shiites."

After this endless stream of unending evidence from scholars of the umma, I would like to point to those who attempted to reiterate the fatwa of Ibn Taymiyya against the rejecters of the faith[34]—they attempted to apply it to the Twelvers—thus exploiting it against the Islamic revolution in Iran. It consists of several important errors:

---

[32] Abd al-Wahhab Khalaf (1888–1956), Egyptian jurist and professor at Cairo University.
[33] Ahmad Ibrahim Bakk (1874–1945), Islamic jurist.
[34] Rejecters of the faith (*al-rāfiḍa*), a derogatory term mainly employed by Sunnis to characterize Shiites as they do not recognize Abu Bakr, Umar, and Uthman as legitimate successors of Prophet Muhammad.

1. They did not ask why they could not find a fatwa such as this in the history of Islam before Ibn Taymiyya, although he came in the thirteenth century, more than six centuries after the emergence of the Shiites.
2. They did not understand Ibn Taymiyya and the contradictions the Muslim community was facing as it was confronted by an external invasion.
3. In the midst of their hatred against the Islamic revolution in Iran and their political position derived from it, did they attempt to find out if the word "rejecters" mentioned by Ibn Taymiyya applies to the Twelvers or not? Professor Anwar al-Jundi writes in his book *Islam and the Trajectory of History* that "the rejecters are neither Sunni nor Shiite." Imam Muhammad Abu Zahra reviews some of the Shiite sects such as the Zaydis and Twelvers in his book *Ibn Taymiyya*, without referencing any negative position of Ibn Taymiyya. He does mention the Isma'ilis,[35] however, as he writes: "This is the sect whose members Ibn Taymiyya had positions against… So he fought them with his knowledge, tongue, and sword." It is because of Ibn Taymiyya's position against this sect that we find Imam Abu Zahra talking at great length about it in his study, as he himself states.

This was the position some Islamic movements and leaders derived from this fabricated pandemonium on the issue of Shiites and Sunnis… The Iranian revolution, which erupted in early 1978, awakened the spirit of the Muslim umma along the axis stretching from Tangier to Jakarta. The Muslim masses looked to Teheran and their memory was swept by the marvelous triumphs brought forth by Islam… As the revolution advanced, its appeal to the masses increased, and these masses expressed their joy and delight in the streets of Cairo, Damascus, Karachi, Khartoum, Istanbul, around Jerusalem, and everywhere the Islamists were present.

One of the historical leaders of the Muslim Brotherhood, Professor Issam al-Attar who was in West Germany, is well known for his sincere devotion, the might of his jihad, and his revolutionary purity… This man who had spent his entire life without reconciling with a ruler and who did not approach the castle of an emir, he writes a whole book about the history and roots of the revolution. He stands beside the revolution in support and he wrote more than once to Imam Khomeini to congratulate, bless, and support him. His recorded conversations in support of the revolution were distributed among young Muslims on cassettes.

The magazine *The Pioneer* also played an important role in supporting the revolution and explaining its position. The position of the Muslim Brotherhood in Sudan and of the Islamic Youth of Khartoum University was one of the most wonderful positions witnessed in the Islamic capitals in which they came out in demonstrations of support. Dr. Hassan al-Turabi[36]—the movement's leader in Sudan, known for his

---

[35] Isma'ilism, branch of Shiite Islam derived from Imam Isma'il ibn Ja'far. While Isma'ilis accept Isma'il ibn Ja'far as the successor to Ja'far al-Sadiq, Twelvers accept Musa al-Kazim, the seventh of the twelve imams.
[36] Hassan al-Turabi (1932–2016), Sudanese politician, Islamic intellectual, and leader of the Sudanese National Islamic Front.

cultural capacity and political wisdom—travelled to Iran where he met the imam and declared his support for the revolution and its leader.

The magazine of the Islamic movement in Tunisia, *Consciousness*, stood beside the revolution. They blessed it and called upon all Muslims to support it. The leader of the Islamic movement there, Rashid al-Ghannouchi,[37] even wrote in the magazine nominating Khomeini to lead the Muslims, which led to the magazine being closed down and to the arrest of the movement's leaders by the Bourguiba government. Professor al-Ghannouchi considers the modern Islamic trend as "taking shape"—taking shape at the hands of imam al-Banna, Mawdudi, Qutb, and Khomeini—to represent the most important of the Islamic trends in the contemporary Islamic movement (in the book *The Islamic Movement and Modernization*). He considers that "the success of the revolution in Iran commences a new civilizational role."

He writes under the headline "What do we mean by the term 'The Islamic Movement'?" in the same book:

> However, what we stipulated from that trend, which stems from the understanding of Islam's comprehensiveness, is the goal of establishing a Muslim society and an Islamic state based on that comprehensive idea: This understanding stems from three great currents: "The Muslim Brotherhood, the Islamic groups in Pakistan, and the movement of Imam Khomeini in Iran."

He then writes: "A process commenced in Iran, perhaps the most important thing that could happen in the liberation movements' march in the region, namely, the liberation of Islam from the dominance of the authorities, working to employ it in the face of the region's revolutionary tide."

In Lebanon, the Islamic movement's support for the revolution was one of the most obvious and profound positions, and its leader, Fathi Yakan, and its unique magazine *The Pact*, took an Islamic, revolutionary, and glowing position on the revolution. Professor Yakan visited Iran numerously, participated in ceremonies, and held lectures in its support.

The general supervisor of the Muslim Brotherhood in Jordan, Muhammad Abd al-Rahman Khalifa,[38] declared his support for the revolution before and after his visit to Iran... Just as Ibrahim Zayd al-Kilani[39] called upon King Hussein to assume the path of revolution (!). Professor Yusuf al-Azm[40] recited his famous poem, published in more than one magazine, including *The Pact*, in which he called for pledging allegiance to Imam Khomeini.

---

[37] Rachid al-Ghannouchi (1941–present), Tunisian politician and intellectual. Co-founder of the Tunisian Islamic party Ennahda, serving as its intellectual guide.
[38] Muhammad Abd al-Rahman Khalifa (1919–2006), the longest serving leader of the Jordanian Muslim Brotherhood from 1953 until 1994.
[39] Ibrahim Zayd al-Kilani (1937–2013), Jordanian Islamic cleric, member of the Jordanian Muslim Brotherhood's political wing, the Islamic Action Front, and Jordanian Minister of Awqaf and Islamic Affairs in 1990.
[40] Yusuf al-Azm (1931–2007), Jordanian Muslim Brotherhood leader, intellectual, and author. Al-Azm was appointed Jordanian Minister of Social Development in 1991 for six months during the Second Gulf War.

The magazines *The Call*, *Adherence*, and *The Islamic Digest* in Egypt stood beside the revolution, affirming its Islamic character, and supporting it and its leader. When Saddam Hussein's invasion of Iran began, *Adherence* wrote on its cover: "Comrade al-Tikriti… the student of Michel Aflaq[41] who desires a new Qadisiyya in Muslim Iran." It wrote in the same issue under the title "The reasons for this tragedy": "Fear of the Islamic revolution spreading in Iraq." It then stated:

> Saddam Hussein saw the transition the Iranian army went through, transforming from an imperial army into an Islamic army, as a golden opportunity to destroy it before it became an indomitable force due to the Islamic creed in the hearts of its officers and soldiers.

Professor Jabir Razaq,[42] one of the most prominent journalists in the Muslim Brotherhood, wrote in *Adherence*, explaining the reasons for the war: "This war broke out at the same time when all the American conspiratorial plans against the revolution of the Iranian Muslim people failed." He then says: "Saddam Hussein forgot that he will fight a people four times the size of the Iraqi people. This people are the only people that have been able to rebel against the Jewish crusader imperialism." He continues:

> The Iranian people in their entirety, with all of their institutions and organizations, are determined to continue the war until victory and until the fall of the bloody Baath party. The spiritual and mental mobilization among all the Iranian people is unprecedented, and the desire for martyrdom takes the form of competition and bravery. The Iranian people are fully confident that the victory will ultimately be that of the Islamic revolution of Iran.

Professor Jabir Razak then explains that colonialism's objective with the war is the attempt to overthrow the revolution. He thus writes:

> With the overthrow of the Iranian revolutionary system, the threat frightening this kind of tyrants disappears, who tremble from imagining the possibility of their people revolting against and overthrowing them, just as the Iranian Muslim people did against the puppet Shah.

At the end of the article, he writes: "The party of God is triumphing, but it requires jihad and martyrdom, for God will surely support those who support Him. Indeed, God is powerful and Exalted in might."[43]

This is consequently the war's essence, and not what the sons of the Saudi era, and some of the good-hearted people who know nothing about this world, say. They say

---

[41] Michel Aflaq (1910–1989), Syrian philosopher and Arab nationalist. Regarded by many as the key ideological reference of Baathist thought, Aflaq believed the Arab world should be united into one Arab nation-state. See Max Weiss, "Genealogies of Baʿthism: Michel Aflaq between Personalism and Arabic Nationalism," *Modern Intellectual History*, 1–32.

[42] Jabir Razak (1936–88), Islamist journalist and member of the Egyptian Muslim Brotherhood.

[43] Razak is here referencing sūrat al-ḥajj: 40.

that Shiite Iran wants to storm the Sunni regime in Iraq… How sad is this blindness, and how criminal is he who sows this ignorance and hatred in the hearts of the people?

Adherence wrote on its cover in January 1981: "The revolution that restored the accounts and shifted the balance." The magazine wondered: "Why is the Iranian revolution the greatest revolution in modern times?" At the end of the article, which was written on the second anniversary of the Iranian victory, and after the author had spoken of the imperial army's strength and its repressive means, he stated: "Thus triumphed the Iranian revolution after thousands of martyrs had fallen… Thus it was the greatest revolution in modern times with its efficacy, and with its positive results and their effects, which restored the accounts and shifted the balance."

From Egypt to the position of the International Organization of the Muslim Brotherhood, which made a statement: "To those responsible for all Islamic movements around the world." It stated during the spy hostage crisis:

> If it was about Iran alone, it would accept a compromise after figuring out what was going on. Yet, the issue is Islam and its people everywhere. It has become the responsibility of the only Islamic rule in the world, which imposed itself with the blood of its people in the twentieth century to consolidate the rule of God above the rule of rulers and above the rule of colonialism and international Zionism.

The statement points to the vision of the Iranian revolution for those attempting to weaken one of them:

> If a Muslim fails to absorb the age of the Islamic flood, and still lives in the time of surrender, then he must thus seek forgiveness from God and try to supplement his incomplete understanding of the meanings of jihad and glory in Islam. Or if he is an agent mediating the interest of Islam's enemies at its expense, boasting about brotherhood and the concerns for it… Or if he is a Muslim moving without opinion or will… Or a hypocrite betting between these and those.

When the clashing invasion on Muslim Iran commenced, the International Organization of the Muslim Brotherhood issued a statement addressed to the Iraqi people, attacking the infidel atheist Baath party. To quote the statement, which also said:

> Also, this war is not a war of liberation for the oppressed among men, women, and children who cannot do anything and who cannot find a way. So the Iranian Muslim people liberated themselves from oppression and from the American-Zionist colonialism by a heroic wondrous jihad through an Islamic revolution, overwhelming and unique in human history and under the leadership of a Muslim imam who undoubtedly is the pride of Islam and of Muslims.

Then the statement talks about the objectives of the clashing aggression: "Striking the Islamic movement and extinguishing the flame of the Islamic liberation emanating from Iran." At the end, it addresses the Iraqi people: "Kill your hangmen, for the opportunity has come. Throw away your weapons and join the camp of the revolution. The Islamic revolution is your revolution."

The position of the Islamic groups in Pakistan is represented by a fatwa about the Islamic revolution in Iran, published in the magazine *The Call* by Abul Ala' al-Mawdudi. It is an answer to a question posed to the magazine about the Islamic revolution in Iran by the mujtahid scholar al-Mawdudi, whom the Islamic movement has unanimously identified as one of the most prominent pioneers of this century. It states: "Khomeini's revolution is an Islamic one, and those in charge of it are an Islamic group and youth who received education in the Islamic movements. All Muslims in general and Islamic movements in particular must support this revolution and cooperate with it in all fields."

So the legal position on the revolution is as proposed by al-Mawdudi: We must support and cooperate if we want to be committed to Islam… As for the counter-revolution and waging a suspicious crusader war against it, by whom? From groups belonging to the Islamic movement… So this is a legal fabrication of the great mujtahid's fatwa.

Regarding the position of al-Azhar, its previous sheikh declared in an interview with the newspaper *al-Sharq al-Awsat*, published in London: "Imam Khomeini is a brother in religion and a sincere Muslim." He then said: "Muslims of different sects are brothers in religion, and Khomeini stands under the banner of Islam just as I do."

In his last book, which is circulated by the youth of the Islamic movement, *The ABCs in the Conceptualization of Strategy in Islamic Work*, Professor Fathi Yakan reviews the conspiracies of colonialism and the international forces against Islam. He thus writes: "Recent history is a witness to what we are saying, which is the experience of the Islamic revolution in Iran… This experience, which gathered all infidel forces on Earth to battle it and abort it, which continues, because it is Islamic, and not eastern or western." See to whom the Muslim youth listens today: to Abul Ala' al-Mawdudi and Professor Fathi Yakan or to semi-literate claimants of Islam, sometimes with dubious interests!!

The last thing we have in our hands is the magazine exiled in Austria, *The Call*: "There is in the world today a comprehensive Islamic awakening with the Islamic revolution in Iran as one of its effects, which despite its stumbling blocks was able to undermine the largest and most powerful empires hostile to Islam and Muslims." Thus, in one of its most recent issues, *The Call* considers the Iranian revolution to be Islamic and to be one of the effects of the comprehensive Islamic awakening, which we referred to in the beginning of this study. The stumbling blocks are in my opinion the difficulties that colonialism is trying to put in the way of the revolution to influence its path. It is thus the duty of committed Muslims to remove them.

This is the position of the scholars and intellectuals of the Islamic Sunni movements… On the other hand, we will suffice with the words of imam Khomeini who after his arrival in Paris answered a question about the origins of the revolution. He said: "The cause driving Muslims to either a Sunni or Shiite side is no longer there. We are all Muslims. This is an Islamic revolution. We are all brothers in religion."

Professor Ghannouchi quotes imam Khomeini in the book *The Islamic Movement and Modernization*: "We want to rule by Islam as it was revealed to Muhammad, peace be upon him. There is no difference between the Sunnis and the Shiites as the legal schools did not exist in the era of Prophet Muhammad."

At the fourteenth congress for Islamic thought in Algeria, the representative of imam Khomeini, Mr. Khosrow Shahi, spoke:

> O brothers, the enemies do not differentiate between Sunni and Shiite as they want to eradicate Islam as a global idea and ideology. Therefore, any call or action to divide the ranks in the name of Sunnis or Shiites means to stand beside infidelity and against Islam and Muslims. It is thus, as the legal ruling issued by imam Khomeini, impermissible and Muslims must resist it.

After all this, how can we understand the essence of the revolution, its historical objectives, and its divine duty...? Islam rises anew in confrontation with the modern Western challenge. The Iranian Islamists are today carrying the banner of revival beside all committed and aware Islamists in order to achieve the victory of Islam on Earth and to achieve the ultimate goal of our lives: to please God Almighty. Let us listen to the Egyptian Christian intellectual and Marxist, Ghali Shukri, who in his attack on the Islamic revolution elucidates parts of its divine mission. He writes in his article published by *Islamic Studies*, quoted by the magazine *Political Signs*: "Ironically, intellectuals who knew their Marxist history turned into violent Islamists in the blink of an eye... Intellectual Christians turned into extremist Muslims in a moment, and intellectuals belonging culturally to the West and its modernity turned unconditionally into the eastern fanatics." Thus did rows of Arab intellectuals gather under Khomeini's banner in the name of reexamining the universals, in the name of returning to authenticity after all estrangement, Westernization, and alienation, and in the name of "the failure that Marxism, secularism, liberalism, and Arab nationalism suffered"!!

At the end of this article, we can only repeat what Imam Khomeini said approximately seventeen years ago in his sermon in 1965:

> The dirty hands spreading division among Shiites and Sunnis in the Islamic world are neither Shiite nor Sunni. They are the hands of colonialism that wishes to capture the Islamic countries from our hands. The colonial states, the states wishing to plunder our wealth by various means and numerous tricks, are the ones inventing division in the name of Shiism and Sunnism.

12

Excerpts from *Facts and Stances*

2007, published by mu'assasat al-aqṣā al-thaqāfiyya, Damascus, p. 71–83.

PIJ was accused of both Shiism and of being Iranian agents in the Palestinian struggle. Initially proposed by the Muslim Brotherhood in the early 1980s, the accusation stuck for decades. The fact that Iran became the main patron of the movement did not help. Indeed, throughout the early and mid-1990s, al-Shiqaqi was asked numerously by journalists about the alleged inclination of his movement toward Shiism and about its relationship with Iran and Hezbollah. As this excerpt from Facts and Stances *shows, this was still the case in 2007.*

Yet, the support for the Iranian revolution was not so much about theology, as it pertained to toppling a regime allied with the United States and Israel. It was, moreover, a great inspiration because it was not a military coup d'état carried out by army officers, but a revolution by the Iranian Islamic masses. Consequently, PIJ would presumably have supported a similar revolution if it had erupted in Syria, Egypt, or Jordan. Essentially, as the relationship between the two is governed by their shared interests on the ground, it is continued Iranian support for the Palestinian cause that matters.

This excerpt matters for three reasons. First, the two preceding texts on Khomeini and the Iranian revolution are documents related to the debates raging in the late 1970s and early 1980s. They may thus be less accessible due to the references employed and the actors being targeted. Both are also authored by PIJ's first secretary-general, al-Shiqaqi, who had far greater intellectual ambitions than Shallah. The language of this text is thus far less esoteric, and Shallah addresses the accusations head on with refreshingly clear language (and not without some sarcasm). Second, Shallah presents a similar view on the Shiites and the necessity of conciliation between them and Sunnis. He thus demonstrates that this is a persisting feature in the ideology of PIJ. Third, because this document was published recently, it is a "revisit" of Iran and the Iranian revolution within the framework of contemporary events. It shows how PIJ understands and analyzes Iran after the so-called War on Terror, the Second Intifada, and the division between Fatah and Hamas. Shallah thus reframes the "Iranian issue" as a facet of the Palestinian political division between the West Bank and the Gaza Strip. Moreover, it addresses the curious fact that the Palestinian Muslim Brotherhood accused PIJ of being Shiites in disguise, while its successor, Hamas, also became funded by Iran.

☾

Some of the Palestinian parties accuse you of being determined to continue launching rockets; for your refusal to participate in the political process; and of implementing an Iranian agenda, as they point to the special relationship that binds you to Iran.

First, who accuses us of implementing an Iranian agenda, whether through our persistence in the resistance or not engaging in the Oslo authority? It is the faction implementing the American-Zionist agenda, and it is a faction present in Palestine and abroad as well. It is nonetheless dangerous and unfortunate to trust this accusation and to be dragged behind it, behind rumors, and behind smear campaigns against the resistance project—against some of the good people of the Islamic movements and currents in the Arab and Islamic world. Yet, why do they believe such rumors and charges as these? We must discuss frankly in order to answer this question and connect the dots to elucidate the historical source of this charge against us in the Palestinian arena.

I regret to say, although obliged, that the brothers in the Muslim Brotherhood in the Gaza Strip were the first ones to accuse us for our relationship with Iran and the Shiites—and I say the Brotherhood because the accusation came before the establishment of Hamas—that is, when they worked under the name The Islamic Center.[1] When they saw this group of young people who formed Palestinian Islamic Jihad, they departed from their approach and declared a war. Certainly, I do not want to reopen the wound by going over the details, particularly since we have laid it all behind us since then. The headache connected to the accusation about our relationship with Iran and the Shiites must nonetheless end, and we must present it in our argument to the people, and to God Almighty before that.

Yes, we did support the Islamic revolution in Iran, just as millions of other Muslims did. All we said that day was that this revolution, which toppled a regime that was one of the strongest allies of the Zionist entity in the region and the world, could be a source of support for us in our jihad for the liberation of our usurped homeland. What we said approximately twenty-five years ago was that which applies to the brothers in Hamas today by virtue of their relationship with Iran and the Shiites. Even if we climbed to the top of the highest minaret in the world, and if we stated or issued our positive positions about Iran or Hezbollah, we would still never keep pace with the Egyptian Muslim Brotherhood's supreme guide—whom we love, appreciate, and respect—in his praise of Hezbollah's bravery in the previous July War.[2] It is in our view a correct position, although many Sunnis do not sympathize with these words. Yet, no one accuses his eminence the supreme guide, and no one accuses the Muslim Brotherhood or Hamas of implementing an Iranian agenda!

---

[1] The Islamic Center (*al-mujamma' al-islāmī*), founded in the Gaza Strip in 1973 and legalized by the Israeli occupation in 1978. In 1988 described as an "all-encompassing centre for social, educational, religious, and cultural functions," the Islamic Center was directly under the control of the Palestinian Muslim Brotherhood. Mohammad K. Shadid, "The Muslim Brotherhood Movement in the West Bank and Gaza," *Third World Quarterly* 10, no. 2 (April 1988): 673.

[2] The 2006 Lebanon War, known in Lebanon as the July War, mainly between the State of Israel and Hezbollah.

There are unfortunately those today who accuse Hamas of being loyal to the Shiites and for implementing an Iranian agenda in Palestine! Yet, the strange and bizarre thing is that the secular movements such as Fatah are now issuing this accusation! Why has Fatah resorted to accusing Hamas of its relationship with the Shiites although it may be described as ridiculous and laughable!? Chanting it at political rallies and marches, which is broadcasted by satellite TV and received by millions!? The reason is, in all simplicity, that Fatah realized how lethal this accusation was when employed against Palestinian Islamic Jihad, particularly as it was employed in a framework of mobilizing sectarianism, which confronted the Iranian revolution, and which accompanied the Iraq-Iran War. Just as it is employed in this current period with the Iraqi tragedy and its bleeding wound. How effective has this accusation not been in depleting the movement, distorting its image and reputation, despite the fact that Palestinian Islamic Jihad is made by the blood of martyrs and the sacrifices of jihad!?!?

Whether this accusation is directed against us by Hamas, or by Fatah against Hamas, it is still a tenuous and ridiculous charge, undeserving of any answer. The motives in the two cases are, unfortunately, partisan motives. They are not issued because of genuine convictions as they lack any roots on the ground or any credibility. In reality, neither Palestinian Islamic Jihad nor Hamas are Shiites, and Fatah is not a garrison protecting the "Sunnis" in Palestine. The story is that of a faction accusing Hamas or Palestinian Islamic Jihad, or anyone else for that matter, for their special relationship with Iran. This faction is the protector of "Israel" and its agenda is to separate and polarize in the region. Indeed, this accusation has become a registered trademark in the Palestinian field against all the resistance movements rejecting the approach of settlement and surrender. The accusation about Iran has become a scarecrow with which the others attempt to cover up the American and Zionist dictates forced upon them. In reality, it did not anger us when the agents of the American and Zionist agenda in the region issued the accusation against us. It is, instead, a testimony that we are correct, and that pleases us…

The position persists, however, in the position of some Islamists who do not bother to examine or to inquire, but, instead, embrace these rumors without learning the truth and goals of these accusations, which primarily aim to irreversibly eliminate the Arab and Islamic dimension of the Palestinian cause… In their conviction, it is forbidden for any Muslim or Arab to extend his hand to the Palestinian cause! It is, instead, the right of America and the whole Western and pagan world to extend their hands to this cause in order to liquidate it, and it is not the right of Iran or the Arab and Muslim countries to do the same to help Palestine or the resistance in any way! So the problem is not Iran. The problem is the absence of resistance. Otherwise, would the country be accused of supporting the resistance—such as Turkey, Egypt, Saudi Arabia, or Morocco? Would they be redeemed for that? Of course not.

Considering the nature of our relationship with Iran, then, there is nothing particular about it as Iran has relationships with every party in the Palestinian field today, whether Islamic or nationalist; whether the Palestinian National Authority (PA) or even independent persons. Despite all of that, we have a good relationship with Iran, and we do not deny it. Nor are we ashamed of it. Indeed, we are adamantly clear on the background, goals, and dimensions of this relationship… All of those who know Palestinian Islamic Jihad realize that we do not talk with two tongues about this topic…

Iran is in our view a Muslim country, and it is their right and duty to extend their hand to help Palestine… When Iran does so, and Palestine obtains a presence in the Iranian agenda, is it then the right of those absent from Palestine and the resistance to accuse others for their intentions!? What is the sin of Palestinian Islamic Jihad in that!? When the entire world besieged us, and when the doors of our umma's capitals were closed to us and, instead, were opened for the Jews and Americans, we found Iran opening its doors and extending its hand in help and support. Were we supposed to reject that while directing our attention toward our central cause—the cause of the entire umma—Palestine!?

The umma is the last castle and fort remaining in front of colonial encroachment under the sweeping American-Zionist attacks in the region. It is so under the launch of the US "constructive chaos" policy to redraw the map of the region and to create the "New Middle East" built on the rubbles and ruins of the American war portending to further fragment and dismember the umma (even within a single country), fighting the umma in its religion, identity, and Islamic creed. Under these circumstances plaguing the region—with the classification of those loyal to the American-Zionist policies as moderates, while the opposition and resisters are categorized as fundamentalists and "terrorists"—it is natural for us as a resistance movement to find ourselves against America and "Israel." Those who want us to antagonize Iran and Hezbollah, they want to bring us to the camp loyal to America and the camp of those implementing the American-Zionist agenda in the region under false pretexts.

Are Muslims required to wrestle with the past and the strife that occurred, while the enemies rob us of everything in our present and fight us in the aspiration to own our own future!? Our future, and the future of our umma, its sanctities, wealth, and status among nations!? Are we required to close our eyes to what America and its stepdaughter, "Israel," represent and are doing to us!? Or should we open our eyes and turn on the spotlights to examine Iran and its intentions for Palestine, for the Arabs and Sunnis? Should we hold it accountable for what they do and do not do!? Does it make sense to ignore "Israel" as a real danger and reality, which is not merely in front of our eyes, but verily sitting on our chests? Should we, instead, put our efforts and energies against a perceived threat called Iran, as Shimon Peres[3] and Condoleezza Rice[4] warn us!? Is it possible that the Arabs and Muslims have become partners and are providing facilities in the possible American-Zionist war against Muslim Iran—accusing Iran of seeking nuclear capabilities posing a threat to "Israel," which itself has hundreds of nuclear warheads!?

Is this truly in the interest of Islam and Muslims? Or is it a literal implementation of the American-Zionist agenda in the region!? It is a question to be asked of the mind, awareness, and conscience of everyone who listened, and who was a martyr!

---

[3] Shimon Peres (1923–2016), Israeli politician and twice prime minister of Israel. President of Israel from 2007 until 2014.
[4] Condoleezza Rice (1954–present), the sixty-sixth US secretary of state under US president George W. Bush.

Yet, there are those who accuse Palestinian Islamic Jihad of having Shiite tendencies in the movement, and that this explains the Iranian support for you. What is your response!?

Let me start with the support and its meaning. I do not wish to defend Iran, regardless of the support, its size, and the exaggeration of it. I stand with what some of its opponents say, that Iran does not support the Palestinians for the sake of it, but because Iran wants a role in the Palestinian cause as a way of serving its particular interests and goals… Assume that this statement, which deprives Iran's position of a motivation based on a religious and humanitarian duty, is a great injustice… Assume that this is true and that Iran merely desires a role in Palestine. Assume that the others in the umma are fearful of this role and do not want to take it upon themselves. Then what wrong have we as resistance movements done, and what is the accusation against us? Do you slam the door in the face of Iran and wait for someone else to open it while the keys are in the pockets of America and "Israel"?

We are an independent, Islamic, jihadist movement, and we cannot mortgage our decision to any side in the world. Those who wish to test the sincerity of our words, try to budge our principles, our convictions, and our approach just an inch, and they will see what the result will be! We are a project of martyrdom and triumph, and we cannot compromise our creed and principles in any way.

Regarding the inclinations toward Shiism, then this is a sensitive and serious topic—rumored in the context of the war against Palestinian Islamic Jihad. It is therefore necessary to talk about it clearly and frankly by emphasizing the following points:

First: Everybody knows that Palestinian Islamic Jihad is an Islamic Sunni resistance movement. Our creed is the creed of the Sunnis, and the movement is on the creedal and doctrinal map of the umma, the creed of Muslims, which is devoid of any other Islamic doctrines. This is the doctrinal identity of Palestinian Islamic Jihad, which embraces thousands of mujahidin who are known by their Islamic descent and origin and their social and familial ties. They are attested by the mosques crowded by them among their family and people in Palestine and everywhere, and they are attested on the battlegrounds of jihad and redemption in the fight against the Zionist enemy.

Second: Palestinian Islamic Jihad—acknowledged far and wide for its courage for the truth, its clearness, and its insistence to adhere to its principles—chant what it believes is just for every citizen, no matter how many opposes it and whatever the consequences. If Palestinian Islamic Jihad had any inclinations toward, or adhered to, any principle, idea, or belonging other than that to the creed of the Sunnis, it would belong to the great Islam. If this were the case, then, thanks to God Almighty, it would have the courage and self-confidence to disclose so without any hesitation or fear of anyone.

Third: We in Palestinian Islamic Jihad do not excommunicate anyone from the umma who says "There is no god but God, and Muhammad is the Messenger of God." The weapon of excommunication is in our view the most dangerous weapon that today kills the umma from the inside and our faith in it. Since the inception of the movement, the creed of the Sunnis has been careful and guarded against excommunication because of the potential consequence of bloodshed and confiscation of money, property, and sanctities. Imam Abu Hamid al-Ghazali—peace be upon him—said: "The mistake of neglecting one thousand infidels is less than the mistake of shedding the blood of Muslims." Sheikh Muhammad Abduh—peace be upon him—said beautifully when clarifying the position of Muslims on the issue of excommunication: "It is known among Muslims, and it is known from the rules of their religion, that if there are a hundred possibilities of infidelity, and there is only one possibility of faith, then only faith is considered and infidelity should not factor in."

Fourth: Regarding the Shiites, our position is that of the majority of the umma, which considers them Muslims, part of the people of the *qibla*. There are differences between us and them. Yet, they have not departed from the religious community. All books and sources of the Sunnis on Islamic sects affirm that the Shiites, except for the fanatics, are a part of these, and none of these books expel them from Islam. The Mecca Document[5] stipulated under the auspices of the Organization of Islamic Cooperation[6] October 1, 2007, regarding the strife in Iraq: "A Muslim is he who states that there is no god but God, and Muhammad is the Messenger of God. This testimony protects his blood and property, and that entails both Sunnis and Shiites." Regarding the difference between Sunnis and the Shiites, the document decided that "there is no difference in the principles of the faith and the pillars of Islam. No Muslim may excommunicate the other, and he may not legally condemn a doctrine because of the crimes [of] some of its followers."

Fifth: Palestinian Islamic Jihad is a resistance movement with the primary and direct duty to fight the Zionist enemy in Palestine. We are thus with everyone who fights "Israel" or antagonizes it, whether Sunni or Shiite. Even those who are not Arab or Muslims. Any intrusion into issues of doctrinal or creedal struggle, and the creation of perceived enemies in our minds and in our Palestinian arena (which is devoid of Shiites), aims to produce strife that creates enemies with the goal of dismantling the umma and blowing it up from within. The doctrinal differences between us and our Shiite brothers were not born of this moment but are deeply rooted in history. If exhumed and stimulated by any party in Palestine, it would provoke a strife that would only serve our enemy. The result would lead us to divert our attention from our real enemy and our jihad from its intended destination: namely, pushing out the Zionist aggression from our people and our land. Thus, delving into issues of doctrinal differences is not in our jurisdiction but, rather, that of scholars and jurists who have the right and duty to identify them for the people. Yet, it is not the right or duty for us, the mujahidin, to be preoccupied by it at the expense of our jihad, or to make it an obstacle or a barrier for cooperation between the Shiite Muslims and us. Nor to make it an obstacle or a barrier for cohesion and standing united against "Israel," challenging its ambitions and plans against the umma.

Sixth: Yes, we supported the Iranian Islamic revolution, just like the rest of the Arab and Muslim people. Those who opposed it and fought it were the regimes

---

[5] The Mecca Document formed on October 20, 2006, sought to end sectarian violence with the participation of both senior Sunni and Shiite Iraqi leaders. The Document was carried out under the auspices of the Organization of Islamic Cooperation and the International Islamic Fiqh Academy.

[6] Islamic Organization of Islamic Cooperation, international organization founded in 1969.

fearing it would become a model. Our support for the revolution in those days, or our relationship with it, was not on a doctrinal background, evidenced by the fact that the revolution overthrew the shah of Shiite Iran with whom the Sunni Arab rulers sympathized, whom they supported, and sheltered! The revolution's lesson for us was the lesson about the rise of the people to change evil and recover their lost rights by their own hands—regardless of the doctrinal or creedal affiliation of these people. This applies to our relationship with Hezbollah, which sees its victory against the Zionist entity in 2000 and in 2006 as a victory of the Arabs and Muslims. This was a victory with a significant impact on the oppressed and broken masses of the umma, who felt that Hezbollah had restored their dignity, raised their heads, and proven that there is no invincible enemy if jihad, will, faith, and sacrifice exist.

These are the pillars summarizing our vision on this sensitive issue, and which govern our relationship with Iran and Hezbollah. They are at the core of our principles and our creed, and to violate them or to abandon them is to abandon the approach of the movement. This is well known to the sons of Palestinian Islamic Jihad, and this is well known to everyone among the sons of our people and our umma who knows the movement closely.

Then, from where comes the talk about inclinations toward Shiism? Unfortunately, it seems someone took a decision for some unknown reason that Palestinian Islamic Jihad should remain the main prey for this falsehood based on our relationship with Iran and Hezbollah, which does not deviate from the previous rules. Our relationship with them does not exceed what we have with anyone else in the Palestinian field. It unfortunately succeeds in polarizing some good people who have a religious and creedal zeal, and who are not well experienced in political manipulation...

To all those fearing doctrinal winds coming over Palestine or Palestinian Islamic Jihad, I say: rest assured... The Palestinian people—the people with the awareness, faith, and insight to prevent the flames of strife—search for those helping them to liberate the homeland and freeing it from injustice. The Palestinian people are not changing their doctrine, they are in no doubt about the validity of their faith, and they realize that victory or defeat is not enough to turn a creed and sin further. Otherwise, what about the creed of those allied with America in Iraq or abandoning its resistance, which, by the way, include Sunnis and Shiites?

The tendentious propaganda war was raised intentionally and premeditated against Palestinian Islamic Jihad by some to distort its picture... I do not exaggerate if I say that its impact was far greater on the hearts of our mujahidin than the Zionist war, which pursued them with assassinations, imprisonments, and all forms of aggressions! That unfortunately falls in under the framework of morally liquidating Palestinian Islamic Jihad, its leaders, and its symbols when "Israel" is incapable of liquidating them physically—that is, a moral assassination that accompanies the assassinations carried out by the enemy against the mujahidin.

Those who participate in this impermissible war against the mujahidin, they turn away from the path of God in terms of knowing or not knowing. This is not an exaggeration or alarmism, but a fact. For Palestinian Islamic Jihad is with all of its humility an Islamic movement that dedicates itself to God. There is no path or road except that of fighting the enemies of God, the usurpers of our Prophet's point of departure for his midnight journey to the seven heavens and our first *qibla*, Palestine. Those who discourage the people from Palestinian Islamic Jihad, including intrigues, fabrications, and lies about the movement, they discourage them from the religion of God and jihad in His path.

We sacrifice thus in anticipation of God Almighty's reward in the Hereafter for He is sufficient for us and He is the best Disposer of affairs. To all those who believe they are doing so well and are defending Islam by slandering Palestinian Islamic Jihad and alienating the people from the movement, we remind them to fear God in their souls and in their brothers, the mujahidin. We remind them to examine critically and consider carefully before striking the mujahidin with their ignorance, and to submit themselves to the words of the Almighty: "And do not pursue that of which you have no knowledge."[7] To abide by the evidence and to rise above the morals that God revealed about them: "[They are] avid listeners to falsehood."[8] God forbid! We ask God to provide guidance and forgiveness for us and for them.

---

[7] See sūrat al-isrāʾ: 36
[8] See sūrat al-māʾida: 42.

Part IV

State, Violence, and Civil Society

13

Restructuring the PLO

The View of Palestinian Islamic Jihad

Published in the book The Palestine Liberation Organization: Evaluating the Experience and Restructuring, *edited by Mohsen M. Saleh (Beirut: Al-Zaytouna Centre for Studies and Consultation, 2007), p. 211–18, by Dr. Anwar Abu Taha, member of PIJ's political bureau*

The relationship between PIJ and the Palestine Liberation Organization (PLO) has always been ambivalent at best. On the one hand, the former always dismissed the secularism of the latter. Moreover, PIJ stated that the political decline of the PLO became apparent long before the concessions of the 1980s and commenced with the introduction of the Ten-Point Program in 1974 instead. On the other hand, PIJ always emphasized and acknowledged the historically important role of the PLO in the 1960s and the early 1970s as the latter restored a Palestinian national sense through armed struggle and by removing the Palestinian cause from the grasp of the Arab regimes.

With the emergence of the main Palestinian Islamic actors in the 1980s, one of the most important Palestinian fault lines was reforming the PLO so it could become a truly representative Palestinian body. Yet, as reform became part of an internal Palestinian struggle between Fatah and Hamas for power and legitimacy, this was always easier said than done—with demands presented from both sides for the inclusion of the Palestinian Islamic actors to be possible.

The following text demonstrates how the ambivalent relationship between PIJ and the PLO always was a question about violence. As Abu Taha asks: "What liberation organization is it that we want?" His answer is simple: the PLO must restore a modus operandi reflecting its name by becoming an armed tool for the liberation of Palestine. Essentially, it must return to the roots it abandoned in 1974, not just for the viability of the umbrella organization but also for the sake of Palestinian unity.

The following text matters for two reasons. First, this is one of the most elaborate and recent texts by PIJ on the PLO, as it presents the view of the former on the reform of the Palestinian umbrella organization. Second, it matters because the text presents a historical analysis through which the position of the Palestinian Islamic movement overall is presented: from those representing the "absolute rejection" of the PLO to the two versions of "non-absolute rejection." Abu Taha thus shows that the Palestinian

Islamic position has never been united, nor has it been constant, as the realities on the ground have been dramatically transformed since the 1980s.

What is the position on the Palestine Liberation Organization (PLO) and entering its framework and institutions? How do we understand this issue, and how do we deal with it?

First: The Position of the Islamists on Entering the PLO

The call of the Islamic forces to enter the PLO in order for it to become the umbrella framework of all our people's forces and political and militant activities is not new. Historically, the position of the Palestinian Islamists has vacillated between the following regarding this call:

1. The absolute rejection of the PLO's formation due to ignorance and infidelity, like that of any Arab regime that does not rule by Islam. This is essentially the position of some Islamic forces and currents that are not included in the call to join the PLO because they are not present on the map of struggle or in the jihad of the Palestinian people.
2. The position of non-absolute rejection, which leaves the door half-open to accept the conditions related to the identity of the PLO, its political program and its struggle, on the one hand, and what share will be given to the Islamic faction that will join the PLO, on the other. This is the position of the brothers in Hamas, which entered early dialogues with the PLO during the First Intifada in order to discuss the matter. Yet, there has not been any agreement on the program or representational ratio.
3. The position of non-absolute rejection, which leaves the door half-open to accept the conditions related to the identity of the PLO, its political program, and its struggle without attention to the issues of quotas and representational rates as the primary determinants in the decision to enter the PLO or not. This is the position of Palestinian Islamic Jihad.

It should be noted here that the focus on the ideological perspective in the decision on the PLO is historical. The saying that the Islamic legal position does not allow the Islamists to enter it was mainly because of the Islamic role's absence in the arena of the Palestinian national jihad and struggle since the beginning of the contemporary Palestinian revolution. Indeed, discrediting the PLO as secularist, as opposed to Islam as an antidote, helped the "Islamic conscience" to remove itself from the field of action and justified its moving away from the arena of jihad and resistance.

This picture changed with the establishment and prominence of Palestinian Islamic Jihad and Hamas since the First Intifada, and the prominent role played by the two movements in the arena of jihadist action, especially in the most recent intifada. If there is no longer an emphasis on the role of Islam in the Palestinian cause, then the PLO is required to provide it in its documents and literature after it was written with the blood of Hamas and Palestinian Islamic Jihad's martyrdom-seekers in the field of struggle and confrontation. In other words, the Islamists are no longer required to rehabilitate Islam, its role, and its position in the conflict after the martyrdom-seekers drew the features and horizon of this role in the time of Jenin and Rafah, the time of Yahya Ayyash[1] and Mahmoud Tawalba.[2]

Second: The Need for a Comprehensive National Framework

The starting point for determining the position of the Islamic forces to join the PLO is the ability to answer the following question: Is there an Islamic or national need for such a step in this circumstance? Or is there a need to restructure the PLO so that it fits to take in all the forces of our people, including Hamas and Palestinian Islamic Jihad in what will serve the Islamic current in the long term?

The answer is certainly: Yes…

In this particular time, when the international, regional, and local situation differs from any circumstance experienced by the Palestinian cause, the need to create a comprehensive framework for the struggle of the Palestinian people, involving all forces, is more urgent than ever.

Should the PLO be this framework, however? All the years of experience and debris during which the PLO has left behind a series of failures on more than one level make it difficult for the pure national feeling and conscience, as well as the Islamic one, to accept the PLO as the solution and as the desired framework. However, the same position on the PLO's experiences, its history, and its reality should not obscure a number of objective facts for us that make the PLO the only framework available to the Palestinian people today. They are the following:

1. The PLO has Arab, Islamic, and international recognition, which in the current circumstances is impossible to be obtained by any new or alternative framework, whether it is the framework of a faction or a group of factions.
2. Unlike the Palestinian National Authority (PA), which was produced by an agreement with the occupation, the PLO is a Palestinian Arab achievement, and it is as such not an instant emergency or a flash in the pan. Regardless of any ideological and political reservations, it is in its origin an instrument stemming from the Palestinian need and necessity to fight for the right of Palestinian people in their land, and to build their national political entity on the whole of this land.
3. Since the signing of the Oslo Accords, this comprehensive framework has been exposed to a systematic process to marginalize and to end it, effectively transforming the PLO into an empty and paralyzed apparatus of power. The revival of this framework, of its reconstruction, and of its composition in order

---

[1] Yahya Ayyash (1966–96), chief bombmaker of Hamas and leader of its military wing, the Izz al-Din al-Qassam Brigades, in the West Bank. He was assassinated by Shin Bet on January 5, 1996.
[2] Mahmoud Tawalba (1979–2002), PIJ military field commander in the Second Intifada, responsible for several suicide bombings planned and executed from Jenin. He was killed in Jenin during Operation Defensive Shield in April 2002.

for it to become qualified to absorb all forces in and outside Palestine means to rescue and to protect this framework, which some want to get rid of or to simply preserve as a decoration without any effectiveness. The PA that was created on parts of the West Bank and the Gaza Strip cannot take upon itself the full responsibility for the cause of a people divided between the territories occupied in 1948, the territories occupied in 1967, and the diaspora where more than five million Palestinians live.

4. With the influence of the Islamic forces (Hamas and Palestinian Islamic Jihad) – from the presence and influence from the Palestinian street – their entry into the PLO with the legitimacy they enjoy, and what will come of it after its development, does not mean that these forces will join the PLO with its current program. Rather, this is the approach to make a program of resistance, adopted by the Islamic movement, which is the program of national consensus—that is, the establishment of the resistance project as the articulated option of the Palestinian people's will, and not as an isolated and separated option that is required to be struck and liquidated under the terms of the "road map" and the requirements of the American war on the so-called "terrorism of the world!"

Therefore, the call to enter the PLO is not an expression of a surrender to the status quo or a response to the vulgar political reality that has been marked since the signing of Oslo. It is an expression of a nationalist need, and the necessity for struggle.

Third: Requirements for Restructuring the PLO

If we, within the aforementioned background, recognize the need to rebuild the organization with the entry of the Islamic forces, the important question remains: What liberation organization are we talking about, and what organization of liberation is it that we want?

To answer this question first, we are well aware of what our entry into the PLO means. We are therefore not prepared to relinquish any of our principles that constitute the determinants in our position on the PLO. Therefore, we have no illusions about the possibility of easily restructuring the PLO to become a united framework that includes all the forces of the Palestinian people, headed by Hamas and Palestinian Islamic Jihad. The Cairo Agreement[3] approved the formation of a committee to discuss the process of developing and restructuring the PLO agreed upon by all forces. With this agreement, the movement attended the preliminary meeting held in Gaza for this purpose, in the hope that it would be followed up by other meetings abroad, attended by the factions' secretary-generals in order to discuss the new foundations for the reconstruction of the PLO.

---

[3] Palestinian Cairo Declaration (2005), declaration signed by the main Palestinian factions reaffirming the status of the PLO as the sole representative of the Palestinian people with the implication of including Hamas and Palestinian Islamic Jihad into its structure through a future reorganization.

Thus, joining the PLO is not an easy mechanical process to be achieved with a stroke of the pen as some think. It is a long, arduous, and complex journey as we are still placing our feet and our first steps on the threshold of a strenuous dialogue.

We realize, and the others also, that there are a number of conditions and requirements that must be met before we say that we have become part of the PLO. This brings us closer to the direct answer to the question that we presented: What liberation organization is it that we want?

Perhaps the obvious answer to this question is the following: The PLO must fully reflect its name on the ground—that is, it must be a jihadist tool aimed at "liberating Palestine" and a comprehensive framework that does not work according to a formula derived from the equation of neutralizing the resistance project, but, instead, becomes a real representative of it. To join the PLO, then, does not mean to waiver our principles but, instead, to save the unity of our people and of the land, both struck by the Oslo Agreement and the compromise approach.

This is from our point of view evidenced by the lines and requirements for discussion in the reconstruction process, the most important of which are the following:

1. The charter: There are forces in the PLO talking about a return to the national charter, and demanding the withdrawal of some of the clauses initiated in the presence of Clinton, which were not endorsed by Yasser Arafat before his death. If the old charter is actually installed, we will still need a new charter that takes the Islamic dimension of the Palestinian cause into account and reflects the current scene in the Palestinian arena today. It is not easy to reach this goal in light of the positions of the (official) PA (according to the Oslo Accords), Fatah, and its factions in this matter, particularly because the establishment of the PA has focused on the formulation of a Palestinian "constitution" that sees the Palestinian entity as an authority in the transition process to a state rather than an "organization" leading a phase of national liberation.
2. Decisions of previous national councils: Whatever the commitment of the official authority or the PLO factions to these decisions, it is ultimately the result of the political will produced at a particular time, and there is no logic in placing them on top of the Palestinian people. They are thus in our view a part of the relapses of a closed political moment and do not constitute a sacred legacy that cannot be bypassed or changed.
3. The political program: The PLO does not have a clear political program today. Its program can alternatively be summarized in one word, "compromise," which is implemented through the PA. To rebuild the PLO means that the political program should reflect the vision of the constituent forces of the organization. Therefore, the entry into the PLO by Hamas and Palestinian Islamic Jihad means the current political agenda of the PLO should be the representative will of the Palestinian people.
4. The relationship between the PA and PLO: One of the requirements for reconstruction is a complete disengagement and separation between the PLO and the PA. It is not only a question of positions, but also the elimination of all kinds of interference. The PA has limited powers, no consensus, and it must in any case

be under the supervision of the PLO, instead of the PLO being one of its organs. The PA cannot impose its program on the PLO or employ the PLO in order to serve it.

5. The structure and mechanism of restructuring: In light of the necessity of disengaging the PLO from the PA, it is not fitting to adopt participation in the elections to the PA's legislative council as a way to reach the Palestinian National Council (PNC) as it is now. This mechanism suffers from several problems such as the following:

   a. The willingness of any movement not involved in the PLO to participate in the legislative elections, which means engaging in the PNC, without agreeing to the other requirements of membership concerning the identity (the Charter), the political program, and the fighting role, thus ignoring the necessity of making fundamental adjustments on these subjects. This is what happened in the position of our brothers in Hamas and their participation in the legislative elections.
   b. There are fundamental forces in the Palestinian streets with a role in the resistance (Palestinian Islamic Jihad) that do not participate in the legislative elections in the framework of the current circumstances. Other forces (the Popular Front for the Liberation of Palestine[4] and the Democratic Front for the Liberation of Palestine)[5] have participated, but their presence in the council has been weak due to the intense competition between Fatah and Hamas. How can the representation of such forces and others in the PNC be dealt with, if the only way to reach it is through the Palestinian Legislative Council (PLC)?[6]
   c. The new PLC includes 132 members from the West Bank and the Gaza Strip. So what about the Palestinian people in the diaspora? How can the elections for the legislative council be carried out there?

Generally, how will the Palestinian National Council and the rest of the organization's institutions be reconstituted, and what mechanisms are needed to include all the forces, including Hamas and Palestinian Islamic Jihad?

Accordingly, in the light of the PLO's legacy, which has evoked skepticism from its constituent forces, and in light of the current complexities of the Palestinian situation at all levels, the reconstruction of all its components and needs is not an easy process and cannot be achieved solely with wishes and desires. It is a complex and arduous process in need of a real effort and the hard work of all for the "rebirth" of the PLO. To reach this, all the forces, including Palestinian Islamic Jihad, face the fateful demands and challenges imposed by this stage and by the role of the resistance movements,

---

[4] Popular Front for the Liberation of Palestine (PFLP), a secular Palestinian Marxist-Leninist organization founded in 1967, and the second-largest faction of the PLO.
[5] Democratic Front for the Liberation of Palestine (DFLP), founded in 1968 and headed by Nayif Hawatma. DFLP initially splintered from the PFLP as its founders believed the latter had become too focused on military struggle while neglecting ideology and its grassroots bases.
[6] Palestinian Legislative Council (PLC), the legislature of the Palestinian National Authority.

which cannot afford to run back or get out of the equation and wait again on the "platforms of dreams!"

Naturally, dialogue between the various forces is the starting point when confronting these demands, and it is the key to reaching the goal—that is, a serious, responsible, and constructive dialogue based primarily on the sincere and genuine intentions of all. It means there is a willingness from everyone. It means there is a possibility of moving to a new stage of domestic Palestinian relations in which national unity is not merely a slogan, but, rather, moving to an institutional embodiment by finding the inclusive framework and actual legitimate representation for all forces of our Palestinian people—that is, providing the elements of strength and capability in order to continue the march of our people's struggle and jihad until their full rights are achieved in the whole land of Palestine.

Finally, we hope that we have answered some of these questions about the situation of restructuring the PLO—a sensitive issue at this critical stage in the age of our umma, our people, our cause, and our movement.

We ask God Almighty to bless us all with faithfulness and acceptance.

14

Principal Notes on the Issue of a Palestinian State

Pamphlet published by Palestinian Islamic Jihad, Beirut, April 1989. Author unknown.

This article was presumably written due to the commencement of the US-PLO meetings in Tunisia, in December 1988. With the December meeting in 1988 being the first direct talk between US representatives and PLO officials on peace in the Middle East, it was largely the result of Yasser Arafat renouncing terrorism and recognizing Israel. The following text is thus a historical piece insofar as it demonstrates how certain segments of the Palestinian Islamic movements reacted to these developments at a time when the First Intifada still rumbled through the Occupied Palestinian Territories.

Although the author remains unknown, Fathi al-Shiqaqi is probably a good guess. Indeed, there is something conspicuously "Shiqaqian" about this piece, as the unknown author delves into the longer historical lines in order for the reader to understand contemporary events—employing Europe and its ("natural") historical development as a mirror image to the one imposed on the Arab-Islamic world through Westernization and secularization. Who but al-Shiqaqi would present PIJ's view on a future Palestinian state by discussing the Roman Empire?

This assumption is strengthened by the fact that a common theme in al-Shiqaqi's oeuvre is repeated once more: The Western colonial project managed to fragment the region through Westernization and secularism, which weakened the Islamic creed—the only thing capable of withstanding the Western attack. This attack could only be sustained, and persist, with the establishment of Israel as a natural partner of the colonial project to impose control in the region.

The following document matters for three reasons. First, it is one of the earliest texts written by PIJ on the developments leading to the Oslo Agreement. It thus demonstrates how one of the main Palestinian Islamic actors reacted and how they justified this reaction. Second, the text is of interest because it underlines the extent to which PIJ employed secular analysis and arguments when confronted with the PLO-US meetings. As opposed to the many PIJ communiqués throughout the First Intifada, which employed religious references to mobilize the Palestinian masses, this piece has no Qur'anic references. What is presented is, instead, a historical-secular analysis of the Palestinian situation, the issues at stake, and the possible pitfalls.

Last, the text matters because of al-Shiqaqi's following prophecy: "Such a state, if established, will move the battle against the enemy to one in the Palestinian arena itself, as the form of the state and the compromise will lead to a split within." Eighteen years later, this document has become tragically prescient as the deep political split remains between the West Bank and Gaza, and between Fatah and Hamas.

Preface

The Palestinian state... how? The state... through what road? A state in Gaza and the West Bank? A federal or confederate state? A state with what constituents? Many more questions now circulate in the Palestinian and Arab arena, and occasionally the international one as well. Perhaps the commencement, or the introduction, of the subject concerns the chaos of priorities, so to speak. There are those who want, in good or bad faith, consciously or unconsciously, to ask the tenth question before the first; to turn assumptions into axioms; or even to ask all the questions simultaneously and concurrently.

The only loser in that case—I believe—will be our people, our umma, and our history, and this will certainly lead us to a chaos of priorities. It is easy in such a situation to find those who defend the constituents of a state in the West Bank and in the Gaza Strip. Why not? There are many who live on their services to tourists, on their dependence on the world order, or on the necessity and efforts of this system. Why not? The political thought of the Palestinian national project has had no desire to change or to be replaced since the mid-1970s—not realizing that the intifada itself is capable of changing it! It still adheres to minimalist positions, despite the historical changes we are witnessing in the struggling march of our people. Again, why not? There is a broad current of the political forces of our people, in one way or another ignoring their vision and thesis.

The beginning, as we will see, is not about the constituents of the state, nor is it about the strategy to reach the heart of the enemy front, in which we have become a party in Israeli elections. The beginning is not about the options of the state and its political framework, independent or "liberated." The beginning is far beyond that!

What State? The Historical Paradigm

The modern and contemporary nation-state is a state that originated and developed within the European post-Renaissance context. It is thus a part of the Western civilizational development, in the same way as the separation of religion from governance; a parliamentarian multi-party political system; social classes with economic roots; religious wars; and the conflict over foreign trade markets, etc. Its inception is related to all of this and more. Even if we wished to go into the details of modern European history, this is hardly the place. It is, however, essential for us to discern the main stations that led to the formation of the modern nation-state in Europe. "Central and Mediterranean" Europe lived under the Roman state for centuries, led by a feudal "Roman" ethnic elite—consecrating the supremacy of the center over its peripheries, and consecrating command of the outside's resources and wealth in favor of the inside. In its time, Rome was "the mistress of the world," as the Romans used to say, with the world as a simple appendix.

After the Roman state collapsed under the blows from the northern tribes, no one was more willing to inherit it than the Catholic Church. It was the most organized in the barbaric chaos, the only institution capable of absorbing the northern tribes. In the end, it represented "the Kingdom of God" and "the gate to salvation" as St. Augustine of Hippo[1] deemed it. The European imperial constitution (the Holy Roman Empire) was thus restored—first under the authority of the Holy See and its enormous ecclesiastical network, and then the feudal kings and lords. The Church was to lead the project of the crusader wars and then to open the road for invasion to the east. Then came trade and translations, to launch the Renaissance, and the growth of the Italian commercial city-states. In the Renaissance, the first arrows were directed against the spirit, morals, values, and dominance of the Church. As Western historians note, a process of rationalizing Christianity commenced (Thomas Aquinas[2] being the most famous proponent) paving the way for the Protestant revolution. This revolution did not merely conclude the battle against the spirit of the Church, but it fought a fierce war against its body.

We do not wish to enter an ideological debate on who made the other: whether the bourgeoisie produced Protestantism or whether the latter established the body of the modern bourgeois class and provided it with its ideology. What matters is that the collapse of the Church's authority, and subsequently the destruction of the framework of the Holy Roman State, led to independent churches and independent provinces around them after a series of massacres (most notably the Thirty Years War). It also unleashed the emerging bourgeoisie toward foreign looting, including the colonization of the Americas; the enslavement and looting of, and trade with, the Africans; and then the colonization of the Far East.

The modern state did not commence establishing its final, or even semi-final, form until the nineteenth century. It did so after the defeat of Napoleon, when the aspirations of the new class moved to unify their domestic markets, and to build larger armies and more complex systems that were capable of fighting the conflict (abroad) over its markets, colonies, and wealth. Even if it is understood that the historical context that established the Western nation-state was a logical sequence, each stage carrying the next inside it, we should not lose sight of the fact that this nation-state is not based on the unity of races, but in most cases on the control of the strongest race. Problems such as the economic deterioration of the British north (Scotland) in favor of the south (England), and those in Northern Ireland, the Basque Country, Corsica, Cyprus, and

---

[1] St. Augustine of Hippo (354–430), North-African Christian theologian and philosopher whose works partly laid the foundation of Medieval philosophy and theology.

[2] Thomas Aquinas (1225–74), Italian Christian theologian and philosopher. On both St. Augustine of Hippo and Aquinas, see Ellen Meiksins Wood, *Citizens to Lords: A Social History of Western Political Thought from Antiquity to the Late Middle Ages* (London and New York: Verso Books, 2008).

the dominance of the Russian white minority in the Soviet Union are all examples of this.

What happened in our country was different, however, at all levels. Our country never knew a state consisting of class- or ethnic elites, nor of a higher religious body. After the break with the tribal era, and the defeat of the Persians and Romans, the Islamic world knew the state of sharia, the rule of law—with all the transgressions of some of its rulers and emirs. True, but even in those periods, the most powerful rulers and sultans—no matter how false, sycophantic, or cowardly—were careful to base their position on sharia—because the legitimacy of the regime was based on Islamic law. An "institutional" religious class-elite had not monopolized this Islamic law, but a man from among the freed slaves could become a great jurist standing in front of the Sultan, and a small merchant in Baghdad could become the greatest jurist of his time, and the umma could rally around him greater than it rallied around any sultan or ruler. The umma was the depositor of Islamic legislation and law.

Our country did not differentiate between the inside and the outside. Everything inside the state's borders was inside, and there was thus no center—in the European sense—dominating the peripheries and absorbing them. When it was the capital of the world, Baghdad had dozens of cities from Cordoba to Khorasan, and from Medina to Bukhari and Samarkand. Throughout the Islamic era, our country did not produce a socioeconomic class, and our history thus did not know the struggle of a new class against feudalism and the Church. Indeed, the Church of Augustine itself did not know the Islamic history or anything like it in any way. Arabs, scholars, ministers, deputies, and officers were partners in authority and governance, as were the Turks, even in the worst stages of Ottoman rule.

The Western colonial conflict toward it had not begun, and the Turkish Westernized elite commenced the process of transforming the Ottoman Empire into something similar to the Roman Empire. This was, of course, after the removal of Sultan Abdul Hamid II, who was not as oppressive as the Arab Westernized elite were! How then did the idea of the nation-state enter the mind and reality in our region and in the rest of the Islamic world?

Imposing the Fragmented State on Our Country

The answer is not so simple. Yet, the important thing is the demise of civil and military force, and the intellectual stagnation in the Islamic world, which commenced after the seventeenth century AD, although numerous causes had accumulated since the first Hijri centuries. This demise was met by the growing vitality of Europe and the crystallization of the Western colonial project. While colonialism had penetrated much of the world with relative ease, the Islamic wall was still unyielding and capable of resistance, despite the accumulation of weakness, and it resisted for more than two entire centuries.

As the imbalance of power grew, this wall had to collapse. However, its collapse was accomplished only through an overly complex and comprehensive process. First, the Western colonial project succeeded in seizing a large section from the Islamic world's elite for the benefit of its cultural and civilizational authority. Second, it then proceeded to tear up the Islamic world by force—the force of arms, soldiers, and bloody occupation, from the battles of the coast of Oman to Libya and Egypt to the First World War. Third, the Western colonial project succeeded in planting the state of the Zionist entity in the Arab and Islamic heart to guarantee the permanence of fragmentation, dependence, annexation, and domination.

The contemporary nation-state in the Islamic world was not a demand by the masses. Nor was it the result of the development of a historical context and domestic factors in our country. It was, instead, a part of the global Western colonial project, imposed with violence and the force of arms. Deceitfully, before and after the stage of direct colonialism, it was handed over to a Westernized elite whose authority was imposed on the masses, most often with violence—a Western state violence in a historical context of its central power represented by its repressive apparatuses and instruments.

We must not lose sight of the fact that Western colonialism—which approved of, and desired, the formation of nation-states in the Islamic world—was rejected and resisted in the Arab region. The former imposed another barrier between the Arabs and their national unity, the small and limited nation-states, although they enjoyed the greatest ethnic harmony—not only compared to the other "third world" countries, but also to the European countries themselves. It was for the simple reason that the Arab basin is the reservoir of creed, history, and civilization, which must be prevented by all means from forming a major power capable of reuniting the diaspora of the umma anew and resisting the project of Western domination.

There is no doubt, however, that the state of the Zionist entity was, and remains, a representative of the Western attack's fundamental pillar in the region. Here is a state, an idea, a system, and a people erected, all of which are an integral part of the Western project itself. A long historical context thus brought "Israel" to our country—from the emergence of the Protestant Church and the revival of the biblical text in modern Europe, and the return of the Jews to the market and power in capitalist society, to the convergence of the Zionist project's goals with those of the Western colonial project. The long context makes it futile to separate colonial domination, annexation, and dependence of the West from the Zionist entity. Certainly, it was not possible to establish this entity without defeating the last Islamic wall (the Ottoman Empire), without the formation of a Westernized elite linked to the outside of our country, and without the establishment of the state of fragmentation.

It was therefore not vanity when our movement—Palestinian Islamic Jihad—raised the slogan: Palestine is the central cause of the contemporary Islamic movement. Here is found a deep historical awareness, rather than an arbitrary selectiveness. If independence, unity, and defeat of fragmentation is to be achieved; if there is to be a total renaissance without attachment or dependency; if there is to be a reunified state of the umma, then it is necessary to fight the battle against Westernization and fragmentation to the end, and against the center of the attack and its base in the state of the Zionist entity. Our movement did not wait for positive changes to take place in the region, but, instead, proceeded to form a spearhead in the direct confrontation with the enemy since the early 1980s—perhaps to eventually ignite the spark of resurgence.

Simultaneously, we find it useless and ahistorical to base the Palestinian national project on the regional and international power balance in order to realize the right (or some parts of it as is said today) in Palestine. The international system is not prepared to give up the center of its domination or the regional system with fragmentation, subordination, and dependency. Indeed, fragmentation was a condition for the establishment of the state of the Zionist entity, so how can balancing its power be a tool against it?

The difficult question is made apparent here. Why do we as Muslim Palestinians have to accept giving up a large part of our country, the holiest land on Earth in Islam? Why do we have to give up a great part of our people in return for the nation-state's identity; the completion of dependency circles; and adding a new system to the group of subordination and dependence? Even until 1920, and afterward, did our people not demand a separate state, but wished to be a part of the Arab umma in its entirety, or at least a part of the Levant, regardless of the implications this may have had on the current Arab political situation. Al-Hajj Amin al-Husayni—May God have mercy on him—did not see that he and his people were only responsible for Palestine in 1931, but called on all scholars of the Islamic umma and its personalities to the Jerusalem Conference to consider what should be done.

We thus see from the outset that the process of reducing the conflict, and separating it from its historical context, now leads some to present this unjust and invalid compromise to our people: a nation-state and a national identity in return for abandoning a part of the right, the largest part—ultimately, to live under the shade of Western colonial domination.

The system of the regional state and the state of fragmentation is completely alien to our historical context, and the umma will eventually get rid of it once its complete renaissance is achieved. Why should we accept it in exchange for losing most of Palestine and its people?

On the Palestinian State

Even so, we in Palestinian Islamic Jihad realize that the set of negative developments since the First World War has created a reality that must be dealt with in order to develop it for the better. We are therefore aware that the conflict cycles have led a large segment of our struggling people at this stage to see Palestinian national independence in its final form to mean the dismissal of the Zionist project. We are therefore first with Palestine, all of Palestine from its river to its sea, independent and free, if there must be an independent Palestinian entity from the rest of the umma. We are also with an Islamic Palestine, however, because it truly guarantees independence from the Western project and its dominance, ensuring movement toward unity.

Whether things are moving in that direction or not, we believe that there are three basic directions from this stage onward to where the Palestinian question may be moving:

The first direction: That the Palestinian national project actually succeeds in achieving its goal of establishing a Palestinian state in the West Bank and the Gaza Strip, or a confederation with Jordan. Before we define our position on that situation, however, we find it necessary to mention the caveats concerning the continuation of that project in the Palestinian, Arab, and Islamic arena:

1. From the onset, we see that the regional and international power balance (hence, the link between the Zionist project and the Western colonial project; the factors of ideology; and the religious and political myths within the Zionist entity) does not indicate that there is any tendency in the enemy to provide such a concession. We see that some of the local and international forces, and some of the Zionists, push the PLO to continue moving toward the state project with the previous concessions and compromises. Essentially, it only aims to rip the Palestinian struggle further apart, attempting to abort the renaissance of our people and their jihad.
2. Such a state, if established, will move the battle against the enemy to one in the Palestinian arena itself, as the form of the state and the compromise will lead to a split within.
3. This state will not only disclaim the rest of Palestine if established, but it will also never be a state for all the Palestinian people abroad and in the occupied 1948 areas. If it was, then it would be incapable of accommodating them all. Just as it will be incapable of withstanding the framework of annexation, dependence, and subordination under the great powers; indeed, under the small ones too!
4. This state, whether in federalism with Jordan or independent, will only lead to the eruption of internal Jordanian-Palestinian conflict given the complex circumstances surrounding the two countries and their political entities. It will additionally raise tensions on all levels in the Levant at the very least.
5. The great disaster in such a situation, however, is that the state will become a true bridge to expand the Zionist civilizational, cultural, and economic project toward the entire Arab region, and even the Islamic world as a whole. If the Palestinians kneel before compromise and peace with the Zionist entity, who will then be able to withstand it?

In spite of all the caveats, everyone has ignored our raised voice, and we have already found ourselves confronted with that situation. Our position will thus be the following:

- At the level of conflict with the enemy, our movement will be of the opinion that nothing has changed and that the military, political, and cultural struggle with it, by all other means, is still open until this project is completely defeated. We will continue to call upon our people and entire umma to continue the jihad no matter what obstacles are put in front of us. We therefore stress that our battle is with the Zionist enemy and its project, and it will never be with any part of our people or our umma.

- At the level of the internal Palestinian situation, we will call to raise the banner of Islam and its system—in other words, first and foremost calling to please God Almighty. This will guarantee the continuation of the conflict until the end, and that it will continue with hundreds of millions of our umma united by Islam, and united around Palestine for decades. It is with emphasis that we view the Christian Palestinians as partners of one homeland, one history, one civilization, and one battle against the Western-Zionist project. At all levels, we reject the attempts of straining the relationship between Muslims and Christians in Palestine—not today, tomorrow, or anytime. The history of Islam and its civilization is not a history of disavowing the others and torching them. It is the history of an exceptional legal civilization, which recognizes creedal plurality, coexistence, and its codification.

This will be so if the issues move in the first direction.

The second direction: This is what we call upon all forces of our people under the circumstances of the current phase and the inability of the Arab and Islamic region to move comprehensively—in short, a structured, serious, and genuine mobilization of all political forces, and all forces and bases of our people, on all levels, to continue the conflict against the Zionist enemy until the end. To drive it from our land, inch by inch, village by village, city by city, till the Mediterranean coast, so that a form of political system will be established on every liberated spot with the continuation of the conflict without compromise, without recognition, and without negotiation for them, unless the enemy approaches us to negotiate the dismantling of its project and its eternal departure from our country.

The third direction: This is considered by our movement its main strategic project, corresponding with the context of the conflict's history in our country, and between our umma and the Western-Zionist project. It is for our people and mujahidin to continue in the confrontation with the enemy politically and militarily, and with all means until the potentials of the umma burst out toward renaissance, unity, and independence under the great banner of Islam—to mobilize the potentials of our whole umma, and even parts of it, toward the battle taking place in Jerusalem and its surroundings.

15

Fundamentalism and Secularism

Lecture held by Fathi al-Shiqaqi in the Ghassan Kanafani Hall in al-Yarmuk refugee camp, Damascus, on July 10, 1995, with Tayyib al-Tizini. The seminar was organized by the Committee for the Defense of National Culture and Friends of Ghassan Kanafani. The lecture was subsequently published in the newspaper al-Hayat on July 28, 1995.

Little has been published by PIJ on future Palestinian society and its political organization once the occupation is ended. Instead, one often finds general outlines such as the principle to establish Islamic rule in the land of Palestine guided by consultation in accordance with divine law. Many could thus easily assume that the movement desires an Islamic state, which from the top down enforces Islamic law and jurisdiction.

The following text challenges many commonly held assumptions about the movement's ambitions for future political rule. Employing the historical struggle between society and ecclesiastical power (the Church) in Europe as a mirror against the Arab-Islamic experience, al-Shiqaqi attempts to analyze the problem of centralized authority in the Middle East. While al-Shiqaqi perceived secularism to have liberated Europe from the domination of the Church over state and society, the opposite was true for the Arab-Islamic experience. There, the institution of scholars was able to protect society from the perceived tyranny of the state before colonially imposed secularism dismantled the existing checks and balances.

This text thus matters for two reasons. First, it is one of the very few texts in which PIJ elaborates on future Palestinian society, its contradictions, and what it perceives as a just political system. Second, this lecture shows that PIJ deemed the greatest threat to Islamic law and values to be the state itself. As al-Shiqaqi postulates in what follows: "The state is repressive by nature, or a tool of repression against the government classes as defined by Lenin. It is the most dangerous instrument of power created by human society." The movement correspondingly outlines a society in which the state is inherently weak in order to avoid despotic rule to develop.

It is uncertain who influenced al-Shiqaqi in this direction. One possibility is the Tunisian Islamist intellectual Rachid Ghannouchi, given the similarity of their just societies. It is a possibility as al-Shiqaqi met Ghannouchi more than once. Another possibility is the influence from the Iranian politician Abolhassan Banisadr—as al-Shiqaqi refers to him in "The Revolution and the State in Iran" (unfortunately not included in this book). This uncertainty notwithstanding, the following text shows that PIJ believes in an Islamic society nurtured from below rather than imposed from above. As al-Shiqaqi suggests: "This society has to be built with a great degree of independence from the state, in which the former is given strength in confronting the state."

I would first like to register my reservations and observations—not only about fundamentalism but about two terms as they both store a particular European experience. At least, I am described here as an Islamist and not as a fundamentalist, as I will talk about Islamism and not about fundamentalism. This term, Islamism, which has passed into our culture today. This term some are silent about, as they believe it means a return to the Islamic fundamentals and principles, or they identify it with the term "fundamentalists," which in our history means the group of jurists engaged in the principles of jurisprudence.

Fundamentalism is a term storing experiences, symbols, and inspirations that have nothing to do with us, but which is, instead, linked with European history and Christian textual culture—adhering literally to the texts, and sometimes reflecting the application of violence in order to achieve its objectives. The Arabic word *al-uṣūliyya* is a poor translation of the English "fundamentalism," which in the dictionaries is described as the doctrine of individual infallibility and thus a reference to the Protestant movement. We are thus facing a Western term carrying Western-Christian connotations, and when the Westerner calls me a fundamentalist, there is little room for any positive suggestions. Simply, he wants to reduce me within a particular and distinct inflexible Christian European experience and to affix its negative connotations to me. It distinguishes at the same time between Christian, Jewish, and Islamic fundamentalist phenomena, and it can even be said to be a Marxist fundamentalism. All of this excludes the possibility of a practical and impartial rendition, and it makes tackling the issue subject to inflammatory incitement against Islamism or against the Islamic phenomenon far from any historical, scientific, or objective context.

Before I drop this remark, I should point out that the term "Islamist" does not mean that those who are not characterized as such are not Muslims, which is the majority of the umma's Muslims. The term is here meant for designation and for ejection from Islam. The term describes, or pertains to, those preoccupied with the general Islamic concern and with the alternative of the Islamic thought and system as a cause of struggle.

The other remark concerns the term "secularism," which is a non-Arabic word. It was carved out equivocally, and employed narrowly by the elites, without looking at the circumstances or the background of the original word. Indeed, it emerged as a theory against the social and political domination of the church in its miserable historical image, and it put forth liberation of the mind and body after a long war with the church. We cannot pass this term into our culture and into our lives, except on two conditions:

1. That the church resembles the mosque in content, role, and working method, and that the ecclesiastical authority resembles the authority of the religious scholars (the Muslims).

2. That the forces of the emerging European civil society at the time and its bourgeoisie vanguard, the carrier and product of the Industrial Revolution, resemble similar forces in our own historical experience.

Because none of these conditions apply, it will be difficult to pass the term "secularism" scientifically or objectively into our culture and lives.

I may add that the origin in the conflict leading to secularism's emergence—as the basis for building the modern state—was not the presence of religion itself or even the church, the religious body, or the intellectual values derived from this religion. Instead, it arose from the domination of the church over the affairs of state and society. This tense relationship between religion and the state, and the contradiction between their values, are nothing but an exception in history. Islam did not experience it; nor did Buddhism and Confucianism experience it.

Either way, if I have the right not to employ the term fundamentalism, then it is not my right to prevent others from employing the term secularism. I will continue my discussion of it in a historical and analytical context in order to proceed to the cries and calls for secularism in the context of the modern Arab renaissance movement, which moved in a different direction than the trajectory of the European Enlightenment and Renaissance. We are thus facing two different contexts—one European and the other Arab-Islamic—and the systems, results, and discourse of the former were copied and applied to a different context. We thus washed our hands of our own heritage before reviving it—that is, before discovering it and its active and living values in society.

The problem in the European experience was the domination of the church over society and state, and its despotism, with illusions and superstition. The problem in the Arab-Islamic experience was the state's attempt to dominate society (that is, from controlling education, legislation, the market, the waqf, and the religious heritage) up to its almost complete hegemony, with the emergence of the nation-state from the labor pains of the nationalist dreams, especially today.

Indeed, the two problems are different. Secularism in the European context attempted to liberate man and society. It did not do the same thing in the Arab-Islamic context, however, but, instead, worked to break the mode of the Islamic society until it reached a stage of fragility, paving the way for the state to control everything. Secularism thus contributed more to the cementation of the patriarchal autocratic regime than to human liberation—perhaps because of its claims against the theocratic religious authority and against the allegedly tyrannical Caliph becoming God on Earth.

Were these claims valid? Jamal al-Din al-Afghani says: "There is no such thing in Islam called a religious authority, but Islam is a religion and law. It has placed limits and rights." The Caliph "is charged with establishing limits and justly implementing the ruling of the judge." Regarding any executive authority, it is "not infallible or the cradle of revelation, and it does not have the exclusive right to interpret the Qur'an and the sunna… It is not permissible to confuse the Caliph among Muslims with what is called western theocracy." That is, the divine ruler "is for them the only one to receive the law from God and who has the right to choose legislation, and he is the only one the people can obey. Not by allegiance or for the justice and protection of the state, but by virtue of faith. As long as the believer is a believer, he does not have the right to disobey." In the view of Muhammad Abduh, the Caliph is "a civilian ruler of all."

The state is repressive by nature, or a tool of repression against the government classes as defined by Lenin. It is the most dangerous instrument of power created by human society, so Islam worked to sort out a mode of human society depriving this state of its power and domination, and thus making it weaker than, and accountable to, society even if the most powerful caliphs and sultans controlled it. After the early period of Islam, and when the institutions of scholars felt the state had begun to become corrupted, they fought it on legislation and kept the state from it. Imam al-Shafi'i[1] devised the idea of consensus[2] as the cornerstone of legislation after the Qur'an and sunna in order to deprive the state of authority on legislation. He told the state that the third source of legislation after the Qur'an and sunna was consensus and not the ruler—the consensus of the umma's scholars. When Ibn al-Muqaffa'[3] attempted to convince the Abbasid Caliph Mansour[4] that the caliph had a political and legislative right, and a right to impose a single jurisprudential and legal system throughout the state, Mansour was incapable of advancing because he understood the strength of the institution of scholars and their opposition.

The institution of scholars was able to protect society from the tyranny of the state and to preserve its cohesive fabric. It oversaw legislation, justice, education, and waqf, and it had closer relations to the market (the bazaars). It even guided the soldiers in war, and the soldiers learned at the hands of the scholars, while our armies today have become Western in culture and in style. Thus, at a time when the secularists wanted to separate religion and state, and to establish civil institutions, they contributed in fact to destroying the mode of Islamic society. For they struck the most important civil institution, which was completely subjected to the state after being dismantled and having its internal strength fragmented. Today, it can no longer move its forces as we saw during the Gulf War. Indeed, the most important manifestations of support for the Palestinian intifada in the region took place in Tel Aviv and not in an Arab city. Further, the most important manifestations of support against the Israeli invasion of Lebanon were also in Tel Aviv and not in an Arab city.

The "secular" appeal nonetheless continues: "We want a civil society"—despite the fact that we are moving further and further away from civil society. We had a true civil society for fourteen centuries, which was independent from the state and with education, health, waqf, and mosque in its hands. Even with the corruption and moral collapse of the state, with its justice or injustice, it did not leave a serious impact on society. Civil society was struck when they cried and shouted that this was backward and reactionary. So the new civil society was not achieved, and we did not preserve our heritage.

---

[1] Abu Abdallah Muhammad bin Idris al-Shafi'i (767–820), Islamic theologian and scholar, and the first contributor to the principles of jurisprudence.
[2] Consensus (*ijmā'*), agreement among Islamic scholars on aspects of Islamic law.
[3] Abu Muhammad Abdallah ibn Daduya (?–759), Persian author.
[4] Abu Ja'far Abdallah ibn Muhammad al-Mansur (714–75), second Abbasid Caliph and regarded as the founder of the Abbasid Caliphate.

Still, Where Is the Error?

The secular appeals and propositions miscalculated the objective and subjective requirement for the renaissance when they did not restrict the essence of European modernization. Consequently, the essence of the modern Western challenge against us is based on modern science and modern industry. The challenge moved from its true field to another: from the field of modern science to the field of creed; and from the field of modern industry to the field of art, literature, and historical sciences. Thus was the renaissance obstructed because of the dualism, fissure, and societal schizophrenia afflicting the character of the Arab man, destroying it in front of differing creeds, arts, literatures, and cultures. Simultaneously, no attention was paid to the natural sciences, mathematics, and industrialization.

In addition to miscalculating the objective condition, the secular appeals did not understand the required subjective condition for realizing the heritage and reviving it—reviving the concepts and values of the heritage. We cannot renew anything unless man renews himself, and man cannot renew himself through science, industry, and governance, but through spiritual revival and renewing the system of moral and aesthetic concepts and values. Even worse, instead of contributing to the spiritual revival as sustenance for revolution, the attack was carried out against our spiritual values and enabled the Western culture. Thus, instead of responding to the sentiments of the Muslim masses and the calls of the great revolutionaries such as Jamal al-Din al-Afghani, European liberal thought was imitated: Islam and reason; Islam and science; Islam and development; Islam and politics; religion and state; and Islam and democracy.

Further, the failure to recognize the subjective requirement prevented the commencement of a genuine and serious dialogue with the West, and it prevented us from conducting a process of cultural exchange with it. We knew neither our principles, nor the principles of Western thought.

What Do the Islamists Want? What Is Our Islamic Project Today?

1. Our project is to rebuild the community, the society, and the umma. It must remain a top priority for the Islamic movement to contribute strongly and effectively to rebuild the community. The society whose civilizational and historical fabric, position, and role were destroyed by the attack of the (aspiring) state, and which the notables—Westernized, on the one hand, and connected to the states, on the other—justified. This society has to be built with a great degree of independence from the state, in which the former is given strength in confronting the state so that civil society supervises education and has authority over media, communication, and affairs. We are in need of a constitutional review of the state's objectivity in our country.

    Rebuilding the community and actualizing its cohesiveness will make accomplishing the rest of the goals a matter of time.

2. The conflict with the Western-Zionist alliance certainly affects the existence of the umma, its presence, its identity, and its historical right to its homeland and independent decision. Without resolving the conflict about Palestine, all attempts to achieve the renaissance or independence will be aborted or besieged. The Islamic current in Palestine thus affirms, along the Arab-Islamic basin, its non-recognition of the Zionist entity's legitimacy, as well as the necessity of continuing the conflict in all its civilizational, economic, political, and military dimensions. This settlement is rejected as it opens up the doors of the Arab and Islamic capitals for the Israeli invasion without any resistance, and the invaders aim for the region's fragmentation. They tear the region apart—nation by nation, sect by sect, and doctrine by doctrine, reshaping it anew on an economic basis. The aggressors thus transform the civilizational conflict in one of the most dangerous regions of the world into relations of consumer and vendor in a market controlled by transnational corporations and subjected to the mechanisms of contemporary capitalism.

   Changing the unjust power balance working for the enemy must remain a strategic objective that we seek on all levels, and we must constantly work to achieve a balance of terror with the enemy until we achieve it.
3. Fragmentation and the establishment of the Zionist entity were the most prominent features of the colonial project in our country. In context of our resistance against the Zionist entity, we stress the necessity of unity within the nationalist, Arab, and Islamic circles—realizing the urgency of Arab unity by fulfilling its components and necessity.
4. The Islamic current calls for the widest popular alliance including all forces against the Zionist-imperialist project. It calls for the commitment of these forces, as the conflict with the hostile world outside is the absolute priority. Domestic ideological or political variations are solved through dialogue far from violence. It calls on all fighting currents to reread each other without disavowal and without referring to the outside. The Islamic current is itself called upon to reevaluate some of the Arab nationalist and secularist experiences. It is itself called upon to reinforce its political alliance with the serious nationalist forces to create a broad nationalist front in the confrontation with the regime of countries and dependence, which became a pliable tool in any formation or fate intended for the region, or in any other of the colonial West's perceptions.
5. Development is society's course to reach the renaissance, and to escape economic and political dependence—for "underdevelopment" is today the essence of our problem. The inevitable alternative is thus development and progress based on the science, industry, and the rationality of the system depending on them without any prejudice against our moral values. Nor against our creedal or ideological system required for the revival of man as an element and component for major development.
6. The Islamic current rejects political oppression, it calls for the widest popular political participation, and it allows consultation, for Islam considers it a divine obligation and not merely a human right. Islam thus makes it one of the

rules of Islamic law and a component for judgments. Al-Qurtubi[5] states in his interpretation of the verse "and Consult Them in the Matter": "Consultation is one of Islamic law's principles and a component for judgment. If someone does not consult the community of scholars, then dismissing him becomes a duty. This is beyond dispute." In fact, Islam commends consultation, making it a path to infallibility when the Prophet said: "My umma will not agree on misguidance."

Indeed, one of the most important things Islam did was solving the problem of "power" without centralizing it. Islam thus removed the fangs of the state: legislation, education, and the market, and it imposed the pillar of waqf. Democracy, on the other hand, in the Western sense, does not give a true indication of people's participation. So they go to the ballot boxes every four or five years, and less than eighty percent of the people participate. Consequently, the leaders rise to power with thirty percent of those having the right to vote!

In any case, the problem that some Islamists have with democracy is with the term and not with the principle of consultation and political participation. Nor do they have a problem with the mechanisms, means, systems, institutions, and experiences achieving the purposes and objectives of democracy. It is well known that sovereignty in legislation is that of God. Yet, man remains the authority in accordance with this divine law: elaborating it; and codifying its tenets, its rules, its principles, and sectioning it. As such, man has the authority of independent reasoning in what is not revealed in heavenly law, as long as human authority remains governed by the philosophy of Islam in legislation (what is allowed and what is prohibited).

The Islamists are today the most prominent victims of political oppression and the absence of democracy, which means the participation of the masses in the street and in politics. This means the return of Islam with what it represents of identity, steadfastness, and independence.

No one has a greater interest in democracy than the Islamists. It will remain in their interests to preserve democracy; the principle of political pluralism; and the rotation of power within the framework of respecting the will of the umma and the constitution that the umma freely agrees upon, which defines its reference.

7. Generally, the Islamic current rejects domestic, internal violence completely; it does not consider violence an Islamic option. Violence is a historical and global phenomenon, and it should be dealt with not in an ideological context but in a social and political one. Perhaps the left and Marxism were the most prominent embodiment of the phenomenon of violence in the twentieth century, which is found in their basic texts and in their practice across the world. The Islamic current sees the most serious and worst violence as that which Western colonialism practiced for two centuries against the people in the region. The colonial West murdered one million people in just one decade and in one spot of our homeland: in Algeria. It is the same West that supported and backed the military coup d'état against democracy in the same place (Algeria), which has led to more than 40,000 being killed and tens of thousands arrested until now.

---

[5] Abu Abdallah al-Qurtubi (1214–73), Islamic interpreter, scholar of hadith, and jurist.

Colonialism left behind us a state of systematic violence against society as a whole and against the opposition in particular. The violent course of the state and its organized terrorism (which it practices in more than just one place) are the key causes of domestic violence. The Islamists work better in conditions of domestic peace, which is in greater harmony with their political and ideological organizational structure as they address a society with their understanding, and which receives their vision. The Islamists do not need violence to impose their vision on society. Those who employ violence against the Islamists are the ones fearing the Islamic project, and they cannot find any help in society in their calls against the Islamists.

The absence of freedom creates a tension and an anxiety making some environments or groups consider violence, and there is no way to stop this except by spreading true freedom among all.

16

Excerpts from "The Islamic Movements and the developments of the Palestinian Cause"

Interview with Fathi al-Shiqaqi published in the newspaper The Objective (al-Hadaf) *in September 1995.*

With bits and pieces existing on future society, this interview with al-Shiqaqi is in many ways an elaboration of the lecture held in Damascus three months earlier. There, al-Shiqaqi talked about the need to construct a civil society independent from the state as the latter inevitably had to turn despotic. Here, he elaborates on the role of civil society and the role of religion in the negotiation and implementation of politics.

Al-Shiqaqi maintains that PIJ supports democracy, freedom of elections and opinions, and the protection of human rights. The movement rejects political oppression, which is suggested to be antithetical to religion, and it supports popular political participation. That is, PIJ does not oppose democratic mechanisms and systems as they are all in the interests of Islamists. This should not be particularly surprising given that al-Shiqaqi himself had felt the effects of authoritarian rule when he was arrested twice in Egypt for publishing his booklet about Khomeini and the Iranian revolution.

Yet, there are questions about the democratic potentials of PIJ's future society. As the excerpt from this interview shows, al-Shiqaqi does support free elections and political participation. Yet, religion is also perceived to be over and above politics, with little room for maneuver outside of its confines. Consequently, as religion is the basis and framework of legislation, al-Shiqaqi suggests that Islam must remain the identity of the umma and its reference. "All currents that recognize one authority [Islam] for the umma are a part of it and have the right to express themselves in the appropriate manner." We may thus question to what degree secular and Marxist parties would be able to participate in, and to negotiate, the framework of the political system.

This interview matters for two reasons. First, little is written by PIJ about its conception of future society and how it envisions a just political system. This interview is thus a much-needed elaboration of the preceding lecture by al-Shiqaqi. Second, while al-Shiqaqi stresses the need for democratic practices and freedom, this interview highlights how there are certain structural limitations to that vision. As he notes: "As long as there is respect for the [Islamic] constitution, and the issue is a disagreement of interpretation, then there will not be a problem." The answer thus seems to be "no."

C

In your debate with Dr. Tayyeb Tizini[1] on the twenty-third anniversary of Ghassan Kanafani's[2] martyrdom, you said: "In truth, we are moving further and further away from civil society. We have had a true civil society for thirteen centuries, which was independent from the state and with education, health, waqf, and mosque in its hands." Is it reasonable of you to consider separating education and health from the state, particularly as such sectors require substantial and increasing support in such a way that no one, no matter how powerful, can provide such services except the state?

What was meant was that when the nation-state—also a remnant of the colonial stage—dominated society, it destroyed its structure and fragmented its internal fabric that gives society its vitality. The state's responsibility to the people—particularly in providing the opportunities of life, health, and education—is fixed according to Islamic jurisprudence and law. We are talking about separating legislation from the executive power, however, so that not everything is placed in the hands of the ruler. The state controls everything today from legislation to jurisdiction and executive power. There is thus no legislative authority independent from the state preventing the latter from infringement, particularly since unlimited security apparatuses support this state.

Take Press Law no. 93 of 1995 in Egypt, for example. The state imposed the law on the Egyptian parliament despite the comprehensive opposition. Legislation has today become subjected to the state or the executive power, while under Islam it was subjected to the class of scholars and judges, and others qualified to appoint or depose a ruler.[3]

In your opinion, who should have legislation in their hands today?

Legislation should be in the hands of the umma and its representatives. It should not be in the hands of the state, and it should remain under the Revelation, and thus under the sovereignty of God and under Islamic law. The umma is the source of its jurisdictions, however, and there is no deputy for God to govern as he himself wishes.

Will the authority of the umma be through parliament, for example?

Yes, what prevents that?

Can religion rule as it did in previous times, or will it have to adjust to the times as happened with the Christian democratic parties in Europe?

---

[1] Tayyeb Tizini (1934–2019), Syrian Marxist philosopher.
[2] Ghassan Kanafani (1936–72), Palestinian author, poet, and a leading member of the Popular Front for the Liberation of Palestine.
[3] Al-Shiqaqi employs here the term "the people of loosening and binding" (*ahl al-ḥall wa-l-'aqd*), which refers to those qualified to appoint or depose a caliph. See Oxford Islamic Studies, "Ahl al-Hall wa'l-Aqd," http://www.oxfordislamicstudies.com/article/opr/t125/e73 [accessed: October 21, 2019].

Islam offers a comprehensive approach to solve human problems, and this approach is based on basic principles and constants. The details, on the other hand, are influenced by time and place in the context of these principles, but they never depart from them. Let us say, for example, that Christianity is a religion and that Marxism is an ideology and an economic and political idea. Islam combines both: the purely religious creed and the economic, political, social, and legal ideas. The secular elites are ignorant of Islam and fill themselves and the people with fear of a specter that does not exist. As the Marxists advocate their idea, so do we call upon the people to our idea and try to convince the people in a friendly manner, believing that Islam's ruling in our lives will bring happiness to the people, guarantee stability, and preserve their identity.

I want to know your opinion on issues that are considered the pillars of modern civil society, such as freedom of opinion and expression, pluralism, and the rotation of power. What is your view on these traditions?

I believe that Islam forms the umma's identity and its civilizational heritage, which cannot be abandoned, and which simultaneously is its reference. With the recognition of this reference, then, there is no problem with pluralism. Islam does not mean this party or that movement. All of these Islamic movements and organizations do not equate to Islam but are only a part of it. All currents that recognize one authority for the umma are a part of it and have the right to express themselves in the appropriate manner. We therefore believe in pluralism and the rotation of power within the framework of all recognizing the authority of the one umma and the constitution on which the umma agrees. After that, if there are a number of independent reasonings and interpretations, even in the understanding of the constitution and religion itself, there is still no problem.

Some say that the constitution must be the Qur'an?

It is intended for the Qur'an to provide the constitution with the basis and principles on which the constitution is based. However, the Qur'an is not simply a law book.

Some say that your position on pluralism and rotation of power is only tactical?

This position is a principled one for us, and it has been established for a long time, since the appearance and maturity of our political idea. We persistently defend it, and we are paying a price for it. Nor did anyone attempt the opposite. Pluralism is a natural issue and it is not possible to suppress it. As for the rotation of power, it is acceptable and it even pushes the Islamists to innovate and avoid stagnation, and those doubting the Islamists' position are either those in power or those who support them without any pluralism or rotation.

Suppose you were the ruling party and let us assume the umma adopted a constitution largely considered to represent your opinions. Will you allow others to introduce their point of view on hot issues on the Islamic law such as hudud-punishment, for example, demanding civil penalties instead of stoning and flogging? I mean if these people did not use violence in order to change the constitution, will you allow them to use peaceful methods to reach their goals, such as expressing their views publicly, forming parties, and negotiating with you?

As long as there is respect for the constitution, and the issue is a disagreement of interpretation, there will not be a problem. The important thing is to respect the will of the umma, through the one authority and the constitution that is freely accepted. After that, I do not see any obstacle to pluralism and for others to seek power. I can disagree with you, but I will not oppress you or eliminate you with force.

℃

17

Creedal and Intellectual Foundations for the "Culture of Resistance"

Lecture held by Dr. Anwar Abu Taha at the Center for Arabic Culture in Damascus, 2009, organized by Dar al-Fikr under the title "Jerusalem is the responsibility for all of us."

PIJ is often referred to as a revolutionary movement. Yet, if "revolutionary" signifies something more than "violent"—the aspiration for the complete transformation of society—how accurate is it to describe the movement as such? As this lecture by Anwar Abu Taha shows, much indicates that the violence PIJ employs is not particularly different from that of other Palestinian factions such as Hamas and Fatah. Instead, Abu Taha proposes a violence that is preservative rather than transformative. The goal of PIJ is hence not to create a radically new utopian society but, rather, to revive and conserve perceived customs, traditions, and values of the past. If there is anything absent in this text, it is the future. Drawing on numerous religious and historical references, Abu Taha also discusses the legality of resistance in general by outlining a thesis of resistance as a universal and inalienable natural right by virtue of man being God's creation.

As the PIJ founding fathers came to believe in the Islamic creed as a liberation ideology, Abu Taha attempts to discuss and outline the conditions for a successful resistance. As he notes, the resister must be free and responsible, which can only be achieved by embracing religion. As religion is the frame of reference, it imposes on its members to resist any form of subjugation, oppression, and injustice. It is, as Abu Taha writes, "a religious obligation in all spheres of life."

This document matters for three reasons. First, and most important, it serves to question the allegations that PIJ and its violence is revolutionary. If the term 'revolutionary' means the intent to radically transform existing society, this sentiment is difficult to discern in the following lines. Rather, Abu Taha's emphasis is on the past and its culture, traditions, and customs. Similarly, there is little to suggest that the justification for PIJ's violence is principally different from that of other Palestinian factions. Second, because al-Shiqaqi wrote so little about violence, we must necessarily approach other theoreticians in the movement. Further, while the text is rife with religious references, Abu Taha the academic discusses the issue on a philosophical level that few in his movement are capable of matching. Third, the text matters because it shows how PIJ theoreticians employ a wide variety of *references: from the Qur'an to British historical theory; from Arab-Islamic history to Palestinian poetry. PIJ is thus—like many other Islamist movements—not relying solely on religious references—mainly because it is a political movement, and not strictly a religious one.*

Permission [to fight] has been given to those who are being fought, because they were wronged. And indeed, God is competent to give them victory.[1]

The act of resistance and its legitimacy have three principles: natural, societal, and cultural. In the first principle, the natural one, we can define resistance as "the instinctive effort to preserve the basis of existence." It is thus a natural, principal, and fundamental act in all creatures to preserve their existence, their life, their being, and their effectiveness in this presence. It is a human act, which is conscious and aware to preserve the condition of human existence's effectiveness in terms of humanity or the meaning of its existence. Human nature thus requires self-defense to preserve life and to preserve the self. This is an inherent and inalienable right of everybody subjected to aggression: "the right to self-defense", "the right to defend legitimate interests."

As for the second principle relating to society, no human community accepts attacks on its life, on its rights, on its interests or those of its members. It considers the preservation of its collective in order for it to be safe and independent as its primary and highest goal. The human community does not accept a stranger as its leader, to say nothing of the stranger occupying its land, threatening to take its resources and its goods. The most important resisting act of the community and of nations is to defend their identity and themselves against what threatens them. The right to a distinct identity of the individual or society was thus a right defended by all societies. Yet, nations make the preservation of self-prosperity a higher goal than the preservation of life and of the self.

Nations' act of resistance is related to the law and custom of "defense" as stated in the Holy Qur'an: "And if it were not for God checking [some] people by means of others, the earth would have been corrupted."[2] "And were it not that God checks the people, some by means of others, there would have been demolished monasteries, churches, synagogues, and mosques in which the name of God is much mentioned."[3] It is a divine principle with which the role and deed of the Concealed manifest themselves in history without canceling human will or the role of human action. Nations thus respond with resistance whenever the challenge of aggression appears, or what Arnold J. Toynbee[4] described as the "law of challenge and response."[5]

---

[1] See sūrat al-ḥajj: 22.
[2] See sūrat al-baqara: 251.
[3] See sūrat al-ḥajj: 40.
[4] Arnold Joseph Toynbee (1899–1975), British historian and philosopher of history.
[5] Approaching the study of history as a holistic endeavor, in which national history had to be studied in terms of nation's "societal" or "civilizational" whole, Toynbee hypothesized that civilizations progressed "as their members generated creative 'responses' to the 'challenges' they faced during their history." When the endeavor failed, civilizations declined and were overtaken, and "dying civilizations" were "replaced by newly born societies." See Ian Hall, "Challenge and Response: The Lasting Engagement of Arnold J. Toynbee and Martin Wight," *International Relations* 17, no. 3 (2003): 389–404.

The third principle is the cultural one: Culture is the product of society's ideas, customs, traditions, ideals, and experiences, which defines society and its members' relationships and perceptions of their identity and of the world. Culture later becomes independent of the society, although it is produced by it. Its most important characteristic is that it is a living thing borrowing qualities of the human self in terms of uniqueness, independence, altruism, and diversity. Hence, every culture is based on consolidating its categories and refuting challenges against them.

There is a disparity between cultures, however, in the degree of their cohesion and particularity. This is the most important question and introduction lying at the heart of our search for the "culture of resistance," which is the desired and hoped for culture. This indicates that there are multiple cultures of resistance culture—such as a culture of compromise; a public culture; a private culture; an independent culture; a dependent culture... and so on.

The culture of resistance relates specifically to vibrant nations emphasizing their uniqueness and leadership, and which resist assault and aggression. It rises through various means and levels of confrontation—from spreading the comprehensive intellectual, cultural, and civilizational foundation to sharp strategic analysis giving the umma a path, vision, and a project, ending with the simplest mechanisms of confrontation.

Our discussion today about consolidating the culture of resistance is not because of fear of it, or of the cultural invasion to which it is subjected—with cultures of humiliation, surrender, subordination, and consumption. Rather, the purpose of this study comes after real and clear victories for the culture of resistance with its spread and dissemination in the Arab Muslim public. The logic of this conversation is thus one of strength, and not one of weakness. It is a positive one, not a negative one. With participation, and not with absence. It is a logic of initiative, and not one of defense. Action, not reaction. Resistance and its culture continue to have legitimacy, power, and influence in theory and in practice, which is denied only by the blind and the hypocrite.

We have from the onset referred to the necessity of liberating the "culture of resistance" from incorrect reduction and shortening in violation of the concept, such as when it is constrained to armed resistance or to that which only resists aggression and occupation. For the concept of resistance is a comprehensive civilizational concept, and it seeks to preserve and distinguish the existence of a nation on all levels, and it then confronts all forms hindering liberation, renaissance, development, and progress.

"The culture of resistance" is a state of complete human civilizational advancement in order to achieve a free, dignified, and secure way of life for man: "Save them from hunger and free them from fear."[6] It confronts all forms of aggressions against it: against occupation, invasion, and settlements; against racial discrimination and its regimes; against economic and capitalist interference; against the transformation of man into a commodity; against immorality and ill behavior; against any act degrading human dignity; against intimidation and terrorization; against all manifestations and methods undermining the freedom, security, stability, good development, and righteous struggle

---

[6] Abu Taha refers here to sūrat al-quraysh: 4.

of man. The culture of resistance is thus both the thought and act of life, and it does not cease as long as man struggles for his earthly interests and his otherworldly salvation. It is a culture affecting all aspects of human existence and all of its levels. Resistance is culture because the concept of a comprehensive civilizational resistance is a cultural concept at the root of its activity. It is a cultural concept in the ability of resistance itself to continue and to spread. It is a cultural concept in the activity of resistance, which has an impact on individuals and communities—even on the fronts against the will of the resistance.

Yet, the necessary and important condition for the culture of resistance to be achieved culturally and practically is "the condition of freedom and responsibility." Thus, for the resister to be a true resister, there is no doubt he must be both free and responsible. Is it possible for us to imagine man as a dependent and commanded slave, or as a person who does not feel any obligation toward his own existence as a decent human being, or toward his community or umma in its confrontation against injustice, aggression, corruption, and ill behavior? Or can we imagine man as harmonious, participating with the community or umma in raising the values of justice, benevolence, truth, and integrity? Can we imagine a free resister without this?

The Holy Qur'an provides us the example of the oppressed and subjugated umma, whose ability to revive and walk in the line of liberation and faith was deprived by enslavement. This is exemplified by the story of God's prophet Moses with the pharaoh, who seized the Tribe of Israel and oppressed them, killed their sons, and enslaved their women. This long enslavement had the negative impact of producing a shattered nation incapable of acting, resisting, and responding to this humiliation. So it failed to revive the right by following Moses and Aaron (peace be upon them): "And when the two companies saw one another, the companions of Moses said, "Indeed, we are to be overtaken!"[7] "O Moses, make for us a god just as they have gods."[8] "So go, you and your Lord, and fight. Indeed, we are remaining right here."[9] The impact of slavery was in other words great in terms of destroying the will of the Israelites to resist and to transform.

Antarah ibn Shaddad[10] was fully aware of this impasse. When his father told him: "Charge, Antarah," he responded: "The slave does not know how to invade or how to defend but is only good for milking goats and serving his masters." So, his father said: "Fight and you will be free." Ibn Shaddad thus fought, and then said:

---

[7] See sūrat al-shuʿarāʾ: 61.
[8] See sūrat al-aʿrāf: 138.
[9] See sūrat al-māʾida: 24.
[10] Antarah ibn Shaddad (526–608), born in Najd, ibn Shaddad was the son of Shaddad al-Absi from the tribe of Abs in the Arabian Peninsula and of Zabiba, an Abyssinian slave. Born into slavery, ibn Shaddad obtained freedom for his courage in battle, and became famous for his poetry.

I, Antarah, am a half-breed	Every man protects his freedom[11]

We found him to be brilliant, and his humanity radiated, and he thus became an example of excellence and of chivalry. The enslavement by any state or ruling elite deprives the umma of its impenetrable fortresses, suppresses the culture of resistance, and isolates it until it loses its components.

God's generosity for His creation bestowed on him the ability to protect his existence and continuity, and to defend it. The generosity of the Almighty was the greatest and highest when He sent His messengers to strengthen this presence in the form of power, sincerity, and freedom. Here comes the culture of resistance's frame of reference for fulfilling the condition of the resisting act, which is freedom and responsibility. Islam constituted the most sublime frame of reference (or so it should be) for each act, declaration, and sacrifice of Muslim man. It formed the frame of reference for the culture of the Muslim who is not sincere in his religion except by resisting. For resistance in religion is not a matter of choice or abandonment in the circle of action or neglect, but a religious obligation in all spheres of life.

Islam fulfills the condition of freedom and responsibility of man—commencing with the creed via legislation to ethics and systems. The starting point for your adherence to religion is to liberate you from the tyrant, whatever tyrant there is—whether it is a god other than God; a tyrant or a ruler; or Satan: "Indeed, Satan is an enemy to you; so take him as an enemy."[12] Whether it is a desire and longing: "Have you seen he who has taken as his god his [own] desire."[13] Whether it is lust and pleasure: "Whoever emigrated to God and His messenger, his emigration will be for God and His messenger. And whoever emigrated for worldly benefits or for a woman to marry, his emigration would be for what he emigrated for."[14]

The faith in God, the true and complete faith, the saving faith, does not become correct, valid, and complete except by completely denying everything of one's own perception: harm and benefit; giving and dispossession; rule and submission; or riches and poverty.

The declaration of the oneness of God—"There is no god but God and Muhammad is the Messenger of God"—is the greatest declaration liberating man from the captivity of all tyrants. It provides man with real freedom in thought and action, as resistance is virtually the indissoluble link in Islam: "So whoever disbelieves in the tyrant and believes in God has grasped the most trustworthy handhold"[15] required to fulfill the faith. However, its condition is completely denying everything of one's own perception, resisting it, and not allowing it to have any effect on thinking and human life.

---

[11] Antarah employs the word half-breed (*al-hajīn*), a term commonly employed for both animals and human beings—in the latter case often referring to a person "whose father was Arab and free and whose mother was a foreign slave." Lewis argued that the term is social rather than racial in content, "expressing the contempt of the highborn for the baseborn." See Bernard Lewis, *Race and Slavery in the Middle East: An Historical Enquiry* (Oxford: Oxford University Press, 1990), 39–40.

[12] See sūrat al-fāṭir: 6.

[13] See sūrat al-jāthiya: 23.

[14] Hadith narrated by Umar bin al-Khattab, Riyad al-Salihin, Book of Miscellany, Hadith 1.

[15] See sūrat al-baqara: 256.

Islam brought freedom of creed and thought, and it fought coercion in its creed. All coercion is unlawful as is everything established by falsehood. Islam stood against all forms of authority and coercion commencing in the belief in Him, which must be a voluntary and optional faith free from coercion. "There is no compulsion in religion";[16] "You are only a reminder. You are not over them a controller."[17]

Man is liberated through his faith, rejecting any manifestation of polytheism, even if it is ever so small in the source of the faith, its intention, its aspiration, or its orientation. For polytheism is a worship of falsehood and usurpation for the forces of falsehood seeking to conquer the self and subject it for their authoritarian purposes. Any adherence to idols, false symbols, or any earthly man-made creed is nothing but the subjugation of man's freedom—isolating him from the arena of confrontation and the field of resistance. Equally, rejecting any manifestation of loyalty to falsehood and the forces of evil: "Do not take the Jews and the Christians as allies. They are [in fact] allies of one another. And whoever is an ally to them among you—then indeed, he is [one] of them."[18]

Denying any manifestations of loyalty to, and the innocence of, the oppressors at all levels, affirming that the act of love, of giving, of sincere affection, and of support and assistance is only for the believers and their priorities. It is only for Truth, benevolence, and good—without falsehood and corruption.

If the highest degree of resistance is the act, then Islam encouraged it and called for it by connecting the authenticity of the faith with its demonstration in practice—combining and attaching theory with practice, saying with doing, and faith with true belief: "Say, I believe in God—and then be steadfast."[19] "O you who have believed, why do you say what you do not do?"[20] "Indeed, those who have believed and done righteous deeds."[21]

| You disobey God, yet claiming to love Him | Truly, one of wonders. |
| If your love were true, you'd have obeyed Him | for the lover is ever obedient of the one he loves.[22] |

The essence of Islam in its creed is a comprehensive and true revolution: a revolution when it liberates man from polytheism… Liberating his mind from superstition and myths… Liberating him from the subjection to ignorance, its manifestations and values… Liberating him from the tyrant, his might and authority… Liberating him from the love for life and the attachment to it… Liberating him from luxury, extravagance, and lavishness… Liberating him from pathological self-love… Liberating him from the fear for livelihood… and the fear of death…

---

[16] See sūrat al-baqara: 256.
[17] See sūrat al-ghāshiya: 22–3.
[18] See sūrat al-mā'ida: 51.
[19] From Imam al-Nawawi's collection of hadith, no. 21.
[20] See sūrat al-ṣaff: 2.
[21] See sūrat al-kahf: 107.
[22] Poem by Abu Abdallah al-Shafi'i

At the level of religious rituals and worship, then, it is a consecration of this believing and liberating method of the resister in worshipping conduct. The slogan "God is great" in prayers, in talbiya[23] during hajj, when fasting for God during Ramadan, and when purifying the self, the body, and spirit by dismissing possessions—all these forms of worship raise man and liberate his spirit and soul from any obsession or servitude toward children, possessions, kin, or wealth.

Regarding the conduct of people toward each other,[24] then, the slogan of Islam "Indeed, God orders justice and good conduct and giving to relatives"[25] calls for resistance to any form of aggression, injustice, and oppression—any lack of justice. The Islamic legislative and moral system was established on the theoretical and practical foundations that fully achieved "the condition of responsible freedom."

The aim of Islamic legislations and values, which strengthened the resisting act in the political society of Muslims, was to make authority subject to the will of the umma, acting on its behalf by ruling on what God revealed and by establishing justice among people. It established a system based on consultation, rotation of power, general oath of allegiance,[26] and the people's election of the imam. The function of office is thus a contract, an oath of allegiance, and an election. It adjudicates in acts of injustice and reimburses the afflicted, imposes *hisba*[27] on its citizens in order to consecrate the duty to resist falsehood and to confront it, and it calls for advice from the imams of the Muslims and the general public. It commands right and forbids wrong, corrects the corrupt, and guides the crooked: "I only intend reform as much as I am able."[28]

In the defense of the umma, the homelands, the properties, and the interests, Islam enjoined jihad in the path of God to eliminate aggression and remove injustice. The value and standing of jihad were elevated to make it the peak of religion: "Permission [to fight] has been given to those who are being fought, because they were wronged. And indeed, God is competent to give them victory. [They are] those who have been evicted from their homes without right—only because they say, 'Our Lord is God.'"[29] The martyr, and martyrdom, was exalted in Islam as it negated his death by affirming his activity in life and existence. "And never think of those who have been killed in the cause of God as dead. Rather, they are alive with their Lord, receiving provision."[30] "And do not say about those who are killed in the way of God, 'They are dead.' Rather,

---

[23] Talbiya, devotional prayer by pilgrims during hajj.
[24] Anwar Abu Taha is here juxtaposing human relations (*muʿāmalāt*) with worship (*ʿibādāt*), the conduct of men toward God.
[25] See sūrat al-nahl: 107.
[26] When a ruler died or was deposed, a small circle of leading officials would pledge their allegiance (*bayʿa*) to the new ruler in a private ceremony (*al-bayʿa al-khāṣṣa*), after which a public ceremony was organized to pledge a general oath of allegiance (*al-bayʿa al-ʿāmma*).
[27] *Ḥisba* (literal meaning: calculation), commonly believed to originate from the Qurʾanic concept of "commanding right and forbidding wrong" ("*al-amr bi-l-maʿrūf wa-l-nahy ʿan al-munkar*"), more commonly referring to upholding public law and order. See Kristen Stilt and M. Safa Saraçoğlu, "Hisba and Muhtasib," in *The Oxford Handbook of Islamic Law*, eds. Anver M. Emon and Rumee Ahmed (Oxford: Oxford University Press, 2018); Oxford Islamic Studies, "Hisbah," http://www.oxfordislamicstudies.com/article/opr/t125/e851 [accessed: October 24, 2019].
[28] See sūrat al-hūd: 88.
[29] See sūrat al-ḥajj: 39–40.
[30] See sūrat āl-ʿimrān: 169.

they are alive, but you perceive [it] not."[31] Islam depreciated the value of those staying behind, of those remaining seated, of the sullen, of the sluggish, and of the apologetic hypocrites. It called for patience on suffering and to bear it for God. Islam extolled the importance of transcending reality by citing the glad tidings: "So do not weaken and do not grieve, and you will be superior if you are [true] believers."[32] "If a wound should touch you—there has already touched the [opposing] people a wound similar to it. And these days [of varying conditions] We alternate among the people."[33] It made otherworldly recompense the fullest, best, most rewarding, most beneficial, most lasting, and greatest recompense of all.

We were warned against conflict and division as we confronted occupiers and aggressors, for in it is great distress and blind strife. Confronting the enemy is thus unquestionable, and efforts must be united far from the lust for power. Indeed, internal injustice is incapable of achieving a consensus in confronting the enemy, the way we achieve it when confronting occupation and foreign injustice, which target you in the principle of your creedal existence, the umma, and its life project.

> If dispersed, the arrows are broken   If one day gathered, they will not break.

Man bears a great responsibility on his shoulders with all the preceding values and legislations toward his religion, spirit, society, umma, and homeland. They answer those wondering about the cause of this umma's persistent commitment to resistance, as those creedal, legislative, moral, and intellectual factors prevent surrender and the acceptance of occupation, defeat, and colonialism. The West managed to subordinate some people to it intellectually, politically, and economically. Some of them have become traditional colonies under the influence of the West. It was unsuccessful, however, in occupying the conscience, mind, or will of the Arabs and Muslims. They thus continue to resist imperial domination in its various expressions. The modern Arab state has not succeeded in suppressing and shaping the awareness of the umma and the individual, leading to its complete capitulation, as happened in the Western experience. It so happened because the conscience and awareness of the umma is still alive with the values of the great religion.

The culture of resistance is a culture of peace. No one believes that resistance is synonymous with violence and killing. The true aim of resistance is for people to live good, safe, and peaceful lives—a life of peace. Resistance is an act to stop murder, crime, aggression, injustice, corruption, depravation, fraud, deceit, delusion, and so on.

The culture of resistance is a culture of life. A culture of peace, and not one of war. It is a culture of safety, and not one of intimidation. A culture of security, and not one of fear. A culture for the triumph of Truth, and not one of submission to falsehood. A culture of true order, and not one of chaos. A culture of justice, and not one of injustice. A culture of freedom, and not one of slavery. A culture of Truth, and not one of falsehood.

---

[31] See sūrat al-baqara: 154.
[32] See sūrat āl ʿimrān: 137.
[33] See sūrat āl ʿimrān: 140.

This culture is incompatible with the peace promoted by the regimes of injustice, by the international forces of falsehood, and the intellectuals of the US Marines, who do not bring Truth and do not achieve justice. For justice is not achieved by the begging of the weak, but by the power, steadfastness, and resistance of the strong. Peace today is one of cowards and the defeated, a peace of humiliation and degradation. True peace is the peace that is based on Truth and that which is protected by the power to endure. It is the peace capable of restoring the rights. It is a peace of the living, and not of those whose hearts have died or who have surrendered to the occupying invaders. It is a peace its adherents are capable of defending if threatened by aggressors, over whom they will be able to triumph. "And those who, when tyranny strikes them, they defend themselves."[34]

The culture of resistance is one against death, and it does not sow it. It is a culture of peace and of life. This brings me to the words of the Palestinian poet Muin Bseiso:[35]

> Yes, we will never die. Yes, we will live
> If the shackles gnaw into our bones
> If torn by the whips of tyrants
> And if they set our bodies on fire
> We will never die. Not at all,
> We will uproot death from our land.

---

[34] See sūrat al-shūrā: 39.
[35] Muin Bseiso (1926–84), Palestinian Gazan-born poet.

18

The Philosophy of Martyrdom

Published by the media department of Palestinian Islamic Jihad, 2000. Subsequently disseminated by the Palestinian Islamic Jihad institution Muhjat al-Quds, an interest organization for Palestinian prisoners and martyrs.

PIJ writes little about the use of violence despite this being its principal means of resistance. It is, most often, in periods when violence becomes contentious that the movement actually discusses its necessity and legitimacy, and the arguments partly depend on what debate or to which period one refers. The targeting of civilians and suicide bombings is a case in point. While the Palestinian Islamic factions were the main actors organizing suicide bombings in the 1990s, most Palestinian groups chose to adopt the strategy following the militarization of the Second Intifada—whether Islamist (Hamas and PIJ), traditionally secular-nationalist (Fatah), or Marxist (Popular Front for the Liberation of Palestine).

The Palestinian use of suicide bombings against Israeli civilians made Israel launch massive reprisals in the Second Intifada—harming the Palestinian civilian population far more than the militants. As the military response of Israel intensified, Arab governments became increasingly anxious that violence would spill over and dispatched their clerics to cool down popular enthusiasm. Indeed, both Sheikh Muhammad Sa'id Tantawi, head of the Egyptian al-Azhar Mosque, and Sheikh Muhammad bin Abdallah al-Sabil, member of the Saudi council of senior ulama', decried Palestinian suicide bombings and rejected any attempt to take human lives. As Tantawi postulated, Islamic law "rejects all attempts on human life, and in the name of the shari'a, we condemn all attacks on civilians, whatever their community or state responsible for such an attack."[1]

Although Abdallah al-Shami, the author of this text, does not address anyone specifically, it seems clear that it was in this particular context that he wrote this piece. Presumably a response to a number of (unnamed) Islamic scholars arguing that suicide bombings were just another form of suicide and thus impermissible, al-Shami's main endeavor is to show that the perpetrators are martyrs who will find their reward in paradise. Indeed, because al-Shami presumably addresses the counterarguments of other Islamic scholars, this text is particularly filled with Islamic references. Similarly, as a number of attacks in the Second Intifada were retaliations

[1] Haim Malka, "Must Innocents Die? The Islamic Debate Over Suicide Attacks," *Brookings*, March 1, 2003, https://www.brookings.edu/articles/must-innocents-die-the-islamic-debate-over-suicide-attacks/.

for Israeli state violence against Palestinians, we find this equally reflected in al-Shami's piece. The justification for violence must thus be read in the context of the reality PIJ found itself in, in the early 2000s.

This document matters for three reasons. First, this is one of the few PIJ texts employing a mainly religious justification for violence, while the preceding ones provide a secular analysis by stressing deterrence, revenge, and a balance of terror. Second, this document is an example of how PIJ adjusts its argument and justification for violence depending on what debate it participates in and in what period it occurs. This text should thus be compared to the next one written by the PIJ West Bank leader, Muhammad Arif al-Hajj Muhammad.

Preface

The martyrs in the history of our modern and ancient umma have drawn vivid paintings of honor, of courage, and of valor. Our umma produced a great history of triumph and of defeating the forces of injustice and misguidance—whether they were polytheists, crusaders, or colonialists. The martyrs have occupied a place today befitting them in the memory of our umma and of our subsequent generations. This could not have happened, were it not for the higher value of martyrdom. Our Islamic creed implanted martyrdom into the hearts of its children for it to become a public culture understood by the youth before it was understood by the adults, the common people, and the scholars. Martyrdom has become a higher goal to realize which the sons of the umma seek to outdo one another—perhaps they will succeed in doing so or ascend to the rank of martyrs.

Although the meaning of martyrdom and its features are clear, we are nonetheless required to discuss it and reveal some aspects of its philosophy. Particularly so, as we are engaged in a fierce struggle with the Zionist enemy, which includes land, man, and faith in its various aspects. With physical force, with control over the mass media (dominating most of the international outlets), and by greatly influencing the formation of culture and people's convictions, this enemy attempts continuously to cast doubt on the martyrdom operations by considering it a kind of suicide. It is assisted in that endeavor by some of our umma's imposters of science, by the bribed, and by those moving to serve emaciated political projects that promote the usurping occupier and accept coexistence with it.

At this time, we aspire to present the stand of the mujahidin, the legitimacy of jihad, the meaning of martyrdom and its philosophy, the stand of the martyrs and their role in reviving the umma. We hope to contribute to refuting some of the false rumors and delusions promoted by the occupation and its agents. We also hope to contribute in pushing the sons of our people to carry out their obligation of jihad and martyrdom against all enemies, even if they differed in names and color.

Introduction

God Almighty says at the beginning of surat baqara: "This is the Book about which there is no doubt, a guidance for those conscious of God—Who believe in the Concealed, establish prayer, and spend out of what We have provided for them."² By reflecting on the preceding verses, we see that faith is based on two basic rules:

The World of Martyrdom: It is the witnessed world in which we live, in which we take cover under its sky, and in which we live with its natural phenomena and its living beings: "[He is] Knower of the unseen and the witnessed; and He is the Wise, the Acquainted."³ This world cannot be denied by anyone, because it means to deny one's own existence. Consequently, there would be no obligation to believe in it as the obligation is derived from the necessity to reflect upon it: "Indeed, in the creation of the heavens and the earth and the alternation of the night and the day are signs for those of understanding."⁴ The second fundamental rule upon which faith is based is thus:

The Concealed: Faith is not achieved but by the faith in the Concealed, and anyone who denies this is not considered a believer—he is not a Muslim at all. For the religion is based on the testimony that there is no god but God, and Muhammad is the Messenger of God. The faith in God Almighty is one of the pillars of the faith in the Concealed. As stated in the hadith of God's messenger—peace and blessings of God be upon him—when he answered someone asking about faith: "It is to believe in God and His angels, His books, His messengers, the Last Day,⁵ and the Divine Will and Decree,⁶ both good and bad." This text includes the pillars of faith in the Concealed.

However, there are other concealed issues of faith in which we are commanded to believe. Whoever disbelieves in them has disbelieved in what was revealed to Muhammad—peace and blessings upon him—for it is a necessary component of the religion such as the faith in heaven and hell, as well as the world of jinn.⁷ One of the issues of faith dealt with by the Holy Qur'an is the issue of death, where the Qur'an told us that all things on Earth, including human beings, will die. As God Almighty states: "Everyone upon the earth will perish."⁸ Death is destined for man at a prescribed time that only God knows: "And it is not [possible] for one to die except by permission of God at a decree determined."⁹ Man is subjected to death, which he shares with all beings as he is not set apart from them in any way. He can neither advance death by an hour nor postpone it. This applies to other objects as well: "And for every nation is

---

2   See sūrat al-baqara: 2–3.
3   See sūrat al-in'ām: 73.
4   See sūrat āl al-'imrān: 190.
5   The Last Day (al-yawm al-ākhir), also known as the Day of Judgment (yawm al-qiyāma) or the Day of Resurrection (yawm al-dīn), the end of time and God's final judgment of man and his deeds.
6   The Divine Will and Decree (al-qaḍā' wa-l-qadar), the belief that everything is preordained by God and that everything happens according to his will, that God knows all things, and that everything was created by God.
7   Jinn (jinn), supernatural creatures in Islamic theology invoked for magical purposes and often held responsible for miraculous or unusual events. See Oxford Islamic Studies, "Jinn," http://www.oxfordislamicstudies.com/article/opr/t125/e1204?_hi=1&_pos=2 [accessed: October 29, 2019].
8   See sūrat al-raḥmān: 26.
9   See sūrat āl al-'imrān: 145.

a [specified] term. So when their time has come, they will not remain behind an hour, nor will they precede [it]."[10]

This is a fact of faith (related to the eternity of death and its concealment). Man is taught courage and to eliminate manifestations of weakness and fear, and he is pushed toward valor. For he knows that if the umma is united, it would still be incapable of preceding its end or postponing it. So why the fear of the end of life? Why the cowardice in confronting falsehood? Why the negligence of resistance against tyranny and aggression?

The Legitimacy of Jihad

God Almighty imposed jihad on the Islamic umma in order for them to fulfill their religious obligation to spread Islam and to remove tyrannical systems interfering between the people and the freedom of belief. For these systems work to preserve their existence and their self-interests, whether political, economic, or social. These systems will therefore never allow Muslims the freedom of proselytization or movement but, instead, put obstacles in their way; dig trenches; terrorize the people; and prevent them from joining the new religion, in which there is true freedom and salvation from all forms of serfdom.

In order to confront the tyrannical systems and this network of interests, God Almighty imposed jihad on the Muslims and their desire for it. He impelled them concerning the collective commitment to fight the infidels and the polytheists by stating:

> Fight those who do not believe in God or in the Last Day and who do not consider unlawful what God and His Messenger have made unlawful and who do not adopt the religion of truth from those who were given the Scripture—[fight] until they give the jizyah willingly while they are humbled.[11]

For God knows with His absolute knowledge that political or diplomatic "advocacy" work cannot remove these regimes, and that it cannot lead to the transformation of whole societies toward Islam. If Islam does not have the power and might to deter the aggressors and tyrants, then their will can never be broken, and their plots and schemes can never be shattered. There are accordingly two conflicting approaches: the approach of God and that of the tyrant. "Those who believe fight in the cause of God, and those who disbelieve fight in the cause of Taghut. So fight against the allies of Satan. Indeed, the plot of Satan has ever been weak."[12]

The abodes of Islam, on the other hand, will remain vulnerable to the aggression by adversaries and enemies, those lurking and trembling. These enemies need a force to deter them and to break their power so the abodes of Islam can live in peace and

---

[10] See sūrat al-aʿrāf: 34.
[11] See sūrat al-tawba: 29.
[12] See sūrat al-nisāʾ: 76.

safety—its people freely practicing their rituals and worship. One aspect of jihad in the path of God thus means self-defense and the defense of land and honor: "Fight in the way of God those who fight you."[13] God Almighty prescribed jihad to protect the weak and the poor in the land, as well as those who are subjected to oppression, tyranny, usurpation, and contempt:

> And what is [the matter] with you that you fight not in the cause of God and [for] the oppressed among men, women, and children who say, "Our Lord, take us out of this city of oppressive people and appoint for us from Yourself a protector and appoint for us from Yourself a helper?"[14]

God Almighty thus prescribed defensive jihad in defense of the sanctities, the mosques, and places of worship: "And were it not that God checks the people, some by means of others, there would have been demolished monasteries, churches, synagogues, and mosques in which the name of God is much mentioned."[15] Jihad is consequently a deterrent to those outside of, and fighting against, the Islamic community:

> Indeed, the penalty for those who wage war against God and His Messenger and strive upon earth [to cause] corruption is none but that they be killed or crucified or that their hands and feet be cut off from opposite sides or that they be exiled from the land. That is for them a disgrace in this world; and for them in the Hereafter is a great punishment.[16]

Jihad in the path of God is the realization of Truth and the destruction of falsehood. Truth is understood here as "that which God's law and his method signifies" in conflict with falsehood. Truth is not achieved, and the spread of falsehood will not be opposed, but by the power of the defenders God calls upon. As God Almighty stated: "And prepare against them whatever you are able of power and of steeds of war by which you may terrify the enemy of God and your enemy and others besides them whom you do not know [but] whom God knows."[17]

Truth thus requires power in order to terrorize falsehood and its agents, near and far:

> [Remember, O believers], when God promised you one of the two groups—that it would be yours—and you wished that the unarmed one would be yours. But God intended to establish the truth by His words and to eliminate the disbelievers. That He should establish the truth and abolish falsehood, even if the criminals disliked it.[18]

---

[13] See sūrat al-baqara: 190.
[14] See sūrat al-nisāʾ: 75.
[15] See sūrat al-ḥajj: 40.
[16] See sūrat al-māʾida: 33.
[17] See sūrat al-anfāl: 60.
[18] See sūrat al-anfāl: 7–8.

The realization of Truth and the destruction of falsehood is only a confrontation between the group of Right and the group of falsehood: "[Remember, O believers], when God promised you one of the two groups—that it would be yours—and you wished that the unarmed one would be yours."[19]

We have, however, not addressed the required stages of jihad in this discussion. What concerns us here is clarifying the purpose of this obligation and what reward God Almighty has prepared for the mujahidin.

The Duty of Jihad

God Almighty prescribed jihad because it fends off evil, upholds rights, and protects beliefs and abodes, which forms a fundamental basis for the freedom of worship. In occupied abodes, or in abodes where the people do not believe in Islam, we see that the reality of Muslims is difficult. They cannot worship freely, and if worship is performed, then it is under pressure and threats. We have witnessed this clearly against our people in Jerusalem throughout the occupation and until now where the occupation soldiers intervene to determine who is allowed entry to pray in the al-Aqsa Mosque and who is not.

We see that they usurped the Ibrahimi Mosque in Hebron. This usurpation and this prohibition require defense and jihad by the mujahidin until this country and these holy places are liberated so that Muslims can perform their rituals and worship freely. "And were it not that God checks the people, some by means of others, there would have been demolished monasteries, churches, synagogues, and mosques in which the name of God is much mentioned. And God will surely support those who support Him."[20]

Without the law of repulsion, one cannot deter falsehood and one cannot shake its power. It was for this reason that God impelled Muslims to jihad and to leap into the fields of death. If they fall as martyrs, they will rise to the heavens and enter the highest part of paradise. He who neglects jihad and does not plan it will die an ignorant death. As the Prophet—peace and blessings be upon him—said: "He who did not fight or think of fighting, he dies an ignorant death." In another account: "He dies on one of the branches of hypocrisy."

For this reason, we see that the companions of the Prophet—peace and blessings of God be upon him—strove to outdo each other in jihad. They would pull arrows[21] with their sons in order to go out to fight. This is what happened with the honorable companion Khaythama ibn al-Harith when he told the Prophet of God—peace and blessings be upon him:

---

[19] See sūrat al-anfāl: 7.
[20] See sūrat al-ḥajj: 40.
[21] Abdallah al-Shami employs the verb *yastahim*, derived from *sahm* (arrow). It refers to the practice of chance-based divination in pre-Islamic Arabia in which a group of arrows with instructions were randomly selected, thus settling a matter. Al-Shami is likely referring to arrows with names of those volunteering for jihad. See Robert G. Hoyland, *Arabia and the Arabs: From the Bronze Age to the Coming of Islam* (London and New York: Routledge, 2001), 154–7.

The Battle of Badr escaped me, and I was, by God, so eager for it that my son participated in the attack. His arrow appeared, and was thus blessed with martyrdom. Yesterday, as I slept, I saw my son at his best, roaming freely among the fruits and rivers of paradise. My son said: Follow us and join us in paradise. So I have found what my Lord has promised me. O God, O Messenger of God, how I long to accompany him in paradise. I have grown old and my bones have become soft. How I wish to meet God. I pray, God, O Messenger of God, to give me martyrdom and to accompany Saʿd in paradise.

So the Messenger of God—peace and blessings be upon him—called on him, and he died a martyr.

Our distinguished scholars have strived to determine the status of jihad in Islamic legislation. They say that the rule of jihad in Islamic law serves as a communal obligation. If a group of people carries out the obligation, then others become exempted. The communal obligation becomes an individual obligation on three conditions:

1. If the enemy attacks the land of the people, then jihad becomes their duty.
2. If the imam calls upon a certain group of people, then jihad becomes a duty for them.
3. If the mujahidin are present on the land of battle, God Almighty says: "O you who have believed, when you meet those who disbelieve advancing [for battle], do not turn to them your backs [in flight]."[22]

According to these conditions, we see that jihad is an individual obligation for the people of Palestine. That is, an obligation for everyone to carry out. Whoever does not perform his jihadist obligation is a sinner. According to this ruling, a woman has the right to leave the home without her husband's permission, and the son can leave the home without the permission of his parents.

Jihad in the Land of Palestine

All these three issues are combined in the land of Palestine—where the law of God is absent; where the land of Muslims is usurped; and where the enemies are practicing corruption and ruin, killing worshippers, seizing their wealth, and threatening its people with death and displacement. Fighting against the enemies on its land is thus a legal obligation by all Qur'anic and prophetic evidence, such as the saying of God Almighty: "Permission [to fight] has been given to those who are being fought, because they were wronged. And indeed, God is competent to give them victory."[23] And we are certainly being fought, and we are certainly being wronged. "[They are] those who

---

[22] See sūrat al-anfāl: 15.
[23] See sūrat al-ḥajj: 39.

have been evicted from their homes without right—only because they say, 'Our Lord is God.'"[24] Certainly, we have been evicted from our homes without right.

This is supported by the Messenger of God—peace and blessings of God be upon him—when a man came to ask him: "O Messenger of God, what shall I do if a man comes to me to take my property?" The Prophet replied: "Do not give it to him." The man then asked: "What shall I do if he fights me?" The Messenger of God said: "Then you fight him." The man asked: "What shall I do if he kills me?" The Messenger of God replied: "Then you will be in paradise." So the man asked: "And if I kill him?" The Prophet replied: "Then he will be in hell."

God therefore prescribed jihad and He made the reward for the mujahidin too great to be described, and the Messenger of God—peace and blessings be upon him—made jihad the peak of Islam. In order to defend oneself and the belief. In order to defend the land and honor. In order to defend the oppressed in the land. In order to drive back the usurpers of God's Truth and his dominion on Earth. In order to exalt the authority of God and spread His religion on Earth. As narrated by Abu Hurayra, a man said: "O Messenger of God, teach me a good deed that will earn me the reward of the mujahidin in the path of God." The Prophet asked: "Are you able to pray continuously and fast without breaking it?" The man answered: "O Messenger of God, I am too weak to do so." So the Prophet—peace and blessings of God be upon him—said: "By He in Whose hands is my soul! Even if you were able to do it, you will not achieve the reward of the mujahidin in the path of God."

For jihad in the path of God is greater than seventy years of prayer. As narrated in the hadith of Imam al-Tirmidhi:[25] A man surrendered himself to solitude. The Messenger of God said: "Do not do so. For indeed one of you standing in the path of God is more virtuous than seventy years of prayers in his abode. Do you not wish for God to forgive your sins and admit you into paradise? Then fight in the path of God, for whoever fights in the path of God for the time it takes for two milkings of a camel, then Paradise is obligatory for him." The Messenger of God—peace and blessings be upon him—stated: "The mujahidin are the best of people." As narrated by ibn Abbas,[26] the Prophet—peace and blessings of God be upon him—asked: "Shall I not tell you what distinguishes the best of people… The man holding his horse's rein in the path of God." When the Prophet—peace and blessings of God be upon him—was asked: "Who is the best among the people?" he answered: "A believer who struggles his utmost in the path of God with his life and property."

Jihad in the path of God is not a picnic. It is not a banner to be raised or a slogan under which one seeks the shade. It is far more than that. Jihad in the path of God is a struggle for the soul and for its longing, yearning, and connection to the land. Jihad in the path of God is hateful to the soul for it means its destruction, and the destruction of property and of the offspring. As stated by the Lord of Glory: "Fighting has been enjoined upon you while it is hateful to you. But perhaps you hate a thing and it is good

---

[24] See sūrat al-ḥajj: 40.
[25] Abu Isa Muhammad ibn Isa al-Sulami al-Darir al-Bughi al-Tirmidhi (824–92), Persian Islamic scholar and collector of hadith from present-day Uzbekistan. He composed *Jāmiʿ al-Tirmidhī*, one of the six canonical hadith collections.
[26] Abdallah ibn Abbas (619–87), uncle of Prophet Muhammad.

for you; and perhaps you love a thing and it is bad for you. And God Knows, while you know not."[27] As the Messenger of God said—peace and blessings of God be upon him—Satan comes to man as he marches, reminding him of his family and offspring, discouraging his resolve and demurring to his order.

When Is Jihad in the Path of God?

God wanted all of his worshippers to worship Him; He wished them not to believe in any of his creatures, and not in any of those who themselves believe they are deities to be worshipped or who believe they are equal to God because of their ignorance. We thus find all Qur'anic legislations and creedal texts removing doubt about the oneness of God Almighty, commencing from His saying: "Say, "He is God, [who is] One, God, the Eternal Refuge. He neither begets nor is born."[28] Proceeding to refute the claims of Jews and Christians when they claimed: "The Jews say, 'Ezra is the son of God'; and the Christians say, 'The Messiah is the son of God.' That is their statement from their mouths; they imitate the saying of those who disbelieved [before them]. May God destroy them; how are they deluded?"[29] Refuting the claims of the polytheist with his saying: "Or have they taken gods besides Him? Say, [O Muhammad], 'Produce your proof. This [Qur'an] is the message for those with me and the message of those before me.' But most of them do not know the truth, so they are turning away."[30]

God Almighty thus created the greatest foundation for joining Islam: "The testimony that there is no god but God and Muhammad is the Messenger of God." According to the mentioned hadiths about the Messenger of God—peace and blessings be upon him—which impel Muslims to devote their deeds and their intention to God alone, he narrated what his Lord said: "I am the One most free from want of partners. He who does a thing for the sake of someone else besides Me, I discard him and his polytheism."[31]

It was narrated by Abu Sa'd ibn Abu Fadala (one of the Prophet's companions—may God be pleased with them):

> When God assembles the first and the last on the Day of Resurrection, a day of which there is no doubt, a caller will cry out: "Whoever used to associate anyone else in an action that he did for God, let him seek his reward from someone other than God, for God is so self-sufficient that He has no need of any associate."

According to this introduction—as jihad is a worship through which the servant comes closer to God Almighty—jihad in the path of God must be free of personal fortunes or material gains, for which the mujahid might aspire through his jihad. The mujahid

---

[27] See sūrat al-baqara: 216.
[28] See sūrat al-ikhlāṣ: 1–4.
[29] See sūrat al-tawba: 30.
[30] See sūrat al-anbiyā': 24.
[31] Narrated by Muslim ibn al-Hajjaj al-Naysaburi.

might sometimes like being seen among the people or being pointed to as a mujahid. He may aspire for a position or influence through his jihadist participation. All of this thwarts the deed and squanders the reward. Our evidence is one man's question for the Messenger of God—peace and blessings be upon him—when he asked: "O Messenger of God, I fight in the path of God and I like my status being seen among the people." So the Prophet—peace and blessings be upon him—answered: "The one who fights so that the Word of God be exalted is the one who fights in the path of God." This is strengthened by the hadith of the Messenger of God—peace and blessings be upon him—in which he said:

> The first of men whose case will be decided on the Day of Judgment will be a man who died as a martyr. He shall be brought before the Judgment Seat. God will make him recount His blessings bestowed upon him and he will recount them and admit having enjoyed them in his life. Then God will say: "What did you do to requite these blessings?" He will say: "I fought for Thee until I died as a martyr." God will say: "You have told a lie. You fought that you might be called a 'brave warrior.' And you were called so." Then orders will be passed against him and he will be dragged with his face downward and cast into Hell.

Consequently, the mujahid must, in the path of God, exert himself and deem himself until he is free of all attachment to the self and to material things. All of his actions, whether small or large, must be in the path of God until he obtains the full reward, which does not involve anything but God. When our imam in this position, Imam Ali—may God be pleased with him—seized one of the polytheists and was to kill him, the polytheist spat in his face. So Imam Ali left and then returned. When he was asked why he did not kill the polytheist, he answered: "I feared that I would kill him in retaliation for myself, and not for God."

We note in this regard that our distinguished scholars have divided the martyrs into three categories:

1. **The Martyr of This World and the Hereafter:** It is he who is killed in the path of God, and is sincere in his intention. As described by the Messenger of God—peace and blessings be upon him—the one patient for God's reward in the Hereafter when attacking is considered a martyr by God and by the people.
2. **The Martyr of the Hereafter:** It is he to whom the hadith of the Messenger of God—peace and blessings be upon him—applies when he asked his companions: "Whom do you consider to be a martyr among you?" They replied: "O Messenger of God, one who is slain in the path of God is a martyr." The Messenger of God said: "Then the martyrs of my umma will be small in number." They asked: "O Messenger of God, who are they?" He said: "One who is slain in the path of God is a martyr; one who dies in the path of God is a martyr; one who dies of plague is a martyr; one who dies of cholera is a martyr." Ibn Miqsam said: "I testify to the truth of your father's statement that the Prophet—peace and blessings be upon him—said: 'One who is drowned is a martyr.'" Thus, he who dies in the path of God seeking knowledge or when in

exile, he is a martyr. He who dies of plague or cholera; who drowns; or dies in the fire, and so on, he is a martyr… They are by God considered martyrs, but they rank lower than the martyrs who fall on the battlefield. In the sense of the people, and in their worldly conscience, they are not considered martyrs. Or, at least, they are not treated as martyrs of battle and resistance. That is, they are washed, dressed for the grave, and prayed for."

3. **The Martyr of This World:** He is considered a martyr by the people because he fell in battle, and he fought zealously and bravely. However, he fought on an ideological foundation other than that of Islam, such as the ideas of secularism or Marxism. If he believes in these ideas and fights under their umbrella, then he will become a martyr of this world if he is killed. There is nothing for him in the Hereafter as the hadith applies to him: "I am the One most free from want of partners."

It appeared in the hadith narrated by al-Nasa'i[32] about al-Irbad ibn al-Sariya, in which the Messenger of God—peace and blessings be upon him—said:

> The martyrs and those who died in their beds referred a dispute to our Lord concerning those who die of the plague. The martyrs said: "Our brothers were killed as we were killed." And those who died in their beds said: "Our brothers died in their beds as we died." Our Lord said: "Look at their wounds; if their wounds are like the wounds of those who were killed then they are of them and belong with them." And their wounds were like their (the martyrs') wounds.

The meaning of the hadith is that the martyrs killed in the path of God ask God Almighty whether those who die from the plague are like the martyrs receiving the great reward of the Hereafter, which is promised to the martyrs by God. They say: "Our Lord, our brothers are those killed as we were killed in your path. For they patiently waited for God's judgment until they died from the plague, which is God's judgment. Just like the martyrs who patiently waited in war and stood firm, they ask for the reward of martyrs."

Those who died from the plague in their beds say: "Our brothers died as we died. That is, in their beds. So how are they given the reward of martyrs who sold themselves to God and were killed in His path?" So God says to them all: "Look at their wounds caused by the plague. If their wounds resemble the wounds of martyrs, then they are martyrs alongside the others." So they looked at their wounds to see if they were like those of the martyrs, and they are—as mentioned—called martyrs of the Hereafter only. They are not bestowed with the verdict of the martyr in battle, including washing and praying for them.

We wish for our mujahidin brothers that their intention and firm will is directed toward God alone in the hope of attaining martyrdom in this world and the Hereafter,

---

[32] Abu Abd al-Rahman Ahmad ibn Shu'ayb ibn Ali Sinan al-Nasa'i (829–915), collector of hadith and the author of *al-Sunan*, one of the six canonical hadith collections.

and of receiving full recompense from God and exaltation from the worshippers in this world.

The Motivations of the Mujahidin

Man cannot overcome restraints by the self and by Satan: the love of survival, of money and offspring, of waste and possessions, and of women. "Beautified for people is the love of that which they desire—of women and sons, heaped-up sums of gold and silver, fine branded horses, and cattle and tilled land. That is the enjoyment of worldly life."[33] Satanic restraints are Satan intimidating the mujahidin when they march out for battle by reminding them of their property and of their children, and that their wives will have intercourse after their death, and so on…

Man can get rid of these restraints only if he is filled by faith, and only if the motivations for what he expects are far greater than the restraints. The greatest motivation prepared for the mujahidin by God is paradise and the highest level of heaven,[34] which the Messenger of God—peace and blessings be upon him—described: "God has in paradise prepared for the worshippers what no eye has seen, what no ear has heard, and what has not occurred to the human heart." "And the Hereafter is better for you than the first [life]. And your Lord is going to give you [that], and you will be satisfied."[35]

When the Messenger of God—peace and blessings be upon him—passed the family of Yasir (Yasir, his wife, and his son Ammar), God was pleased with them as they were tormented, and the Prophet only said: "Patience, O family of Yasir! Your meeting place will be paradise."[36] When the Messenger of God—peace and blessings be upon him—made the second pledge to Islam at al-Aqaba to protect and to defend it, as they defended themselves, their families, and their properties, they asked him: "What will it be for us if we do so?" The Messenger of God—peace and blessings be upon him—said just one word: "paradise." So they said: "We will not revoke, or seek the abrogation of, the pledge of allegiance." So God Almighty refused to equate providing drinking water to pilgrims during hajj and the Great Mosque of Mecca with the believing mujahidin, by saying:

> Have you made providing water for the pilgrim and the maintenance of the Great Mosque of Mecca equal to [the deeds of] one who believes in God and the Last Day and strives in the cause of God? They are not equal in the sight of God. And God does not guide the wrongdoing people. The ones who have believed, emigrated,

---

[33] See sūrat āl ʿimrān: 14.
[34] Al-Shami is referring here to *firdaws* (also referred to as *ʿilliyūn* in the Qur'an, sūrat al-mutaffifin 18–19), which is the highest level of paradise, closest to the throne of God.
[35] See sūrat ḍuḥā: 4–5.
[36] The story refers to Yasir ibn Amir, one of the Prophet's companions. Captured by the Tribe of Makhzum, Yasir and his family were tortured in order to make them abandon their faith.

and striven in the cause of God with their wealth and their lives are greater in rank in the sight of God. And it is those who are the attainers [of success].[37]

Worship thus does not, even in the sacred abode of God, amount to the reward bestowed upon the mujahidin in the path of God. We cite the words of the mujahid Abdallah ibn Mubarak[38] addressed to the worshipper al-Fudayl ibn Iyad:[39]

O Worshipper of the Two Holy Mosques!	Had you witnessed us in the battlefield
You would have known that, compared to our Jihad,	Your worship is child's play.
For every tear you have shed upon your cheek,	We have shed in its place, blood upon our chests.
You are playing with your worship,	While worshippers offer your worship
Mujahidin offer their blood and life.	The smell of nice perfume is for you,
And our perfume is the dust and dirt,	And it has reached us from the sayings of our Prophet,
The martyr is not dead,	This is a true saying, in which there is no lie.
The dust of God's people is never equal,	To a thousand men, whilst the smoke is climbing.
This is the book of God between us,	The martyr is not dead – and this is no lie.[40]

Among the motivations impelling Muslims to jihad, it is that mentioned by one of the Prophet's men—peace and blessings be upon him—when he asked: "What from the worshipper makes the Lord laugh?" So the Messenger of God—peace and blessings be upon him—answered: "To plunge at the enemy unarmored." That is, to fight in the path of God without weapon and shield.

The Meaning of Martyrdom

Amid the great creedal causes connected to death and distinguished from life is the "cause of martyrdom." It means "to be killed in the path of God," which also means that the believer plunges into the fields of death to raise the religion of God or for the Word of God to be exalted. As the Messenger of God—peace and blessings be upon

---

[37] See sūrat al-tawba: 19–20.
[38] Abdallah ibn Mubarak (726–97), one of the early Muslims and a collector of hadith.
[39] Al-Fudayl ibn Iyad (d. 803), renowned Arab bandit who later renounced his crimes and converted to Islam.
[40] The translated poem has been taken and amended from Kalamullah, "O Worshipper of the Two Holy Masjids," https://www.kalamullah.com/yaabidalharamain.html [accessed: October 31, 2019].

him—said: "The one who fights so that Word of God be exalted is the one who fights in the path of God." The word of God's oneness is the Islamic approach, which essentially means to resist injustice, tyranny, oppression, and corruption on Earth.

> "Go, both of you, to Pharaoh. Indeed, he has transgressed."[41] "Indeed, Qarun was from the people of Moses, but he tyrannized them."[42] "Indeed, Pharaoh exalted himself in the land and made its people into factions, oppressing a sector among them, slaughtering their [newborn] sons and keeping their females alive. Indeed, he was of the corrupters."[43]

Repelling aggression from the land of Muslims if invaded is also in the path of God, as is the defense of self, of property, and of honor. It is as mentioned in the hadith about Sa'id ibn Zayd[44] when the Messenger of God—peace and blessings upon him—said: "He who dies while defending his property is a martyr; he who dies defending his blood is a martyr; he who dies defending his family is a martyr."

☪

The Noble Deeds of the Martyrs

God Almighty bestowed blessings and virtues upon the martyrs, recompensing their patience and sacrifices many times over. He confers the gifts and endowments they desire as they rapidly take the path of martyrdom, for they might catch up with the caravan of martyrs. If we attempt to enumerate the most important of these blessings, then we find:

1. The life they live after they die is spent in the heavens, sitting in the shade, eating fruits, and walking freely by its rivers. "And never think of those who have been killed in the cause of God as dead. Rather, they are alive with their Lord, receiving provision."[45]
2. Despite the terror of the calamities, the flashing of swords, the roar of explosions, and dismemberments, the Prophet—peace and blessings be upon him—said: "The martyr experiences no more pain in being slain than what one of you experiences from the stinging of an ant."
3. God Almighty recompenses the martyrs with peace on the day of greatest terrors[46] in compensation for the intensity of wars' horrors—whether by the

---

[41] See sūrat al-ṭaha: 43.
[42] See sūrat al-qaṣaṣ: 76.
[43] See sūrat al-qaṣaṣ: 4.
[44] Sa'id ibn Zayd (593–671), one of the Prophet's companions.
[45] See sūrat āl 'imrān: 169.
[46] The greatest terrors (al-faza' al-akbar) refers to sūrat al-anbiyā': 103: "They will not be grieved by the greatest terror, and the angels will meet them, [saying], 'This is your Day which you have been promised.'"

mobilization of armies, the clatter of swords, the shelling of artillery, the wheeze of bullets, the clamor of aircrafts, and the sound of explosions. It was mentioned in the hadith when the Messenger of God—peace and blessings be upon him—asked Gabriel—peace be upon him—about this: "And the Horn will be blown, and whoever is in the heavens and whoever is on the earth will fall dead except whom God wills."[47] Who is it that God does not want to fall dead? He said: They are the martyrs of God.

4. The martyrs are forgiven from the first drop of blood they shed from their pure bodies, when the martyr is forgiven for all his sins—even great sins against the religion. As the Messenger of God—peace and blessings be upon him—said in the hadith narrated by Abu Qatada that he had heard the Messenger of God—peace and blessings be upon him—reminding them that jihad in the path of God and the faith in God are the greatest deeds. Then a man stood up and asked: "O Messenger of God! Tell me, if I am killed in the path of God, will all my sins be forgiven?" The Messenger of God—peace and blessings be upon him—replied: "Yes, if you are killed in the path of God while you are patient, hopeful of your reward, and marching forward not retreating." Then the Prophet—peace and blessings be upon him—said to him: "Repeat what you have said." The man asked: "Tell me if I am killed in the path of God, will all my sins be remitted?" He replied: "Yes, if you are martyred while you are patient, hopeful of your reward, and marching forward without retreating, but if you owe any debt, that will not be remitted. The angel Gabriel—peace be upon him—told me that."

5. The martyr is saved from the torment of the grave. As mentioned in the hadith about the Messenger of God—peace and blessings be upon him—people are tormented in their graves and subjected to the pressure interlocking their ribs. The martyr, however, is not tormented in the grave. As mentioned in the hadith: "A man asked the Messenger of God—peace and blessings be upon him: "Why will the believers be tested in their graves except the martyr?" So the Messenger of God answered: "The flashing of the swords above his head is trial enough."

6. The martyr is honored by being crowned with the crown of dignity whose gems are greater than the world and what is in it. For he rebelled against this world, its comfort, and its possessions—hoping for it to be for God Almighty. God Almighty therefore bestowed this crown upon him, with gems greater than the world and what is in it.

7. The martyr marries seventy-two virgins and he visits them in one night where he is given the capacity to do so. And they are not like the women of this world, for they have the greatest beauty, grace, tenderness, and exaltedness. If just one of them looked at this world, it would be illuminated and shine from the brightness of her face.

8. The intercession of the martyr will be accepted for seventy members of his family as a mark of honor for the martyr, and God honors them through him—his father, his mother, his brothers, his sisters, and his close companions. There they will have two intercessions, one intercession of the Messenger of God—peace

---

[47] See sūrat al-zumar: 68.

and blessings be upon him—and one of the martyr. It is mentioned in the hadith narrated by al-Miqdam bin Ma'di Yakrib—may God be pleased with him—that the Prophet—peace and blessings be upon him—said: "The martyr has six things (in store) with God: He is forgiven from the first drop of his blood that is shed; he is shown his place in Paradise; he is spared the torment of the grave; he is kept safe from the greatest terrors; he is adorned with a garment of faith; he is married to (wives) from among the wide-eyed houris; and he is permitted to intercede for seventy of his relatives."

The Martyrdom Operations

The Qur'an tells us that the Tribe of Israel fights only within fortified cities or from behind walls since the Almighty said in surat al-hashr: "They will not fight you all except within fortified cities or from behind walls. Their violence among themselves is severe. You think they are together, but their hearts are diverse. That is because they are a people who do not reason."[48]

By studying the practical reality in their wars, we see that they are protected in fortified forts, like the forts of Khaybar, the Tribe of Qurayza, and the Tribe of Nadir—just like the Bar-Lev Line,[49] which they installed on the east bank of the Suez Canal. Today, we see that they have the latest tanks and airplanes, and they work to provide their soldiers with armor and the latest means to avoid being killed or injured. For the human element is scarce and dear to them, and they are not as concerned about material losses as they are about human losses.

In light of this great fortification, and in light of our son's resistance against the occupation, our losses were always greater. Their losses, on the other hand, particularly on the human level, were little. In order to inflict the greatest number of human losses and to overcome the Zionist forts, fortifications, and tanks, our mujahidin brothers—whether in Lebanon or Palestine—were the first to embark upon the martyrdom operations. This places control in the hands of the martyrdom-seeking mujahidin to detonate whenever and wherever they please, which ensures the greatest number of human losses in the ranks of the occupation's military forces and its settlers.

These operations were highly successful against both the US Marines[50] and the headquarters of the Zionist authorities in Tyre and Sidon[51] shortly after the Zionist invasion of Lebanon. This has also been the case against the Zionist forces in Palestine

---

[48] See sūrat al-ḥashr: 14.
[49] Bar-Lev Line, a chain of fortifications constructed at the eastern side of the Suez Canal following the Israeli occupation of the Sinai Peninsula commencing with the Six-Day War in 1967.
[50] 1983 Beirut barracks bombing, al-Shami is presumably referring to the double suicide bombings against US and French service members of the Multinational Force in Lebanon on October 23, 1983.
[51] Tyre headquarters bombing, al-Shami is presumably referring to two suicide bombings against the headquarters of the Israeli army in Tyre, southern Lebanon, on November 11, 1982, and on November 4, 1983.

as happened with the Beit Lid operation of Anwar Sukkar and Salah Shakir,[52] the Kfar Darom operation of Khalid al-Khatib,[53] the Netzarim operation of Hisham Hamad,[54] or those among its settlers and civilians such as the Jerusalem operations and those in Dizengoff,[55] Hadera,[56] and others.

These Operations Have Had Many, Very Important Results

First: The Zionist enemy always struck the Arab-Islamic depth with its tanks and planes without any Arab armies or planes capable of reaching its depth in order to shake its internal security. The martyrdom operations reached this depth and blew it up, contributing to the emergence of a "balance of terror" with the Zionist enemy.

Second: These operations shattered the myth of internal security for the Zionist society insofar as the Zionist entity became unable to protect its military or civilian security. It enabled the mujahidin to raid all military checkpoints and electronic monitoring systems, and to bypass mobile security forces, and then to strike forcefully against the targets with great success.

Third: These operations managed to achieve the desired success after selecting the targets with great precision, and they were executed with great volition and control—making the Zionist death toll significant. It made the enemy recognize its weakness despite having the latest tools, the most powerful armies, and the latest technology. Former Prime Minister Rabin proved this weakness when he said: "How do you stop someone who wants to die?"

Fourth: These operations made Zionist society live in a state of hysteria, and in fear and terror of everything. Many of this society's sons are thinking of fleeing from it for security and preserving their lives. It confirms the declaration of God: "And you will surely find them the most greedy of people for life—[even] more than those who associate others with God."[57] They verify the words of God Almighty: "but [the decree of] God came upon them from where they had not expected, and He cast terror into their hearts [so] they destroyed their houses by their [own] hands and the hands of the believers. So take warning, O people of vision."[58]

Fifth: These operations quenched the believers' thirst for revenge who had suffered the falling of many martyrs because of the occupation's crimes and the destructive

---

[52] Beit Lid operation, refers to the double suicide bombing of PIJ against Israeli soldiers at the Beit Lid Junction on January 22, 1995. The attacks were carried out by Anwar Sukkar and Salah Shakir, and the operations subsequently led to the assassination of PIJ's founding father and secretary-general, Fathi al-Shiqaqi, on October 26, 1995.
[53] Refers to the suicide bombing of Khalid al-Khatib (PIJ) carried out on April 9, 1995, at the Israeli settlement Kfar Darom in the Gaza Strip.
[54] Refers to the suicide bombing of Hisham Hamad (PIJ) carried out on November 11, 1994, against an Israeli military checkpoint by the Netzarim junction in the Gaza Strip.
[55] Al-Shami is presumably referring to the suicide bombing of Ramiz Ubayd (PIJ), who blew himself up in the Dizengoff Center, Tel Aviv, on March 4, 1996.
[56] Al-Shami is presumably referring to the suicide bombing of the PIJ militants Usama Nimr Darwish and Hilal Abd al-Sattar Sabah on May 25, 2001, in Hadera.
[57] See sūrat al-baqara: 96.
[58] See sūrat al-ḥashr: 2.

means in the hands of its soldiers and settlers. On the other hand, it has become an important motivation for the sons of Islam to walk the path of these martyrdom-seekers and to carry out similar operations. In other words, these martyrdom-seekers became a model to be followed and they became an ideal for the mujahidin following in their footsteps.

Sixth: These operations were a deterrent to the occupation, which unleashed its security apparatuses and its soldiers to assassinate our people and liquidate our people's symbols and their mujahidin. The retaliatory martyrdom operations thus restrained the enemy from the whim of continuing its operations, and they made it hesitate a thousand times before committing its crimes for fear of the martyrdom responses. The enemy recognized its inability to stop them or to predict where and when these operations would be carried out.

This martyrdom-seeking effort caused great embarrassment to the occupation and its apparatuses, with its near-complete inability in dealing with it and minimizing its threat. It found no other means but to focus on the security coordination with the Palestinian security services, which were able to dismantle many of the military cells and to strike them before they could reach the depth of the occupation. Moreover, the enemy attempted to cast doubts on those executing these operations, and their fate, by designating them "suicide bombers." For the enemy knows that those who commit suicide do not enter paradise. Instead, according to the belief of Muslims, they enter hell. The enemy thus wants to fill others motivated to carry out such operations, or who want to join those executing them, with doubt. The Zionist enemy therefore gives special emphasis to the word "suicide" instead of "martyrdom."

The Arab media and some mercenaries unfortunately commit an injustice in the name of religion and science, considering this act to be suicide which is forbidden by Islam. They attribute it to the economic and social failure of those carrying out these operations. Their most misleading inference is that these operations target civilians, whom the Messenger of God—peace and blessings be upon him—forbade being exposed to wars and battles. We will discuss these false and misleading conclusions in turn in order to reject the claims of the Zionists and to expose the falsity of the claims of the profiteers of religion, the preachers of the sultans, and start from the last point.

Targeting Civilians

We must first establish a fact understood by all: that the Zionist society is a military one. He who is not a soldier in combat zones is thus a reservist, whether a man or a woman, called upon in an emergency. Zionist society is furthermore an armed one as well, with weapons spread to almost every home. It is thus a society of war. Its civilians are, moreover, even greater usurpers than its soldiers are. They usurped our homes, houses, and arable land after they displaced our people with the force of arms and with the threat of slaughter and massacre. This is in addition to the settlement activities where the Zionist civilians attack the rest of our land under the protection of the occupation soldiers and their tools—with all its killings and devastation.

Is it then not right to strike those civilians in order to respond to the aggression in accordance with the Qur'anic logic: "So whoever has assaulted you, then assault him in the same way that he has assaulted you?"[59] So we respond to the Zionist aggression and we send another message to all those among the Zionist Jews who consider coming to live in the occupation state in the place of our displaced people: that their fate is death and that their future is uncertain; that the Zionist entity is killing our people, our children, and our women; and that we have the right to deal with them in the same manner.

The Claim of Suicide

It is true that Islam forbids suicide, and that it threatens those doing so with eternity in the flames of hell—whether it is suicide with a knife or poison, by throwing oneself from a mountain or a building, or by shooting oneself or taking chemical drugs. Suicide is the attempt to end one's life because of one's personal failure at the social or economic level, or because of psychological issues, or because of despair and frustration. This leads the person to flee from life, as he is unable to face it or his frustrations.

The martyrdom-seeking mujahid, on the other hand, is one of the most optimistic and most successful at the creedal, social, and economic level. He is one of the most moral, and with the purest behavior. He is one of the most successful at the level of social relations. He is thus far from what they call a social or economic failure, and if he boldly embarks upon this deed, then he does not leave the life of this world, but moves to another life in which there is blessedness and immortality: "And the Hereafter is better for you than the first [life]."[60] "No! But you love the immediate And leave the Hereafter."[61] Where you will find the best and purest of companions: "And whoever obeys God and the Messenger—those will be with the ones upon whom God has bestowed favor of the prophets, the steadfast affirmers of truth, the martyrs and the righteous. And excellent are those as companions."[62]

Moreover, these martyrdom-seekers boldly embark upon their courageous deed; and they aim to inflict the greatest losses on Zionist society and the greatest number of deaths. They are thus not committing suicide and it is unlawful for Muslims to employ this term. They are, instead, martyrdom-seekers striving for God, hoping to join the messengers, the righteous, and the martyrs before them…

"Do Not Throw [Yourselves] with Your [Own] Hands into Destruction"

Among the discouraging words and demoralizing propaganda attempting to cast doubts on the martyrdom operations, there are sayings such as "Do not throw

---

[59] See sūrat al-baqara: 196.
[60] See sūrat āl-ḍuḥā: 4.
[61] See sūrat al-qiyām: 20–1.
[62] See sūrat al-nisā': 69.

[yourselves] with your [own] hands into destruction,"[63] as promoted by some ignorant people and collaborators prevalent in the Palestinian circles and institutions. They claim that embarking upon such operations is subject to punishment by divine prohibition, particularly as this is an incomplete part of the Qur'anic verse found in surat al-baqara: "do not throw [yourselves] with your [own] hands into destruction [by refraining]. And do good; indeed, God loves the doers of good."[64]

This verse informs that Muslims are commanded to spend in the path of God, and that not doing so in response to the divine commandment equals throwing oneself into destruction. Especially since the preceding verse comes after the verses impelling the Muslims to fight in the path of God against the aggressors and infidels. The fighting must be comprehensive so that there is no strife—not in religion, not in the self, and not in property. As the verses of surat al-baqara state:

> Fight them until there is no [more] fitna and [until] worship is [acknowledged to be] for God. But if they cease, then there is to be no aggression except against the oppressors. [Fighting in] the sacred month is for [aggression committed in] the sacred month, and for [all] violations [it] is legal retribution. So whoever has assaulted you, then assault him in the same way that he has assaulted you. And fear God and know that God is with those who fear Him. And spend in the way of God and do not throw [yourselves] with your [own] hands into destruction.[65]

The spending here is in the sense of spending in the path of God, spending in response to aggression and oppression, and spending in fighting to avoid strife. Not doing so means throwing oneself into destruction.

If this incomplete part of this verse is employed in such an illegitimate way, it would nullify the obligation of jihad in the first place. For jihad is fighting and it involves killing; and killing involves destruction. According to those who are ignorant, there is an obligation not to fight the aggressors and oppressors, because it would mean throwing oneself into destruction. It is thus decided not to fight in the path of God, and not spending to fight in the path of God, for that would lead to throwing oneself into destruction, as evidenced by the verses in the Qur'an.

The Legal Evidence

God Almighty impelled the Muslims to jihad in His path and to resist the oppressors and the unjust. He instructed that there is killing in His legislation of jihad, whether for Muslims or enemies. He has ruled so clearly in His distinguished Book: "Indeed, God has purchased from the believers their lives and their properties [in exchange] for that they will have Paradise. They fight in the cause of God, so they kill and are

---

[63] See sūrat al-baqara: 195.
[64] See sūrat al-baqara: 195.
[65] See sūrat al-baqara: 193–5.

killed."⁶⁶ Thus, there is no guarantee for the Muslim entering battle to leave unharmed. He, instead, wishes for God Almighty to bestow martyrdom upon him, for he knows the martyr's status and esteem by God, and that his life will continue.

This is one of the Prophet's companions, al-Bara' ibn Malik,⁶⁷ in the Battle of Shustar⁶⁸ against the Persians. When one of his companions said:

> O Bara'… Do you remember the hadith of God's Messenger, peace and blessings upon him, who said: "Many a person with disheveled hair, covered with dust, possessing two raisins, if he swears by God then He shall fulfill it. Among them is Al-Bara bin Malik…" He said "Yes." He said: "May God grant us victory over them." So he stated: "God has enabled us to overcome them and triumph over them… And I swear by You to bestow martyrdom upon me in Your path."

So it came to pass that he fell a martyr in this battle and God responded to his prayer. He is, however, not the only one wishing for martyrdom from God, but we see that all Muslims pray day and night to God to be granted martyrdom in His path.

On the day of Badr, the Messenger of God—peace and blessings be upon him—stood instigating the Muslims to fight the polytheists and impelling them to be patient and steadfast. He said: "By Him in Whose Hand is my life and fights them while he is patient, hopeful of his reward and marches forward without retreating, he will enter paradise if he is killed." Umayr bin al-Hamam—may God be pleased with him—heard these words, so he asked: "O Messenger of God…Is nothing between paradise and me but for one of them to kill me?" So the Messenger of God—peace and blessings be upon him—answered: "Yes." So Umayr threw his dates from his hand, fought the polytheists, and achieved martyrdom…

Jihad in the path of God is based on the killing of polytheists and the killing of Muslims. We find wonderful models of persistence and patience on the battlefield in our Islamic history. One, for example, dug a hole for himself to be in so that he could not flee from fighting. Others tied their feet so as not to think of escape or retreat, until the divine warning of fleeing from the battlefield did not apply to them.

> O you who have believed, when you meet those who disbelieve advancing [for battle], do not turn to them your backs [in flight]. And whoever turns his back to them on such a day, unless swerving [as a strategy] for war or joining [another] company, has certainly returned with anger [upon him] from God, and his refuge is Hell—and wretched is the destination.⁶⁹

---

⁶⁶ See sūrat al-tawba: 111.
⁶⁷ Al-Bara' ibn Malik al-Ansari (d. 640), one of Prophet Muhammad's companions. By appearance, ibn Malik is described as so thin that people turned away in disgust. Yet, he was renowned for his valiance in battle.
⁶⁸ Siege of Shustar (ma'rakat Tustur), battle from 641 until 642 between the Persian Sasanian Empire and the Rashidun Caliphate.
⁶⁹ See sūrat al-anfāl: 15–16.

We also find this in the position of the great companion al-Bara' ibn Malik in the Battle of Yamama[70] against Musaylima the Liar[71] and his soldiers, which supports our evidence. Musaylima and his soldiers were exposed, and they fled to a "garden fort" intended for that purpose, barricading themselves there. The resolve of the Muslims was about to weaken when al-Bara' ibn Malik rushed to ask his brothers to carry him on their spears and throw him into the fort so that he could open the gates for them, which they did not expect. He climbed the walls of the fort and plunged himself into the middle of the enemies defending it. He fought with a sword in one hand and tried to open the fort's gate with the other until he was able to do so in the end. He did so, however, only after his pure body had been hit with eighty-two strikes, stabs, and shots...

Some cowards may portray this act as careless and heedless. Yet, it was one of the great companions with great faith and extraordinary courage who executed it, and the Muslims achieved a great victory and a glorious conquest. This companion, who understood the truth of Islam, the truth of sacrifice, and the truth of trading with God Almighty.

The act of the aforementioned companion supports our preceding evidence; however, the sheath of his sword broke as he extended his greetings to the companions, but he fought until he was killed. Another evidence is the companion asking the Messenger of God—peace and blessings be upon him—about the worshipper's deed making the Lord laugh. So he—peace and blessings be upon him—said: "Plunging at the enemy unarmored." To seek martyrdom in the path of God is plunging into the enemy with your hands, bones, and blood without armor and shield. For this is one of the greatest deeds making the Lord laugh.

The most important point on which we rely to deduce the legitimacy of the act of martyrdom is the hadith of the Prophet—peace and blessings be upon him: "Actions are judged by their intentions, so each man will have what he intended..." The intention of this martyrdom-seeker is thus to infuriate the enemies by inflicting the greatest losses possible on them in response to God's repeated calls in the Holy Qur'an such as: "So let those fight in the cause of God who sell the life of this world for the Hereafter. And he who fights in the cause of God and is killed or achieves victory—We will bestow upon him a great reward."[72] In response to the guidance of the Messenger of God—peace and blessings be upon him—in defense of the oppressed men, women, and children on Earth, and in defense of the sanctities violated by the enemies of God.

If this is his intention, he will receive recompense for that, which is martyrdom and paradise, and he will be gathered with the messengers, the steadfast affirmers of Truth, the martyrs, and the righteous. And excellent are those as companions.[73] This has been

---

[70] Battle of Yamama (632), following the death of Prophet Muhammad, a number of Arabian tribes refused to acknowledge Abu Bakr as the new caliph and rebelled. Some of the rebels chose to follow Musaylima the Liar, a self-proclaimed prophet, instead of Abu Bakr, leading to the Battle of Yamama where Musaylima was killed.

[71] Maslama ibn Habib, Musaylima the Liar (d. 632), one of several persons claiming prophethood following the death of Prophet Muhammad. He was killed in 632 as a part of the Apostasy Wars (ḥurūb al-ridda) at the Battle of Yamama.

[72] See sūrat al-nisā': 74.

[73] Reference to sūrat al-nisā': 69.

stated in legal opinions by many sincere Muslim scholars. Martyrdom has thus become a wish for all Muslims, and they call upon God Almighty to bestow it upon them at every time and at all times. Martyrdom has therefore also become an inherent value in the hearts of our sons, fathers, and mothers who all rush to its places. May they receive this honor and reward. For this has made our people's sons a model of sacrifice and redemption, of life, and of revival and emulation for our entire umma.

We therefore ask everyone not to neglect this value, and not to renounce this dignity, for in it is the highest glory and victory in this world and in the Hereafter. In it is infuriating the enemies and healing the breasts of the believers. Everywhere and all the time, we preserve the word of God Almighty:

> Say, "Never will we be struck except by what God has decreed for us; He is our protector." And upon God let the believers rely. Say, "Do you await for us except one of the two best things while we await for you that God will afflict you with punishment from Himself or at our hands? So wait; indeed we, along with you, are waiting."[74]

We thus hope for one of the two best things, victory or martyrdom, and there is no third option.

If we relinquish the desire for martyrdom, and for seeking martyrdom in the path of God, then we will remain in the circle of weakness and degradation. Nations will fall upon us as the eaters fall upon the food plate—neither giving us any distinction, nor shedding a tear for us. For nations respect only the strong, and the first path of strength stems from lacking fear of death and storming forward for its values. This is what the first caliph, Abu Bakr—may God be pleased with him—wanted to teach us when he said: "Strive for death endowing you with life."

Praise be to God.

---

[74] See sūrat al-tawba: 51–2.

19

Excerpt from *The Jihadist March of Palestinian Islamic Jihad*

Excerpt from Yusuf Arif al-Hajj Muhammad's book The Jihadist March of Palestinian Islamic Jihad, published by the Muhjat al-Quds Institute, September 2011 (p. 79–86).

Although PIJ commenced employing suicide bombings in 1993, their number was limited throughout the 1990s. However, suicide bombings would largely define the Second Intifada—with photos in international news outlets of Israeli buses, cafés, restaurants, and nightclubs torn sunder. The targeting of Israeli civilians was often framed as a means of deterrence and a balance of terror (Israel would have to think twice before attacking Palestinians), as revenge (against the demolition of the Jenin refugee camp in 2002, for example), or to create leverage in negotiations. Violence and suicide bombings were thus a legitimate means of the resistance.

Within days following the terrorist attacks against the United States on September 11, 2001, the military attacks against the Palestinians intensified as Ariel Sharon suggested that the Palestinian resistance was equal to that of Usama bin Laden and al-Qaida. The Israeli suppression of the Second Intifada was not just about defending Israeli lives, according to Sharon: "The fight against terror is an international struggle of the free world against the forces of darkness who seek to destroy our liberty and our way of life."[1] With Israel as a partner of the United States in the "War on Terror," it now constructed a narrative of itself as a Western outpost struggling against the evil forces of radical Islam.

The Palestinian factions in general and PIJ in particular thus attempted to distance themselves and their practices from that of al-Qaida shortly after the attacks. Yet, to do so posed a theoretical conundrum for the movement, as PIJ had to disassociate itself from the attacks on US civilians while simultaneously avoiding delegitimizing its own attacks on Israeli civilians. As we see in the following excerpt, the PIJ West Bank leader Yusuf Arif al-Hajj Muhammad did so by developing an interpretation of jus in bello with which the legality of violence depended on the existence or absence of alternative channels for political influence. Because Muslims, Arabs, and Palestinians had alternative channels for voicing discontent and applying political pressure in the United States, violence was illegitimate there. Conversely, these channels did not exist

---

[1] Derek Gregory, "Palestine and the 'War on Terror,'" *Comparative Studies of South Asia, Africa and the Middle East* 24, no. 1 (2004): 184.

for Palestinians under Israeli occupation, and violence was hence the only viable means to resist.

This document thus matters for two reasons. First, this document is one of the most elaborate writings by PIJ on the terror attacks of September 11. It clarifies the position of the movement, as well as explaining why they reject these attacks. Secondly, this document is also interesting because al-Hajj Muhammad largely employs the United States as the negative mirror image of Israel in order to elucidate the situation and position of the Palestinians. The United States is a democracy, Israel is a settler-colonial state. US citizens have alternative democratic channels to apply political pressure, the Palestinians do not. Violence against US civilians is thus prohibited, while violence against Israelis is permitted.

☪

The September 11 Attacks—The Events That Shook the United States

The attacks on the World Trade Center on September 11, 2001, was a turning point in the American policies toward all that is Arab or Muslim. The United States removed its mask of civilization, civility, and secularism after it turned out that al-Qaida, led by Sheikh Usama bin Laden, had planned and executed these surprisingly sophisticated and thoroughly implemented attacks. US president George W. Bush declared a war against the Islamic world and described it as a crusade. He commenced with Afghanistan, and then turned to Iraq, before he began putting pressure on Syria and Iran. Bush then proposed the Roadmap[2] for the Palestinians, which included establishing a small state for them on a part of the West Bank and the Gaza Strip. The Palestinians and Israelis were to negotiate the plan in order to determine the size of the state, and the degree of sovereignty and independence it would enjoy. The Arab states would in return recognize Israel and establish normal relations with it. All of this was one of the direct effects of the events of September 11, in addition to what the American authorities practiced of arrests in the ranks of Arabs and Muslims, with the various forms of oppression.

There are certain questions pertaining to the events of September 11, the position of Palestinian Islamic Jihad on these bombings, the legal responsibility of Arabs and Muslims for these events, and the future of the Arab and Islamic relationship with the United States and the West in general after these events.

Regarding the position of Palestinian Islamic Jihad, the movement does not understand how al-Qaida's action was right, or how it was in the interests of the Palestinians, the Muslims, or the Islamic call. True, the successive American administrations are criminal concerning the rights of the Palestinians and the

---

[2] The road map for peace, a plan first outlined by US president George W. Bush in 2002 to resolve the Israeli-Palestinian conflict and to establish an independent Palestinian state.

Palestinian cause. It is also true that they are very hostile to Islam and Muslims, and that they sponsored and protected corrupt regimes against its people, in the entire world in general, and in the Islamic world in particular. The administrations are additionally the main sponsor of the Zionist entity with unlimited support for it, and thus an accomplice in all the crimes this entity has committed. Hence, the United States bears full responsibility for every drop of blood shed by this entity in and outside of Palestine. In addition to the crimes in Palestine, the United States' crimes extend to the entire Islamic world. It suffices to note that the regime of Iraqi president Saddam Hussein—which the United States deposed—had received all technological, financial, and intelligence-related backing, support, and assistance in the war against its neighbor Iran following the overthrow of the shah and the establishment of the Islamic republic.

The US policies against the Islamic world in its entirety incite the hatred and intense anger of Muslims, against which they consider to be in a war. Yet, each war has its own domain adequate to the circumstances of the belligerents, the opportunities, and the type of war: military confrontation with army against army; the popular liberation war against an occupier; or an economic war, which is a form of boycott exposing the enemy's economy, targeting it, and attempting to destroy it. One form of economic war is to obstruct the export of certain goods to the enemy and to refrain from buying its goods and products.

Because of the nature of the demography of the United States—based on large and small ethnic and religious groups and blocs—there is another form of war inside, which is the war of influence. It is the confrontations between conflicting economic, ethnic, or religious blocs, such as the war between the Jewish sect and its followers, on the one hand, and the Palestinians, Arabs, and Muslim communities, on the other. It is a war that does not employ arms, but, instead, uses the weapons of money, the media, interests, and the use of influence. It is only natural for the Arabs and Muslims to wage a war (within the law) inside of the United States against the overwhelming Zionist influence, which is maintained by the unlimited support of Christians in general, and of right-wing Christians, known as Christian Zionists, in particular.

However, the Muslim communities have remained negligent in this field. It is true that their influence in the United States does not equal that of the Zionists and their supporters among the Christian Zionists, which is equally true of their financial status. Yet, the Arab and Muslim communities are not few in numbers, their possibilities are not slim, and they do not lack supporters in US society. They are nonetheless in need of a unity of purpose, a strong incentive for such confrontations, and the generosity of time, effort, and money toward this very purpose. It is therefore the Jewish pressure groups and their supporters who are unparalleled with regard to their dominant influence in the American administration and Congress, and who have played a key role in guiding American policy to support Israel and to oppose Arabs and Muslims—steering the war machine against Islamic country after country.

Despite the difficult situation for the Arabs and Muslims in the United States—particularly after September 11, which provided the Jews and their supporters the task of drawing the worst image of all that is Arab and Muslim in the American citizen's imagination—they still have the possibility of fighting this battle. They can do so with the possibility of winning supporters and put an end to the influence of the Zionists and Christian-Zionists. It is a battle that requires them to fight with all their might and influence within the laws permitted in that country if they wish to achieve self-esteem, respect, and decent lives for themselves, which they lost after the events of September 11. They must serve the causes of their country, particularly the cause that must be at the heart of every Muslim's attention, and that is the Palestinian cause.

The entire Islamic world can wage a war against the United States with the greatest damage and without a powerful military machine. This war is economic war: the war of boycotting the American economy. The Islamic world is also negligent here, just as in its negligence in the war of influence. It lacks the will, the awareness, and the sincere leadership to fight a war of this kind. But it is not too late. Certainly, it is necessary for Muslims to fight such a battle day after day. Just as striking the US forces occupying this or that Islamic country through guerilla operations is very effective. What happened to the US forces in Lebanon and in Saudi Arabia, and what they experienced in Afghanistan and in Iraq, is clear evidence of the legitimacy and effectiveness of the guerilla war against US forces.

Nonetheless, what happened on September 11, 2001, was another form of war. It was an extreme violence and it was inflicted on a people outside the arena of confrontation. Among them were people who did not know anything about the Palestinian cause and who had not caused any harm to Muslims. There were also Muslims among them, and there were, of course, also people there against Muslims and Islam. That is, the strike was directed against civilians outside the Occupied Palestinian Territories, killing thousands of people, including many innocents who had never harmed anyone. It is unacceptable in Islam for the innocent to assume the offense of the criminal: "And [of] Abraham, who fulfilled [his obligations]—That no bearer of burdens will bear the burden of another."[3]

Palestinian Islamic Jihad thus rejects this kind of war and considers it unnecessary and not a priority. The movement believes that the attacks have seriously damaged the reputation of Islam, and that they have made it easier for the enemies to pass their lies about the ugliness of Islam and the terrorism of Muslims. Minds without any idea of Islam have become ready to accept the notion of it as a religion of violence and aggression.

It is true that the September 11 attacks dealt a blow to the prestige of the United States, and that they inflicted a great wound on its pride. It thus felt some of the wrath of the entire world's people who had suffered injustice and oppression, and not only in the Muslim countries. Yet, the amount of damage to the enemy is not the measure of legitimacy or illegitimacy in Islam. Islam has identified causes for war and rules regulating it, as well as the manner of dealing with the infidel during and after war. Islam is thus a reference for Muslims.

The United States made Islam and the entire Islamic umma responsible for what happened in September. It no longer hid its hostility but, instead, launched wars and hatred against them. It bestowed support, armament, and aid upon their enemies—Jews, Hindus, Russians, and others waging unjust wars against the Muslims—although the responsibility for what happened does not rest with every Muslim. Sheikh Usama

---

[3] See sūrat al-najm: 37–8.

bin Laden did not hold a conference for the Muslims where he presented the plan to strike the World Trade Center in New York and obtained a mandate from the Muslims to carry out this deed. If this were the case, then the Muslims would have been held responsible for what happened. The fact is, however, that the United States is an old and known enemy of Islam and Muslims, and of the Palestinian people in particular. Its support for their enemies, and especially for the Zionist enemy, has made every Muslim earnestly concerned with his religion and the honor of his umma, feeling resentment and hatred against this hostile and aggressive country—feeling that he is at war with the United States and wishing to see its humiliation and destruction with his own eyes.

If the United States has united the feelings of the Muslims against it, then it has also made many of them search for ways to respond to it and punish it for the crimes committed against the entire Islamic world. Among them emerged someone with a particular mindset, who had great possibilities and capabilities, and who had the will to act against the main Muslim enemy. He was Usama bin Laden, the leader of al-Qaida, who carried out several operations of destruction against America's objectives before carrying out the greatest of them all, which shook the whole world.

The feelings of the Palestinians—particularly their lack of sympathy with the United States as they witnessed the dignity of the country and the reputation of its central intelligence wallow in the mud—were a people's natural feeling against a strong and powerful state appointing their enemy to kill, imprison, and displace them, destroying their homes and confiscating their land.

It is clear that the events of September 11, 2001, formed an important historical turning point on the international level and on the level of the American–Zionist conflict with the Islamic world. If this conflict has acquired the character of violence and defiance as the United States gradually and deliberately works to impose its control—and thus Zionist control over the entire Islamic world—then there is a positive factor emerging little by little calling for optimism no matter how intense the American aggression against the Palestinian people and the Islamic umma is. This positive factor is the beginning of the Islamic people's awakening, and their readiness to go into battle. The Muslims know for certain they will eventually win this battle, God willing.

ℂ

20

Anwar Abu Taha on the Arab Spring and PIJ's Position

Author's interview with Anwar Abu Taha, member of PIJ's political bureau, in Beirut, Lebanon, March 19, 2018.

A number of the preceding texts may have given the impression that the Iranian connection has mainly been a cause of nuisance for PIJ—ranging from accusations of being Shiites to that of being Iranian agents in the Palestinian arena. Yet, PIJ has benefitted from Iranian funding, which has facilitated its armed action against the Israeli occupation. Although this funding has never caused the growth of the movement, it has nevertheless sustained it. PIJ has consequently suffered in times of conflict between the movement and its patron when funding has decreased. This was increasingly the case from 2015. Struggling to fund its militants; its media workers; and employees, PIJ leaders such as Muhammad al-Hindi travelled unsuccessfully to Turkey and Algeria to find alternative sources of finance. Consequently, although the movement is careful to keep a certain ideological and political distance from its patron in order to preserve its organizational independence, the aftermath of the Arab Spring proved that it had grown increasingly dependent on its patron.

Hamas disavowed the Syrian regime and moved its leadership from Damascus once Iran, Hezbollah, and the regime of al-Assad were drawn into the Syrian civil war. PIJ, on the other hand, was far more careful, and its leadership only left Damascus after allegedly conferring with Iranian and Syrian leaders. Yet, Iran later began to pressure PIJ to choose a side in its many regional conflicts. But because it persisted in its neutrality and avoided making the Palestinian cause a part of any regional conflict, tensions between the patron and PIJ increased.

This is an unpublished interview by this translator with a member of PIJ's political bureau, Anwar Abu Taha. Refreshingly honest, Abu Taha discusses the Arab Spring, the Syrian civil war, and its relationship with Iran. The document thus matters because it offers a unique insight into the thought and practice of PIJ regarding the region and the Arab Spring. The document also matters because it addresses a paradox of the movement. On the one hand, PIJ postulates that it supports democracy and free elections. It also declares its opposition to the Arab regimes—both due to their autocratic form and because they are perceived to be stooges of the West and too lenient toward Israel and its occupation. Consequently, PIJ supports the Arab Spring and the popular protests. On the other hand, the movement has never denounced the Arab regimes and it was careful not to weaken its alliance with Iran, Syria, and Hezbollah.[1] How does PIJ reconcile these two contradictory positions? This interview with Abu Taha thus highlights how real political considerations affect the ideological positions of the movement.

☪

What is PIJ's position on the Arab Spring? How has the position developed from the inception of the uprising until today?

The position of PIJ has not developed; it has been constant. We are with the people against oppression, against tyranny. We support freedom, democracy, a circulation of power, and we are against corruption. We support political liberalism in the administration of internal affairs. We are for multiple freedoms against tyranny, and we support transparency and accountability. These Arab regimes are authoritarian, they kill their people, and they are the agents of the West—taking their orders from the White House, from London, and from Paris. The [Arab] presidents are not democratically elected, and we support a democratic political life in the Arab world under free and fair elections, and with a circulation of power. We support economic independence, and we are against corruption and theft. We are against the close union with foreign European and American alliances at the level of foreign policy, and we support the Islamic countries fulfilling their own interests, and not the interests of those who want the oil on the level of all economic and internal policies. So, we support those who rose up, we support the Arab revolutions, and we support the Arab Spring.

In Syria too?

Everywhere, even Syria. However, we are against turning the Arab Spring into an armed conflict although we do support the Arab Spring everywhere, even in Syria. We want dialogue between the people and these regimes. What happened in Syria? There are armed groups there supported by Saudi Arabia, Turkey, and Qatar, so I want to ask you: Are Saudi Arabia and Qatar democratic states? How do you support non-democratic countries [such as these] that support parties against a non-democratic regime [Syria], and which later took up arms? In our position on Syria, we call for a political dialogue between the Syrian opposition and the regime without the use of weapons and without the foreign supporters. This is our position, first. We are in principle with the freedoms of the people and with justice, but we are against the use of weapons and the financing from a foreign party whether they are Arab, undemocratic, have a king or an emir. We support political dialogue; we do not want the killing of the people.

The second most important issue is that PIJ is a Palestinian movement and we do our utmost for Palestine and we do so inside Palestine. Even abroad, we worked to garner political, financial, logistical support, and so on to benefit the resistance inside Palestine. We do not intervene in any Arab affairs. It is a difference between

---

[1] For a historical analysis of this period and how it affected PIJ, see Skare, *A History of Palestinian Islamic Jihad: Faith, Awareness, and Revolution in the Middle East*.

the ideological and political position and the practical work. In practice, we will never interfere. But you asked for our position: Our position is with freedom, with justice, and with the political dialogue. On the practical level, however, we do not interfere in any Arab affairs. Why? Because if we intervened it would not benefit any party. Today, if I entered Syria, would it affect the battle? No. It would cause strife, and my effort against Israel's occupation would be harmed. I leave the Arab people to decide their fate as they want.

And how did the Arab Spring affect your relationship with Iran?

The Arab Spring affected our relationship not only with Iran but with all parties. Because all the parties in the Arab world… if you are not with us 100 percent then you are against us. The Arab regimes do not accept that you are with them halfway, this is the Arab culture. In Europe, I can agree 5 percent with you in this situation, and it is okay. Fifty percent and it is okay. This is how the Arab world is. We are not able to support this. So, the financial support was weakened in response, but not cut completely. We stand firm, however. The Arab Spring thus affected all relationships. For example, in Egypt and the Gulf there were counterrevolutions, but we say that everything that the United Arab Emirates and its puppets do is against the Arab Spring. Yet, we go to Egypt in the interests of the political geography as it is next to the Gaza Strip, and we interact with the Egyptians. Yet, we do not care about Egyptian internal affairs; this is for Egyptians and we do not interfere in it. I have dialogue with the regime of al-Sisi about Palestine, Gaza, the blockade, and the border crossing.

℃

Bibliography

Abou Jalal, Rasha. "Islamic Jihad Gains Support in Gaza as Hamas Declines." *Al-Monitor*, April 10, 2014. https://www.al-monitor.com/pulse/originals/2014/04/islamic-jihad-support-gaza-expense-hamas.html.
Abu-Amr, Ziad. *Islamic Fundamentalism in the West Bank and Gaza*. Bloomington, IN: Indiana University Press, 1994.
Akbarzadeh, Shahram, ed. *Routledge Handbook of Political Islam*, 1st ed. New York: Routledge, 2011.
Ansari, Ali M. *Modern Iran: The Pahlavis and After*, 2nd ed. Harlow: Pearson Education lmt., 2007.
Anthony, Sean W. *The Caliph and the Heretic: Ibn Saba' and the Origins of Shī'ism*. Leiden and Boston: Brill, 2012.
Arjomand, Said Amir. *The Shadow of God & the Hidden Imam. Religion, Political Order, and Societal Change in Shi'ite Iran from the Beginning to 1890*. Chicago and London: The University of Chicago Press, 1987.
Ashour, Omar. "Myths and Realities: The Muslim Brothers and Armed Activism." *Aljazeera*, August 12, 2014. https://www.aljazeera.com/indepth/opinion/2014/08/myths-realities-muslim-brothers--20148129319751298.html.
Baconi, Tareq. *Hamas Contained: The Rise and Pacification of Palestinian Resistance*. Stanford: Stanford University Press, 2018.
Brenner, Björn. *Gaza under Hamas: From Islamic Democracy to Islamist Governance*. London and New York: I.B. Tauris, 2017.
Bunzel, Cole. "The Kingdom and the Caliphate: Duel of Islamic States." MA: Carnegie Endowment for International Peace, 2016.
Busse, Heribert. "The Sanctity of Jerusalem in Islam." *Judaism* 17, no. 4 (Fall 1968): 441–68.
Caridi, Paola. *Hamas: From Resistance to Government*. New York: Seven Stories Press, 2012.
Crone, Patricia. *God's Rule: Government and Islam: Six Centuries of Medieval Islamic Political Thought*. Columbia: Columbia University Press, 2004.
Dunning, Tristan. *Hamas, Jihad and Popular Legitimacy: Reinterpreting Resistance in Palestine*. London and New York: Routledge, 2016.
Eagleton, Terry. *Ideology: An Introduction*, new ed. London and New York: Verso Books, 2007.
Elamir, Norah Sonya. "The Theological Concept of 'Isma from the Early to the Modern Period of Islam." Master's thesis, The University of Texas at Austin, 2016.
Encyclopædia Britannica. "Māturīdīyah." No date. https://www.britannica.com/topic/Maturidiyah.
Encyclopædia Britannica. "Iblīs." No date. https://www.britannica.com/topic/Iblis.

Ende, Werner. "Sunni Polemical Writings on the Shi'a and the Iranian Revolution." In *The Iranian Revolution and the Muslim World*, edited by David Menashri. Boulder: Westview Press, 1990.

Ende, Werner. "al-Jundī, Anwar." In *Encyclopedia of Islam* III, edited by Kate Fleet, Gudrun Krämer, Denis Matringe, John Newas, and Everett Rowson. http://dx.doi.org/10.1163/1573-3912_ei3_COM_32879.

Esposito, John L. *The Islamic Threat: Myth or Reality?* 3rd ed. New York and Oxford: Oxford University Press, 1999.

Esposito, John L. and Emad al-Din Shahin, eds. *The Oxford Handbook of Islam and Politics*. Oxford: Oxford University Press, 2016.

Gregory, Derek. "Palestine and the 'War on Terror.'" *Comparative Studies of South Asia, Africa and the Middle East* 24, no. 1 (2004): 185–98.

Gunning, Jeroen. *Hamas in Politics: Democracy, Religion, Violence*. London: Hurst & Company, 2009.

Haider, Najam. *Shī'ī Islam: An Introduction*. Cambridge: Cambridge University Press, 2014.

Hall, Ian. "Challenge and Response: The Lasting Engagement of Arnold J. Toynbee and Martin Wight." *International Relations* 17, no. 3 (2003): 389–404.

Hatina, Meir. *Islam and Salvation in Palestine*. The Moshe Dayan Center for Middle Eastern and African Studies, Tel Aviv University, 2000.

Hatina, Meir. "Restoring a Lost Identity: Models of Education in Modern Islamic Thought." *British Journal of Middle Eastern Studies* 33, no. 2 (2006): 179–97.

Haykel, Bernard. *Revival and Reform in Islam: The Legacy of Muhammad al-Shawkānī*. Cambridge: Cambridge University Press, 2003.

Hegghammer, Thomas. "Jihadi-Salafis or Revolutionaries? On Religion and Politics in the Study of Militant Islamism." In *Global Salafism: Islam's New Religious Movement*, edited by Roel Meijer, 244–66. Oxford: Oxford University Press, 2013.

Helbawy, Kamal. "The Muslim Brotherhood in Egypt: Historical Evolution and Future Prospects." In *Political Islam: Context versus Ideology*, edited by Khaled Hroub, 61–85. London: Saqi, 2010.

Holbrook, Donald, ed. *Al-Qaeda 2.0: A Critical Reader*. London: Hurst & Company, 2017.

Hourani, Albert. *Arabic Thought in the Liberal Age 1798–1939*. Cambridge: Cambridge University Press, 2003.

Hoyland, Robert G. *Arabia and the Arabs. From the Bronze Age to the Coming of Islam*. London and New York: Routledge, 2001.

Hroub, Khaled. *Hamas: Political Thought and Practice*. Washington, DC: Institute for Palestine Studies, 2000.

Hroub, Khaled. "Introduction." In *Political Islam: Context versus Ideology*, edited by Khaled Hroub, 9–19. London: Saqi, 2010.

Høigilt, Jacob. "The Palestinian Spring That Was Not: The Youth and Political Activism in the Occupied Palestinian Territories." *Arab Studies Quarterly* 35, no. 4 (Fall 2013): 343–59.

Ingram, Haroro J., Craig Whiteside, and Charlie Winter. *The Isis Reader: Milestone Texts of the Islamic State Movement*. London: Hurst & Company, 2019.

Jensen, Michael Irving. *The Political Ideology of Hamas: A Grassroots Perspective*. London: I.B. Tauris, 2010.

Jewish Encyclopedia. "Zechariah ben Jehoiada." No date. http://www.jewishencyclopedia.com/articles/15201-zechariah-ben-jehoiada.

Kalamullah. "O Worshipper of the Two Holy Masjids." No date. https://www.kalamullah.com/yaabidalharamain.html.
Kepel, Gilles and Jean-Pierre Milelli, eds. *Al Qaeda in Its Own Words*. Harvard: Harvard University Press, 2010.
Kifner, John. "Five More Dead in Arab Protests." *New York Times*, February 8, 1988. https://www.nytimes.com/1988/02/08/world/five-more-dead-in-arab-protests.html?searchResultPosition=1.
Lahoud, Nelly. *The Jihadis' Path to Self-Destruction*. London: Hurst & Company, 2010.
Lewis, Bernard. *Race and Slavery in the Middle East: An Historical Enquiry*. Oxford: Oxford University Press, 1990.
van Linschoten, Alex Strick, and Felix Kuehn, eds. *The Taliban Reader: War, Islam and Politics in Their Own Words*. London: Hurst & Company, 2018.
Livne-Kafri, Ofer. "Jerusalem in Early Islam: The Eschatological Aspect." *Arabica* 53 (2006): 382–403.
Malka, Haim. "Must Innocents Die? The Islamic Debate Over Suicide Attacks." *Brookings*, March 1, 2003. https://www.brookings.edu/articles/must-innocents-die-the-islamic-debate-over-suicide-attacks/.
Mansfield, Laura. *His Own Words: A Translation of the Writings of Dr. Ayman al Zawahiri*. Old Tappan: TLG Publications, 2006.
Mejdell, Gunvor. "Kulturelle og språklige utfordringer i oversettelse av arabisk litteratur." *Babylon. Nordisk tidsskrift for Midtøstenstudier*, no. 2 (2012): 8–19.
Milton-Edwards, Beverley. *Islamic Politics in Palestine*. London and New York: I.B. Tauris, 1999.
Milton-Edwards, Beverley and Stephen Farrell. *Hamas: The Islamic Resistance Movement*. Cambridge: Polity Press, 2010.
Mishal, Shaul and Avraham Sela. *The Palestinian Hamas: Vision, Violence, and Coexistence*. New York: Columbia University Press, 2006.
Mitchell, Richard P. *The Society of Muslim Brothers*. Oxford: Oxford University Press, 1969.
Nafi, Basheer M. "Abu al-Thanaʿ al-Alusi: An Alim, Ottoman Mufti, and Exegete of the Qurʾan." *International Journal of Middle East Studies* 34, no. 3 (2002): 465–95.
The Noble Qurʾan. "The Noble Qurʾan." No date. https://quran.com..
Noe, Nicholas, ed. *Voice of Hezbollah: The Statements of Sayyed Hassan Nasrallah*. London and New York: Verso Books, 2017.
Oxford Islamic Online. "Ahl al-Hall wa'l-Aqd." http://www.oxfordislamicstudies.com/article/opr/t125/e73.
Oxford Islamic Online. "Dervish." No date. http://www.oxfordislamicstudies.com/article/opr/t125/e523.
Oxford Islamic Online. "Hisba." No date. http://www.oxfordislamicstudies.com/article/opr/t125/e851.
Oxford Islamic Online. "Ijtihad." No date. http://www.oxfordislamicstudies.com/article/opr/t125/e990?_hi=1&_pos=1.
Oxford Islamic Online. "Jinn." No date. http://www.oxfordislamicstudies.com/article/opr/t125/e1204?_hi=1&_pos=2.
Oxford Islamic Online. "Marja al-Taqlid." No date. http://www.oxfordislamicstudies.com/article/opr/t125/e1437.
Oxford Islamic Online. "Murid." No date. http://www.oxfordislamicstudies.com/article/opr/t125/e1622.
Oxford Islamic Online. "Musnad." No date. http://www.oxfordislamicstudies.com/article/opr/t125/e1654.

Oxford Islamic Online. "Naskh." No date. http://www.oxfordislamicstudies.com/article/opr/t125/e1721.

Oxford Islamic Online. "Qisas." No date. http://www.oxfordislamicstudies.com/article/opr/t125/e1931.

Oxford Islamic Online. "Shura." http://www.oxfordislamicstudies.com/article/opr/t125/e2199.

Reynolds, Gabriel Said. "On the Qur'an and the Theme of Jews as 'Killers of the Prophets.'" *al-Bayān* 10, no. 2 (2012): 9–32.

Rizvi, Sayyid Muhammad. "Muhibb al-Din al-Khatib: A Portrait of a Salafi-Arabist." Master's thesis, Simon Fraser University, 1991.

Rogan, Eugene. *The Arabs: A History*. London and New York: Penguin Books, 2011.

Routledge Encyclopedia of Philosophy. "Averroism." 1998. doi:10.4324/9780415249126-B012-1.

Roy, Sara. *Hamas and Civil Society in Gaza: Engaging the Islamist Social Sector*. Princeton, NJ: Princeton University Press, 2011.

Seikaly, May. *Haifa: Transformation of an Arab Society, 1918–1939*. London: I.B. Tauris, 1998.

Sela, Avraham. "The 'Wailing Wall' Riots (1929) as a Watershed in the Palestine Conflict." *The Muslim World* LXXXIV, no. 1–2 (April 1994): 60–94.

Seliger, Martin. *Ideology and Politics*. London: Allen & Unwin, 1976.

Shadid, Mohammad K. "The Muslim Brotherhood Movement in the West Bank and Gaza." *Third World Quarterly* 10, no. 2 (April 1988): 658–82.

Sing, Manfred. "Brothers in Arms: How Palestinian Maoists Turned Jihadists." *Die Welt des Islams* 51 (2011): 1–44.

Skare, Erik. *A History of Palestinian Islamic Jihad: Faith, Awareness, and Revolution in the Middle East*. Cambridge: Cambridge University Press, 2021.

Skovgaard-Petersen, Jakob. *Defining Islam for the Egyptian State: Muftis and Fatwas of the Dār al-Iftā*. Leiden and Boston: Brill, 1997.

Stilt, Kristen and M. Safa Saraçoğlu. "Hisba and Muhtasib." In *The Oxford Handbook of Islamic Law*, edited by Anver M. Emon and Rumee Ahmed. Oxford: Oxford University Press, 2018.

Al-Sudairi, Mohammed. "Mao in the Middle East: Hadi al-'Alawi, Scion of the Two Civilizations." *Middle East Report 270* (Spring 2014): 19–20.

Tamimi, Azzam. *Hamas: Unwritten Chapters*. London: Hurst & Company, 2009.

Villa, Luisa. "A 'Political Education': Wilfrid Scawen Blunt, the Arabs and the Egyptian Revolution (1881–82)." *Journal of Victorian Culture* 17, no. 1 (2012): 46–63.

Weiss, Max. "Genealogies of Ba'thism: Michel 'Aflaq between Personalism and Arabic Nationalism." *Modern Intellectual History*: 1–32.

Wood, Ellen Meiksins. *Citizens to Lords: A Social History of Western Political Thought from Antiquity to the Late Middle Ages*. London and New York: Verso Books, 2008.

Zahid, Mohammed. *The Muslim Brotherhood and Egypt's Succession Crisis: The Politics of Liberalisation and Reform in the Middle East*. London: I.B. Tauris, 2012.

Index

Abd al-Baqi, Ahmad Hilmi (Prime Minister of All-Palestine Government) 72
Abd al-Hadi, Awni (politician) 72
Abd al-Raziq, Mustafa (Egyptian philosopher) 159
Abd el-Krim, see also Al-Khattabi, Muhammad ibn Abd al-Karim (Moroccan leader)
Abdel Raziq, Ali (Egyptian scholar) 138
Abduh, Muhammad (jurist and reformer) 60–1, 180, 203
Abdul Hamid II (Sultan of the Ottoman Empire) 136, 195
Abu Hurayra, see al-Dawsi, Abd al-Rahman ibn Sakhr (Prophet's companion)
Abu Qatada (Prophet's companion) 235
Abu Taha, Anwar (PIJ political bureau member) 185–6, 249–51
Abu Zaabal bombing (Egypt, 1970) 117
Abu Zahra, Muhammad (Egyptian lecturer) 165, 169
Adherence (magazine) 171, 172
Al-Afghani, Jamal al-Din 57, 60, 61, 137, 202
Afghanistan 82–4
  American aid to 85
  Marxism in 86
  and Soviet Union 84–7
Algeria
  Islamic revolution in 80, 133, 137–8
Ali bin Hussein (Sharif of Mecca) 136–7
Ali ibn Abi Talib (Caliph) 103
al-Alusi, Abu al-Thana' (Iraqi Islamic scholar) 60
Amin, Hafizullah (President of Afghanistan) 86
apostles and prophets 29, 46, 104, 107–8
Al-Aqsa Martyr's Brigades 20
Al-Aqsa Mosque (Jerusalem) 12, 96–7, 101, 102, 106

Arabism 48, 125, 136
Arab Muslims 29–30
Arab Spring 44, 249–51
Arafat, Yasser (PLO Chairman) 189, 192
armed jihad, *see also* jihad
  and Islamic movements 55
  and PIJ 12–13, 34
  and PLO 37
  and Qassamists 80
Al-Ash'ari, Ali bin Isma'il (theologian) 51 n.5
Atlit settlement 80
Al-Attar, Issam (Muslim Brotherhood leader) 169
Averroism 138 n.26
Awad, Louis (Egyptian author) 58, 139
Awda, Abd al-Aziz (PIJ leader) 9, 14
Aws, Tribe of 112
Al-Azhar (magazine) 105–7
Al-Azm, Yusuf (Jordanian intellectual) 170

Al-Bahnasawi, Salim (Egyptian jurist) 159, 165–6
Bahr al-Baqar primary school bombing (Egypt, 1970) 117
Bakk, Ahmad Ibrahim (jurist) 168
balance of terror 237, 244
Balfour Declaration (1917) 69, 70
Al-Banna, Hassan (founder of Muslim Brotherhood) 62, 65, 67
  rapprochement with Kashani 145, 159–60
  vis-à-vis Shiites-Sunnis reconciliation 158–9
Al-Bayir, Hassan Ibrahim (Palestinian militant) 78
Beirut Reform Society (*Jam'iyyat Beirut al-Iṣlāḥiyya*) 68
Beit Lid Operation 20
Ben Badis, Abdelhamid (Algerian reformer) 137

Ben Bella, Ahmed (President of
    Algeria) 133
Bin Laden, Usama 245, 247–8
Boumédiène, Houari (President of
    Algeria) 133
Britain
    Afghanistan policy 84–5
    and Arab nationalism 68–70
    and Ottoman Empire 136–7
    al-Qassam's views on 77, 79
Buraq Operation (Oct 1986) 13
Buraq Uprising (1920 Arab Riots) 77

Caliph
    role and functions of 202–3
The Call (magazine) 171, 173
Canaanites 29
capitalism 93–4
Catholic Church 194, 195
challenge and response (Toynbee) 213
Christianity
    and Palestinian Muslims 30
    Westernised and estranged
        Christians 58
Christian Zionists 246–7
civil society 203, 208, 209
Cold War 90
communism 93–4, 131
compromise 35–6
Consciousness (magazine) 170
Consensus (*ijmā'*) 203
consultation (*shūra*) 206
The Covenant Society (*Jam'iyyat
    al-'Ahd*) 68
conversion to Islam 48–9
culture 214
culture of resistance 214–16
    frame of reference 216–20

al-Dajani, Arif Basha (Palestinian
    politician) 70
al-Dawsi, Abd al-Rahman ibn Sakhr
    (Prophet's companion) 102,
    228
The Decentralization Party
    (*Hizb al-Lāmarkaziyya
    al-Idāriyya*) 68
democracy 206, 208
    and Islam 48

Democratic Front for the Liberation of
    Palestine (DFLP) 25, 190
dialogue
    and Islamic movements 142–3
    PIJ's views on 41
diaspora 40
Al-Dinawi, Muhammad Ali 160–1

economy in Islam 49
Egypt
    French campaign in 134–5
    Islamic movements in 133, 141
    and Israel 117–18
    liberal ideas in 139
    and Ottoman Empire 135–6
    and PIJ 44
    Press Law no. 93 (1995) 209
    and Soviet Union 92
    support for Iranian Revolution 171
Egyptian Communist Party 90–1
Egyptian Islamic Jihad (EIJ) 44
elections 190
Ethiopia 88, 91
excommunication (*takfir*)
    in Islam 47
    PIJ's views on 179–80

Fada'iyan-e Islam (militant group) 144
family and Islam 49
Al-Faruqi, Suleiman al-Taji (politician and
    activist) 70
Fatah 189, 221
France
    Egyptian campaign 134–5
freedom and responsibility 216–19
fundamentalism
    Western notion of 201
funding 249
future Palestinian society 6, 200–1,
    204–7

Gate of Moors Operation (Oct 1986) 13
Gaylani, Rashid Ali (Prime Minister of
    Iraq) 144
Gaza Central Prison
    escape from 13
Al-Ghannouchi, Rashid (Tunisian
    politician) 170, 200
Al-Gharabli, Zuhdi (Fayiz) 13

1920 Riots (1920)   71
  in Qur'an   101, 102, 103–4, 112–13
Jews   33, *see also* Israel, Tribe of
  Arab/Muslim reconciliation
    with   47–8
  early 20th century uprisings
    against   71–2
  expulsion from the Arabian
    Peninsula   109–10, 112
  Mandate years   76–7
jihad, *see also* armed jihad
  duty of   226–7
  and Islamic movements   21–2, 55,
    64 n.38
  Islamic principle of   47, 218
  legitimacy of   224–6, 240–1
  and Palestine   227–9
  in Path of God   229–32, 235
  and PIJ   23, 34–5
Jordan   198
  and Israel relations   117
  support for the Iranian
    Revolution   170
Al-Jundi, Anwar (Egyptian
    journalist)   166–7, 169
Jurisprudence (*fiqh*)   168

Kamil, Mustafa (Egyptian activist)   61,
    62, 136
Kashani, Abol-Ghasem (Ayatollah)   144–5, 159–60
Khalaf, Abd al-Wahhab (Egyptian
    jurist)   168
Al-Khalidi, Husayn (Mayor of
    Jerusalem)   72
Khalifa, Muhammad Abd al-Rahman
    (Jordanian Muslim
    Brotherhood)   170
Khalil, Ibrahim al-Sheikh
    (Qassamist)   75
Khalil, Sami al-Shaykh (PIJ militant)   13
Khan, Amanullah (King of
    Afghanistan)   83–4
Kharijites   51 n.8
Al-Khatib, Muhibb al-Din (Syrian
    intellectual)   158
Al-Khattabi, Muhammad ibn Abd
    al-Karim (Moroccan
    leader)   138 n.23
Khazraj, Tribe of   112

Al-Khoei, Sayyid Abu al-Qasim
    (Ayatollah)   166
Khomeini, Ruhollah (Ayatollah)   137,
    142, 145
  Islamic and revolutionary position
    of   146–51
  and Palestinian cause   151–3
  on Shiite-Sunni sectarianism   173–4
  support for   169–71, 173
Khrushchev, Nikita   93
Al-Kilani, Ibrahim Zayd (Jordanian
    cleric)   170
Kishk, Abd al-Hamid (Egyptian
    preacher)   105–6

League of Nations   89
Lebanon   152
  mujahidin   236
  support for Iranian Revolution   170
legislation
  status of jihad in   227
  and umma   209
liberalism   6, 135, 250
  in Egypt   139
  failure of   131, 139, 174
Libya
  nationalist movement in   138
The Light (al-Nūr) (magazine)   11

McMahon, Sir Henry   68–9
Al-Mahdi, Muhammad Ahmad (1844–85)
    (Nubian religious leader)   59–60
Al-Makhzumi, Mahmud Salim
    (Qassamist)   79
Mandatory Palestine   70, 76–7
al-Mansur, Abu Ja'far Abdallah ibn
    Muhammad (Caliph of
    Baghdad)   203
martyrs and martyrdom   218–19, 222–3
  categories of   230–1
  legitimacy of   240–3
  meaning of   233–4
  operations   19–20, 34, 236–7
  operations' consequences   237–8
  propaganda against   239–40
  rewards of   234–6
Marxism
  in Afghanistan   86
Maturidi (theological school)   51 n.6

Al-Mawdudi, Abul Ala' (Pakistani jurist and scholar)   173
Maymuna bint al-Harith (Prophet's wife)   102
The Mecca Document (2006)   180
Medina
    Jewish tribes in   109–12
    moral infallibility (*'isma*)   166
Morocco   138
Mossadegh, Mohammad (Prime Minister of Iran)   144
Mudayn, Farih Abu (Mayor of Beersheba)   70
Muhammad, Prophet
    campaigns against Tribes of Israel   109–10
    on jihad   228
    on martyrdom   234, 235, 236
    and Qur'anic dimension of Palestinian cause   100–1, 102, 103 n.15, 106
Muhammad, Yusuf Arif   244–5
Muhammad Daoud (President of Afghanistan)   85–6
Muhammad Nadir Shah (King of Afghanistan)   84
Muhammad Zahir Shah (King of Afghanistan)   84, 85, 86
mujahidin   239, *see also* martyrs and martyrdom
    motivations of   229–30, 232–3
    rewards for   228
Mukhtar, Umar (Libyan resistance leader)   138
Mulay Slimane   60
Musaylima the Liar (false Prophet)   242
Muslim Brotherhood   55
    1st generation   62–3
    2nd generation   63–4
    3rd generation   64–5
    and Shiite relations   160–8
Muslim Brotherhood in Egypt   55, 131 n.4, 141, 160
    and Afghan cause   82
    PIJ's conflict with   153, 176
Muslim Brotherhood in Jordan   170
Muslim Brotherhood in Palestine   9, 55, 138
    accusation of PIJ as Iranian agent   154, 175–8

and jihad   21–2
    PIJ's conflict with   120–1, 122–3, 154–5
Muslim Brotherhood in Sudan   169–70
Muslims
    influence in US   246–7
    secular   57–8
    traditional   57
The Muslims (magazine)   161–2
Muslim societies   50
Mu'tazila (theological thought)   51 n.7
Muzzafar, Muhammad Rida (jurist)   166

Al-Nadim, Abdallah (Egyptian journalist)   62
Nadir, Tribe of   110
Nadwi, Abul Hasan Ali Hasani (Indian scholar)   167
nakba
    1948   73
    1967   73–4, 116
Napoleon Bonaparte   134–5
Al-Nasa'i, Abu Abd al-Rahman (collector of hadith)   231
Al-Nashashibi, Raghib (politician)   70
Al-Nashashibi family   77
Nasif, Sulayman (Protestant entrepreneur)   70
Nasser, Gamal Abdel (President of Egypt)   133
National Defense Party (British Mandate of Palestine)   70, 71
nationalism/nationalist movements   77, 79
    Arab nationalism   68–9
    and Islam   48, 63–4, 124, 137–8
    in Ottoman Empire   136–7
national partnership   38–9
nation-state
    formation of   193–5
    and Islamic world   195–7
    and secularism   202
    al-Shiqaqi on   209
Nebi Musa Riots (Jerusalem) (1920)   71
Nebuchadnezzar II (King of Babylon)   104, 106–7, 109

oppression and oppressed   215–16
Oslo Agreement   1, 37–8

Ottoman Empire 67–9, 88, 195
  and Egypt 135–6
  fall of 98, 114–15, 136–7
  Khomeini on 148
  secret Arab societies in 114

PA, *see* Palestinian National Authority
The Pact (Magazine) 170
Pakistan 62, 88
  Pakhtusa Crisis 85
  support for Iranian Revolution 173
Palestine 26, *see also* Palestinian cause
  1967 state 35 (*see also* Palestinian state)
  internal situation 36–8
  and Islam 29–30, 45–6
  and jihad 227–9
  land 27–8
  national issues and tasks 39–40
  national relations 38–9
  people of 28–9, 117
Palestine Arab Congress (Jan 1919) 70
Palestine Arab Party 71
Palestinian Cairo Declaration (2005) 188
Palestinian cause 33–4, 74
  allies of 79
  centrality of 40, 66–7, 96, 97–100, 120–1, 196
  historical dimension of 95, 113–16, 121
  as internal Islamic concern 96–7
  Iran's support for 179
  and Khomeini 151–3
  Qur'anic dimension of 95–6, 100–7, 120, 121–2
  role of Islam in 186–7
  Western position on 42
Palestinian Christians 28, 199
Palestinian Islamic Jihad (PIJ) 1–3, *see also* al-Shiqaqi, Fathi
  decline of 17
  formation of 6, 9–11, 18–20
  formative stages of 11–15
  identity of 27
  ideological literature of 3, 4–5
  ideology and nature of 179–81
  as moderate player 154–5
Palestinian Liberation Organization (PLO) 18, 37
  and Islamists 186–7
  need for comprehensive national framework 187–8
  PIJ's position on 15–16, 185–6
  recognition of Israel 43
  requisites for reform 188–91
Palestinian National Authority (PA) 1, 17, 25, 36, 37–8, 187, 188
  and PLO 189–90
Palestinian National Council (PNC) 15, 190
Palestinian state 193, 197–9
Pan-Islamic Congress (1931) 71
Party of Union and Progress (İttihad ve Terakki Fırkası) 68, 114
peaceful coexistence 90–1, 93
peace treaties 35
  abolition of 42
PFLP, *see* Popular Front for the Liberation of Palestine
PIJ, *see* Palestinian Islamic Jihad
The Pioneer (magazine) 169–70
pluralism 210–11
PNC, *see* Palestinian National Council
political ideologies 3–4, 25–6
political participation 205–6
politics
  role of Islam in 210–11
  role of religion in 208
Popular Front for the Liberation of Palestine (PFLP) 25, 190, 221
power rotation 210
prisoners
  liberation of 39

Al-Qaida 244, 245
Al-Qassam, Izz al-Din (Syrian preacher and revivalist) 71, 72, 75, 138
  death and funeral of 81
  and revolution 77–81
  as symbol of faith 75–6
  as thinker 76–7
Al-Qassam, Kamal 78
Qaynuqaʿ, Tribe of 109
Al-Quds Brigades 20
Qur'an 46
  custom of "defense" in 213
  death in 223–4

and Palestinian cause   95–6, 100–7,
      120, 121–2
and Qassamists   75–6
Shiites'   165–6
Qurayza, Tribe of   110
Qutb, Sayyid (Egyptian revolutionary
      Islamic theorist)   64, 151
   influence on al-Shiqaqi   66–7

Rabin, Yitzhak (Prime Minister of
      Israel)   13
Razak, Jabir (Egyptian journalist)   171
refugees   31
religion and politics   208, 210–11
renaissance   62–3, 99–100, 202, 205
resistance   47
   legitimacy of   212, 213
   notion of   213
   principles of   213–20
revolution(s)   64–5
   in Algeria   133, 137–8
   and al-Qassam   77–81
   in Sudan   133–4, 137
revolutionary nationalist
      movements   63–4, 137–8
revolutionary socialism   139
right of return   31
Russia, *see* Soviet Union

Al-Sabil, Muhammad bin Abdallah
      (member of Senior Council of
      Ulama)   221
Sadat, Anwar (President of Egypt)   129
Al-Sa'di, Nimr (Palestinian militant)   78
Safavi, Navvab (Iranian cleric)   159,
      160–2
Sa'id ibn Zayd (Prophet's
      companion)   234
Salafism   51, 57, 58–9, 60–1
Salah, Abd al-Latif (Nablus-based
      leader)   72
Al-Salih, Subhi (author)   164
Salim, Abd al-Majid (Mufti of
      Egypt)   159
Samuel, Herbert Louis   70
Al-Sayyid, Ahmad Lutfi (Egyptian
      intellectual)   139
science and Islam   49
Second Intifada, *see under* Intifada

sectarianism
   Israel's role in   177
   Mecca Document   180
   Sunni-Shiite   41, 160–1, 166–7, 169,
      173–4
   Sunni-Shiite reconciliation   158–60,
      162–4, 175
secularism
   emergence of   202
   and Islam   48
   and Islamic society   202–4
   Western notion of   201–2
Sennacherib (King of Assyria)   104, 106,
      107
Al-Senussi, Muhammad Ibn Ali
      (theologian)   59
Senussist movement   59, 138
September 11 attacks (9/11 attacks)   245–
      8
settlement agreements   35
Al-Shafi'i, Abu Abdallah Muhammad bin
      Idris (theologian)   203
Al-Shak'a, Mustafa   165
Shallah, Ramadan Abdallah (PIJ
      secretary-general)   17, 44–5,
      175
Shaltut, Mahmud (Grand Imam of
      Al-Azhar)   159, 162–3
Al-Shami, Abdallah (PIJ leader)   2, 9,
      221–2
Sharif-Emami, Jafar (prime minister of
      Iran)   149
Sharon, Ariel   244
Al-Shawkani, Muhammad (Yemeni
      jurist)   60
Shiism/Shiites   51, *see also* sectarianism
   Hamas' allegiance to   177
   and Iranian Revolution   156–7
   and Muslim Brotherhood   160–8
   PIJ's alleged inclination to   175–6,
      179–82
   PIJ's views on   180
Al-Shiqaqi, Fathi   2, 9, 11, 20, 21–2, 192
   on Afghan-Soviet War   82–3
   arrest of   12–13
   on civil society   208, 209
   on future society   200–1
   influences on   66–7
   on Islamic movements   55–6

on Palestinian cause 95–6
support for Iranian Revolution 154–5
views on international law 83
on Western colonialism 66, 82–3
Al-Shuja'iyya Operation (Jan 1987) 13
Shukri, Ghali (Egyptian intellectual) 174
Al-Shuqayri, Ahmad (PLO Chairman) 15
Al-Siba'i, Mustafa (Syrian Muslim Brotherhood) 160
social ideologies 64
Society of Muslim Youth (Jerusalem) 11
Somalia 88
Soviet Union
    and Middle East 90–2
    strategic interests in Afghanistan 84–7, 93–4
Sudan
    Islamic revolution in 133–4, 137
Sufism 51
suicide bombings 221–2, 236–7, 239, 244
Sunnis 51, see also sectarianism
    and moral infallibility 166
Al-Suri, Misbah (PIJ militant) 13
Syria 250

Al-Tahtawi, Rifa'at (Egyptian scholar and teacher) 114
Ta'ima, Sabir 167–8
Al-Takfir wa-l-Hijra (Group of Muslims) 64
Tal, Ron (Colonel) 13
Tantawi, Muhammad Sa'id (head of al-Azhar Mosque) 221
Taraki, Nur Muhammad (President of Afghanistan) 86
targeting civilians 238–9
Al-Tayyib, Tawfiq 141, 151–2
terror list 42–3
Al-Thaqafi, Abu Mihjan (Arab poet) 23
Al-Tirmidhi (Persian scholar) 228
Truth 225–6
Tuqan, Sulayman Abd al-Razaq (Mayor of Nablus) 70
Al-Turabi, Hassan (Sudanese politician) 169–70
Turkey 68, see also Ottoman Empire

and United States 92
Twelver Shiites 51 n.9, 159, 163, 165, 168
    and moral infallibility ('işma) 166

umma 40–2, 46–7, 178
    1970s 73–4
    and Afghanistan 87
    and authority 218
    consensus of 203
    Israeli threat to 118
    and legislation 209
    Prophet's companions 50
Unified National Leadership of the Intifada (UNLU) 126
United Nations 89
United States of America, see also September 11 attacks
    aid to Afghanistan 85
    American-Zionist agenda 178
    patronage of Israel 42
    and Soviet Union 90–4
    "state terrorism" 41
    and Turkey 92
unity
    of Muslims 148
    of Palestine 38, 99–100
UNLU, see Unified National Leadership of the Intifada

Vanguard of Arab Youth 158
Vienna Conference (1815) 89
violence, see also armed jihad; balance of terror; suicide bombings; targeting civilians
    and internal Palestinian problems 38
    and Islam 48, 206, 207
    necessity and legitimacy of 221–2, 244, 245
    and PIJ 212–13
    revolutionary 212
    use of 6, 9
    and Western colonialism 206–7

Wahhabism 56, 59, 60
Well of Spirits (bi'r al-arwāḥ) (Jerusalem) 103 n.15
Western colonialism
    and Afghanistan 84

and Islamic homeland 97–8, 114–16, 118, 155, 194, 195–6
    Khomeini on 148
    and religion 140
    Soviet colonial interests 90
    use of violence 206–7
    and Zionist project 32, 68, 115–16, 118, 121, 122, 178, 196, 198, 199
Westernization 98
    as colonial tool 84, 114–15, 136–7, 138–9
    of Egypt 135, 139
    and Israel 118
    and Shiite-Sunni sectarianism 166–7
Westphalia Conference (1648) 88
White Revolution (*Enqelāb-e Sefid*) (Iran) 145
women
    and Islam 49
    and PIJ 39

Yakan, Fathi (Lebanese cleric) 161, 170, 173
Yakrib, al-Miqdam bin Ma'di (Prophet's companion) 236
Yasin, Subhi (Palestinian militant) 76
Yasir ibn Amir (Prophet's companion) 232
YMMA, *see* Young Men's Muslim Association
Young Arab Society (*Jam 'iyyat a-'Arabiyya al-Fatā*) 68
Young Men's Muslim Association (YMMA) 71, 76

Zaydan, Abd al-Karim (Iraqi scholar) 165
Zaydism 159
Zayn, Samih Atif 167
Al-Zindani, Abd al-Majid (Yemeni academician and politician) 162
Zionist project
    as component of Western colonialism 31–2, 68, 115–16, 118, 121, 122, 178, 196, 198, 199
    and peace 35
Zuaiter, Akram (Palestinian politician) 81

Printed in the USA
CPSIA information can be obtained
at www.ICGtesting.com
CBHW050024070924
14141CB00008B/393